£3

The church of Our Lady and the English Martyrs, Cambridge after completion, October 1890.

# Catholics in Cambridge

To Our Lady of Grace
and the Martyrs
of Cambridge

# Catholics in Cambridge

edited by

## Nicholas Rogers

GRACEWING

First published in 2003


Gracewing
2 Southern Avenue, Leominster
Herefordshire HR6 0QF

ISBN 0 85244 568 7

Typesetting by
Action Publishing Technology Ltd, Gloucester, GL1 5SR


Printed by
Newton Printing Ltd, London W1G 8PX

# Contents

# Illustrations

## Plates

2a. St Michael's church, Cambridge, exterior of the chantry chapel of Hervey de Stanton, founder of Michaelhouse, built *c.* 1327. Photo: Malcolm Underwood.

2b. Corpus Christi College, Cambridge, the gallery built between 1487 and 1515, linking the College with St Bene't's church. Photo: Malcolm Underwood.

3a. Master's lodge and chapel, Sidney Sussex College. Detail from David Loggan's view of the College, showing its appearance during Joshua Basset's mastership.

3b. The Huddleston miniature chalice and paten, *c.* 1660. Used for Masses celebrated at Sawston Hall during penal times; the miniaturization was intended to assist concealment. It was probably made in London, but submission for hallmarking could not be risked owing to the 'knop' on the stem of the chalice, a distinctive Catholic feature. The paten is engraved with the sacred monogram within rays. Now in the Victoria and Albert Museum, London, on loan from the Huddleston Collection. Photo: © V & A Picture Library.

4a. The chapel, Sawston Hall. The chapel on the ground floor of Sawston Hall, fitted out by Richard Huddleston *c.* 1801, superseding the attic chapel of 1584. Photo: *The Connoisseur*.

4b. Sawston Hall, a drawing by R. Relhan, early nineteenth century. Relhan was a prolific, if primitive, recorder of Cambridgeshire scenes in the early nineteenth century. His view shows Sawston Hall during the ownership of Richard Huddleston. C.A.S. Collection: Relhan Drawings. By permission of the Cambridge Antiquarian Society.

5a. Canon Thomas Quinlivan (1816–1885), Rector of the Cambridge mission 1843–1883. OLEM Parish Archives.

5b. Canon Christopher Scott (1838–1922), Rector of the Cambridge mission 1883–1922. OLEM Parish Archives.

6a. The visit of Ugandan dignitaries to Cambridge, 7 June 1914. 00 L. to r: Canon Scott, Chief Stanislaus Mugwanya of Buganda, Prince Joseph of Buganda and Bishop Henry Hanlon. OLEM Parish Archives.

6b.   The funeral of Canon Scott, February 1922. The coffin, preceded by Bishop Cary-Elwes of Northampton, is borne along Hills Road to its final resting place in the church grounds. OLEM Parish Archives.

7a.   Mrs Yolande Marie Louise Lyne-Stephens (1813–1894), foundress of the church of Our Lady and the English Martyrs, painted in her later years by the eminent French artist Charles-Emile-Auguste Carolus-Duran. OLEM Parish Archives.

7b.   Mrs Lyne-Stephens, shown in her earlier career as the ballet dancer Pauline Duvernay, when she often appeared on the stage of the Paris Opéra and at the Drury Lane Theatre in London. She is depicted here taking the title role in *La Belle au Bois Dormant*. OLEM Parish Archives

8.   A 'War Requiem' held on 5 November 1916. Edward Conybeare's diary describes how thirty soldiers held candles before a catafalque and a cadet guard of honour fixed bayonets at the Gospel. Those commemorated were Pte Stephen Ryan, Pte Ernest Freeman, 2nd Lieut Nelder, Cpl J. J. Mayle, Pioneer Bert Edmund Rogers, Lieut Goss, Joseph Poulissen and Alambert Daenen. OLEM Parish Archives

9a.   Cardinal Bourne, Archbishop of Westminster, arriving at the west door for the inauguration of the Catholic Bible Congress, Saturday 16 July 1921. The iron railings seen surrounding the church were to be removed in 1942 as part of the war effort, leaving only the gates surviving, a concession for church premises under the requisitioning regulations. OLEM Parish Archives.

9b.   Catholic Bible Congress Committee, 1921. L.to r. (seated) Mrs Thorneley, Dom Bede Camm, OSB, Rev C. M. Davidson, Mgr C. Scott, Archbishop Keating of Liverpool, Rev J. B. Marshall, Rev J. McNulty, Mr E. Conybeare, Miss Bell; (standing) Messrs G. N. Fitzgerald, C. T. Wilkins, F. W. Apthorpe, G. Litchfield, L. McA. Westall, J. McDowell, J. A. Naylon, B. Raston. OLEM Parish Archives.

10a.   Baron Anatole von Hügel (1854–1928). OLEM Parish Archives.

10b.   John William Edward Conybeare, (1843–1931), parishioner, honorary canon of the Northampton diocese, former Anglican clergyman. Reproduced by permission of the Conybeare family. OLEM Parish Archives.

11a.   Robert Hugh Benson (1871–1914), assistant priest 1905–08. OLEM Parish Archives.

11b.   Canon James Bernard Marshall (1879–1946), Rector of the Cambridge mission 1922–46. OLEM Parish Archives.

12a.   Men's Retreat, Spring 1937, given by Fr Cyril Martindale SJ. L. to r. (back row) Messrs A. Leach, Mullet, Bates, Asquith,{?}, {?}, { ? }, M.Wilkins, Mayes, Corbett; (middle row) Messrs {?}, Boot, F. Leach, Clark, Col Lucas , Smith, J. Wilkins, Polleti, Markham, B. Wilkins, Venables; (seated) Messrs Hornsby, Ryan, Goddard, Gifford, Britchard, Canon Marshall, Fr Martindale, Arnold, MacGilary, Golding, Pope, H. Lister; (front) Messrs {?} , Kreise, Angel, Irvings, Glendal, Britcher, Egan, Hogan. This group photograph was taken in front of the stage access of the Houghton Hall, as completed in the summer of 1936 with a roller shutter. OLEM Parish Archives.

12b.   Corpus Christi Procession, Sawston Hall, *c.* 1937. Bishop Youens of Northampton addresses the assembled parishioners and their clergy in the grounds of the Hall. Most parish organizations and religious communities of the day appear to be represented. OLEM Parish Archives.

13a.   A wartime wedding: Corporal Gene Mazzini USAAF to Miss Vera Kester, 2 June 1945, Canon Marshall officiating. The windows in the church are boarded up owing to the bomb damage sustained by the stained glass in 1941. Until repairs could be carried out after the war, all services in the church were conducted by artificial light. OLEM Parish Archives.

13b.   Canon Stokes with St Andrew's School first Holy Communion group, Corpus Christi, Thursday 16 June 1949. Also shown are the headmaster, Mr J. P. Bates, and a class teacher, Miss Mary Venables. Photo: Cambridge Studio. OLEM Parish Archives.

14a.   Canon Edmund Harold Stokes (1888–1961) parish priest
1946–61. Photo.: *Cambridge Evening News*.

14b.   Canon Diamond with first Holy Communion group,
30 April 1967. OLEM Parish Archives.

15a.   Passion tableau in St. Laurence's church, Chesterton, Good
Friday, 1951. Photo.: *Cambridge Daily News*. Margaret Plumb's
photograph album.

15b.   Opening of the new church of St Laurence, Milton Road,
24 August 1958. Procession along Ascham Road. L. to r: Mr
Bowman, Mr Plumb, Fr Wallace, Bishop Parker, Mr Hales Tooke,
Mr Wilkin, Mgr Grant, Mr Curtin, Canon Stokes, Mr Gifford,
Dean Thompson. Margaret Plumb's photograph album.

16.   Enclosure of the Carmelite convent at Waterbeach,
14 September 1937. The ceremony was performed by Bishop
Laurence Youens of Northampton. OLEM Parish Archives.

17   Corpus Christi procession, Lensfield Road, Cambridge.
The feast of Corpus Christi, on 23 May 1940, was marked by a
procession along Lensfield Road, Panton Street and Union Road,
Cambridge, 'The first Corpus Christi procession in the streets of
Cambridge since the processions of Corpus Christi College 400
years ago', wrote Canon Marshall in the *Cambridge Catholic
Magazine*, Aug. 1940. OLEM Parish Archives.

18a.   Margaret Plumb in Paston House uniform on the steps of
her grandmother's house, Russell Street, 1943. Margaret Plumb's
photograph album.

18b.   Fr Gilbey opening St Laurence's fete, Saturday, 19 June
1954. The old St. Laurence's church is in the background.
Margaret Plumb's photograph album.

18c.   Sports Day, St Mary's School, 28 June 1951. Mary Hawke
receiving sports medal from Sister M. Christopher IBVM.
Margaret Plumb's photograph album.

18d.   St. Laurence's May procession, 1954. Elizabeth Kidman
crowning the statue of Our Lady in the grounds of the church.
Margaret Plumb's photograph album.

19a.   The interior of St Andrew's church, Union Road. This shows the church as originally designed by Pugin. Note the wrought iron dividing screens between the sanctuary and the side chapels and the absence of clerestory windows (added during the reconstruction at St Ives in 1902). OLEM Parish Archives.

19b.   Dismantling the redundant St Andrew's church, 1902. All the distinctive architectural components of Pugin's design were carefully preserved and transported by barge to St Ives, Hunts., for incorporation in the church of the Sacred Heart. This was not, however, a 'brick by brick' removal, St Andrew's church was built in white Cambridge brick while red brick was used for the Sacred Heart church in St Ives. OLEM Parish Archives.

20a.   The sanctuary, Our Lady and the English Martyrs, April 1954, showing the baldacchino carved by R. L. Boulton and painted and gilded by N. H. J. Westlake. Photo.: James Darragh. OLEM Parish Archives

20b.   'The Canon's playpen'. The sanctuary after re-ordering in 1972–3. Photo.: Michael Wilkins. OLEM Parish Archives

21a.   St Jerome and the Lion. A carving on the pulpit by Ralph Hedley of Newcastle, *c.* 1890. Photo: Christopher Jackson.

21b.   Display of roof bosses in Rattee and Kett's workshop prior to installation. OLEM Parish Archives.

22a.   Ancient statue of the Virgin and Child. Located adjoining the Holy Souls Chapel and mounted two feet higher up the wall following a malicious incendiary attack in 1970. Much uncertainty surrounds the provenance of this statue, which is now believed to be Netherlandish or German work of the mid-sixteenth century. It is held in high regard by the congregation. Photo: Christopher Jackson.

22b.   South aisle window, showing St John Fisher receiving the deed of foundation of St John's College from Lady Margaret Beaufort. Photo: Christopher Jackson.

23.   Figure of St Andrew crucified. A votive offering by A. W. Pugin to St Andrew's church in 1843. Moved to the north transept of the present church in 1890. Photo.: RCHME Crown Copyright.

24.   The Abbott & Smith organ. Photo.: Chris Burton.

25.   The opening of the chapel at St Edmund's House, 16 October 1916. L. to r. Revd T. C. Fitzpatrick, University Vice-Chancellor, Revd Fr Thomas Williams, Principal, St Edmund's House, A. C. Benson, Master of Magdalene College (brother of Fr Hugh Benson), Edward Conybeare, Baron Anatole von Hügel. Photo.: Ramsey & Muspratt Ltd. By kind permission of the Master and Fellows of St Edmunds College, Cambridge.

26a.   Fr Sebastian Bullough OP. Blackfriars, Cambridge.

26b.   St Michael's Priory, Cambridge, autumn 1939. The Bullough house, designed by H. C. Hughes, before additions. Blackfriars, Cambridge.

27a.   Altar of the lower chapel, Blackfriars, May 1939. Blackfriars, Cambridge.

27b.   Mass in the Dominican rite celebrated by Fr Thomas Gilby in the upper chapel, Michaelmas 1962. Blackfriars, Cambridge.

28a.   The boys of the Union Road School, unknown date (1890s). The group includes Canon Scott and the headmistress, Miss Trehearne. OLEM Parish Archives.

28b.   The girls and mixed infants of the Union Road School, unknown date (1890s). This group also includes Canon Scott, two schoolteachers, (Miss Trehearne and possibly Miss Webster) and two monitors or pupil teachers. OLEM Parish Archives.

29.   The Union Road School (St Andrew's 1936-1962, St Alban's from 1962), completed 1936. The upper floor contains three classrooms and the ground floor houses the Houghton Hall. This is a post-war view showing the later alteration to the stage access. OLEM Parish Archives.

30a.   St Bede's School, laying the foundation stone, 26 July 1961. The site foreman keeps watch while Bishop Leo Parker of Northampton performs the ceremony. Photo.: *Cambridge Evening News.*

30b.   St Bede's School: a technical drawing class in progress in the 1972 extension under Mr Tony Froud, one of three members of the secondary team at St Andrew's School, Union Road to be appointed to St Bede's in 1962. Photo.: *Cambridge Evening News.*

# Acknowledgements

Mr Colin Ball, former Deputy Head, St Bede's School; Mr Roger Boon, Headteacher, St Bede's School; Mrs Barbara Britton; Mr Joe Britton; Lord Camoys; Dr Geoffrey Cook, Vice-Master, St Edmund's College, Cambridge; Mrs Dora Cowton, Assistant Archivist, Diocese of East Anglia; Mrs Mary Dicken; Fr Ian Dickie, Archivist, Archdiocese of Westminster; Dr Bruce Elsmore, St Edmund's College, Cambridge; Mr Roland Fernsby; Mrs Stella Fox, former Head of Infants' Department, St Alban's School, Cambridge; Mr Duncan Galley, Archivist, St Edmund's College Ware; Dr Pierre Gorman, Curator of Cambridge Book Collection, University of Melbourne; Miss Catherine Green; Sister M Gregory Kirkus and Sister M Ursula Murphy, both of the Institute of the Blessed Virgin Mary; Revd Petroc Howell, Archivist, Archdiocese of Birmingham; Mr Chris Jakes, Curator of the Cambridgeshire Collection, Central Library, Cambridge; Mr Melvin Jefferson; Mr George Kent, former Head, St Bede's School; Fr Raymond Kerby; Mr T. Kubiakowski; Mr William Lack; Fr Derek Lance, Diocese of Northampton; Mr Julian Limentani; Mrs Diana Lindsay; Fr Frank McHugh, The von Hügel Institute, Cambridge; Miss Molly Marshall; Mr Peter Meadows; Fr Aidan Nichols, OP; Mrs Anna-Maria Norman, Polonia House, Cambridge; Mrs Margaret Osborne, Archivist, Diocese of Northampton; Mrs Lynn Quiney, Librarian, The Law Society; Dr Richard Rex, Queens' College, Cambridge; Mrs Charlotte Rogers; Canon Timothy Russ; Miss Anne Rutherford; Dr Philip Saunders, Deputy Archivist for Cambridgeshire; Mr W. A. Scott; Mrs Marilize Snyman-Harvey; Mrs Elizabeth Stazicker, Head of Heritage and Archives for Cambridgeshire; Fr Anthony Symondson, SJ; Mgr Harry Wace; Mr Victor Walne; Fr John Warrington; Mr Peter Warrington; Professor David Watkin; Fr Allan White, OP, former Chaplain, Fisher House,

Cambridge; and Jo Ashworth of Gracewing Publishing for her care in the preparation of this text for publication.

## Living Memory Contributions

The following individuals allowed their memories to be taped as part of the preparation for this History and their contributions are gratefully acknowledged:

Mr Anthony Brotchie, †Mrs Patricia Mulhern, Mrs Margaret Navin, Mrs Joan Osborne, Miss Margaret Plumb, †Mrs Mary Prior, Mr William Scott, †Mrs Daphne Spencer, †Mrs Rosella Walne, †Mrs Catherine Wilkins, Mr Gerard Wilkins, Sister M. Gregory Kirkus, IBVM, Sister M. Ursula Murphy, IBVM.

†Requiescat in pace.

## Other Assistance

The support and assistance of the following members of the Cambridge Catholic History Group is also gratefully acknowledged:

Kate Carpenter, Imelda Clift, John Firth and the late Professor Peter Parish.

# Foreword

*The Most Revd Maurice Couve de Murville,*
*Archbishop Emeritus of Birmingham*

I welcome this book as a collection of detailed, wide-ranging and well researched studies, produced mostly by contributors from Cambridge parishes, with a sprinkling of academics. From the three dozen essays contained in this book an account written from a 'town' viewpoint emerges.

In the introduction to an earlier work, *Catholic Cambridge*, published in 1984, Philip Jenkins and I acknowledged that our subject was vast and our sketch impressionistic. In choosing to follow where we had begun, the present authors have succeeded in filling many of the gaps, but this is in no sense a complete history. There is plenty more for future generations to write about.

The writers of this book have chosen an episodic approach to subjects such as the extent of religious observance in medieval Cambridge, the eclipse of the Catholic faith following the Reformation, the slow and cautious rehabilitation during the eighteenth and nineteenth centuries, and the sometimes difficult relations between town and gown where Catholicism was concerned. Especially interesting are the lively and intimate portrayals of personalities and events from the late nineteenth and early twentieth centuries, when the Catholic community was moving from obscurity to a certain public exposure. It is recorded of that period that 'some non-Catholics considered that a religion so recently outlawed ought to avoid making itself conspicuous' (see pp. 110–11). How grateful we must be for the failure of this approach, thanks to men and women like Thomas Quinlivan, Christopher Scott, Yolande Lyne-Stephens, Robert Hugh Benson, Mother M. Salome Oates IBVM, Edmund Nolan, Anatole and Margaret von Hügel, Edward Conybeare, Alfred Gilbey, Mrs Holmes and many others mentioned in these pages. These were figures of stature, devoted to the Church, often holy, upholding principle, self-opinionated, seeking to be heard in spite of the unpopularity of their views, determined against long odds because of their faith in the future of the Church, many of them great conversationalists, never boring. The one thing they could not do was to make themselves inconspicuous. The record of their service to the Catholics of Cambridge is one of the most appealing aspects of this book.

The impressionistic canvas which Philip Jenkins and I left unfinished, all those years ago, has been replaced by these valuable cameos and by many other remarkable studies. To all those who have contributed to the production of this book, especially Mgr Anthony Rogers who initiated the project, Mr Christopher Jackson the co-ordinator and Mr Nicholas Rogers the diligent editor, I express my admiration and gratitude.

*+ Maurice Couve de Murville*

# Prelude

## *Nicholas Rogers*

We shall never know the name of the first Christian in Cambridge. He may have been a priest, sent by one of the early popes or British bishops. He may have been a merchant or soldier, bringing news of salvation from the other end of the Roman Empire. He may even have been a she. The history of early Christianity, from apostolic times onwards, is full of examples where the women of a household were the first to embrace the Faith, and the Roman Canon serves as a constant reminder that several of the most famous Roman martyrs were women.

There are scarcely any visible traces of the practice of the Christian religion in the Roman town of Durolipons. The deliberate destruction of a pentagonal temple on the site of the future churchyard of All Saints by the Castle presumably marks the official adoption of Christianity in Cambridge. A lead tank found 'near Cambridge' has been interpreted as having been used for baptism. Similar tanks have been found at Willingham and Burwell. More obviously Christian is the pewter *tazza* apparently discovered near Sutton in the Isle of Ely, decorated with Chi Rho, alpha and omega, and peacocks, and bearing an inscription which has been interpreted as referring to bishop and clergy. But this paucity of evidence could be changed by a chance archaeological find. This is illustrated by the discovery at Water Newton near Peterborough of a hoard of Christian liturgical silver, including the earliest surviving chalice in the world. We do not know the location of the *sanctum altare* to which the Water Newton vessels were dedicated. Nor do we know the reason for their concealment. It has been suggested that they had been looted from a church at a time of pagan resurgence. After the end of Roman rule Christianity survived in some parts of Britain but not in Cambridge, where a thick layer of loam covered the deserted town.

The first reference to what became the present-day city of Cambridge occurs in Bede's *Ecclesiastical History of the English People*. Sixteen years after the death of St Etheldreda her sister Sexburga, who had succeeded her as abbess of Ely, decided to place Etheldreda's bones in a new coffin inside the church. She sent some of the brothers to look for suitable blocks of stone from which to fashion a coffin. They went by boat to a 'small deserted fortress' called Grantacæstir, and there, near the walls of the fortress, they found what must have been a Roman marble sarcophagus. On their return it was discovered that the body of St Etheldreda was incorrupt and fitted the coffin 'as if it had been specially prepared for her'.

Most probably in the time of King Offa in the late eighth century a Mercian *burh* was established on the site of the old Roman town. It seems that there may have been a minster church associated with this *burh*, perhaps the ancestor of the house of canons regular at first established at St Giles's. Substantial numbers of tenth-century grave covers have been found near the presumed site of the church. Following the death of St Edmund, king of the East Angles, in 869 Cambridge was occupied by the Danes; traces of this period remain in the name Kettle's Yard and perhaps in the dedication of a church to St Clement. After 921, when 'the army that belonged to Cambridge' chose Edward the Elder as their lord, the area south of the river was developed as a trading centre, of which the tower of St Bene't's church (the dedication to St Benedict doubtless reflecting a continuing link with Ely) stands as a reminder (Pl. 1).

Cambridge, which provided a coffin for St Etheldreda, has seen many saints pass by. On the site now occupied by Sidney Sussex College the Subtle Doctor John Duns Scotus, beatified by Pope John Paul II in 1993, taught for a while before moving on to Oxford and then Cologne, where his relics are now enshrined. It was most probably on the earliest site occupied by the Carmelites in Cambridge, near the castle, that St Simon Stock was favoured with his vision of the Our Lady which resulted in the bestowal of the Scapular privilege. Henry VI, the royal saint whose canonization process was interrupted by the Reformation, is remembered in the chapel of King's College, of which he laid the first stone on 25 July 1446. Three of his recorded miracles are linked with Cambridge: the healing of a man in the parish of Great St Mary's, shot through the eye by an arrow, the restoration of sight in the left eye to a woman while hearing Mass in the Austin Friars; and the preservation from death of an innocent man hanged on Castle Hill and taken away by friars (most probably the Franciscans) to be buried.

Above all Cambridge is associated with the martyrs of the English Reformation. In the chapel of Fisher House is an inscription, composed by Canon Corboy, commemorating the some thirty members of the University 'who preferred the truth'. These include three of the five protomartyrs of the Henrician Reformation, John Houghton, prior of the London Charterhouse, Richard Reynolds, the 'Angel of Syon', and John Hale, vicar of Isleworth and fellow of King's Hall. Later martyrs include the schoolmaster-poet St Richard Gwyn, briefly at St John's at the beginning of the reign of Queen Elizabeth, St Philip Howard, the ancestor of the Duke of Norfolk who contributed half of the cost of the site of Our Lady and the English Martyrs, and St Henry Morse, who ministered to plague-stricken Londoners in 1636. But the chief of the martyrs of Cambridge is St John Fisher, Bishop of Rochester and Chancellor of the University. As a fellow of Michaelhouse he would have said Mass in St Michael's church in Trinity Street. He had hoped to be buried in a chantry chapel at St John's College, but instead, his body was tumbled into a nameless grave first outside All Hallows Barking by the Tower and then in St Peter ad Vincula, and his head displayed upon London Bridge, whence it was cast down into the Thames to make way for the head of St Thomas More. The hammer blows on the remains of his chantry chapel preserved in the new chapel at St John's speak eloquently of the malignity of Henry VIII and his creature Thomas Cromwell, the new Chancellor of the University.

In more recent times Cambridge can lay claim to the Passionist missioner Venerable Ignatius Spencer, superior of the Order in England, who, as the Hon. George Spencer, graduated MA from Trinity in 1819.

And then there are the saints whose names are known to God alone. Whether in parish church or college chapel, the upper room at Sawston Hall, the chapel chamber at Sidney Sussex College, the Pugin chapel of St Andrew, Union Road, or the more magnificent setting of Our Lady and the English Martyrs, the faithful have always sought the sanctifying grace of the sacraments. This book is about them, the Catholics of Cambridge.

# Chapter 1

# The Religious Life of the Townsmen of Medieval Cambridge

*Roger and Marie Lovatt*

Cambridge is full of ghosts. Walking down Regent Street from the Victorian church of Our Lady and the English Martyrs, which stands on what were fields in medieval times, you will arrive at Emmanuel College, the site of the great Dominican friary. Turning left into Downing Street and then right into Free School Lane, you will pass the one-time site of the Austin friary. Continuing onwards past the Arts Theatre, you will walk over the spot where in 1381 the peasants burned the records of the University and the property of Corpus Christi College. Passing the Guildhall, you will come close to the site of the earliest Franciscan house in Cambridge, and proceeding across Market Hill and down Market Street, a turn left down Sidney Street will take you past Sidney Sussex College, the site of their second and larger friary. Continuing further will bring you to St John's College, where the town hospital once stood, and to the Round Church of the short-lived fraternity of the Holy Sepulchre, an echo of the crusading movement. And so it goes on. In Cambridge, there is so much history beneath your feet. But for the townsmen of Cambridge, what was it like to live here in medieval times? What churches did the town possess? When and why were they founded? Where exactly were they situated? What was the nature of the devotional practices that went on within their walls? Such questions are easy to ask, but some simply cannot be answered for lack of evidence. It is the task of the historian to set out the factual bones as they stand, and to try to make them live.

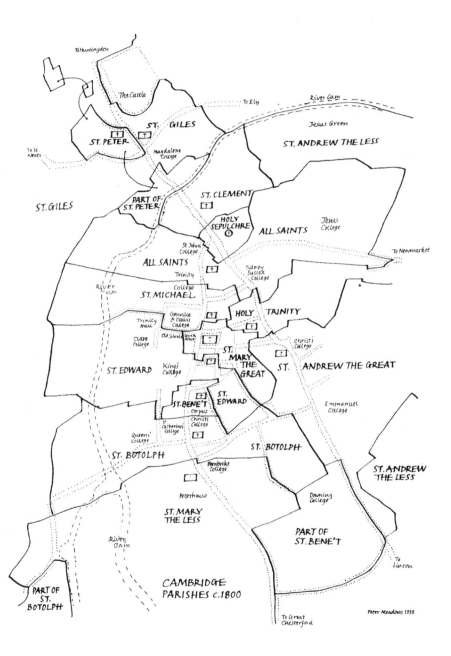

Fig. 1. Map of Cambridge Parishes

## The Parish Churches

The religious lives of the citizens of medieval Cambridge naturally revolved primarily around their parish churches, so it is appropriate to begin by giving some account of them. However, when one goes to Domesday Book, that great survey of 1086 undertaken by William the Conqueror, and an obvious source for this time, it becomes clear that, while Domesday contains a considerable amount of information about Cambridge, it makes no mention of any churches there at all. This is clearly an omission on the part of the compilers, for the great Anglo-Saxon tower of St Bene't's (situated in Bene't Street) must have been constructed in about 1000. Indeed, there are sufficient Norman remains in four Cambridge churches – St Giles and St Peter to the north, and Holy Sepulchre and Little St Mary's to the south – for us to be certain that the town was relatively well provided with substantial stone-built churches at least within a generation or so of the Norman Conquest.

We have to wait another two centuries for the next great survey of England, the so-called Hundred Rolls of 1279, for a complete picture of the town's parishes, but the wait is well worthwhile. By a happy chance, this survey is particularly full for Cambridge; in fact, no other town in medieval England is described in such detail. We are provided with information about every plot of land in the town, who owned it, how it had come into their possession, and what rents and dues were owed from the property. The impression is one of a prosperous borough. In terms of its extent, the town had probably reached the limits of its pre-nineteenth-century expansion, and was perhaps more thickly populated than at any other time before the early seventeenth century. Indeed, it had already burst out from behind the confines of the city walls, and there were populous suburbs on many sides, taking the form of a characteristic 'ribbon development'. To the east, and beyond the Barnwell Gate, by Christ's College and St Andrew's church, Cambridge had expanded towards Jesus Lane and the Newmarket Road. To the south, and beyond the Trumpington Gate (which stood at the junction of Mill Lane and Pembroke Street) settlement was now extending towards the sites of Old Addenbrooke's Hospital and the Leys School. The main commercial centre of the town, then as now, lay around Great St Mary's church and the market place, and here also were the municipal buildings, the guildhall and the town gaol. So crowded was the centre that houses had been built right up against St Mary's church itself. The most fashionable area lay just to the north, in St Michael's parish, but again the town spread much further in this direction, too, past the Jewry near the Round Church, from which the town's Jewish community had recently been expelled, over the bridge, past the present Magdalene College and up the hill towards the castle.

The survey of 1279 also gives a vivid picture of an active property market amongst the citizens of the town. They were inheriting, buying and selling town houses, shops and small plots of agricultural land in the surrounding fields. Single families can be seen rapidly accumulating groups of shops and houses only for their estates to be just as rapidly dispersed as a result of financial difficulties or the lack of an heir. This rapid turnover in property can largely be attributed to the fact that most town houses were small and modestly built. Even the better houses were timber-framed with an infilling of clay and reeds, while many one-storey cottages had mud-built walls. All were thatched with straw or reeds, with the result that fire was a chronic hazard. Some stone houses did exist – a remarkably lavish example is the so-called School of Pythagoras at the back of St John's College – but they were a conspicuous indication of wealth, given the absence of stone quarries in the region, and were sufficiently striking to be remarked upon in documents of the day and in the survey of 1279. By contrast, the characteristic house might have a frontage of only some twenty feet, and in the less densely-populated parts of the town would often also possess a long thin garden, or 'croft', stretching back behind it.

The growth of the town, and its economic prosperity in 1279, were based on a wide range of economic activities. Unlike its rival Oxford, for example, Cambridge was never dependent upon a single trade, such as wool and cloth, and was therefore economically more resilient, surviving such economic disasters as the Black Death (1349) much better than many other English towns. Manufacturing, apart from brewing, had little place in Cambridge. Rather, the commercial life of the town was partly focused on a variety of trading and partly on its role as a regional market for agricultural produce. The men of real wealth were the grocers, the mercers, the vintners, the spicers, the goldsmiths and the innkeepers. Similarly, Cambridge was at the heart of a region of fertile agriculture, as well as possessing substantial fields of its own. Many agricultural labourers lived within the town walls, and flocks of farm animals would have been a familiar sight on the streets of Cambridge, as they were until the early nineteenth century. Naturally the town possessed its own market, for the sale of foodstuffs and the exchange of its craftsmen's products for the goods of the countryside, but the nearby Stourbridge Fair was one of the greatest commercial occasions of medieval England. What is more, the proximity of the river meant that food and other goods could readily be carried further afield, or even exported through the ports of East Anglia.

It is essential to stress the buoyancy and vigour of the commercial life of medieval Cambridge, because it is this which provides the essential backdrop to any account of the provision of parish churches in the town, as well as to their changing history. The survey of 1279 lists almost 550 occupied house plots in the city, together with seventy-five shops. From these figures it is reasonable to estimate that the total population of the town at that time must have amounted to some four or five thousand. For their religious worship there were fourteen, or perhaps fifteen, parish churches situated within the town walls. The vast majority, a dozen in all, were situated – as one might expect – along the main highway of the town, the spine of Cambridge and only about one mile in length, which we now know successively as Trumpington Street, King's Parade, Trinity Street, St John's Street, Bridge Street and then Castle Hill. This pattern accurately reflects both the settlement pattern within the town and the circumstances of the foundation of these churches. They were placed on, or alongside, the central commercial artery of the town. The churches, and their parishes, take streets and road junctions as their core. They are at the heart of natural, smaller communities within the larger town. They reflect real concentrations of people, genuine social units, before parochial boundaries came to be frozen by about 1200. Yet this multiplicity of parish churches, one every hundred yards or so along the main street, is striking to us and was unusual even in the Europe of its own day. The towns of medieval England were positively crammed with small parish churches. There were around fifty parish churches at the time in such larger towns as Lincoln, Norwich and Winchester. But there is no parallel for this proliferation of small churches in contemporary Italy or elsewhere in northern Europe.

To some extent, it may be explained by the circumstances of the foundation of these churches. No overall ecclesiastical plan for the town was formulated by the church authorities. All was circumstantial and spontaneous. Most of the churches in Cambridge were founded between the tenth and the twelfth centuries. They were built, and endowed with revenues to support their parish priest, by groups of citizens, perhaps led by a particularly wealthy individual or by a local landowner with urban property in co-operation with his tenants and his neighbours. In this way, the churches and their parishes were the instinctive product of their communities, the religious focus, the social heart, even the status symbol, of their own natural environment. So informal and personal was their creation that these churches in their early days were actually regarded as the property, or proprietorial churches, of their founders and benefactors. Hence we find wealthy citizens of Cambridge in the early Middle Ages not only appointing the parish priests of what they saw as *their* churches, but also bequeathing the churches and their property themselves, or giving them to other individuals, or, subsequently, donating them to religious communities in the area. A curious record from around 1200 tells how a group of leading Cambridge citizens testified that the church of Little St Mary's, then known as St Peter's, had originally been 'held' by one Langlinus who also acted as its priest, that Langlinus had then given the church 'in the manner then customary in the city of Cambridge' to a relation, Sigar, who held it for more than sixty years and also served as its priest, and that Sigar had then in turn given it to his son Henry who held it for another sixty years until he eventually gave it by charter to the brethren serving the town's hospital.

None of this was unusual at the time, although it does vividly illustrate the circumstances in which such churches were founded. Nor were the dedications that these founders chose for their churches at all unconventional. Two churches were dedicated to All Saints, St Mary, St Peter and St Andrew respectively, and one to St John the Baptist, the Holy Trinity, St Michael, St Benedict, St Clement, St Edward King and Martyr, and St Botolph. There is little that is surprising here. St Clement, a popular Scandinavian saint, may represent the Viking influence present throughout East Anglia, and St Botolph, whose cult was widespread in the region, was naturally – as the patron of travellers – to be found in Cambridge as elsewhere adjacent to the town gate.

These fifteen or so churches provide the bedrock for the parochial life of medieval Cambridge. Of course, over several centuries there was change, although in general the parish system throughout the country, once established, was remarkably stable. A church of St George, which briefly appears early in the twelfth century, apparently soon disappeared and made way for the Round Church. Similarly, after 1279, two other parish churches succumbed, although for very different reasons. The parish of All Saints-by-the-Castle was severely depopulated by the plague in 1348-9, and as a result the Bishop of Ely united the parish with its neighbour St Giles, and All Saints church then fell into ruins. More violent was the fate of St John Zachary, which once stood at the western end of what is now King's College chapel and was simply pulled down when the chapel was built in 1446.

## Religious Houses

But these were relatively minor events. More substantial changes to the religious lives of the citizens of Cambridge came from two other directions: the foundation of new religious communities in the town, and the growth of the University and its colleges. Two religious houses had already been in existence for well over a century when the survey of 1279 was made. In about 1092 Picot, Sheriff of Cambridgeshire, had built the church of St Giles by the castle and installed there a small community of Augustinian canons. Within twenty years they had moved outside the town to a larger site at Barnwell, where the community grew rapidly, constructed substantial buildings and steadily acquired a rich endowment. By 1200 it had become by far the largest religious house in the neighbourhood of the town. Then, in the 1130s, a community of Benedictine nuns, the priory of St Radegund, was established on an extensive site directly adjacent to the town walls, where Jesus College now stands. Both houses, Barnwell and St Radegund's, received numerous endowments from the citizens of Cambridge at the time of their foundation and soon afterwards, with the result that both came to own considerable amounts of property within the town. But by 1279, this flow of benefactions from the citizens had virtually ceased and, as both houses were actually situated on the outskirts of the town, their role was perhaps largely restricted to that of absentee landlords.

A very much greater impact was made on the internal religious life of the town by the massive influx of the various orders of friars during the course of the thirteenth century. The friars constructed substantial convents in the heart of the town, partly because their communities were so large, and partly because their very *raison d'être* – unlike that of the canons or the nuns – brought them into the most immediate contact with their urban neighbours. The Franciscan friars were the first to arrive in about 1225. Initially they settled in a small house, perhaps previously the town gaol, given to them by the townsmen and near to the present Guildhall in the market place. The site was cramped, even for the three friars who formed the first community, and we are told that the chapel was 'so exceedingly humble that a carpenter in one day set up the fourteen pairs of rafters' which formed its roof frame. Not surprisingly, by the 1260s the Franciscans had moved to a much larger and permanent site in what are now the gardens of Sidney Sussex College, near the corner of Jesus Lane. The Franciscans were followed by the Dominicans (the Black Friars) who had arrived by about 1238 and set about constructing what was to become their very substantial convent on the present site of Emmanuel College. The Carmelite friars arrived in 1247 but had a rather restless early history until finally settling, in the 1290s, on a site at the back of Queens' College, next to the river. The last to arrive were the Austin friars, who built their convent during the 1290s where the old Cavendish Laboratory now stands, behind Corpus Christi College.

So by 1300 all four major orders of friars were established in Cambridge, as well as a number of minor orders which did not survive for long. Three of these major orders occupied large central sites inside the city walls, and the Dominicans were only just outside by the Barnwell Gate. Immediately, they set about building substantial accommodation for themselves: churches, cloisters, refectories, dormitories and libraries. As a result, these convents of friars would have presented an inescapable and striking physical presence to the townsmen. When Parliament met in Cambridge in 1388 it sat in the Dominican friary. The University itself, which had no safe place for its valuables, secured some of them in a chest within the Carmelite friary. And important university ceremonies came to be held in the capacious church of the Franciscan friars.

Yet, apart from this physical presence, what did the friars mean to the life of the townsmen? This is a difficult question to answer, because all four convents were also houses of study, to which young friars were sent from houses all over the country to complete their education. So the convents were, in a sense, satellites of the University; and indeed it was the presence of the University which partly explains why the friars were so quick to come to Cambridge. Equally, they saw the talented young men studying there as fertile ground for their recruitment. Sheer numbers of friars would certainly have made their impact on the town, and at their height, there were between two and three hundred friars in Cambridge. The houses of two largest orders, the Franciscans and Dominicans, might have contained as many as sixty members each. So at the very least, the friars would have been a ubiquitous presence in the streets of the town.

Their relationship with the townsmen was a closely reciprocal one. The two communities both gave and received. The friars were vowed to poverty: such property as they had was formally vested in the hands of the papacy. For everything, the sites of their houses, the money to build and their daily maintenance, they were dependent upon their own efforts at begging and the generosity of their well-wishers. And it is here that the reciprocal relationship is most vividly revealed. The Cambridge convents were large; the cost of their upkeep and that of their members was expensive. To support themselves, the friars developed an elaborately structured system of begging. Each house was permitted to canvass a specific area. Certain friars, presumably those skilled and experienced in the delicate matter, were specially appointed to conduct the begging, and these friars were expected to present fortnightly accounts of their success to their convents. So the townsmen of Cambridge would regularly have been confronted by the entreaties of the friars. The evidence is that they responded generously. The Franciscans' first small house by the Guildhall was provided by the townsmen. Similarly, their later, substantial six-acre site in Sidney was the gift of a large number of separate benefactors. Later, the order – and doubtless the other orders – were sustained by a multitude of gifts, large and small, from a wide variety of donors. The king made grants, as did members of the nobility, but much came from the local community: substantial sums from wealthy Cambridge merchants, gifts from local clergy, and pennies and halfpennies from modest and anonymous townsfolk. Many made gifts in kind, often food such as barley and wheat, or cloth for the friars' habits, or materials for their new buildings. Other gifts often took the form of legacies, from £10 from an earl to 2d. from a Bottisham man; but such benefactions were often accompanied by requests that the donors should be buried in the friars' churches and that Masses should be said there for the repose of their souls. Here, once again, is reciprocity in action. Others gave themselves and entered the orders. It would seem that all the Cambridge friaries contained many local men.

In return, the friars themselves gave much. In particular, they preached. At a time, particularly in the thirteenth century, when preaching was not widespread, the friars made it their special vocation to preach. Indeed, so skilled were the Dominicans in this respect that they came to be known generally as the Friars Preachers. Similarly, the characteristically large, open-plan, barn-like design of the friars' churches was intended to provide an ideal forum for preaching to large congregations. Their pastoral success, particularly in preaching but also in hearing confessions and attracting burials, was so great that it sometimes provoked friction with the parish clergy, and caused the ecclesiastical authorities to impose limitations on the friars' activities. In other words, although the friars clearly formed a massive presence in medieval Cambridge, they were only as successful as the support and generosity of their benefactors in the town and elsewhere enabled them to be.

## The University

The growth of the University also had a profound, and of course more permanent, effect on the lives of the townspeople. The first scholars seem to have arrived in Cambridge, in exile from Oxford, in 1209, and thereafter the University grew rapidly. By the fourteenth century there may well have been close to a thousand masters and students. In other words, they amounted to something like a quarter of the total population of the town. In comparative terms, it was as though the University of today was approximately double its present size. Naturally this rapid and massive influx deeply affected the townsmen. But both citizens and scholars needed each other. Again, as with the friars, their relationship was one of reciprocity, but a reciprocity which was at times expressed in rivalry and even conflict. In some ways – economically, certainly – the scholars were at the mercy of the townsmen. They needed the accommodation, the food and the multiplicity of other services which only the townsmen could provide. And in order to redress this economic vulnerability the University acquired numerous rights, privileges and immunities by grant from a royal government anxious to protect the nursery in which its future ministers, diplomats, civil servants and bishops were being raised. The townsmen resented the control which the members of the University thereby obtained over their markets and their commercial life. They disliked the extensive judicial authority of the chancellor and his court. They were provoked by the legal immunities enjoyed by the scholars. At times these resentments boiled over into serious outbreaks of violence between town and gown. Yet this was uncharacteristic. The citizens needed the trade of the scholars, just as the scholars needed the services of the townsmen. It was a relationship symbolized by the foundation of Corpus Christi College, in 1352, by two guilds of Cambridge townsmen.

However, the relationship, though reciprocal, was not symmetrical. The presence of the University transformed the town in a multitude of ways. Not least, the University – or rather its colleges – revolutionized Cambridge's appearance, its layout and its architecture. The Backs, as they now stand, are the creation of the University. But while this is immediately apparent, it is much more difficult to measure the precise influence of the University on the religious life of the townsmen. How can one assess the role of the large number of priests and theologians brought to the town by the presence of the University? Personal contacts must have been frequent but any evidence of their effects is virtually non-existent. Rather, the impact of the University must be sought in another direction. We are accustomed today to think that members of the University worship mainly in their own institutions, whether college chapels or the Catholic chaplaincy. In the Middle Ages this was either not the case, or only gradually came to be so. Most members of the University were not members of colleges, and the first colleges did not even possess their own chapels; rather, their members were expected to worship, like their neighbours, in their local parish church. The earliest chapel built exclusively for collegiate purposes, that of Pembroke, does not seem to have come into use until the end of the fourteenth century.

The existence of colleges was, however, to have a profound effect on the nature of many of the Cambridge parish churches. The connection between the members of the early colleges and their churches was not merely that of the normal parishioner within his parish church. Often these parish churches were appropriated (to use the legal term) to their neighbouring colleges by their founders or by later bishops. Eventually, half the parish churches of Cambridge came to be linked with colleges in this way. As a result, such churches came to serve a dual role, acting both as parish churches and as college chapels. The substantial corridors which link Little St Mary's with Peterhouse, or St Bene't's with Corpus Christi College (Pl. 2b), exemplify a much deeper bond than mere bricks and mortar. Appropriation involved a fundamental change of status for the church. When a church was appropriated to a college, that college not only acquired all the endowed revenues of the church which had previously gone to support the rector, but also obtained the right to appoint a vicar to whom they paid a fixed – and much smaller – stipend. From a financial point of view, this involved a large hidden transfer of wealth from the towns-men, who had originally endowed their churches, to the colleges who now took the surplus revenues from these endowments. It also meant that, in effect, the colleges came to acquire a controlling influence over something like half the parishes in medieval Cambridge.

Collegiate control was partly administrative in nature, although none the less important for that: the absorption of parochial revenues and the right to appoint incumbents were not trivial matters. But it also had a more tangible aspect. This was not usually expressed as destructively as in the demolition of St John Zachary by King's College, but it took an equally physical and visible character. To put it simply, many colleges remodelled or rebuilt 'their' parish churches to suit their new roles as college chapels. When the old church of St Peter, for instance, which belonged to Peterhouse and gave the college its name, became ruinous in the middle years of the fourteenth century, it was entirely rebuilt on an extended site and re-dedicated to the Blessed Virgin Mary. So decisive was the college's influence in this process that the new design entirely reflected its needs. The church as it now stands was planned to serve solely as a chancel for the use of the scholars, with a nave at the western end for the use of the parishioners. Characteristically, perhaps, this projected nave was never built, and the parishioners were obliged to fit themselves into the western end of the scholars' new chancel. The relative roles of college and parish had thus been reversed, and the cuckoo had taken over the nest. In the church of St Edward King and Martyr, a somewhat similar transformation took place. When the church came to serve as a chapel for Clare College and Trinity Hall, both colleges added substantial aisles at either side of the chancel for their own use. The most dramatic example of such a collegiate take-over is that of St Michael's church, which was completely rebuilt during the first half of the fourteenth century to suit the requirements of its college, Michaelhouse, which was later to become part of Trinity College (Pl. 2a). The plan of the new church is unique : the chancel arch was placed so that the chancel became more than twice the length of the nave. In consequence, the parishioners were to be confined to a very small nave with its side aisles while the fellows of Michaelhouse enjoyed a substantial chancel in which their stalls were placed. Once again, the parishioners had become, as it were, exiles within their own church, relegated for the benefit for their new collegiate masters.

## The Guilds

Yet the townsmen of Cambridge were not simply the passive victims of collegiate imperialism. In all sorts of ways they also made their own contributions to the religious life of the town. In tangible terms at least, this contribution took two main forms: the improvement of the fabric of their parish churches and the foundation of parish guilds. During the Middle Ages the principle came to be firmly established that the rector of a church (a college or a religious house when a church was appropriated) was responsible for the maintenance of the chancel of that church, while the parishioners were responsible for the upkeep of the nave (usually, of course, a much more substantial burden). This obligation was fulfilled, as one might expect, by a large number of small donations, often in the form of legacies, by the members of the parish. Such donations became ubiquitous in the wills of the later Middle Ages; in fact, it is a rare will of the day that fails to make some such provision. It is clear that the parishioners took their responsibilities seriously in this respect, and gloried in maintaining and beautifying their churches. Indeed, so numerous did such gifts and legacies become that the office of churchwarden came to be established largely as a representative administrative officer whose main role was to receive and account for these gifts and to control their expenditure on the fabric of his church.

In fact, relatively few wills of the townsmen of medieval Cambridge have survived, but the physical evidence of their pious generosity is overwhelming. Some churches have disappeared, and some were completely rebuilt during the nineteenth century, with the result that we can know nothing of their medieval fabric; in fact, none of the extant churches of medieval Cambridge has survived in anything like its original form. Everywhere there has been substantial remodelling and extension, if not complete rebuilding; and even where an early medieval feature has been preserved because of its striking character, such as the tower of St Bene't's or the circular nave of the Round Church, the rest of the church has been rebuilt or refashioned. Some of this work was sponsored, and no doubt in part funded, by the University: colleges, or their founders, played a large part in rebuilding Little St Mary's and St Michael's, and in the same way the University rebuilt Great St Mary's between 1479 and 1519 with the support of a national appeal which attracted donations even from Richard III and Henry VII. But even here, it was a local apothecary who left money to provide a window in the new church glazed with the story of King Edward the Confessor; and elsewhere, the contribution of the parishioners was total, or at least substantial. What is more, as any visitor to Cambridge's churches can see, these new churches of the later Middle Ages were built on a much more lavish scale than were their predecessors. If one looks at the exterior, they are marked by all sorts of expensive elaboration, often massive towers, large porches, pinnacles and battlemented roofs, clerestories and decorated buttresses. The same picture holds good for the lavish decoration of the interior. We now find stained glass windows, elaborately-carved wooden roofs, and the provision of pews and pulpits. Roofs are raised on slender arches, and side aisles are added to the north and south. This increasing elaboration reflects changing styles of architecture and taste, and the increasing generosity of the parochial patrons, but it also mirrors changing devotional practices. The addition of side aisles and the multiplication of subsidiary altars were made for a purpose, and that was to house the processions and Masses sponsored in increasing numbers by the parochial guilds.

Guilds have now disappeared from our consciousness, and their curiously hybrid nature is difficult for us to recapture; but to put it briefly, they were in part religious communities, in part friendly societies, in part dining clubs, and in part sometimes almost business associations or trade unions. The members were both men and women, and were predominantly lay but also normally included priests. They were formed under the protection of a particular saint or religious festival, such as Corpus Christi, and met at least once a year to celebrate their patronal festival with a Mass, with processions with candles and torches, and with a feast. Many met much more frequently for occasions of this sort. Guild members attended the funerals of all their brethren who had died, and also regular Requiem Masses for their departed brethren and benefactors. They elected officers from amongst their more senior and wealthy colleagues to control their finances and to administer their affairs. Members thus obtained spiritual benefits from their guilds, but were themselves also able to contribute to their spiritual life. Most frequently, the guilds maintained lights or candles before the altars in their parish churches, and also hired chaplains either permanently or on a temporary basis to say Masses for them – particularly on their death – and for their departed brethren. But the benefits of membership had to be bought. There were entry fees to be paid, and also annual subscriptions. Equally, membership was carefully controlled by those who already belonged. In return, the members enjoyed some temporal as well as spiritual benefits. Those who became too poor to pay for their own funeral expenses might have them provided by the funds of their guild. And some guilds also made regular payments to those members who fell into poverty (although guild funds cannot always have been sufficiently buoyant to sustain this obligation).

Thus these guilds were the natural, spontaneous expression of the religious and social enthusiasms of the medieval laity: in Cambridge there were more than thirty guilds, each attached to a particular parish church, with the larger churches containing perhaps three or four guilds. All fell into the general pattern which existed throughout the country, but some had their own peculiarities. Some were more or less exclusive in character, forbidding membership to women, priests and even bakers! One went in for some trading activity, another put on a play, and a third had its own livery. Some were vigilant about their members' behaviour, threatening expulsion to those who refused to desist from haunting the streets at night or from playing chess. Yet at the heart of each was the parish church and the regular round of religious observance, of candles maintained before altars, and of processions and Requiem Masses.

## The Evidence of Wills

What can we say about the private religious feelings of the individual citizens of medieval Cambridge? In general, as one might expect, the answer is very little. But occasionally the veil is lifted. The religious sentiments of individuals are revealed most clearly in their wills. Of course, this source has to be used with great caution. Only the relatively wealthy made wills in the first instance, so this form of evidence is biased towards a minority of the rich. More important certainly is the fact that it was the custom, in the Middle Ages, to make wills 'in extremis'. Death-bed sentiments may well be an inadequate guide to life-time attitudes. This particular problem is also compounded by the fact that, not unnaturally, such wills were often made under the supervision of a priest. All such pressures combined to produce a situation where religious motivations were likely to be intensified, and acts of piety or charity would come to figure more prominently than they may have done in the testator's lifetime. But wills are often all that we have and, bearing these limitations in mind, they can tell us something.

All testators made more or less elaborate arrangements for the conduct of their funerals, normally at the outset of their wills. These would include specifying where they were to be buried, usually the parish church or sometimes a local friary, but would also embrace instructions of varying degrees of detail concerning the service itself. Small sums of money might be set aside for those attending the funeral, often in the form of charitable provision to poor men – almost professional mourners – who were to be clothed in black and bear a candle. But the funeral itself was only the beginning of a series of spiritual precautions designed to safeguard the fate of the soul. Almost all wills laid down arrangements for Requiem Masses to be celebrated subsequently, sometimes on the anniversary of death but often much more frequently. Many clearly believed in the special efficacy of prayers said on their behalf by members of the religious orders. Hence legacies would be given to one or more of the four orders of friars in Cambridge with a request that they might sing a trental for the repose of the soul of the testator; or occasionally, money might be given for the same purpose to a more distant monastery, such as the London Charterhouse, famed for its strict observance. It was equally normal to provide legacies for the church of burial, small payments to the Rood or the Sepulchre, or for candles to burn in a particular place, usually before the statue of a saint. Such bequests often extended to the fabric of the church: gifts for its maintenance, money to provide for a new stained glass window or for the repair of the churchyard. Many Cambridge testators extended their charitable provision to embrace wider needs within their society. Money might be left to provide food for the needy, or perhaps to enable poor folk to pay their taxes. Legacies often benefited prisoners or local hospitals, or – in ways alien to us – were devoted to the repair of local roads and bridges. Finally, the residue, as one might expect, went to the wife of the testator, perhaps in trust, and to his family and relations.

Many of these themes come particularly vividly to life in the will of one citizen of Cambridge, John Harryes. Harryes was a man of some distinction. He had served as MP for Cambridge on two occasions and was mayor of the town three times, and his will reflected both his wealth and his social status. But his concerns resembled those of many others, merely writ large. Like so many, Harryes was dead within only about a month of drawing up his will in February 1418. He asked to be buried near his first wife, Margaret, in Great St Mary's, and made several legacies to that church. He left money for repairs to the fabric, to the parish chapel and to the chantry chapel of St Mary within the church. He also left a gift to the parish clerk, a large candle for the high altar and a substantial sum of money for Masses to be said. £20, a large amount in those days, was to be distributed to the poor who attended his funeral. All four houses of friars in Cambridge received a legacy from him, and their members were all provided with a suitable meal. But Harryes's acts of charity extended much more widely. A legacy went to the leper house in Trumpington Street (situated on the corner with Lensfield Road), and the huge sum of £100 was set aside to provide clothing and blankets for the poor, the blind and the deaf in Cambridge and the surrounding region. Finally in this vein, Harryes left £10 for the repair of the 'vile road' from Cambridge to Barley and Barkway. Harryes's concern for others was spiritual as well as practical. He left a large sum to pay a chaplain to celebrate Mass in Great St Mary's for the souls of all his benefactors, as well as money to support a chaplain for a year to say Mass for the repose of his own soul. After making provision for his servants, he left all his remaining property, including his house (which was situated opposite Great St Mary's church, where the east end of King's College chapel now stands) in trust to his second wife, Isabel, for her life, but instructed that on her death (Harryes was evidently childless) all was to be sold and the proceeds used for the benefit of his own soul and of all Christian souls.

Certain prevailing attitudes come across clearly enough in wills such as these. Yet here we are attempting to measure the immeasurable. Some townsmen were undoubtedly exceptionally pious, others were no doubt perfunctory in their observance. But who can judge this? We know what the Church required: regular attendance at Mass on Sundays and major festivals, and confessions at least once a year before Easter, as well as the minor observances such as fasting in Lent. We know what the Church provided, or perhaps aspired to provide: a daily Mass said by every priest and the performance of the canonical hours. And by the later Middle Ages preaching would have become an increasingly familiar element in the Church's ministry. We know that the laity in Cambridge responded in abundance to the Church's message, by founding, endowing and later rebuilding and beautifying their parish churches, by supporting at least in part the earlier canons and nuns and the massive communities of friars, and by sustaining numerous religious guilds to supplement and elaborate the Church's own provisions. We may therefore conclude that the citizens of

Cambridge were as devout as any, and perhaps more so than many. Virtually no heresy is recorded amongst the laity of late medieval Cambridge, unlike those of many other towns. And the churchwardens of Great St Mary's church subsequently proved very reluctant, in the changed circumstances of Elizabeth's reign, to sell such physical survivals of the old religion as the Eucharistic canopy, the Lenten veil, the censers and the pyxes. But beyond this, we can say no more, nor make windows into men's souls.

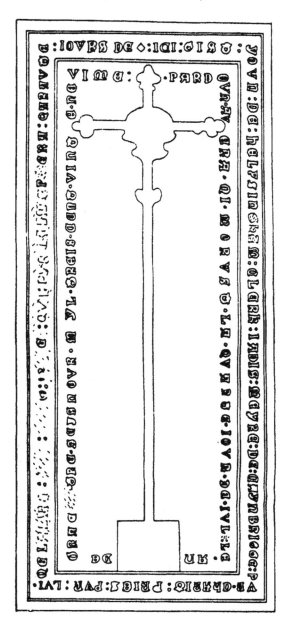

Fig. 2.  Indent of brass of Eudo de Helpringham, Mayor of
Cambridge, d. 1329, formerly in St Clement's.

# Chapter 2

# Religion and the University to 1535

*Malcolm Underwood*

## Town and Gown

The townsmen who shared parish churches with the students of medieval Cambridge also knew them as neighbours, lodgers and customers. Within twenty years of the first migration of scholars from Oxford in 1209 the gownsmen were recognizable as that characteristic form of medieval urban organization – the guild. In their case the guild was composed of teachers of the liberal arts, and of philosophy, theology, law and medicine, led by a Chancellor who, initially at least, was appointed by the local bishop, the Bishop of Ely. These teachers trained as their 'apprentices' a body of up to six hundred or so students, some of whom were eventually admitted to the guild to become teachers in their turn. All were bound together by a succession of scholastic exercises and oaths, much as a tradesman progressed through the various stages of his craft.

The town of Cambridge had a guild merchant which regulated the affairs of all its various trades, but it also had a number of guilds with a rather different purpose. These were associations which aimed to support their members in time of sickness, to provide for their funerals and burials, and even to act as forums of arbitration in case of disputes. These guilds were closely connected with the parish churches, in which lights were placed at their expense and the souls of deceased members commemorated.

Colleges of scholars, which began to be founded in Cambridge from 1284, had, besides their educational aims, social and religious ones similar to those of the fraternal guilds. They were originally societies predominantly of university graduates, since most undergraduate students lived in lodgings or university hostels rented from the landlords of the town. The college communities consisted of very small groups of men studying and passing on learning, who at some point would become priests and serve the Church and civil society as parish clergy or administrators. While at college one of the scholars' functions was to pray for the founders and benefactors of their house, who had provided their means to study usually in exchange for intercession for kin and friends. Hence the religious aim of these foundations was quite as strong as the educational one.

Before the Reformation, therefore, the scholars shared with the townsmen forms of association rooted in Catholic belief and practice. A direct link was forged by the foundation of Corpus Christi College by two town guilds in 1352. A glance at the history of the foundation of Corpus Christi College shows us both the intimacy and the occasions of conflict between the two communities. In 1344 the property of Sir John de Cambridge, a wealthy townsman, was made over to the Guild of St Mary to provide five chaplains to celebrate Mass in Great St Mary's church for the souls of the king and queen, the brothers and sisters of the guild and their heirs and for the faithful departed. The affairs of the Guild of St Mary, however, were soon taken over by the energetic officers of a new guild, that of Corpus Christi, which in 1349, during the months of its first promotion, spent money on masks for the Corpus Christi play. These officials seem to have had in mind from the first the founding of a college, and they invoked the patronage of the Duke of Lancaster in order to secure their objective. The two guilds were formally united, and Corpus Christi College founded in 1352. Three chaplains who were officers of the guild became the first fellows of the College, also with a duty to pray for the members of the guilds, who took part in the acquisition of property on its behalf. At a later date, in the 1370s, the local connection was overwhelmed by the patronage of a circle of London courtiers, so much so that some of the townsmen claimed that the College was misapplying the rents it collected, called candle rents, to pay for church lights, and joined in pillaging it during the famous riots of 1381.

Nevertheless, a spark of great significance remained from the dampening of relations between townsmen and college. Each year the Cambridge Corpus Christi procession set out from St Bene't's church, bearing shields of arms which displayed the symbols of the Passion. The Master of Corpus Christi College followed, sheltered by a canopy, as he bore the Host in a tabernacle of silver-gilt. There came afterwards the Vice-Chancellor, fellows and scholars of the College and other members of the University, the mayor and town council, and inhabitants of the town. They made a circuit of the town as far as Magdalene Bridge, and returned to St Bene't's, next to which at

Corpus a feast was provided for the participants. This demonstration of faith continued until abolished by government order in 1549. It then became an object of contention, being revived under Queen Mary and abolished finally under Elizabeth, its last appearance saddened by fire striking the canopy as it passed the Falcon Inn in Petty Cury.

The founding of Corpus Christi and the procession is an outstanding and isolated example of the practice of a common faith. The history of town and gown is of course full of examples of conflict between the communities, and instances when charity grew very cold, in 1381 and long afterwards. Yet a powerful sense of the habit of intercession remains, and the University and colleges in their ceremonies, buildings and statutes reflected obligations to all those who endowed them.

## The University as a Religious Community

The university year was divided into terms marked by religious feasts, which determined the calendar of the western world. Michaelmas began the day after the feast of St Denis (9 October) and lasted until 'O Sapientia' (16 December) – after the Vespers antiphon for that day. Lent began the day after the feast of St Hilary (13 January) and continued until the Friday before Palm Sunday. Easter term began on Wednesday after the first Sunday after Easter, and continued until the feast of St Margaret (20 July). These divisions have, with some modifications, set the pattern for the structure of the academical year until the present time. The hours of lectures and other scholarly acts within these terms were announced by the bells of town churches: Great St Mary's and St Benet's, and the bell of the University Schools whose keeper was also the Chaplain of the University. Those studying to be Bachelors of Arts had first to go through a testing time of defending in live debate logically formulated problems. This time, known as 'determination', began on Ash Wednesday and was also known as 'standing in Lent'. It began with a procession to Great St Mary's, a sermon and a prayer, and ended with a final solemn debate on the Thursday before Passion Sunday.

The scholarly community itself was deemed part of the clerical body, and the Chancellor of Cambridge was in origin an official of the Bishop of Ely, from whom during the fifteenth century he gradually acquired independence. This clerical aspect of course long outlasted the Reformation, and is reflected still in the quasi-religious form of degree ceremonies. A seventeenth-century bedell recorded that in his time the last day of the Michaelmas Term was marked by a ceremony of absolution: 'The Vice-Chancellor goeth to the back of his chair, and he first readeth the 67th psalm in Latin to the company, all kneeling, who do repeat the same after him. This done, he sitting in his chair, head covered, and pronounceth the absolution in these words "by the authority committed to us we absolve you from all faults of casual neglect, forfeiture, breach of statutes, privileges and customs, and restore you to God and the sacraments of the Church; in the name of the Father, the Son, and the Holy Spirit [author's translation]."' Another record adds that every person admitted to a degree in any faculty should pronounce the De Profundis and the customary prayers for the dead.

The more solemn and formal scholarly debates, which took place for example on admissions to degrees, were performed in Great St Mary's. This church which, as St Mary's in the Market, was recognized as crucial also to the worship of the town, was repaired towards the end of the fifteenth century on the initiative of the University. Among contributions levied for the project were those from masters when they gained professorships in civil or canon law and from students entering the higher faculties of theology, law and medicine. In 1494 Thomas Barrow, Archdeacon of Colchester, a Doctor of Laws, gave £240 to be divided between the repairs for the church and the maintenance of a chaplain to pray at the anniversary of his death, and also for members of the royal family. From the end of the fourteenth century a new chapel built over a divinity school was also available to the University, and in this formal business was conducted. In 1398 the Chancellor and the University's government agreed to celebrate twice a year the exequies of Sir William and Lady Thorpe by whose generosity the building had been completed. It was in this new chapel that the governors of the University deliberated on proposals in the 'graces' put before them, and their decisions on each were ordered to be proclaimed 'in a loud voice' in the middle of the chapel by one of the proctors or their deputies. There is reference to a small chapel annexed to the main building, which suggests that, as in the design of early medieval hospitals, the sacred and 'business' functions were united under one roof. The chapel windows, before the Reformation, bore inscriptions relating to the prayers for the dead. These were destroyed, following a grace passed in 1565, but those depicting the arms of the Thorpes were allowed to remain.

## The Role of Friars and Monastic Students

The medieval University relied not only upon the church of Great St Mary and its own purpose-built premises to conduct its religious and scholarly affairs, but on the houses of the friars, who formed a very important element in university and town life. The Greyfriars had from the mid-thirteenth century a large and imposing church, ideal for sermons. Between 1479 and 1519, while building operations were carried on at Great St Mary's, scholastic acts for conferring degrees were held there. One took place in 1507 at the creation of twelve doctors over which John Fisher presided as Chancellor in the presence of the King, his mother Lady Margaret Beaufort, and Prince Henry. The Cambridge Faculty of Theology depended much on the excellent preachers and scholars among the friars, who included John Duns Scotus, although their exemption from some aspects of university control led to quarrels with the non-friar students. The Greyfriars had also contributed an excellent water supply to the town in the shape of the conduit that was later to feed the fountain in Trinity Great Court.

The Blackfriars, who began building a church and convent outside the Barnwell Gate of the town in 1238, had by the year 1260 two friars, Siger and William, lecturing in the University, and in the fourteenth century the house hosted visiting foreign scholars reading theology. Outstanding among Dominican scholars was Robert Holcot, who wrote a commentary on the book of Wisdom. The friars also performed the duties of confessors and preachers, and a confraternity is recorded as having used their house as a meeting place. In the late Middle Ages they possessed an image of Our Lady of Grace, before which offerings were made in 1505 and 1507 on behalf of Lady Margaret Beaufort, mother of King Henry VII. It is reputed that the beautiful Virgin and Child which is situated in the Church of Our Lady and the English Martyrs (Pl. 22a) came from the house of the Blackfriars, but its style resembles that of mid sixteenth-century carving, and the point remains unsettled.

The ministry of friars as preachers and confessors embraced other orders. The Carmelites, or Whitefriars, settled first at Chesterton, then at Newnham, and in the 1290s moved to a more central position on what was to become the Walnut Court of Queens' College. The Augustinian Friars were settled on the Old Cavendish site by Free School Lane in the 1280s. Their church, like that of the Franciscans, was used as a venue for scholastic ceremonies in the late fifteenth and early sixteenth centuries.

A direct link between the religious life and the student collegiate life was forged by the foundation of colleges set apart for student monks sent to university by their abbeys or priories. At Oxford such houses were Gloucester College (1283–91), to which came monks from a variety of Benedictine abbeys, Durham College (*c.* 1289), to accommodate those from Durham Priory, and Canterbury College (1361), for those from Canterbury. There followed St Mary's College for

Augustinian Canons (1435), and St Bernard's College (1437) for the Cistercians, who had also been housed at Rewley Abbey from about 1280. At some of these was also an intake of secular students, and in the case of Canterbury College this mixed community led to power struggles. Monastic patronage, however, permitted secular students to attend university who might not have had the means: eight from the vicinity of the city of Durham were supported by the Priory at its Oxford college.

At Cambridge there was only one such foundation. In 1340 the Bishop of Ely set up a hostel for Ely monks there, in Trinity Street, which continued until in 1428 larger premises were acquired by the Abbot of Croyland. The new Monks' Hostel – on the site of Magdalene College – received greater endowments in the 1470s when it became known as Buckingham College. Henry Stafford, Duke of Buckingham, has been credited with this benefaction, but it has recently been suggested that the real benefactress was Anne Neville, dowager duchess and mother-in-law of Margaret Beaufort, to whom she left books in English and French and her personal book of hours. It appears that, particularly for Benedictines, much store was set by university training for some monks, and a large number of them became heads of their houses in the later Middle Ages.

An idea of the importance of the friars and other religious in the life of the University can be gained from a description of the reception of King Henry VII when he visited Cambridge on 22 April 1506: 'As he approached near the University, within a quarter of a mile, there stood first all the four Orders of Friars, and after other Religious, and the King on horseback kissed the cross of every [order] of the Religious; and then there stood all along all the Graduates after their degrees in all their habits, and at the end of them was the University Cross ...'.

## The Colleges as Centres of Prayer and Renewal

The secular medieval colleges were established along the lines dictated by the various statutes of their founders, but all shared a community life, a major aspect of which was prayer. It is worth remembering that these educational bodies we see today, containing teachers and students specializing in a number of disciplines, with the achievement of qualifications as their *raison d'être*, originated in very different circumstances, which yet provided the solid foundation upon which they have developed. The special aim of the University colleges was to provide graduate students with sufficient means to continue the long course of study in the higher faculties: theology, law and medicine.

One of the earliest recorded attempts at endowing scholars was that by Barnwell Priory, which in 1267 was provided with money by the Bishop of Ely to support two students of theology. In 1280 a later Bishop placed scholars in the Hospital of St John the Evangelist on the site of the present St John's College, as a means of funding them in that securely endowed body already under the patronage of the Bishop. In a short time it was discovered that the student and hospital communities could not peaceably co-exist on the same site, and in 1284 the scholars were given separate premises, forming in Peterhouse the earliest Cambridge college.

Nevertheless, wherever endowment took place, it carried with it an obligation to pray for the endowers, their friends, patrons and kinsfolk. Some of the collegians, like the scholars dwelling in the hostels and lodgings of the town, worshipped side by side with the townspeople. At Peterhouse, Corpus Christi, and Michaelhouse the college chapels and parish churches were combined at St Peter's (Little St Mary's after 1352), St Bene't's, and St Michael's in Trinity Street (Pl. 2a). Whether in their own chapels or elsewhere, however, religious observance was a key element in the function of the colleges. The statutes given by Bishop Bateman in 1353 for Gonville Hall, a college whose emphasis was to be the study of canon law and medicine, with theology added in deference to the wishes of its initial founder Edmund Gonville, prescribe a detailed programme of worship. Every fellow must hear or sing Mass daily, repeat the Ave Maria fifty times, and pray for the College's benefactors. Every Saturday the dedication of the College was to be celebrated with a Mass of the Annunciation – a representation of which appeared on its earliest common seal – and the saying of one hundred and fifty Aves. At Queens' College by its statutes of 1475 the accent was placed on the study of theology, and that of law discouraged, a feature common to other late fifteenth-century foundations. Their intention was to supply the Church at large with well-trained priests to balance the large number of clergy with predominantly legal rather than theological backgrounds. The driving force behind Queens' was an energetic Cambridge parish priest, Andrew Dokett, who also established almshouses, improved St Botolph's Church, and successfully solicited the patronage of two queens of England for his project. He was aided in the acquisition of properties by two of his parishioners, Richard Andrew and John Morris, and employed a third – the master mason Reginald Ely – in the design of the College. Two benefactions included obligations to the wider world. A Cambridge cleric in 1459 gave the College land in St Botolph's parish to pay for sermons by theologian fellows of Queens' 'in places where this is of pressing necessity for the salvation and comfort of the greatest number of souls'. A lecturer of the College supported by another benefaction in 1472 had to pray for the benefactress and her husband, and also to preach a sermon every Easter at the London church of St Dionis Backchurch.

A fellow of Queens', John Fawne, was the first holder of the Preachership founded officially for the University in 1504 by Lady Margaret Beaufort, mother of Henry VII. The preachers were to deliver sermons during the year both to members of the University and – when out of term – to travel and preach in several named locations. This was a well-financed foundation, funded like Lady Margaret's professorship in theology from the estates of Westminster Abbey. It supplemented an existing scheme, sanctioned by the Pope in 1503, by which the University could license twelve qualified graduates, priests, to preach throughout England, Scotland and Ireland. One hundred and seventy-five such licences were granted between 1504 and 1522. There is little doubt that the need for wider pastoral care was felt and that it was exercised in the late medieval University, although its impact on national life as a whole is difficult to assess.

Lady Margaret Beaufort, and her spiritual guide and executor John Fisher, Chancellor of the University 1504–35, were leading protagonists of the effort to nourish the Church with life blood from the University. Christ's College and St John's, both founded by Lady Margaret, again aimed to promote the training of learned clergy. The story of the foundation of these colleges belongs to the wider history of education. Lady Margaret rescued the struggling foundation of Godshouse, dedicated to training teachers in Latin grammar, endowed it handsomely and grafted on to its original design provisions for graduate fellows to study arts and theology. She intended another foundation on the site of the hospital of St John, which was carried through after her death by her executors and particularly by John Fisher, as the present St John's College. St John's was planned by Fisher as a seminary and an English 'collegium trilingue' like Louvain, specializing in the renewed studies of classical Latin and Greek, and even the little-known Hebrew, with a view to placing in the hands of its scholars the most up-to-date tools for the exploration of the Bible, and to equip theologically trained priests for the Church.

These two colleges, however, had like others another spiritual dimension as places where the liturgy was celebrated and intercessory prayer maintained. The fellows of Christ's, and indeed the undergraduate scholars who since the late fourteenth century had come to figure in some colleges, were to pray principally for the foundress and her royal kindred. They were also to maintain the chain of prayer for the founder and major benefactors of Godshouse only; they might not be paid to serve as chantry priests for other purposes. The fellows of Godshouse who continued in the new foundation, however, were permitted to accept other stipends to pray for souls. The fellows were to celebrate Mass four times on Sunday: Masses of the day, of the Holy Trinity, of the Blessed Virgin Mary, and a Requiem. On Monday to Saturday the Masses of the day were to be celebrated together with those of the Blessed Virgin Mary and a Requiem. On each day a special Mass was added: on Monday that of the Angels, on Tuesday that of the Martyrs, on Wednesday that of the Apostles, on Thursday that of the Virgins, on Friday that of the Confessors, and on Saturday that of All Saints. Thus the whole company of the Church was represented in the Christ's College liturgy in a weekly timetable.

We have evidence of the wealth of devotional imagery which was to be found at Christ's. In her will Lady Margaret left both fixed and processional crucifixes, which were in fact calvaries, depicting Mary and John as well as the Saviour. She also left communion vessels, and images of the Virgin and Child, St Mary Magdalene, St John the Baptist and St George. Among the altar cloths was one depicting St Gregory's vision of the Passion while he was celebrating Mass, and other vestments figured the monogram IHS, both embroideries witnessing to the special dedication of the College to Christ. The dedication of the place was reflected in another liturgical feature, a permanent Easter Sepulchre. This was finished in 1510 and contained images of Christ, Mary and four knights. It was made by Ralph Bolman or Bowman, freemason, apparently on the premises of the Carmelites, from whence it was carried at a cost of eighteen pence by Nicholas Ap Rice. Images of Christ's Resurrection and of Our Lady we know to have been carved from local Eversden stone. We also have records of the making of a tabernacle for an image of Christ from a great tree, forty-six feet long, and upon this and other works seven carvers were employed in 1510–11. In 1548 and 1551 two assaults were made on the furnishings of the Chapel: a workman was paid for 'helping down with Images and mending the pavement under Christ's Image' (perhaps broken during the work of iconoclasm), and two tabernacles were taken down, the high altar being replaced with a wooden communion table.

St John's also had its chain of prayerful intercession: for its own founders and benefactors; for those of the Hospital which had preceded it; and for the three decayed religious houses – the priories of Higham in Kent and Broomhall in Berkshire, and the Hospital of St Mary at Ospringe on the road to Canterbury – which had been dissolved and whose possessions had gone to increase its endowment. It had also an elaborate provision for chantry Masses, and a special requirement for the preaching obligation of its fellows. Erasmus paid tribute to Lady Margaret and to Fisher as those who supported preachers 'to bring the principles of the Gospel to the people'. The statutes of St John's, given by Fisher in successive codes between 1516 and 1530, prescribed that one quarter of the fellowship should be engaged in preaching in English to the people not less than eight sermons a year, and after their first year an additional sermon in the College chapel. Between 1519 and 1524 we can follow through the College accounts payments to certain fellows for preaching in country churches. After 1524 the form of accounts changes and payments cannot be separately traced, but the appointment of preachers in the College continued. So whether or not this outgoing evangelical enterprise was long maintained, it was a testimony to Fisher's original pastoral concern. He was himself a noted preacher, and some of his sermons reached a wider public through the lively printing trade of the time.

## Dissenters and Reformers

As we now know, that spirit of Catholic pastoral concern either was not widespread enough, or was powerless in the context of the times, to prevent the seismic upheaval in religion, in Cambridge as elsewhere, which we recognize in the long course of the Reformation. Much has been made of the spearhead role of Cambridge in these events. Historians have focused on the importance of the 'cell' of academic dissenters discussing Protestant ideas at their base at the White Horse Tavern, sited between the present King's and St Catharine's Colleges. They have highlighted the conversion of Hugh Latimer, fellow of Clare College, and University chaplain, whose preaching in St Edward's parish church in 1529 brought those ideas to the townspeople of Cambridge. They have traced the tortured and tortuous career of the hapless Thomas Bilney, a fellow of Trinity Hall, through whom Latimer came to his Protestant opinions.

While it is tempting to see in the White Horse radicals, and in Latimer's attacks on Catholic doctrine at St Edward's, the signs of a strong Cambridge movement providing the English Reformation with intellectual ammunition, the truth is almost certainly less neat. The convictions of the reformers were very diverse: there was no Protestant 'party line' in solid conflict with the Church. Thomas Bilney, while he rejected the intercession of the saints and disputed with a friar at Ipswich the veneration of images, maintained to the last his belief in the Catholic doctrine of the Eucharist, in Confession, and in the supremacy of the Pope. Latimer, on the other hand, fully espoused

Lutheran doctrine, and was to be numbered among those who died affirming his Protestant beliefs in the reign of Mary. Conversely King Henry VIII was able to number among those who backed his claim to be head of the English Church William Buckmaster, Vice-Chancellor of the University and otherwise of orthodox Catholic opinions. With hindsight we view a gradually widening gap between opposing camps, based on the subsequent history of western churches; but the men of the time were feeling their way in a battle of diverse opinions.

A strong tradition of obedience to the royal will in matters of church discipline, dating back to the early fifteenth century and before, led many eminent churchmen instinctively to follow their monarch in his resistance to the Pope, while retaining their traditional Catholic faith. Fisher, alone among the English bishops, was prepared to suffer martyrdom for the intimate connection between papal supremacy and the stability of Catholic doctrine. The king himself, sincerely troubled in conscience (whether or not over-scrupulously) about the legality of his marriage with his dead brother's wife Catherine of Aragon, led also by his own desire for a male heir, and captivated by Anne Boleyn, ended his life a schismatic monarch Protestant by policy rather than conviction. It has been suggested that while he was prepared to see most of the private chantries of England stripped of their lands, he was not prepared to witness the dissolution of the Colleges in Oxford and Cambridge, because they included royal foundations bound to pray for the King's soul.

Before the king's personal dilemma brought the whole standing of the English Church's relations with the Church Universal into question, there was at Cambridge a coherent Catholic programme of renewal which was more in evidence than the scattered sounds of Lutheran dissent. We have already seen how Christ's and St John's were dedicated to producing learned clergy, to celebrating the liturgy, and, in the case of St John's, to preaching in the English tongue. As part of the enterprise of renewal and reform Erasmus had been brought to Cambridge by Fisher, held the professorship in theology founded by Lady Margaret Beaufort, and began his work producing a new Greek edition of the New Testament – the *Novum Instrumentum* – with Latin translation, published in 1516. That work was owned by Fisher's old tutor William Melton. It figures in his will, made in 1528, with a variety of works by the Fathers of the Church, and many by up-to-date writers of the Renaissance.

Erasmus's work was an inspiration both to those who in the years to come would reject the Church and to those who would defend it. The sensation of its appearance encouraged people to concentrate afresh on the wording of the text and its substance, rather than simply accepting it as a part of the whole Christian tradition, as had been possible with the long use of the Vulgate. Bilney said that on reading it, 'immediately I seemed unto myself inwardly to feel a marvellous comfort and quietness, insomuch as my bruised bones leaped for joy'. John Watson, Master of Christ's and noted for his opposition to Lutheran teachings, wrote to Erasmus that 'it shed a wonderful flood of light on Christ, and earned the gratitude of all who are devoted to it'. The renewal of classical and biblical scholarship had implications both for Catholic and Protestant programmes of reform.

It was a different matter when it came to editions of the Bible in English, unrecognized by the Church authorities. Those by William Tyndale and Miles Coverdale, an Augustinian friar at Cambridge, were produced by men with known Lutheran opinions, disseminating a text which made no mention of the hierarchy of the Church as it could then be seen in the world. To the bishops it was a matter of interpretation: theological scholars having access to a good Latin text which they could then study and comment on in their sermons, interpreting it with their command of the full range of Church tradition, could only do good. The bare text of the Gospels, placed by the new craft of printing in the hands of those without such training, could be a force for lessening or destroying people's awareness of God's grace mediated through all the sacraments. This was also why scholars such as Bilney and Latimer could be viewed as a danger when they preached to non-university audiences purely from their own readings of the Bible text in these translations. Some trends in Protestant conviction can be seen as the culmination of earlier ones: concentration on the saving Person and Passion of Jesus, embodied in devotion to the Eucharist; regard for the simple of way of life of the first disciples and criticism of worldly churchmen – a recurrent theme throughout the Middle Ages. But there had also been regard for the intercession of the saints, an appreciation of the importance of shrines, relics and pilgrimages as a means of grace and a reminder of holiness. For Bilney to tour the villages of Norfolk deploring these things as meaningless in the light of his own conviction of justification through faith in Christ was seen as harmful to those communities.

The seminal force of the scholars gathered at various times at the White Horse can be overestimated. The most influential attender was Robert Barnes, Prior of the Augustinian Friars, who, along with his pupil Miles Coverdale, came to take a determined stand against the whole range of traditional Catholic teaching. Apart from Bilney and George Stafford, a fellow of Pembroke College who chose to lecture directly on the scriptures rather than on the *Sentences*, their best known traditional medieval commentary, between 1524 and 1528, there were about ten others on whom Barnes could count as supporters. Confronting them were a number of orthodox Catholic scholars of equal dedication, both at Oxford and at Cambridge – where most were connected with St John's College. Among them was Ralph Baynes, who fled the country in 1534 rather than take the Oath of Supremacy which placed Henry VIII at the helm of the English Church.

## The Royal Divorce and its Consequences

During the 1520s it seemed that the Lutherans in the English Universities were an intrepid but not numerous group. Opposed to them were Catholic reformers nourishing knowledge of the scriptural languages in the foundations of St John's College, Cambridge and Corpus Christi and Cardinal Colleges, Oxford. Things were to change decisively in 1530. In the furnace of controversy surrounding the question of Henry's divorce, some shifted their ground: Robert Wakefield and Richard Croke, both originally paid as Hebrew and Greek lecturers respectively by Fisher, became devoted King's men. In Croke's case disaffection had begun earlier, with his opposition to Fisher's own chantry foundation in St John's, and reports of Croke not fulfilling his lecturing duties, gathering select groups apart in his rooms, and absenting himself from the common college hall. At the date of those rumours, in 1526, Fisher wrote of the Lutheran heresy being in Cambridge, and dissociated himself from those who were denying Purgatory. In 1529 he personally confronted Wakefield in open debate on Wakefield's revised reading – favourable to Henry's case – of a text in the Book of Deuteronomy. Eventually the Universities, albeit not without controversy, gave Henry the verdict he desired. For Cambridge the moment came on 9 March 1530, after a close debate. Congregation had been summoned to discuss the question, but dissolved in conflicting opinions without reaching a decision. The Vice-Chancellor, Buckmaster, proposed that the matter be referred to a committee. Those defending Catherine of Aragon's case protested at the selection: the majority were Henry's supporters. Stephen Gardiner, Master of Trinity Hall, defended the choices, and this body made the final decision that Henry's marriage to Catherine was invalid if her previous marriage with Prince Arthur had remained unconsummated.

It may seem a very technical pronouncement, but its consequences were profound. It meant that the University had confirmed the King's opinion of his case in defiance of the Pope, and during the 1530s the tide was to turn in favour of the King's men. The logic of the King's opposition to the Pope had led to his control of the English Church, and also to encouragement of those who proclaimed anti-papal teach-ings in his support. But the issues of doctrine were complex, and men fought and suffered for the whole range of their opinions. To help secure their position Henry and his vice-gerent Thomas Cromwell made nine men with Protestant leanings bishops out of a total of eleven between 1532 and 1536; but Hugh Latimer was disciplined by Convocation for his preaching, when he attacked clerical celibacy and the doctrine of Purgatory. Thomas Bilney continued to hold fast to his discovery of a renewed personal faith through the New Testament, and witnessed to it by preaching in Norfolk, and handing an anchoress at Norwich a copy of the Protestant William Tyndale's English translation of it. This inflamed the authorities to action, and Bilney was burnt at the stake in Norwich on 19 August 1531. Before dying he had heard Mass, accepted confession and absolution and received the Eucharist. His death, after his acceptance of at least a part of Catholic doctrine, is one of the great tragedies of the history of the Reformation. Another is that of John Fisher who, consistent with his Catholic faith to the last, had refused to subscribe to the Acts of Succession and Supremacy, and was executed on 22 June 1535. Since that day in 1506 when he welcomed Henry VII to the University, he had travelled far from the centre of the establishment. He had even, in conversation with Chapuys, the imperial ambassador, discussed the possibility of foreign intervention against Henry VIII. Chapuys had smuggled out of the country Fisher's treatises in favour of Catherine of Aragon.

Within the University a restructuring of learning and allegiance was put into operation in the autumn following Fisher's execution. The King's right-hand man, Thomas Cromwell, succeeded Fisher as Chancellor of Cambridge University. The royal injunctions which he carried out through his deputy, Thomas Leigh of King's College, covered both religious matters and some aspects of the curriculum. An oath of allegiance to the statutes which Fisher had refused to accept was required from all members. Theology lectures must henceforward be given on the bible text, rather than on the *Sentences* of Peter Lombard or his commentators, the choice made privately by George Stafford in 1524. In continuation of the work of renaissance scholars more of the fabric of late medieval scholastic studies was removed, and for it was substituted a greater emphasis on the teaching of classical Greek and Latin throughout the University. The authority of Aristotle himself, however, the major authority in ethics and philosophy, was retained or even enhanced since the refinements of the late medieval philosophers were swept aside. The study of canon law was abolished, since the English schism had logically removed the need to train men in laws made by the universal Church, whose ultimate court of appeal was the Pope. Canon law was still to be practised in English church courts, but by civil lawyers under the Crown.

Explicitly religious and liturgical changes were only beginning in 1535. The injunctions appointed a commemorative Mass in Great St Mary's for the college and university founders and benefactors, and also for the King and 'Lady Anne, his lawful wife and queen of the realm' – sealing a radical political and religious change with a traditional form of celebration.

In the injunction that 'all ceremonies, constitutions and observances that hinder polite learning should be abolished' was sounded the death knell of the medieval university, and a presage of radical change. Over the next decade the houses of friars and other religious in the town were dissolved. The chantry foundation of John Fisher in St John's, which had linked payments to lecturers in Greek and Hebrew to a round of Masses and prayers for its founder and his kindred and friends, was abolished and the lectures were henceforth administered without it, under new statutes given in 1545 by the King. The colleges, saved from the dissolution of chantries in 1546 and in obedience to doctrinal change under Edward VI, shed that part of their prayerful function which was to pray for the salvation of souls and their release from Purgatory. They concentrated instead on prayers for their present sovereign and benefactors, and on commemorating past benefits for the edification and example of living members. Corpus Christi College ceased its annual procession, and sold its vestments and sacred vessels, to the chagrin of townsmen who claimed that the college had been built upon their charity, which the procession clearly epitomised for them. The University Chapel retained its traditional furnishings and vestments until Elizabeth's reign, but eventually sold them in accord with the long-term success of the Protestant changes in form and doctrine.

The story outlined above is part of the larger and complex history of the Protestant Reformation, events which many historians now see as having been a gradual erosion of Catholic England occupying the whole of the sixteenth and early seventeenth centuries. Resistance to the change by a recusant minority was, however, equally enduring, and the universities themselves were re-penetrated by Catholics returning from exile and training at Douai and other centres abroad. We can acknowledge the academic gains of Henry VIII's changes, for all the brutal methods by which they were brought about: the foundation of Regius professorships, and of Trinity College; the scholarship of such men as Roger Ascham, tutor of Elizabeth I, and John Redman, Lady Margaret Professor and Master of Trinity. What was permanently lost was the possibility of continuing and developing the University within Catholic Christendom, enriched with classical and biblical learning, while retaining something of its late medieval scholastic heritage.

# Chapter 3

# A Catholic Interlude: Sidney Sussex College, 1687–1688

*Nicholas Rogers*

## The Death of Catholic Cambridge

The last Mass in Great St Mary's was said in June 1559, to be replaced
by the re-introduced services of the 1552 Prayer Book. The churchwardens' accounts reveal the process of the decatholicization of the
church, always in response to official command. In 1562 Archbishop
Parker ordered the demolition of the rood loft. The image of Our
Lady on the blue velvet altar cloth was removed on the command of
the archdeacon in 1567–8 and sold for 6s. The images in the stained
glass windows were whitewashed, an easily reversible reformation.
Here and elsewhere in Cambridge efforts were made, as they had
been in the reign of Edward VI, to preserve the paraphernalia of
Catholic worship. Most of these attempts were unsuccessful. The
whereabouts of the vestments and other items secreted by John Caius
were betrayed to the authorities by one of the fellows of his college
and put on a bonfire in December 1572. But in Our Lady and the
English Martyrs is a mid-sixteenth-century Netherlandish or German
wooden statue of the Virgin and Child (Pl. 22a) which was apparently
found in a building belonging to Emmanuel College in the nineteenth
century. This may well be a survivor of the Marian re-equipment of
Cambridge churches, perhaps even the 'Image of our lady vppon the
hyghe altar' for which the wardens of Great St Mary's paid 8s. 6d. in
1558.

## Cambridge Recusants

However reluctantly the people of Cambridge may have come to terms with the new ecclesiastical order, within twenty or thirty years constant exposure to the Prayer Book liturgy, sermons and catechetic instruction ensured that the town was thoroughly Protestant. There was little opportunity in Cambridge for a strong urban recusant community to survive. Unlike Winchester or Oxford, Cambridge did not have much in the way of nearby recusant gentry who could provide protection to priests. The Huddlestons at Sawston and the Paris family of Linton, which died out in the reign of Charles II, were the only significant recusant gentry. Unlike Oxford, Cambridge did not lie close to jurisdictional boundaries, which could be of use in evading the authorities. It is naturally difficult to obtain figures about numbers at any point. The one exception is the Compton census of 1676. Although this clearly underestimates numbers, its reckoning of three papists as opposed to 3088 conformists compares poorly with Oxford's thirty-four against 4075 or Winchester's forty-eight against 1815. A more significant minority in Cambridge in 1676 were the seventy-seven dissenters, the product of a long tradition of radical Protestantism in the town's churches. However, small though it was, the Cambridge recusant community produced at least one vocation. On 15 October 1601 Thomas More, born in Cambridge in 1586, the son of Edward and Mary More, was ordained priest in Rome. He later joined the Jesuits and died at Ghent in 1623.

On 5 June 1578 Montford Scott, a newly ordained priest who had studied at Trinity Hall before going on to Douai, was captured in Cambridge with a companion and sent to London by the Vice-Chancellor, 'with all such books, letters, writings, and other trash which were taken about them'. He may have been arrested while endeavouring to minister to Catholics in the town, but it more likely that his aim was the conversion of members of the University. He was eventually released, but in December 1590 he was captured again, while visiting his birthplace in Suffolk, and on 1 July 1591 the Venerable Montford Scott was hanged, drawn and quartered in Fleet Street.

## Catholics in the University

The history of Catholicism in Cambridge in the century after 1559 is largely a University history. Several of those Catholics in the University who were opposed to the Elizabethan settlement went to foreign universities, most notably Louvain, where a Cambridge College was established. For a time some protection to Catholics was provided by conservative heads of houses who stayed, such as Caius or Provost Baker at King's, who eventually had to flee to Louvain in 1570. By the end of the reign of Elizabeth, Cambridge colleges were firmly Protestant and largely Calvinist in their theology. But there was a Trojan horse in the Protestant citadel. As part of their debate with Catholics, Protestant academics needed access to the works of their adversaries. On the shelves of Sidney Sussex College, founded in 1596 as a sort of Anglican seminary, could be found the Douai Bible, John Gibbons's *Concertatio*, which included St Edmund Campion's *Rationes decem*, the works of Robert Bellarmine, and even St Teresa of Avila. Perhaps this was one of the reasons why access to the library was so closely controlled. Blessed Henry Heath, the Franciscan who was executed at Tyburn in 1645, was converted to Catholicism by reading Bellarmine while an undergraduate at Corpus Christi. The armour of Protestantism provided by study at Cambridge was not fully proofed, as St Alban Bartholomew Roe discovered when, as an undergraduate, he entered into debate with a recusant prisoner at St Albans. What happened is recounted by Challoner:

> He applied himself with good success to higher learning; till going to visit some friends at S. Alban's, as Providence would have it, he was there told of one David, an inhabitant of that town, lately convicted and cast into prison for a popish recusant, and was desirous to go and talk with the prisoner, making no question but that he could convince him of the errors and absurdities of the Romish tenets; for he had a sharp and ready wit and a tongue well hung, and withal was full of conceit of his own religion, and with false ideas of the Catholic doctrine.
>
> To the prison therefore he went, and entered into discourse with the prisoner, upon the subject of his religion; who, though a mechanic, yet was not ill read in controversy, so that he was able to maintain his cause against all the oppositions of our young University man, and even pushed him so hard upon several articles, that Mr. Roe soon perceived that he had taken a tartar, and knew not which way to turn himself.
>
> In conclusion, he who came to the attack with so much confidence of victory, left the field with confusion, beginning now to stagger and diffide in the cause.

There was a generational shift in Cambridge away from Jacobean Calvinism which manifested itself both in Laudian Anglicanism and in an increase in conversions to Catholicism. The poet Richard Crashaw, the son of the anti-Catholic divine William Crashaw, ended his days as a canon of Loreto. Quite sharp religious divisions could appear even within families, mirroring the divisions of the Civil War. Walter

Montagu, the brother of the Parliamentary general the Earl of Manchester, was not only almoner to Queen Henrietta Maria but also commendatory Abbot of Pontoise. The ascendancy of the Parliamentarians led to the breaking down of 'popish pictures' by William Dowsing and his associates. Most surviving medieval imagery in Cambridge went at that time, as did the Laudian innovations. The reign of Charles II brought generally easier times for Catholics, until there erupted the foul lies of Titus Oates, preposterous tales that they could all too easily be believed by a people brought up on bugbears such as the Spanish Armada and the Gunpowder Plot. Cambridge gave three victims at the time of the 'Popish Plot': Edward Coleman, the Duke of York's secretary, the Jesuit Anthony Turner, and William Howard, Earl of Stafford, who had studied at St John's in the 1620s.

## Joshua Basset

In 1685, having weathered attempts to exclude him from the succession, James II, who had been a Catholic since 1672, succeeded his brother. One of the contributors to a volume of verses published by the University to mark the death of Charles II and the accession of James (*Mœstissimæ ac lætissimæ academiæ Cantabrigiensis affectus* (Cambridge, 1685)) was Joshua Basset, a fellow of Gonville and Caius College. In the first of his three poems he rejoices that James has survived the attacks of Titus Oates so that he may serve the one, apostolic and Catholic faith. As part of his drive to ameliorate the lot of Catholics, James sought to break the Anglican monopoly in the universities. He seems to have envisaged the academic promotion of Catholicism by the encouragement of free debate.

The man whom James chose to advance the Catholic cause in the University of Cambridge was Joshua Basset. Basset had been born in King's Lynn in 1641, the son of a merchant. In 1657 he had been admitted at Caius, where he became first a junior fellow and then, in 1673, a senior fellow. He had taken Anglican orders and from 1674 to 1681 was dean of Caius. The tenor of Basset's poem on James's accession indicates that he had converted to Catholicism by 1685. This is confirmed by *Reason and Authority: or the Motives of a late Protestants Reconciliation to the Catholic Church, together with Remarks upon some late Discourses against Transubstantiation*, published anonymously by Henry Hills, the King's Printer, in 1687, in which Basset gave a lively account of his theological development. He had attempted to construct a scheme of divinity on rational grounds, which he found resulted in a 'confused Babel of Religion'. The Church of England did not constitute a lawful authority, sufficient to oblige his reason and conscience. Only the Church of Rome provided 'fundamental doctrines, authoritatively imposed, and universally received throughout the whole Christian world'. To the Protestant allegation that the Catholic Church was corrupt in faith and morals Basset replied that, if that were the case, then 'Christ failed of his promise, and so good night to Christianity'. His decision to convert seems to be have been taken after the publication of Tillotson's *Discourse against Transubstantiation* in 1684. A large part of *Reason and Authority* is devoted to a refutation of Tillotson's arguments, and to demonstrating that some Anglican writers, such as Herbert Thorndike, professed a Catholic eucharistic theology.

On the death of Richard Minshull, the aged Puritan Master of Sidney Sussex College, on 31 December 1686, Basset was appointed his successor by a royal mandate dated 3 January 1687. The speed with which James II acted suggests that Basset had already been marked out for preferment. Basset had been instrumental in securing the recantation of Edward Spence, who had attacked the Catholic Church in a University sermon on 5 November 1686. He may have been known at Court before then. In *Reason and Authority* he alludes to attending a sermon at Whitehall in Charles II's reign, and he apparently told the fellows of Sidney that he had liberty to wait on the King, the Queen Consort and the Queen Dowager.

When the fellows of Sidney requested that their new master should take the oath against 'popery and all heresies, superstitions and errors' required by the College statutes, a second mandate was issued on 12 January, which dispensed Basset from taking the oaths of allegiance and supremacy. This was followed on 25 February by a royal warrant again dispensing Basset and other Cambridge converts from the oaths. Joshua Basset was finally admitted as Master on 7 March 1687, the day when the assize judges arrived in Cambridge. Following a further attempt to invoke Sidney's statutes against the Master, those statutes were scrutinized by the Ecclesiastical Commission, which on 13 June 1687 ordered the deletion of the anti-Catholic provisions.

## Life at Sidney Sussex

Much of our information about the impact of Joshua Basset on Sidney Sussex College is derived from letters written by Joseph Craven, a fellow at the time, to Richard Reynolds, Bishop of Lincoln, and John Leng, Bishop of Norwich, in 1725 and 1726, in response to queries from them. Craven reveals that the first royal mandate was brought by Alban Placid Francis, a monk of the English Benedictine monastery of

Lambspring in Germany, who functioned as Basset's chaplain. At first Mr Francis (as he was known) took his meals with the Master, at the king's expense, but after the alteration of the college statutes he was made a fellow commoner, and came to meals in his habit. An attempt was made to award Francis an MA degree, but this foundered in the face of concerted opposition by the University, co-ordinated by the closet Arian and convinced anti-Catholic Isaac Newton. From Caius Basset brought two pupils, who were admitted in November 1687. One, William Thompson, who was made a fellow on the crown's recommendation, was certainly a Catholic, and the other, Valentine Husband, probably was one.

Unlike Magdalen College, Oxford, there was no expulsion of recalcitrant fellows. The library of Thomas Goodlad, one of the fellows, reveals that he was busily buying anti-Catholic tracts at this time to confirm his prejudices. In many ways life at Sidney seems to have carried on much as usual, to judge by contemporary records. Basset began a remodelling of the Master's garden, which can be seen in Loggan's view of the College (Pl. 3a). The College chapel continued to be used for Anglican services, but there were limits. Basset objected to its use for the customary Gunpowder Day service on 5 November 1687:

> He locked the door of the Chappel against us, having the night before taken the key from the scholar who kept it; and so forcibly hindered us from divine service that morning, as we had resolved not to omit it.

Conversation at high table must have been awkward at times. This can be sensed in Dr Craven's assessment of Basset's rule at Sidney:

> As to his government, we found him a passionate, proud and insolent man, whenever he was opposed, which made us very cautious in conversing with him, who saw he waited for and catched at all occasions to do us mischief in what concerned our religion. I don't deny, that he had learning and other abilities to have done us good, but his interest lay the contrary way.

## The Catholic Chapel at Sidney

Basset had one of the rooms in the Master's lodge fitted as a chapel, which was used by the Catholics of Cambridge. The remodelling of the Master's lodge in the early nineteenth century makes it impossible to identify the room exactly. The most likely candidate is the first-floor room known by 1639 as the chapel chamber, which overlooked Chapel

Court. The Cambridge antiquary William Cole, writing in the mid-eighteenth century, stated that he had met several Cambridge people who had heard Mass at Sidney. He also noted that the altarpiece of this chapel, consisting of the IHS monogram in a glory with cherubim about it, was still to be seen, hanging over one of the doors in the audit room. This is presumably the 'old Picture formerly an Altar peice', now no longer extant, recorded in the great chamber (or audit room) in the 1746 inventory of College possessions.

## The 'Glorious Revolution'

On the birth of the Prince of Wales on 10 June 1688, Basset contributed two poems to the *Genethliacon* published by the University. Others were not so loyal. The prospect of a Catholic succession set in train the events that led to the invasion of William of Orange. In mid-November, shortly after William's landing, Basset left Sidney. On 1 December James II, in a desperate attempt to placate his Anglican critics, rescinded the alterations to the statutes of Sidney Sussex College, and authorized the fellows to elect a new master. In December 1688, following the King's flight from London, the mob attacked Catholics and their property in Cambridge. Basset's chapel was despoiled; the college subsequently spent 11s. on 'mending the chamber broken by the rabble'.

Following his departure from Cambridge, Basset first went to King's Lynn, from which he soon moved to avoid the mob, and apparently settled in London, where he earned a living from legal work. Cole records that Basset approached his successor, James Johnson, when the latter was in London, in an attempt to recover his property from Sidney, 'but was roughly made to understand that if he did not desist he would be informed against as a Popish Priest'. There is no evidence that Basset ever took Catholic orders, but it is possible that Johnson threatened him with prosecution under penal legislation. Despite this, Basset evidently still regarded his former college with some affection. In 1714 he presented Sidney with a copy of his newly-published critique of the ecclesiology of Henry Dodwell. According to Cole, Basset lived to a great age and died in London 'in no very affluent circumstances', probably about 1720. Alban Francis retired for a while to Lambspring, but by 1701 had returned to the English mission, and died in England on 27 July 1715.

The 'Glorious Revolution' left Catholics excluded from the University once more, and burdened by further civil penalties. Yet even at this dark time there was a spark of light. In 1689 Basset's fellowship at Caius, which he had retained in addition to his mastership of Sidney, was formally declared void. The same action was taken at the same time against Clement Bolt, the son of a King's Lynn baker, a fellow since 1681, who had evidently converted to Catholicism under Basset's influence. On his expulsion Bolt entered the Venerable English College in Rome on 1 May 1689. He was ordained on 23 November 1692 and sent on the English mission the following May.

Amen, amen, I say to you, unless the grain of wheat falling into the ground die, itself remaineth alone. But if it die, it bringeth forth much fruit (John 12.24–5).

# Chapter 4

# Glowing Embers: Catholic Life in Cambridgeshire in the Century before Emancipation

*Christopher Jackson*

Religious reform may have been the more obvious reason for the onset of the Reformation throughout Northern Europe but in England there were strong political pressures at work as well. Considerations of national security rivalled Protestant orthodoxy as the motivation for establishing the Church of England, along with a Protestant succession to the monarchy, and saw to it that the severity of the penalties against a Church guided from outside the national territory endured rather longer in England than elsewhere. If the Elizabethan authorities saw the Spanish Armada as a papal conspiracy and Catholic priests as agents of a foreign power, their establishment paranoia was at least equalled during the times of James I (the Gunpowder Plot 1604–5), the Civil War and Commonwealth (1642–60) and William III (the Glorious Revolution of 1688). The complicity of individual Catholics during the Jacobite Rebellions of 1715 and 1745 attached suspicion to the entire Catholic community. The cumulative effect of this series of national crises was that the criminal penalties against Catholics in 1750 remained as harsh as in Elizabethan times but the civil restrictions against them taking any part in public life were if anything more severe. As Lord Hardwicke had remarked when Lord Chancellor in 1745: 'The laws against papists as they stand in the statute book are so severe that they are the cause of their own non-execution.'

The Catholics of mid-eighteenth-century Cambridgeshire found that good sense and humanity on the part of the authorities left them for the most part undisturbed. A mere handful of individuals, they were unlikely to pose a threat either to the government of the day or to the Established Church. Archbishop Blackburne of York had probably spoken for many in authority when he had told Lord Carlisle in 1733 that Catholics who 'are quiet and peaceable will find the Penal Act, for my part, as harmless as they can wish'. At least the Order Books of the Cambridgeshire Quarter Sessions during this period show no record of prosecutions being brought in the county under the Recusancy or Anti-Popery Acts from the year 1750 until this legislation was finally removed from the statute book in 1844. The same absence of prosecutions can be shown in the Town Sessions Order Books of the Borough of Cambridge over the same period. Even so, Cambridgeshire Catholics were well aware that sudden crises could sway public opinion or the mob against them at any time, as in 1688. In 1715 the anti-Catholic scare caused by the Jacobite rebellion led to the seizure by the County authorities of the arms and horses of 'Mr Huddleston and Mr Short two Papists of this county', under powers conferred on them by a statute of 1689, 'An Act for the better securing the government by disarming Papists and Reputed Papists'. Perhaps fortunately for the Catholic community, complicity in Jacobite plots was no longer an accusation levelled against them after 1766 when the Vatican withdrew its recognition of the Stuart claim to the throne of England.

## 'The finest hiding place in the country'

The survival of Catholic beliefs and observances in Cambridgeshire while these severe penalties remained on the statute book clearly demanded a high degree of care and caution. Since 1633 the counties of Norfolk, Suffolk, Cambridgeshire and Essex had formed the missionary district of the Jesuit 'College of the Holy Apostles'. In this College a group of priests, whose numbers varied from a maximum of nineteen to a minimum of eight, worked in the missionary district but did not live together. Two were normally assigned to Cambridgeshire and one of these lived at Sawston Hall (Pl. 4b). By 1750 only one of these Jesuit priests, John Champion, was based in Cambridgeshire and had resided at the Hall, the Cambridgeshire seat of the Huddleston family, since 1725. Known universally as 'Mr Champion', he was given additional cover to his true role by serving the family as their estate steward, messenger and legal adviser. Other Catholics, too, were admitted to hear Mass at Sawston Hall if within reach, the celebration being disguised by the designation 'Prayers', behind locked doors. One trusted Anglican friend of the Huddleston family, the antiquary Revd

William Cole of Linton (later of Milton), wrote of the religious arrangements at Sawston Hall after a visit in 1757:

> The private Chapel is a gloomy Garret and no ways ornamented; it is quite out of the way by Design, and in case of any Confusion, the Tabernacle and Altar may easily be removed. Mr. Champion, the Priest, has his Chamber close beyond it, he is a very worthy Jesuit and has lived in the Family these 30 years.

An attic was a popular location for the chapel in a Catholic house. As Cole discerned, the worshippers would then have had the greatest warning of an impending search by the authorities and secret cupboards for sacred items and vestments, along with exits and hiding places for the priest, all had to be provided for emergency use, as they were at Sawston Hall. The earlier Hall, a timbered Tudor mansion, had been burned down by a Protestant mob in 1553, frustrated at the escape of Mary Tudor from their hands. The rebuilt Sawston Hall as it now survives had been completed by 1584, with a number of these purpose-built features, among them two hiding places, already included in the structure. Later, in 1593, when the need to provide secure hiding places was becoming desperate, an additional priest's hole was ingeniously constructed by the Jesuit lay brother Nicholas Owen (canonized in 1970). This erstwhile builder and carpenter was to devote much of his life and his incomparable skill to installing these recesses in Catholic houses around the country. It seems safe to conclude that Cole, who made no mention of the priest's hole in his report, was not brought into this family secret. Even in 1757 searches for Catholic priests were still possible in the aftermath of the 1745 Jacobite rebellion. One therefore has to seek for more recent commentary about this secret feature, such as that of Granville Squiers who, writing in 1933, claimed this to be 'undoubtedly the finest hiding place in the country'. Sir Nikolaus Pevsner wrote in similar vein in the *Cambridgeshire* volume of his *Buildings of England* series: 'The house also contains one of the most convincing priest-holes in the country – a real hole at the top of the newel stairs, small and excellently hidden – and there are two others.'

## The Wider Ministry

The residence of Catholic priests in Catholic houses such as Sawston Hall was a matter partly of convenience and partly of safety. The care of John Champion and the long line of priests based at Sawston before and after him extended beyond the immediate duties of chaplain to the

Huddleston family, encompassing all Catholics in Cambridgeshire wherever they might be found. As mentioned above, the Mass Centre at Sawston was open to all Catholics within reach, though necessarily limited to those within walking or riding distance. This would have included any Catholics living in the town of Cambridge who were able to make the journey. Beyond that distance the priest was obliged to undertake a travelling circuit to maintain contact with his flock, estimated in 1773 at about seventy but spread well beyond a county which at that time (and until 1897) included the towns of Newmarket and Royston as well as the more distant centres of Ely, Chatteris and Wisbech. One of Fr Champion's successors at Sawston Hall, Fr James Taylor wrote on 13 March 1791:

> I have been near three weeks from home on a visit to my little congregations which lie so very distant that my journeys can not be performed in much less time. My rides are near 160 miles every Indulgence. [The eight Indulgences, long obsolete, were the times when devout Catholics would normally receive Holy Communion, being 1. Christmas, 2. The First Week of Lent, 3. Easter, 4. Whitsun, 5. SS. Peter and Paul, 6. The Assumption, 7. Michaelmas, 8. All Saints].

Even though the Catholic population in Cambridgeshire was so small, and six other English counties also numbered one hundred Catholics or even fewer, the picture over the country as a whole was rather different, and warranted organization on a national scale. The population of England and Wales in 1751 stood at 6.2 million of which almost one per cent or 60,000 were Catholics. From 1688 onwards the country had been divided into four Missionary Districts – London, Western, Northern and Midland, each district in the charge of a Vicar Apostolic with all the powers of a bishop but without a formally constituted diocese. A titular bishopric was however conferred on each Vicar Apostolic, and Cambridgeshire fell within the jurisdiction of the Bishop of the Midland District, based (1752–1804) at Long Birch House, Brewood, Staffordshire, later (from 1804), at Giffard House, Wolverhampton. All the missionary clergy and resident chaplains in Cambridgeshire and fifteen other counties (including the priests of the College of the Holy Apostles in the Eastern Counties until disbanded in 1773) came under the jurisdiction of the Bishop of the Midland District until 1840. Then a division took place, the eastern portion became the Eastern District, and in 1850 the Diocese of Northampton.

The penal laws and Protestant indignation gave scant respect to Vicars Apostolic or titular bishops. In 1771 Bishop James Talbot of the London District had been tried at the Old Bailey at the instance of a notorious Protestant informer, William Payne, 'for exercising the functions of a Popish bishop'. Even though acquitted for lack of evidence, the prosecution gave this aristocratic bishop, a brother of the Earl of Shrewsbury, much irritation. Bishop John Hornyold of the Midland District had on one occasion to put on a 'female cap' and throw a woman's cloak over his vestments to escape arrest.

## Family Life at Sawston Hall

The Test Act of 1672, as extended by subsequent Acts in 1714, 1729 and 1735, provides the key to the essential differences identifiable between the lives led by the Huddleston family during the second half of the eighteenth century and those of their neighbours among the county gentry. The Act required that all persons having any offices, civil or military (with few exceptions), or receiving pay from the Crown, or holding a place of trust under it, should take the oaths of allegiance and supremacy, subscribe a declaration against Transubstantiation, and receive the sacrament of the Lord's Supper according to the usage of the Church of England. The Huddlestons were thus excluded from all public activities normally undertaken by persons of their social status, whether sitting on the county bench of magistrates, holding commissions in the army or navy, entering Parliament, receiving the valuable benefits of patronage, or pursuing a career at the Bar. Even membership of Oxford or Cambridge colleges came under the excluded category.

Education, too, was a field where religious scruples provided a differentiation. If positive obstacles existed only at university level, other forms of education available in England were too closely linked to the Anglican religion for comfort. In common with most other Catholic families of similar standing the Huddlestons had often sent their children abroad for a Catholic education. The choice appears to have been quite wide; at least forty schools and colleges had been established in continental Europe in the aftermath of the Reformation, offering a Catholic education for English children. In the 1780s Ferdinand Huddleston chose the Dominican College at Bornheim Priory in the Austrian Netherlands (the present day Bornem in the Belgian province of Antwerp) for the education of his sons Richard, Henry and Edward, and the Augustinian Convent in Bruges for his daughters Mary and Jane. None of these five children chose to follow a religious vocation, although Richard Huddleston had given serious thought to joining the Dominican Order when aged seventeen. Among preceding generations the Huddlestons had produced at least two priests and seven nuns between 1600 and 1760.

These differences apart, the Huddlestons enjoyed all the privileges of country life appropriate to the lords of the manor of Sawston, hunting, shooting and socializing on equal terms with other county families including the Hardwickes of Wimpole and the Pembertons of Trumpington. Parish responsibilities took much of Ferdinand Huddleston's attention in the late eighteenth century, as a trustee of charity lands, parish surveyor of roads and influential, too, in church matters. His son Richard was even involved, in 1794, in an approach to Lord Hardwicke seeking a more remunerative living for his Anglican friend Revd Thomas Cautley, vicar of Sawston. This easy relationship with Anglican neighbours must have helped secure for the much-loved family chaplain John Champion a fitting resting place in Sawston church when he died in 1776 after forty-six years devoted service to his Catholic flock in Cambridgeshire, part of this time as Superior of the College of the Holy Apostles between 1741 and 1758. He is buried in the north chapel under a gravestone inscribed:

Jo Champion

S S I

Ae 82 1 7 7 6

## Keeping an Eye on the Numbers

It is well accepted that any religious denomination will keep count of its numbers, for reasons which may range from morale-building to the proper allocation of resources. It is rather less usual for a running census of religious denominations to be maintained by official agencies, especially if the purpose is to measure the threat which increasing numbers might pose to the State or its legally established religion. Yet it was a well-established practice during the second half of the eighteenth century either for the House of Lords or for Anglican diocesan bishops to call for numbers of Catholics (sometimes Nonconformists, or 'Protestant Dissenters' as well), residing in every parish in England and Wales. Although this practice may seem somewhat intrusive to modern eyes, there is at least the advantage that these carefully compiled returns now survive as a record which might not otherwise have been kept. Owing to the smallness of numbers the returns for Cambridgeshire made in the years 1755, 1767, 1780 and 1783 can be conveniently set out in turn as follows:

## *1755 – Return to the Bishop of Ely*

A questionnaire in twenty-six parts as to the state of each parish in the Diocese of Ely included:

XXV.    Are there any Popish Families in your Parish and how many?
XXVI.   Are any attempts made by their priests to seduce the People from the Protestant Religion?

Only two parishes in the Diocese replied affirmatively to question XXV:

| Parish | Popish Families |
|---|---|
| Sawston | 1 |
| Cambridge | |
| St.Michael's | 1 |

Question XXVI received a negative reply from every parish in the Diocese.

## *1767 – Return to the House of Lords of Papists resident in the Diocese of Ely*

| County | Parish | No | Sex | Age | Occupation | Time of Residence |
|---|---|---|---|---|---|---|
| Towne of Camb. | St.Benedicts | 1 | Female | 57 years | Widow of a Gardener | 18 years |
| Cambridgeshire | Sawston | 6 | Male | 34 | Gentleman | Native |
| | | | Male | 73 | Reputed to be a popish priest | 30 years |
| | | | Female | 55 | Widow of a Gentleman | 35 |
| | | | Female | 65 | Servant | Native |
| | | | Female | 50 | Wife of a Labourer | Native |
| | | | Female | 30 | Wife of a Gentleman | 16 months |
| | Whole number 7 | | | | | |

## *1780 – Return to the House of Lords from the Diocese of Ely*

This required a 'return of Papists or reputed papists within the several Parishes, and any popish School or Schools ... and what number of children of protestant Parents are taught therein'.

Only Sawston provided an affirmative reply on the subject of resident Papists as appears below, but the replies from three other parishes are also worth quoting:

*Pampisford and Sawston*
I have the satisfaction to acquaint your Lordship that in Pampisford I have found no reputed Papist – in the Parish of Sawston there are

five professed papists consisting of Mr.Huddlestone, his wife and two boys, and one woman of inferior rank but no school.

*Ickleton*
My Lord, I have received your Lordship's letter and have the pleasure to inform your Lordship that after diligent enquiry I do not find that there is at present one reputed Papist in my Parish of Ickleton; I therefore presume to conclude that there is at present not one therein who professes or teaches the principles of Popery, as in so small a community no person could long favour such religious tenets un-noticed by the rest of the Parish.

*Fulbourn All Saints*
There is not a papist or reputed Papist in the said Parish – there is a school but nothing taught leading to Popery, to the best of [my] knowledge the daily schollars may be about 14 to 20.

*Linton*
No Popish School, no Papist, no reputed Papist within my Parish of Linton.

*1783 – Deanery Returns to the Bishop of Ely*

*Sawston*
Dissenters: There are two or three families of Dissenters in this Parish; and one Roman Catholic family, Mr.Huddlestone's; which is the only one in the District.

For all the statistical elaboration of these countrywide exercises it seems apparent that the rank and file Catholics of humbler station than the Huddleston family had long learned how to keep a low profile, so avoiding the attention of the Anglican parson when returns came to be made. This seems to be the only way to explain the discrepancy between the number of Catholics, never more than seven, officially reported as resident in Cambridgeshire during this period and the seventy counted by the Midland District and ministered to by the likes of Fr James Taylor during his three-week long travelling circuits.

## Relief and Revolution come to Cambridgeshire

A number of political factors on the national and international stage started to influence the lives of Catholics in Cambridgeshire from the 1770s onwards, mostly for the better. By the mid-eighteenth century the powerful monarchies of continental Europe were beginning to sense a new liberalism in the air, carrying with it the seeds of possible revolution. The enlightened attitudes of the Jesuits were seen as a threat to the established order by the more autocratic rulers, and in 1773 Pope Clement XIV was prevailed upon by Spain, France and Portugal to abolish the Society of Jesus. If this was an attempt to save a political status quo long overdue for reform, in practice it served as little more than a prelude to the French Revolution which started sixteen years later, in 1789. At Sawston in 1773 Fr John Champion was of advanced years and failing health ['worn out and past labour', wrote his friend Fr Edward Galloway] and his change of status from Jesuit to secular priest made little difference to the remaining three years of his life. More active Jesuits continued their ministry, for the most part in the secular priesthood, but the College of the Holy Apostles ceased its collective activities in the Eastern Counties after 140 years of service to its small and scattered congregations.

The Boston Tea Party, which also took place in 1773, marked the start of the struggle of the American colonies for independence. It also gave rise to increasingly serious implications for the security of the British Isles. Ireland was held under British garrison, its population aggrieved by the recusancy and anti-popery legislation imported from mainland Britain and receptive to new talk of independence. Although France had not been in armed conflict with Britain since the Seven Years War ended in 1760, it remained the nation's main threat and natural enemy. Any independence or revolutionary movement in Ireland would have risked the exposure of Britain's flank to possible invasion from Europe, the problem made worse by the transfer of English garrison troops to fight in America. Concessions to the Catholic population were seen as one means of keeping the situation in Ireland stable. So it was that the Catholic Relief Act was brought to the statute book in 1778, the same year that the American Republic allied itself with France and Spain in its conflict with Britain, and the same year too that a volunteer force was raised in Ireland to defend the country against France. The Catholic Committee, with members drawn from the English Catholic aristocracy, had been pressing for similar objectives during the 1770s but would never have achieved such rapid results by its own lobbying had the political climate not provided the Government with pragmatic grounds on which to concede their claims.

The Catholic Relief Act of 1778 applied only to England and Wales, not Scotland. It took steps to ease the practice of the Catholic faith by repealing legislation dating from William III's reign which had provided for the prosecution of 'Popish Bishops, priests, Jesuits or Papists', life imprisonment for 'Papists who keep Schools' and disabling Papists 'to inherit land by Descent'. The remainder of the Act was concerned with a mitigation of the Test Acts so as to permit

Catholics to serve in public office if they were prepared to take a specially formulated oath of loyalty to the Crown. The oath did nothing to conceal Protestant suspicions, belief in papal conspiracies and continuing national paranoia, but at least it was a step in the right direction. Oaths were to be taken before any court in England and Wales and 'A Register [was] to be kept of the taking and subscribing of the same'.

Ferdinand Huddleston, a member of the Catholic Committee, evidently had sufficient inside information of the coming into force of the Act to attend within a very few days afterwards before Cambridge Quarter Sessions to take the new oath, alongside other applicants keeping to the older-established forms, as appears from the Quarter Sessions Order Book:

31st July 1778 by adjournment at the Rose Tavern before William Greaves Esq, Sir Thomas Hatton Bart., Robert Plumtre D.D. Vice Chancellor of the University of Cambridge and others their Companion Justices etc.

THIS DAY Ferdinand Huddlestone and Thomas Mitchell Esqrs, two Roman Catholicks severally personally appeared in Court and did then and there publickly in open Court take the Oath appointed to be taken by an Act made in the eighteenth Year of the Reign of his present Majesty intitled an Act for relieving his Majesty's Subjects professing the Popish Religion from certain Penalties and Disabilities imposed on them by an Act made in the eleventh and twelfth years of the Reign of King William the third intitled An Act for the further preventing the Growth of Popery, and immediately in open Court did subscribe their Names under the same pursuant to the said Statute.

William Stevenson Esq. Capt Cambs Militia, Oath of Allegiance Supremacy & Abjuration (Test Acts)

Rev Thos Parke Jas Stovin & John Jefferson Clerks respectively Fellows of Peterhouse – Oaths of Allegiance Supremacy & Abjuration

Thomas Mitchell was not from Cambridgeshire. He was a close friend and correspondent of Ferdinand Huddleston, normally resident in Yorkshire.

The Catholic Relief Act of 1778 may have been seen as a grudging first step but it still left much to be desired in terms of religious observance. If it spared Catholics from the risk of random arrest on the grounds of their religious affiliation it still left them unable to establish their own places of worship for public celebration of the Mass; this could still take place only in private premises, behind closed doors, and for the sake of common prudence still described as 'Prayers'. The Catholic community may have been left hoping for better times but Protestant feelings that things had been allowed to go too far led two years later to the Gordon Riots, during which 50,000 demonstrators virtually took over the centre of London for seven days of rioting, leading to 850 deaths and the plundering or destruction of four Catholic chapels. Yet increasingly momentous events abroad during the following eleven years achieved for Catholics what the sentiments of their countrymen might not have been ready to allow. The American Revolutionary War had been crowned with success for the colonies. Their victory over the English forces at Yorktown in 1781 led to the Treaty of Paris in 1783 and the recognition of an independent United States of America. Sandwiched significantly between these two events was a major political concession for the Irish people, the establishment in 1782 of a separate Parliament for Ireland. If this succeeded in postponing for a time the more urgent Irish demands for independence, nothing was yet done to accommodate Irish religious grievances. The conditions for Irish Catholics were no better or worse than for their English counterparts save that they constituted an overwhelming majority of the Irish population and their arguments for change were proportionately more vocal and more indignant than in England. The storming of the Bastille at the start of the French Revolution in 1789 was a dire warning to the other European states of the power of the people to overthrow an unpopular regime. Much sympathy was shown not only to refugee French aristocrats but also to French priests escaping from the revolutionaries. Suddenly Catholics from either side of the Channel were seen as natural allies of the existing order on account of the severe anti-clerical measures taking place in France. The scene was set for the passage through Parliament in 1791 of the second Catholic Relief Act. Four years of lobbying by a reconstituted Catholic Committee, with Richard Huddleston among its members, had been rewarded, due it must be admitted, as much to the pressure of external events as to their own efforts.

The Catholic Relief Act of 1791 contained the religious concessions not granted by Parliament in 1778. The oath to be taken by Catholics gave rather more tangible benefits than before, namely specific immunity from prosecution for failing to attend Anglican church services, from the offence of 'being a Papist', and exonerated Catholics from the need to take any oath required by other legislation. Furthermore, Catholic clergy might say Mass and minister to their congregation provided that their name was recorded at the Quarter Sessions, that their place of assembly was certified to the court and that the worship did not take place behind locked doors. Penalties were provided to discourage the disturbing of congregations or the misusing of priests. 'Roman Catholick School-masters' who had taken the oath were allowed to establish schools, provided that their establishment was recorded by the Clerk of the Peace and they did not 'educate in [their] School any Child of a Protestant Father'. Among negative provisions were a prohibition against the founding of any religious orders, schools, academies or colleges by Roman Catholics, and of holding the mastership of any College or School or Royal Foundation (including keeping a School in either of the Universities of Oxford or Cambridge).

'Ministers of any Roman Catholick Congregation' who took the oath were to be exempted from serving on juries, and from various parochial and ward duties. Again thanks to their inside information, Ferdinand and Richard Huddleston, father and son, took the first opportunity available after the Act came into force on 24 June 1791 to appear before Cambridgeshire Quarter Sessions as appears in the court records:

> 15th July 1791 This Day Ferdinand Huddleston of Sawston County of Cambridge Esq, and Richard Huddleston of the same place Esq, person- ally appeared in Court and did then and there in open Court severally take make and subscribe the Declaration and Oath directed to be made taken and subscribed by persons professing the Roman Catholic religion in and by an Act of Parliament 31 Geo.3 c.XXI (The Roman Catholic Relief Act 1791).
>
> This Day Ferdinand Huddleston of Sawston in the said County Esq, delivered into this Court a certificate under his hand bearing date this 15th July instant certifying to the said Justices that a House or Chapel situate in Sawston aforesaid is intended to be used as an Assembly for religious worship by Persons professing the Roman Catholic Religion And further certifying that the Revd. James Taylor is the priest or minis- ter who is intended to officiate in the said Chappel, and desiring that the same may be recorded in this Court pursuant to the Act of Parliament in the case made and provided.

[On this date the registration is also recorded 'of a barn or building, property of Mr. Thomas Hancock in Ludlow Lane Fulbourn intended to be appropriated and set apart as a place of religious worship of Almighty God' – this being a similar registration required of Protestant Dissenters.]

## 'I hear you are fitting up a very pretty chapel'

It was now possible, for the first time since Sawston Hall had been rebuilt in 1584, for the ground floor room intended as the chapel to be fitted out and openly used for that purpose (Pl. 4a). An Italian marble altar was set up containing the altar stone salvaged from the earlier

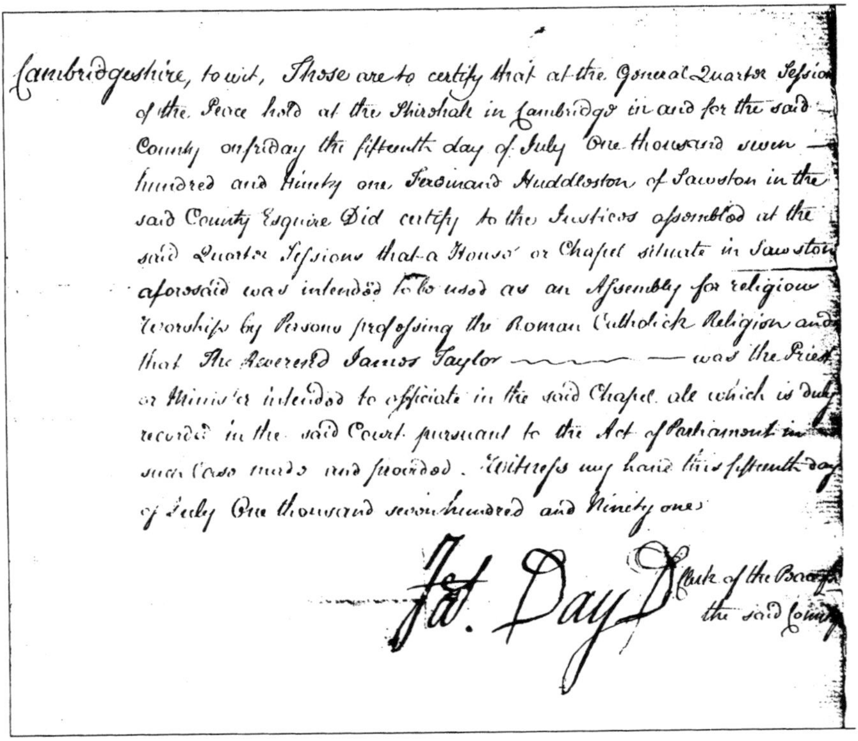

Cambridgeshire, to wit, These are to certify that at the General Quarter Session of the Peace held at the Shirehall in Cambridge in and for the said County on friday the fifteenth day of July One thousand seven hundred and thirty one Ferdinand Huddleston of Sawston in the said County Esquire did certify to the Justices assembled at the said Quarter Sessions that a House or Chapel situate in Sawston aforesaid was intended to be used as an Assembly for religious Worship by Persons professing the Roman Catholick Religion and that the Reverend James Taylor ——— —— was the Priest or Minister intended to officiate in the said Chapel all which is duly recorded in the said Court pursuant to the Act of Parliament in such Case made and provided. Witness my hand this fifteenth day of July One thousand seven hundred and Ninety one

Ja. Day Clerk of the Peace the said County

Fig. 3. Certificate of registration of the Catholic chapel, Sawston Hall, at Cambridgeshire Quarter Sessions, 15 July 1791.

chapel (destroyed in the fire in 1553), above it a gilt tabernacle dating from the reign of Charles II, together with a fine late-eighteenth-century plasterwork ceiling. Curiosity got the better of Richard Huddleston's sister Jane when she wrote to her brother before the work was finished: 'I hear you are fitting up a very pretty chapel pray tell me where it is ...'

The changed climate meant that there was no further use for the previous chapel up in the garret and the practice of saying Mass behind locked doors was no longer permitted. Even so, the traditional disguise of Mass as 'Prayers' continued for many years afterwards at Sawston Hall, possibly a gesture to the memory of more dangerous times.

> *Sawston Hall,* near Cambridge, Rev John Scott. – Prayers on Sundays and holidays at 10.
> – *Laity's Directory,* 1833.

Another sign of the times was the new-found freedom of Bishop Milner of the Midland District to travel openly for pastoral visitations and confirmations following his appointment in 1803: 'Mr. Milner the Bishop spent part of two days with us in his progress. We were much pleased with him, he travels about in the stile of the ancient Bishopps, saddle bags etc'.

## The Sawston Chaplains, 1773–1850

The twenty-six-year period between the suppression of the Jesuits and the outbreak of the French Revolution (1773–1789) was a time in which there was some scarcity of Catholic priests. The sequence of those who served at Sawston was intermittent and often short-lived. There were even times when Sawston was served by monthly visits from other Catholic houses in the Eastern Counties or by members of 'the Riding Mission', a group of priests based at Buckden, Hunts. Those whose names survive as resident chaplains comprise:

> Fr Marshall, resident at Sawston in 1773, evidently overlapping the ageing Fr. Champion but performing the active duties of chaplain.
> Fr John Smith OP, a member of the Dominican Priory at Bornheim who arrived from Leicester in May 1783 and returned to Bornheim the following April.
> Fr Henry Chappell OP, another Dominican who arrived from Bornheim in April 1784 and was assigned to Leicester after eighteen months residence.

It was my humble opinion beforehand that the solitude of Sawston would never suit Mr.Chappell; but experience must show the reality and so it has appeared (L. Brittain OP, Prior of Bornheim to Ferdinand Huddleston, 17 Oct 1783).

Fr.James Taylor came to Sawston in 1791 from the Riding Mission at Buckden, being a priest of the Midland District. His registration as the resident priest at Cambridge Quarter Sessions in July that year has already been mentioned but he was no longer at Sawston in 1793. He moved to other Catholic families as chaplain, among them:

Mr. Taylor is chaplain to Mrs.Fitzherbert – he may have occasion for the wisdom he so often acknowledges having learnt at Sawston (Jane Canning to her brother Richard, 15 Oct. 1803).

The gap which followed before the appointment of the next chaplain was coincidentally linked with the dire events then overtaking the Church in revolutionary France. Faced with the choice of swearing allegiance to a National Church separated from Rome or compulsory exile (sometimes commuted by local initiatives to the guillotine) French priests fled in their thousands in 1792, seeking refuge in every neighbouring country. Of these a first wave of 3000 arrived in England and another 480 as a second wave when the French revolutionary army invaded the Netherlands. Bellenger, writing in 1986, calculated that nearly 7000 French clergy were involved in this mass migration to the British Isles between 1792 and 1814. By 1797 there were 5500 French priests in England of whom only 500 were self-supporting. The rest had to rely on charity which was readily forthcoming from an English population largely Protestant but deeply appalled by the revolutionary excesses across the Channel. On Sunday 7 April 1793 collections for the French clergy were made in Anglican churches throughout the country, and at Holy Trinity Church, Cambridge, alone the collection produced £33. 17s. 6d. In Cambridge in 1792 the University Senate voted a sum of £200 for the relief of the French clergy and the same amount in 1793. The noted Church historian Mgr Bernard Ward wrote that this influx 'brought about results which had a permanent and far-reaching influence on Catholicity in this country'.

Against this background, Ferdinand Huddleston received a letter in French dated 17 January 1793 from an address in Hammersmith, accepting the position of chaplain at Sawston Hall offered to Abbé Martinet, of the Diocese of Paris. Fr Martinet served at Sawston for three years until, in March 1796, he decided to leave and seek a position teaching French in Cambridge. During his three-year stay at Sawston Fr Martinet conducted a correspondence with Richard Huddleston, then serving in various military camps as a lieutenant in the Cambridgeshire Militia Regiment. A final letter arrived from

Cambridge in October 1798 announcing that he was about to be deported on the orders of the Duke of Portland, then Secretary of State for the Home Department: 'The blackest and most infernal calumny (La calumnie la plus noir et la plus infernale) has long followed me. I have strongly protested my innocence. But my enemies have just triumphed, I was told today of an order to leave England.' This episode involved a security lapse, or worse, as Lord Hardwicke later explained to Richard Huddleston in a letter on 18 November 1798: 'I fancy he was guilty of imprudence at Yarmouth; in procuring a letter to be sent to France for one of his Countrymen.' It must be remembered that the country had just passed through a grave national emergency with a threatened invasion from France (partly realized with a landing in Ireland) and could only breathe more easily when news arrived in October of Nelson's victory over the French fleet at the Battle of the Nile. Richard Huddleston continued his military service with the Cambridgeshire Militia (including a spell in Ireland), reaching the rank of major and acting as commandant of the regiment before he returned to civilian life in 1806.

Other French clergy served for brief periods at Sawston between 1796 and 1802, among them Christophe Louvel (Diocese of Rouen), Jean Fleury (Diocese of Boulogne) and Fr Le Breton (*curé* of Valmont), but a turning point came in 1802 when the Concordat between France and the Holy See allowed the refugee clergy to return home without penalty. The situation was further eased for those in England by the short-lived Treaty of Amiens 1802 which brought the hostilities between Britain and France to an end. The flow of returning priests turned into a flood during 1802 and by the end of the year only 900 remained out of the thousands who had sought refuge ten years previously. According to Mgr Ward, of those who remained some had become attached to their work, and the rest were deeply committed to the Royalist cause in France and would only return when the Bourbon dynasty was restored in 1814. The beneficial influence of these priests remained strong for the next fifty years, both for English Catholicism as a whole and for the localized setting of Sawston. Their presence coincided with the dwindling away of the penal conditions so long enforced in England and they encouraged more open observance of the Catholic faith than had been possible at any time since the Reformation.

The positive benefit for Sawston was that French chaplains, either in residence or visiting from other centres, served there for another twenty-five years, from 1802 to 1827. *Père* Tottevin was active at Sawston from about 1804 until at least 1814. During this long residence he earned many affectionate references in family correspondence and took part in their activities. 'My father is pretty well, is gone out riding with Mr.Totevin', wrote Jane Huddleston to her mother Mary Huddleston on 1 August 1805. Of the rest, it is believed that Fr Jean Fleury came over to say Mass at Sawston from the Newhall Convent at Chelmsford between 1814 and 1820, Fr Le Roux is said to have served both Sawston and Cambridge in 1820 and Dom Charles Ferraud, OSB was resident at Sawston from 1824 to 1826. Apart from these active priests there are signs that some elderly French clergy were invited by Richard Huddleston to spend their retirement years at Sawston Hall. This at least would explain the death of Fr Fleury at Sawston in 1828 and Fr Pierre de la Cour in 1846 (aged 88) when other priests held the appointment of chaplain.

## Relief Turns to Emancipation, 1791–1829

Few would have supposed that the Catholic Relief Act 1791 was to be the last word on the subject. Civil disabilities such as the lack of right to vote or to stand for Parliament still remained. The government of the day (and its successors for the next thirty-nine years) had seen the merit of meeting Irish pressure, Catholic pressure and Nonconformist pressure all at one go but repeated attempts to bring further Catholic relief measures to the statute book had all failed, mostly at the last hurdle with the refusal of the monarchs of the day, George III and after him George IV, to give the royal assent. Father and son both felt that to do this was to breach their coronation oath to uphold the Protestant religion. Steadfast in their support of this royal intransigence was the University of Cambridge, which submitted petitions to Parliament against further Catholic Relief Bills in 1807, 1812 (twice), 1817, 1819, 1821, 1822, 1823 and 1825. At last, in February 1829, a final attempt to petition Parliament ended in a symbolic failure by insufficient votes in the Non-Regent House of the University (43 for, 53 against). Meanwhile, closer to the seat of government, King George IV, near hysterical and ill, with only another year to live, reluctantly gave way to the insistence of the Duke of Wellington's Government and on 13 April 1829 gave the royal assent to 'An Act for the Relief of His Majesty's Roman Catholic Subjects', known ever since as the Catholic Emancipation Act of 1829.

The forty sections of the Act may be summarized as permitting Catholics to sit in parliament, to vote in elections (if otherwise qualified) and, with some exceptions, to hold public office. The wording of the oath required of Catholics as a condition for these privileges was considerably toned down by comparison with the two earlier versions, largely in response to a continued, and vocal, dissatisfaction from the Catholic hierarchy and priesthood. It has to be said that religious orders, particularly the Jesuits, were still treated with some severity although breaches of legal restrictions were no longer capital offences. Perhaps in recognition of their loyalty to the Established Church, the universities were spared from any requirement to admit Catholics.

Soon afterwards, in May 1829, the Test Acts were repealed by related legislation. The result of this was that the oaths taken by Anglican office-holders before the Cambridgeshire Quarter Sessions were much modified. From then on they were recorded as a 'declaration for protection of the Protestant Church' when taken for example by Revd John Graham, the University Vice Chancellor (6 April 1832) and Joseph Twiss, the Coroner (6 July 1833). The new order of things permitted 'Richard Huddlestone of Sawston Hall' to take a high office in the county for the first time, filing his appointment as High Sheriff of Cambridgeshire and Huntingdonshire for the year commencing 3 February 1834 and taking the oath provided by the 1829 Act before the Quarter Sessions Court. Less than twelve months later, Richard Huddleston was almost certainly the first Cambridgeshire Catholic to vote in a parliamentary election, held for the Cambridgeshire county constituency on 15 January 1835, having filed his oath at the court three days beforehand.

Notwithstanding the Catholic Emancipation Act, the penal legislation of earlier centuries, although by then a dead letter, was not removed from the statute book until 1844 and some other legal provisions continued in force, such as the requirement dating from 1791 for registration of Catholic places of worship. The habit of keeping a check on numbers also continued, though accuracy may not have been the strongest feature of its results, as appears from the contributions called for by the House of Commons in 1836, to *A Return ... of the ... Registered Roman Catholic Chapels in England and Wales:*

<u>Return of the Clerk of the Peace for Cambridgeshire</u>
There is only one Roman-catholic chapel in this county and I do not find an entry of a licence for that
    9th April 1836                        Christopher Pemberton
<u>Return of the Town Clerk of Cambridge</u>
There are not any Roman-catholic chapels in Cambridge
    22nd March 1836                   Francis J Gunning
<u>Return of the Registrar, Diocese of Ely</u>
    Roman-catholic chapels         None
    8th April 1836                     George J Twiss, Deputy Registrar

## An Awakening in the University

Little has so far been said of Catholicism in the University of Cambridge. Indeed little on the subject could be said when its degrees and fellowships were barred to all save members of the Church of England, required to swear their allegiance to the Crown and their adherence to the Protestant faith. The University had been the cradle of the Reformation in England, rapidly becoming a stronghold of the Church of England and one of the principal sources of candidates for the Anglican priesthood. Very gradually, however, the situation began to change in favour of Catholics. From the early years of the nineteenth century some colleges became more willing to admit Catholics, starting, it has to be said, with a few well-connected young noblemen who took up places as privileged fellow commoners entitled to dine at high table. After meeting the entrance requirement of matriculation, for which no religious test had to be met, these young gentlemen could continue with their academic studies but were unable to proceed to a degree, this being the point at which the religious test was imposed. Thomas Redington from Galway was admitted a fellow commoner of Christ's College in 1832 and arrived in Cambridge with his mother and an Irish chaplain who said Sunday Mass in their rented house to which the Catholics of Cambridge were also admitted.

The only other reason for the appearance of Catholics in the University was the conversion of existing Anglicans, starting with the well-publicized case of a Trinity graduate, Kenelm Digby in 1825. He was soon joined by a newly-converted undergraduate Ambrose Phillips (he assumed the name Phillips de Lisle in 1862) who came up to Trinity in 1826. Believed to have been the only Catholics in the University at this time, both had a strong if romantic vision of a Catholic Church rooted in medieval antiquity. This common bond took them on a twenty-five-mile ride on Sunday mornings in term time to hear Mass at St Edmund's College, Old Hall, Ware, a journey requiring considerable physical stamina in the days when the eucharistic fast started at midnight. The combination of the High Mass liturgy, the welcoming fellowship of the seminary students and the reputedly generous table must have been sufficient attraction for these young idealists to disregard any discomfort, and indeed the much closer destination of Sawston Hall, when embarking on these all-day Sunday excursions. Unlike the robust Kenelm Digby, a pioneer college oarsman, Ambrose Phillips was of a more delicate constitution; his health gave way after eighteen months and he was obliged to move to Italy to recover from these exertions in a milder climate.

A total of 149 Cambridge men are reckoned to have become

Catholics during the nineteenth century according to Gorman. One of the more controversial of these cases involved John Morris and his classics supervisor, Frederick Apthorpe Paley in 1846. Each was received into the Church separately but the twin scandals of a Cambridge undergraduate converting during term time and the undue influence of a College tutor (as imputed by his critics) was almost too much for the Protestant die-hards to bear. Paley was not expelled from St John's College but was recommended by the Master to leave. Ambrose Phillips also had some involvement in the conversion of John Morris and of another Trinity man, Hon. George Spencer, youngest son of 2nd Earl Spencer of Althorp. George Spencer was ordained in Rome in 1832 and later joined the Passionists as Hon. and Revd Fr Ignatius of St Paul, eventually becoming Provincial of his Order.

The position of Catholic undergraduates remained unchanged until 1856 when for the first time all non-Anglicans were permitted to become members of colleges and to proceed to first degrees, as provided by the Cambridge University Act 1856, s.45:

> No Person shall be required, upon matriculating, or upon taking, or to enable him to take, any degree in Arts, Law, Medicine or Music, in the said University, to take any Oath or to make any Declaration or Subscription whatever ...

## Chapter 5

# The Mission in Cambridge: A Tale of Three Bishops and a Determined Priest

*Christopher Jackson*

The expression 'mission' in modern-day parlance carries with it a suggestion of distant countries in which 'missionaries' work to bring the word of Christ to unenlightened populations. In the context of early nineteenth-century England, however, a mission was a Catholic place of worship established in a locality where none had been before, or at least since the Reformation, while a missioner was a Catholic priest working at large among a scattered Catholic population without the benefit of any fixed places of worship. Once a mission had been built, the priest in charge would be given the title 'mission rector' and if a separate house was acquired this would be called 'the mission rectory'. These expressions characterize the development stage of the re-emergent Catholic Church in England. 'Parishes', 'parish priests' and 'parish boundaries' were not used by Catholics in this country with regard to their own churches until authorized by the *Codex Juris Canonici* promulgated in 1914, and dioceses were not divided into territorial units called 'parishes' until 1918.

The sequence of events leading up to the establishment of the mission church of St Andrew in Union Road, Cambridge, begins with a letter written by Bishop Milner of the Midland District on 4 July 1823 to Fr William Foley. Fr Foley, who established the new mission at Northampton later that year, was about to make an extended tour through the Eastern Counties:

> If in your intended journey ... you go into Cambridgeshire, be pleased to make the same enquiries [i.e .the number of Catholics, etc.] respecting the county town and the neighbourhood, of Richard Huddleston Esq., of Sawston Hall, about six miles south of Cambridge.

Bishop Milner died in 1826 without having made any further arrangements or directions with regard to Cambridge. He was succeeded by Bishop Thomas Walsh who took early steps to appoint Fr Edward Huddleston to establish a new mission in Cambridge. Fr Huddleston had been ordained at St Mary's Seminary, Oscott in 1826. He had then stayed on there as a professor and moved to his new appointment in July 1827, taking up residence at Sawston Hall. In effect this member of the Huddleston family was also taking over the position of chaplain at Sawston Hall in succession to Dom Charles Ferraud who had moved on to St Gregory's, Downside in 1826. Having obtained advice from Fr Foley he lost no time in preparing a printed appeal for funds in the form of a circular letter, making particular reference to the fast increasing numbers of Irish Catholics in the Town, the pressing claims of other places which had 'delayed execution', and the intention to build a chapel and a house for the priest.

Notices in this or similar form also appeared at various times in the annual *Laity's Directory* (and in its successor publication the *Catholic Directory* from 1840), over the entry showing Fr Huddleston to be the priest in charge at Sawston Hall, with the Mass times (Prayers) for Sundays and holidays.

By January 1828 Fr Huddleston had succeeded in raising about £900 and it appears probable, though opinions seem to differ, that £400 out of this sum was applied towards the purchase of a pair of cottages, with land at the rear, in Union Road in the parish of Barnwell (or St Andrew the Less), Cambridge. Although Richard Huddleston was responsible for arranging this purchase, the transaction had to proceed with extreme caution, through a nominee. There was every reason to suppose that a vendor, discovering the true identity of the purchaser, or that the property was intended as the site of a future Catholic chapel, would have withdrawn in hostile indignation. Sadly it is impossible to identify the date of acquisition, the name of the vendor or of the nominee purchaser because the title deeds were destroyed by fire in January 1849 while in the custody of the church lawyer Mr Henry Bagshawe. Possibly the confusion as to the acquisition date derives from a letter from Jane Canning to her brother Richard Huddleston (2 April 1841):

> I am glad they have made so good a purchase for Cambridge – Mr Baynham deserves credit for that at least, he is not in the odour of sanctity here owing to his being employed by Dr Walsh. . . .

However, it seems reasonable to suppose that Jane Canning was referring to news of the secret acquisition which had only just leaked out,

TO

# THE CATHOLIC PUBLIC.

LONG before his lamented death, the late Vener‐ able Bishop of the Midland District had entertained the design of establishing a permanent MISSION in the Town of Cambridge.

The celebrity of the place, the daily increasing numbers of resident Irish Catholics, who now amount to more than two hundred, the liberal spirit, which distinguishes the University of Cambridge, in admitting within her Colleges Catholic young Men for the purposes of Education, and the fact of there being no Public Chapel in the whole County, strongly recommended the measure. But the absence of resources, and the pressing claims of other places, delayed the execution. A more favourable opportunity seems now to have presented itself.

Influenced by the above weighty reasons, the present Vicar Apostolic of the District, the Right Rev. Dr. WALSH, has determined to act upon the intentions of his illustrious Predecessor. With this view, his Lordship has already appointed to this arduous and destitute Mission, as the future Pastor of Cambridge, the Rev. EDWARD HUDDLESTON, of St. Mary's College, Oscott.

Under such high sanction, the individual so appointed, presuming that an undertaking thus especially recommended by two successive Vicars Aposto‐ lic, will not be thought either unseasonable or unimportant, appeals to the piety and gene‐ rosity of the Catholic Public; and in the name of his respected Bishop, solicits its liberal support to a measure at once auspicious to Religion and creditable to the Catholic Cause : and he appeals with a confidence higher and greater, in proportion to the acknowledged utility of the measure, and his own destitution of means to complete a work affecting Catholic Interests in the three United Kingdoms.

As soon as sufficient Funds can be raised, it is proposed to build a Chapel in the Town of Cambridge, and a House for the Priest.

---

*⁎* Contributions for these purposes will be thankfully received by the Rev. E. HUDDLESTON, Sawston Hall, Cambridge; the Right Rev. Dr. WALSH, Giffard House, Wolverhampton ; and by Messrs. WRIGHT and Co. Henrietta-street, Covent-garden.——Any article of Church Furniture, Vestments, Tabernacle, Crucifix, Altar Piece, &c. however humble, most gratefully accepted.

Fig. 4. Printed appeal for funds by Fr Edward Huddleston, 1828.

rather than to any more recent purchase. Fr Huddleston moved to St Augustine's, Stafford in 1831 and was replaced at Sawston by Fr John Scott who was also entrusted by Bishop Walsh with the same responsibility for founding a mission in Cambridge. Unfortunately, progress towards this goal was extremely slow during the next ten years. If one attempts to discover the cause, rather than any blame, for this virtual standstill a number of contributory factors emerge. Fr Scott does not appear to have been a born mission-founder. Sawston was his first charge after ordination, aged twenty-seven, in 1831 and he left this quiet backwater twenty-four years later in 1855 to take up his next and possibly last appointment as chaplain to a convent of Visitation Nuns at Westbury-upon-Trym in Gloucestershire. Bishop Walsh was a noted Vicar Apostolic of the Midland District at a time of great expansion of Catholic activity throughout the Midlands, though this trend had not yet reached the Eastern Counties. It is clear that there were a great many calls on his time and attention in burgeoning Midland cities and obvious limits on the time he could spare in planning a way ahead for Cambridge. By 1835 the Jesuits were contemplating the establishment of a chapel in Cambridge, no doubt attracted by the challenge of this celebrated academic centre. Their proposal to Bishop Walsh was received with some enthusiasm but while arrangements were still in the planning stage the Bishop felt obliged to write to the Jesuit superior in January 1837:

> I find that the report of your negotiations at Cambridge is already abroad and that such a storm is gathering around me in consequence that it will perhaps be prudent to suspend our operations at present.

The Bishop evidently preferred peace to conflict but was also prone to vacillation, and by his own admission 'easily led and weak' (Jane Canning). By the time that he raised the subject with the Jesuits again, feeling that the situation was more promising, the opportunity had been lost, his withdrawal had been interpreted as final rather than temporary and by then some of the funds earmarked for the Cambridge project had been allocated elsewhere.

By February 1839 matters seemed to be back where they had started, but this did not deter Bishop Walsh from writing to Richard Huddleston:

> I deeply regret that Cambridge has remained so long a time without a chapel, and that a little temporary opposition, which I could have surmounted, should have prevented the Jesuits from persevering in the plan for establishing a mission there, which I earnestly entreated them to do, as it is quite out of my power to accomplish, for the whole

amount of my funds for the purpose, including your handsome donation, did not amount to more than about £700. It was fully my
intention, as soon as the new proposed division of districts was pointed
out from Rome ... to appropriate a certain portion of the residue to so
desirable an object. It is important that the interest deriving from the
Cambridge Fund should be preserved with care; but I am willing to
allow Mr Scott £15 per annum, or £20 per annum if you judge proper
(9 February 1839).

On 22 April 1839 Fr John Scott, whose stipend had just been arranged
by his bishop, appears to have received a visit from the architect A. W.
N. Pugin, who was responsible for the design of the chapel to be consecrated in Union Road four years later. Pugin's diary shows only the
appointment on this date and no detail of the business discussed, but it
is at least encouraging to suppose that the architect had already been
approached by Bishop Walsh and that something was about to take
place at last.

An event of significant importance to the development of the
Cambridge mission took place on 11 May 1840 when the four Districts
of the Catholic Church in England were divided into eight, reflecting
the ever increasing population and expanding activity and the need to
allocate the consequent responsibilities among a greater number of
Vicars Apostolic. As a result the sixteen counties of the Midland District
were divided into three new districts, the Central District, the Eastern
District, and the District of Wales. Of these Bishop Walsh retained the
Central District and a new Vicar Apostolic, Bishop William Wareing,
was allocated the Eastern District (comprising the counties of
Northampton, Huntingdon, Bedford, Cambridge and Isle of Ely,
Rutland, Lincolnshire, Norfolk and Suffolk).

The differences between these two new Districts could not have been
greater. Retained in the Central District were all the noted and
expanding industrial cities of the Midlands including Birmingham,
Coventry, Nottingham, Leicester, Worcester, Stafford, Derby and the
Potteries, with a Catholic population in the region of 100,000, more
than 100 Catholic churches already established and others being built.
The Eastern District was larger in terms of area but less well endowed
in terms of a Catholic population of 10,000, only twenty-six Catholic
churches and the most modest of plans for further expansion. This,
however, was an unexpected advantage given to the Cambridge
mission as a result of the division. Suddenly Cambridge gained a significance in the Eastern District which it had never previously enjoyed,
Northampton and perhaps Norwich being the only possible rivals
for attention at the time. A building fund was in existence, a site had
been acquired and the services of the architect Pugin had already been

retained by one of his major patrons, Bishop Walsh. These preparations had all been made while Cambridge was part of the Midland District but were now available to the Eastern District. Bishop Wareing lost no time in setting the wheels in motion for this new project, modest in size but attractively significant in its location. The sudden change of pace can be easily seen by comparing the rather leisurely and erratic progress since the appointment of Fr Huddleston thirteen years previously with what took place in the two and a half year period between the formation of the Eastern District in May 1840 and the opening of the newly built St Andrew's church in December 1842.

Bishop Wareing's first step was to appoint a priest to take sole responsibility for establishing the Cambridge Mission. Fr Scott was left in place at Sawston, and the Bishop's choice fell on an Irishman, Fr Bernard Shanley, from the Irish College in Paris. The choice was without doubt appropriate, as Fr Shanley himself would have been the first to agree. In fact his version of events was that, being concerned over the increasing population of 'poor Irish' in Cambridge with no Catholic ministry for their spiritual needs, he had himself approached Bishop Wareing and obtained leave to found a mission. The idea was put about later that the Bishop and Fr Scott both regarded Fr Shanley's efforts as 'impracticable and visionary in the extreme'; but, as Fr Shanley wrote in an appeal for funds during his time in Cambridge: 'the Vicar Apostolic of the Eastern District feels it is his duty to second and support such noble exertions. . . .'.

The truth is that Catholic Cambridge needed both of these reverend gentlemen like the opposite sides of an equation. Bishop Wareing had the site, the funds and the architect; Fr Shanley had the energy, imagination and persuasive fund-raising powers needed to galvanize the local (largely Irish) Catholics into a loyal and effective congregation. For the first time since the Reformation Cambridge had regular Sunday Masses, though starting in somewhat squalid and makeshift premises. Fr Shanley's first Mass for the Catholics of Cambridge was said in an upstairs room in the lodging house of Thomas Patrick Price, general dealer, in Newmarket Road, with a chalice borrowed for the occasion from Richard Huddleston. This venue was not chosen again because the floor threatened to collapse. Next followed sixteen weeks' occupation of a little hut nearly bursting at the seams, before the pair of cottages on the Union Road frontage to the church site became vacant. One cottage served for a time as the priest's residence and the other as the chapel for the duration of the building period.

The Irish presence in Cambridge deserves some attention. It had nothing to do with the painful exodus from Ireland at the time of the Great Famine, which was not to start until 1846. Even so, several generations of Irishmen had responded to the land pressure and general poverty in their own country by seeking employment in Great Britain, some finding work and settling with their wives and families, others taking seasonal work at harvest time, and returning for the rest of the year to their homes and small cultivations. Cambridge had attracted Irishmen from both categories, some being employed in public works such as road-making and fen drainage or in agriculture, others at harvest time only. Some may even have been drawn to the district by opportunities at the annual Stourbridge Fair and to the horse-market at St Ives, the largest in the kingdom. Fr Huddleston had referred to as many as two hundred Irish Catholics resident in Cambridge in 1828 and Fr Shanley had no difficulty in finding one hundred or more to join his congregation from 1841 onwards.

The 'seasonal visitors' were remarked upon condescendingly in the local press when they made their annual appearance, as the following report shows:

Irish reapers As usual at this period of the year, vast numbers of tattered individuals from Ireland have arrived in this part of the kingdom for the purpose of assisting at the approaching harvest. For a fortnight past they might have been seen in groups in our streets and in the lanes surrounding the town, exhibiting every shade of apparent want and raggedness. The services of the men have not been called for at so early a period as they anticipated, and the consequence is that many of them have had no immediate means of subsistence. One meets them begging in every part of the neighbourhood, and we understand that 40 of them have been received into the Union Workhouse. (*Cambridge Chronicle*, 14 August 1841)

This picture can be neatly balanced by the following more sympathetic comment:

At the turn of the [nineteenth] century another class began to swell the numbers of Catholics in England and make their presence and their religious needs felt among their co-religionists. They were the Irish, driven from their native land and attracted to this country by the promise of work and wages. As a consequence they were generally referred to by their hosts as the 'poor Irish' and poor in this world's goods they certainly were. But they enriched the Church in England with something that the English Catholics lacked and needed. With a strong faith and a long tradition of persecution behind them, they found themselves in a foreign country; therefore the practice of their religion was uncomplicated by national affinities or social aspiration; they felt no need, and had no desire, to conform to the customs and ways of thought and life of their neighbours ... (D. Gwynn).

Soon the building money was to find its way through from Bishop Walsh out of the funds of the Midland District:

> Previous to the receipt of your respected communication which I found on my arrival from London at Oscott last week, I had given instructions to Mr. Bagshawe to pay as soon as possible to the Revd. Bp. Wareing the amount of subscriptions to the Cambridge Chapel.
>
> The £500 with interest shall be transferred according to your directions.
>
> It affords me true consolation to learn that the prospects at Cambridge are now so flattering. I trust that 'ere long a most respectable mission will be established in that city.
>
> Availing myself again of this favourable opportunity, I request to assure you how grateful I feel for your repeated acts of kindness to me.
>
> I remain, Dear Sir,
>
> Your obliged faithful priest
>
> and devoted servant
>
>   + Thos.Walsh
>
> (Bishop Walsh to Richard Huddleston, 19 May 1841)

Work was soon to start on the building site at the rear of the two cottages in Union Road, only to be threatened by the celebrated three-cornered confrontation which took place on the night of 5 November 1841 between a body of University undergraduates, representing the Church of England, Fr Shanley and a group of 'valiant sons of Erin', representing the Catholic congregation, and the forces of law and order in the Borough, comprising the Mayor, the Town Clerk and the Clerk of the Peace (Protestant Dissenters to a man and no friends of the Anglican establishment), accompanied by a party of special constables. The declared intention of the first group was to tear down the building enclosure and to tear up the newly laid footings (45 ft x 43 ft) of the chapel, but their way was barred by the second and third groups and they eventually dispersed, their intention unrealized. It should be remembered that in those days undergraduates were required to be back in College not later than 10 p.m. and Fr Shanley's readiness for an all night siege was perhaps over-ambitious. One may guess that the righteous indignation of these undergraduates had been fired earlier in the day at one of the University functions reported in the local press the following day:

> The Fifth of November: Yesterday, being the Anniversary of the Gunpowder treason, a sermon was preached in the morning at Gt. St. Mary's by the Rev. Dr. Hodgson, Master of St. Peter's college on *Acts xxvi.9* I verily thought with myself, that I ought to do many things contrary to the name of Jesus of Nazareth, after which the usual Latin

speech was delivered in the Senate-house by the Rev. James Hildyard
M.A. Fellow and Tutor of Christ's Coll. (*Cambridge Chronicle*, 6 November
1841)

The building work then appears to have proceeded unhindered, with
encouraging progress reports reaching the pages of *The Tablet* from
time to time:

> the walls of the new Chapel at Cambridge are already several feet above
> the foundations. ...
>   The new Catholic church of S.Andrew, now erecting in Cambridge ... is
> progressing rapidly and if the funds are found to be sufficient, will be
> ready for opening by the feast of its patron saint ...

An unexpected event occurred when the end of the building work was
nearly in sight. In October 1842, without any prior warning or subsequent explanation, Fr Shanley was moved from the Cambridge Mission
and shortly afterwards took up a position as chaplain at Coldham Hall
near Bury St Edmunds, Suffolk. He attended neither the opening of
the church on 4 December 1842 nor its consecration the following
April. It is possible to detect in Fr Shanley a great capacity to befriend
or to offend, and it may have been that his successor Fr Norbert
Woolfrey, a Cistercian monk working temporarily in the secular
missions, was seen as better fitted to the testing role of opening the new
Catholic mission in Cambridge. A high priority would have been to
leave, if humanly possible, no-one offended in the process. Fr Woolfrey
was by then quite well acquainted with an inner circle of prominent
'Midland Catholics', among them the Earl of Shrewsbury, Ambrose
Phillips de Lisle, Bishop Walsh and Augustus Pugin, and this may well
have influenced Bishop Wareing's decision. Fr Woolfrey attracted
favourable reactions both inside and outside the Church during his
time in Cambridge, though this was in a strictly interim role
(November 1841–January 1843) until his newly-ordained successor Fr
Thomas Quinlivan was deemed ready to take over the Mission on his
own. Soon afterwards Norbert Woolfrey and his brother Odilo, Abbot
of Mount St Bernard Abbey, both left the country to undertake
missionary work in Australia.

To learn of the details of the opening of the church on 4 December
1842 and its consecration on 27 April 1843 we can only refer, as Fr
Shanley must have done, to the press reports of each occasion, set out
in the Appendix to this chapter. The account of the consecration in *The
Cambridge Independent Press* states that it took place 'on Thursday
morning last, being the festival of St George'. The Thursday before 29
April 1843 was 27 April. Normally the feast of St George is on 23 April,

but in 1843, because of the date of Easter, the feast was transferred to 27 April.

## The Aftermath

To borrow nautical expressions, the Cambridge mission was now launched and under way after so many frustrating years and vicissitudes. It could not however expect plain sailing in calm blue waters for some time yet. The resident and undergraduate populations in Cambridge would need time to adjust and come to terms with this newcomer in their midst and there would be squalls ahead when harsh words would be heard and youthful mischief endured with forbearance.

Fr Shanley may have been suffering from hurt feelings when he wrote an extraordinarily fulsome letter which appeared in *The Tablet* on 1 July 1843, addressed mainly to the congregation he had left behind, praising their (and possibly his) achievements and the donors who had responded to his appeals for funds. The civic leaders of Cambridge were thanked for their support, so too was Major (Richard) Huddleston and even, for some unexplained reason, Daniel O'Connell Esq. MP 'the greatest man in the world', but his reference to Bishop William Wareing accords him only a secondary role in the establishment of the Cambridge mission.

One of the most outspoken opponents of these developments, from his own pulpit, had been Revd Charles Perry, the Anglican vicar at the newly-built St Paul's Church, only two hundred yards away in Hills Road. When he left Cambridge in 1847 to become the first Anglican Bishop of Melbourne, his farewell address to his congregation contained words of honesty and some magnanimity: 'I have done everything in my power to put down "Popery" in my parish, but I have failed. It is now established in the midst of you. Live therefore in peace with the Roman Catholics.'

It is also worth recording that no resident of Cambridge saw fit to object to the choice of St Andrew as patron of the Catholic mission, even though it clearly lay within the boundaries of the ancient, but Anglican, parish of St Andrew the Less. The infant congregation was at least spared this ground for hostile comment.

Richard Huddleston, who together with his predecessors had done so much to keep the Catholic faith alive in Cambridgeshire, died a life-long bachelor at Sawston Hall in 1847. Fr Scott continued to say Mass in the chapel until he left Sawston in 1856, but no replacement priest was appointed and, according to successive editions of the Catholic

Directory, Sawston was for the next seventy years 'occasionally served from Cambridge' a reversal of the situation in earlier days.

## The Restoration of the Hierarchy, or Papal Aggression

The final event to be dealt with in this chapter is the creation (described as 'restoration') of thirteen new territorial dioceses in England and Wales each with a Catholic bishop, in place of the eight Districts with their Vicars Apostolic. This was achieved by Letters Apostolic from Pope Pius IX dated 29 September 1850, and although the rest of his episcopal colleagues would have much preferred a fairly low-key transition, the newly-created Cardinal Wiseman chose to handle the matter rather differently. By his celebrated pastoral letter 'From Out Of The Flaminian Gate', addressed to his faithful of the London District and dated 7 October 1850, Cardinal Wiseman announced the substitution for the eight Apostolic Vicariates of one Archiepiscopal or Metropolitan and twelve Episcopal Sees; and the appointment of Cardinal Wiseman to the Archiepiscopal See of Westminster, giving him at the same time the administration of the Episcopal See of Southwark:

> so that at present and till such time as the Holy See shall think fit other-wise to provide, we govern and shall continue to govern the counties of Middlesex, Hertford and Essex as Ordinary thereof, and those of Surrey, Sussex, Kent, Berkshire and Hampshire with the Islands annexed, as Administrator with Ordinary jurisdiction.

It has to be said that this choice of words was as misjudged as it was misinterpreted. Even Queen Victoria, when she read the announcement, exclaimed 'Am I Queen of England or am I not?' The choice of 'Westminster' was probably the title which gave most offence, seeming to claim some jurisdiction over the very seat of British government. 'Papal aggression' was the favourite phrase chosen by hostile critics to describe the event.

Perhaps predictably, the University of Cambridge was quick to assert its loyal indignation in an address to Queen Victoria which read in part as follows:

> WE, therefore, most humbly beg leave to represent unto your Majesty that it is with deep concern that we have learned that the Bishop of Rome has arrogated to himself the right to intermeddle with the government of this country, and to ignore the ancient episcopacy of our church, by presuming to confer on certain of your Majesty's subjects professing the

Roman Catholic religion the highest ecclesiastical titles, derived from English towns, together with territorial jurisdiction.

By this unwarrantable assumption of power on the part of the Bishop of Rome, not only are your Majesty's high prerogative and the lawful authority and jurisdiction of the prelates of our church invaded and outraged, but the consciences of your Majesty's loyal subjects grievously offended.

Bishop William Wareing, formerly Bishop of the Eastern District but newly established as Bishop of Northampton, felt it necessary to give reassurance to his flock in the face of the general furore. His first Pastoral Letter, dated 5 November 1850, concluded in the following terms:

> While therefore, dearly beloved, we express our gratitude to his Holiness for the favour and distinction wherewith he has honoured us, let us fervently pray that in due time, those of our countrymen whose prejudices and jealousies have been unfairly excited, may see how they have been misled, may lay aside the groundless terrors with which they have been artfully impressed, and be generously disposed to allow us quietly to enjoy the religious liberty which they claim for themselves, and which they profess to be the birthright of every Englishman.

This pastoral letter was read in St Andrew's Church, Union Road on Sunday, 10 November 1850, and was followed after Mass, in accordance with the Bishop's direction, with a Te Deum and the Prayer for the Queen. Although a protest meeting was held in Cambridge Guildhall on 18 December 1850, the indignation died down after a year or two and the Catholics of Cambridge were for the most part spared from the heat of this particular controversy.

Between the vicariate of Bishop Stonor and the episcopacy of Bishop Wareing, Catholic life in Cambridgeshire had changed out of all recognition in the hundred year period which ended in 1850. From a handful of Catholics practising an illegal religion by largely covert means, the passage of time and the abolition of legal restrictions had brought to Cambridge a permanent mission, a resident priest and a congregation attending Mass every Sunday morning, even though the 250 seats in the church would be more than adequate for their needs for some time to come. This was the base from which so much more would be achieved in terms of numbers, buildings and devotional activity, but above all in public acceptance, in the following century and a half.

# Opening of the New Romanist Chapel

from *The Cambridge Chronicle*, 10 December 1842

The Romanist chapel, recently erected in Union Road, New-Town, was opened last Sunday morning. It is a neat little building in the Early English style after a design, we believe, of Mr Pugin. The following account of its opening is evidently from the pen of someone connected with the place – probably from the Priest himself: we give it without alteration and of course are not responsible for its phraseology:–

"On Sunday 4th inst. the Catholic Chapel of St Andrew was opened for divine service, it having been blessed privately (with the especial permission of Bishop Waring [sic] by Rev. H. Woolfrey, etc., its present incumbent. The morning service commenced with the 95th Psalm, with invitatory, after which the acts of Faith Hope and Charity. The Litany for Advent and a short explanation of the holy sacrifice of the mass (for the benefit of strangers). The daily sacrifice was offered, followed by a solemn profession of the Catholic faith, by a lady who has been for some time anxious to belong to that church. The morning service was concluded by the prayers for the penitential time of Advent.

At three o'clock an explanation of the Christian doctrine, as taught in the Catholic Catechism, followed by vespers which were sung. At seven o'clock prayers and an explanation of the Catholic Faith especially as to its unity and the four works of the Church which alone can possess that one faith, leaving the application of those four works to the judgement of each. The text was taken from the Creed of St Athanasius, 'I believe in one holy Catholic and Apostolic Church; This is the Catholic Faith, etc.' The three services were extremely well attended and the attention and respect of strangers excellent.

The reverend gentleman adverted to the distribution of tracts, even through the public market. He supposed that such tracts could not be the production of any members, much less of the ministers of the Church of England, who have had the benefit of a college education, but of some of those individuals whose belief is built on their own airy imaginations. He said with such he should not contend, nor do them the honour of a further reply."

We hear that there is to be a grand and ceremonial public opening at Easter, and rumour affirms that Mr Sibthorp, whose cession from the church created so much ferment last year, will preach on that occasion.

# Consecration of the New Roman Catholic Chapel

from *The Cambridge Independent Press*, 29 April 1843

On Thursday morning last, being the festival of St George, the building situate in Union Road, New Town, which has lately been erected and used as a Roman Catholic place of worship, and which before we have had occasion to notice, was formally consecrated by the Bishop of Ariopolis (Dr Wareing), celebrant, assisted by the deacon and sub-deacon, assistant priest, acolytes, Thurifer and choir, together with the mitre and crozier bearers. These being arranged in the gorgeous and spotless robes pertaining to their office, presented a very imposing, and from the fact of the ceremonial taking place in Cambridge, a University Town, for the first time, a very novel appearance.

The church dedicated to God in honour of St Andrew was built by A. Pugin Esq whose eminent taste as an architect is universally acknowledged. It is in the early English style and though plain is yet perfectly graceful and pleasing. Every feature is real, genuine and natural. All is in accordance; the porch and the font are particularly beautiful, and on entering the visitor immediately sees that Catholic is stamped upon its features. The screen with its cross and figures – the altar, so beautifully carved – the open seats – *in fine*, everything connected with the church recalls to our mind the old times when the Catholic religion was all-in-all. About nine o'clock the procession entered the church with cross-bearer, acolytes, Thurifer, Deacon and Sub-Deacon, assistant priest, choir, etc., and the Right Rev. Dr Wareing, the Bishop of the Eastern District. The consecration occupied about two hours. After this was finished, the candles were lighted on the altar, and a solemn high mass commenced by the Right Rev. Dr Wareing.

The ceremonies were most appropriate and although different from those of the consecration, yet they were quite in accordance with the service. Parts of the mass were chanted by some of the students of St Edmund's College, Old Hall Green, the plain chant being used. After the gospel the Right Rev. Dr Wiseman (Bishop of Melipotamus), so celebrated for his zealous and talented advocacy of Catholic tenets, and as having first introduced the doctrines of Puseyism (now so rapidly spreading) into this country, made his appearance at the altar. He took his text from the 28th chapter of Genesis and the 11th, 12th, 16th, 17th and 18th verses detailing Jacob's dream and his erection and anointing of the altar.

At the conclusion of the sermon the mass was continued. The Bishop intoned the Credo which was sung by the choir. After this, the more solemn part of the service commenced, which it is unnecessary here to describe. Everything was conducted in the most solemn manner. When the mass was finished, a solemn 'Te Deum', in thanksgiving to God, was chanted by the choir and then the Bishop and his attendants left the altar and proceeded down the church in procession in the same order as they had entered. The service was over about two o'clock. Everyone present, whether from curiosity or principle, behaved in a manner becoming such an occasion. There was a very numerous attendance; Major Huddlestone and his brothers, Mr George Cayston, and several respectable strangers and inhabitants of the town, we observed present in the church during the consecration at the close of which the doors were opened to the public, and during the performance of mass the church was densely crowded.

In the afternoon an excellent dinner was provided by Major Huddlestone at the University Inn. The Right Rev. Dr Wareing, Bishop Wiseman, Major Huddlestone and his brother (who was in the chair), Rev. N. Woolfrey, several priests from different places, the students from Old Hall Green, and other gentlemen, sat down to dinner a little after four o'clock. The Queen's health was first proposed and then the Rt Rev. Prelates who officiated at the service. Thanks were also given to Revd Mr. Rolfe and the students of Old Hall for their valuable services. Major Huddlestone's health and the Rev. N. Woolfrey's (the pastor of the church) were also given.

# Chapter 6

# The Rectorship of Canon Quinlivan, 1843–1883

*Tim Glasswell*

## Introduction

Canon Thomas Quinlivan (Pl. 5a) was the first rector of the Catholic mission in Cambridge. He fulfilled this role for forty years, guiding the church through an important and eventful period, during which steady, and at times, impressive progress was made in the position of the Catholic Church in England. Particularly noteworthy achievements during his rectorship in Cambridge were the establishment of the schools and the acquisition of the site for the new church.

## Early Life

Thomas Quinlivan was born on 1 November 1816 in Lisborn, County Clare, Ireland. Sadly, little else is known about the formative years of his life. We are told that this 'gallant son of Erin' began his studies for the priesthood at Maynooth, followed by seminary at Carlow. Moving to England in the late stages of his study, he enrolled at the Seminary of St Felix in Gifford's Hall, situated on the edge of the Dedham Vale in Suffolk. He was ordained as a Catholic priest by Bishop Wareing (then the Vicar Apostolic of the Eastern District) on 10 June 1843. He became a canon of the Cathedral Chapter in Northampton in 1852, and was appointed missionary rector in 1859.

## The Mission, the Breakthrough, and the Man

A significant amount of progress had already been made in Cambridge before Quinlivan's arrival. The first reference to a 'mission' in the area, launched from Sawston Hall by Revd Edward Huddleston, was in 1827. The early attempts at founding such a mission were not particularly successful, yet the determination was never lacking. The *Catholic Directory* of 1833, for example, carried an appeal that justified 'the need to build a chapel, and establish a permanent mission in the town of Cambridge'. The presence of the University in Cambridge played a large part in paving the way for a great increase of Catholicism, both in the city and county. An increasing number of sons from notable and wealthy Catholic families were arriving to study at Cambridge University. With no permanent place of worship within the town, these students 'were consequently deprived of the support and advantages of their religion, at that critical period of youth'.

In 1841, appointed by Bishop Wareing, Fr Bernard Shanley came to the town to make determined efforts to collect funds for a chapel. By 1842, Major Huddleston had managed to acquire a site for, and funds to build, a new church in New Town, an area to the south of the town centre. By the time St Andrew's Catholic church was opened in Union Road in December 1842, Fr Shanley had been replaced by Henry Norbert Woolfrey. The newly ordained Reverend Thomas Quinlivan arrived in Cambridge in July 1843. He was intended as a permanent replacement for Fr Woolfrey, and was quickly appointed 'Pastor of the Infant Mission'. *The Tablet* in January 1844 (at the time of his departure) noted that in his time at Cambridge, Norbert Woolfrey had 'made many converts and removed mountains of prejudice'. Nevertheless, by the time Quinlivan took charge of the mission in the town, the Catholics were still relatively few in number. There was hardly a single Cambridge-born Catholic. However, by all accounts, the mission was on the verge of a great change, with a steady flow of converts, both from the town and university.

Fr Quinlivan quickly became a well-respected and much loved character in Cambridge. Although his chief concern was to help and build upon the faithful Catholic congregation, he was 'noted for his charity and benevolence to all men of whatsoever creed, or none, who needed help and sympathy spiritual or material'. From contemporary accounts it is clear that Thomas Quinlivan was a charming and dedicated individual, with a positive, healthy, open outlook on life. A 'cheery old soul', he possessed a warm sense of humour, his frequent puns and jokes unfortunately often lost in his hearty laughter. A 'clever, popular, excellent and very wide-awake Romish priest', his frank, courteous manner and his generous nature were remarked upon by those who had the pleasure of his acquaintance.

## The Growing Catholic Presence in Cambridge

In comparison to the other great university town, the prospects of conversions in Cambridge were 'hopeful', and the field 'particularly good'. The struggle in Oxford was well documented in the columns of the Catholic press at the time. 'Strong religious prejudices against the Catholic faith', remarked Quinlivan himself, held Oxford in 'strong bonds of delusion'. The relatively more liberal attitudes of the population of Cambridge were reflected in the success of conversions. By March 1857, the number of converts received into the church at Cambridge by Canon Quinlivan was little short of 300.

One of the many explanations for the growing numbers of Catholics in the town was the coming of the railway. In 1845, Cambridge station opened on the Eastern Counties' London to Norwich line, followed in 1847 with a connection to Peterborough and thence to Northampton in 1848. St Andrew's Catholic church was only a few minutes' walk from the railway station. The opening of these rail links would have had a profound result on the mobility of Cambridge Catholics. At the larger scale, there was also immigration from the continent. The congregation at St Andrews included French, Italians, Spaniards, Belgians and Germans, beside English, Irish and Scottish. A significant proportion of the new Catholic congregation in Cambridge were Irish folk, 'with large hearts and empty purses'. Harvest time was traditionally a time of great influx, as was the famous annual Stourbridge Fair held at Barnwell. Casual visitors to these events may have eventually settled in the area, which in turn attracted further immigrants from Ireland. Quinlivan's own Irish background would doubtless have endeared him to these members of the parish. St Patrick's Day in Cambridge was reported as a particularly exciting event. At the same time, there was also emigration. In July 1852, in a letter to the Squire of Sawston, Quinlivan noted that 'several of the congregation were leaving for America and Australia'.

## Opposition and Anti-Catholicism during Quinlivan's Rectorship

The mission's presence in Cambridge, although generally well respected, *was* looked down upon by some quarters of the townsfolk.

The Church was not fully emancipated from the unpopularity that it attracted from the time of the Reformation. Despite Canon Quinlivan's universal respect for Cambridge townsfolk, whether Catholic or not, it was not uncommon for 'young Protestant bloods' to enter the Church and cause a nuisance. This could range from small, daring 'token' acts such as putting 'soot or some black filth in the Holy Water stoup', to the full-scale invasion of a 'noisy scoffing mob kicking up a shindy' at the most solemn moments of Mass and Benediction.

One such source of troublemakers was Cavendish College, which stood on the site of what is now Homerton College. Inaugurated by the Duke of Devonshire in 1876, Cavendish was founded by the County College Association to enable students somewhat younger than ordinary undergraduates to pass through a university course and obtain a university degree. *Kelly's Directory* for 1887 noted that 'there they would train in the art of teaching those students who intended to become schoolmasters and to secure the greatest practicable economy in cost as well as time'. The members of this 'first public hostel' were seen as too young, and discipline was very slack, making it a centre for much that was objectionable. To St Andrew's, the men from Cavendish were especially annoying.

Vespers and Benediction particularly 'became a painful ordeal', when often unruly members of the University were present in force. There was no certainty that the service would not be disturbed by some of the men and girls who made it a rendezvous. These stormy scenes at St Andrew's used to get so out of hand that salutary methods were often necessary. With conduct so abominable, 'detectives' often had to placed in the church to identify the troublemakers, and help physically deal with them. Two undergraduates in the time of Canon Quinlivan had been imprisoned for bad conduct in the church, and their heads had been shaven. They took pipes into church, and when the Canon used the censer, they imitated his movements. This suggests that the intrusions were more akin to adolescent student pranks than deeply rooted religious protests. Indeed, it was reported that in Cambridge in 1850, 'the most perfect goodwill seemed to exist between the members of the Churches of Rome and England'.

However, pockets of strong anti-Catholic prejudice *did* exist in the Cambridge area, and had to be dealt with tactfully. In March 1850, Quinlivan had a difficult case to manage at Exning, near Newmarket. The Church of England parson there took a symbolic stance by refusing to bury a Catholic child. It is obvious that Quinlivan was easily frustrated by such petty attitudes. In return, he planned to go to Exning church to read the service, and see whether the parson meant to persist in refusing the child a grave in the churchyard. In his opinion, this situation was 'ludicrous and absurd in the extreme'. In his frank and forthright manner, he 'wrote the gentleman a rather funny puzzler on the subject of Baptism and threatened to treat him to a card of admission to the Court of Arches and a picnic in the columns of the Evening Mail'.

## Church Life

The ecclesiastical census taken for the Cambridge mission on 30 March 1851 gave the seating capacity of St Andrew's as 230. Attendance at Mass was 210, with 150 at the afternoon service and a further 150 at the evening service. It was estimated that scholars comprised almost a quarter of those present at morning Mass, a third of those at the afternoon service, and a fifth of the congregation in the evening. The chapel at Sawston Hall, 'used exclusively for worship', had spaces for 60 free sittings available for public worship. Fr John Scott preached to 20 persons in the morning, and 30 in the afternoon; 30 to 40 Catholics at Ely were also preached to, fortnightly.

On 6 November 1859 the first episcopal visitation of Cambridge took place, the results of which provide a fascinating 'snapshot' of the mission at that time. In 1858, there were 19 Baptisms, 11 Conversions, 136 Easter Communions, 2 Marriages, and 6 Deaths. The congregation is listed as 'about 290', comprising 210 adults and 80 under-fourteens. The 'return' includes a detailed breakdown of the mission finances, but also information about church life. We find for example that the altar wine was 'English College Lisbon' and that altar breads were fresh every two to three months. Baptismal vows were renewed each week, and the 'last retreat by Father Gaudentius' was about 1850. In the parish there were confraternities of the Living Rosary, the Sacred Heart and of the Scapular. As regards indulgences, the only faculties the Rector had were the 'ordinary ones'.

Mass times at St Andrews stayed regular and consistent throughout Quinlivan's time there. In 1858, Sunday Communion was at 9 a.m., and Missa Cantata started at 10.30 a.m. English prayers were said before and after Mass. Vespers was sung at 3.00 p.m., and the evening service varied between 7.00 p.m. and 7.30 p.m. depending on the season. Mass on weekdays was at 8.00 a.m., and on holy days at 10.00 a.m. Confessions were heard on Saturday evenings and each morning before Mass. Catechism was held in church every Sunday, after which there could be baptisms. Benediction on Sundays required written permission.

The annual income of the rector was £97.10s. in 1858. This was broken down as £16.10s. from the Huddleston Trust, £28 from the bench rents, £25 from the offertory, £12 from Sawston Hall and £16 in casual gifts. Canon Quinlivan was at this time living in a hired house, and, owing to the absence of endowment, was dependent for support upon the offertory. This, he said, 'fell short of the wages of a common mechanic'. Church expenditure amounted to £32.11s.4d., comprising altar wine, breads, gas, rates, 'improvements and repairs', oil and turpentine, washing and cleaning the church, coal for the sacristy, linen, candles, and £10 for the Church organ and choir.

## The Schools and the Sisters

Canon Quinlivan's achievements during his rectorship were perhaps most remarkable in the field of Catholic education. In a town described as 'one of the chief centres of educational growth and religious influence in the British Empire', schooling was seen as very important. Within months of his appointment, he had opened a school for the children of the parish, in two cottages adjacent to the recently opened Catholic church. For the next twenty-five years he was able to keep these schools open, with the help of subscriptions, school pence and his own resources. The Canon was a strong believer that teaching the ways of the faith to little ones was the key to a successful mission:

> Without such schools and without such training Catholicism, instead of flourishing as it now is sure to do, would gradually become sapless and ultimately disappear, as is the case in many ... instances. Missions that some twenty or thirty years ago were prosperous are now little better than the wretched lifeless wreck of Catholicism; and this is because there were no efficient schools to train up and carefully develop and mature the rising hope of the Church in these localities. No schools, no abiding Catholicity.

In 1850, the schools were greatly helped by the arrival of two of the Sisters of the Infant Jesus from their Northampton convent. *The Catholic Standard* on 30 March of that year declared with happiness that 'nuns are again stationed in the University town of Cambridge'. At nine o'clock in the morning of 11 March 1850, the parents of the children assembled in great numbers to hear the arrangements adopted by the good nuns for the future government of the schools. A Mass was celebrated the following Wednesday, by 'the worthy Pastor' Revd Thomas Quinlivan, for the special invocation of the Holy Spirit on the labours of the sisters. The optimism for the schools nurtured an optimism in the mission as a whole, as mentioned in the second annual report of the Catholic Poor Schools Committee in *The Catholic Standard*, 16 March 1850:

> This is glorious news for the Catholics of Cambridge and for the catholic world. It has long been said 'There's a good time coming, if we waited only a little longer', and I think the Catholics of this Mission, after waiting a space of 300 years, may truly say it has come to them at last. Let us hope that this is the beginning of better days for this poor but very important mission, and that under the fatherly care of our venerable pastor, and the prayers of all the faithful, this town may become what it once was, viz. All Catholic.

In a letter of 14 May 1850 to Edward Huddleston, squire of Sawston Hall, Quinlivan remarked that bringing the nuns to Cambridge was 'the best, the wisest and most important step taken since [his] appointment to the charge of souls'. He reports with enthusiasm that 'the Schools are flourishing under [their] holy direction; the children being trained as if by magic'. So fond were the children of their schools and the nuns, 'that, those, whose parents could scarce get them to attend three days before became so regular in their hours that the parents could not get them to stay at home, if they would'.

The presence of the nuns was, however, only ever seen as temporary. Certainly the mission's long-term intention was to erect a convent, and more suitable schools, but this was not realized for a number of years. In *The Catholic Standard* of 17 August 1850, Quinlivan reluctantly announced that one of the good sisters had to leave through ill-health, and that the Bishop had threatened to 'deprive the Mission of the services of Nuns altogether unless they got them larger schools'. This suggests that the nuns' presence in Cambridge was no longer perceived to be a viable and practical posting while they were confined to the present buildings. There is no mention of the nuns in the 1851 *Directory*, suggesting that they had moved back to Northampton by then.

## Mission Finances

Although the mission at Cambridge was regarded as fairly permanently established, much was still needed in the way of support. At times, Quinlivan's position was certainly anything but enviable. Despite many financial difficulties to contend with, he remained characteristically determined to make the mission succeed, in the face of strong opposition and an extreme lack of resources.

The schools in particular must have been a great expense to

Quinlivan, with expenditure regularly exceeding income. Contributions received from the newly created Catholic Poor Schools Committee were minimal, forcing the mission to look elsewhere for financial support. In 1858, for example, an income of £39 for the schools was offset by expenditure of £48. Of this, the schoolmistress required a fixed salary of £27, while other expenses included coals for the schools and teacher's use, repairs, and other small items such as the 'childrens' treat', presents and books to complement the 'small but well selected library'.

Fund-raising events helped in part to raise monies. One such event from 1860 was a party 'for the benefit of the schools attached to the mission' at the Great Room of the Rose and Crown Inn. *The Cambridge Chronicle* reported that the party was 'numerous and respectable. Occupying the chair was the Reverend Thomas Quinlivan, who did ample justice to the toasts or sentiments which included "Our beloved Queen, Pope Pius IX, and success to the Schools".'

Individual benefactions were also welcomed and thankfully received. The 1858 school income, for example, was comprised partly of 'The Cuddon benefaction' and 'John Sutton's gift of £10 for general purposes'. Another individual was Mrs. Elizabeth Dias Santos, who left in her will £300 towards the school fund and £200 for the poor fund. She had also purchased the adjoining property to the west of the church, with the declared intention of handing it over to the church as soon as the purchase money should be paid.

The survival of the mission and its schools was mainly dependent upon precarious subscriptions of the congregation. With rising debts in his mission's hands, Fr Quinlivan made frequent appeals for funds, through the publication of 'pleas' in the *Catholic Directory*. One such entry was directed at 'benevolent friends' to now 'lay their charitable offerings, as sweet incense, on His Sacred Altars for the supply of the educational and other wants of his poor little ones', In another, from 1845, he 'earnestly appealed to the charity of the faithful in support of Cambridge's rising and important mission, which from the poverty of the congregation, was very destitute'. However, no amount of assertive and honestly worded appeals, could disguise the fact that the mission was heading towards financial crisis, and the Canon was getting desperate. The lack of funds threatened to seriously affect the mission's progress. In 1850, with a debt on the schools standing at £52.10s., Quinlivan wrote to Edward Huddleston:

> My principal object in going to town is to beg. I suppose I shall have some doors slammed in my face, but what matter, if I can keep my nose (which is not very prominent, nor a turnip (up) one) at a safe distance.

Do offer up a prayer for the success of a beggar who is woefully destitute
of brass on his face.

Buried in the archives is a well-documented tale that exemplifies the
financial hardship and struggle of the mission. For sixteen Sundays in
early 1850, Fr Quinlivan had ministered to the congregation at
Sawston Hall in the absence of its chaplain, Revd John Scott (who was
taken ill and sent sea-bathing in Littlehampton.) This cover comprised
a Mass of a weekday at the Hall every week (except the first) and three
others, and every other Sunday. These duties became increasingly
laborious and time-consuming, particularly since the duties at St
Andrew's were equally pressing.

Some time after, coming out of church after service one Sunday,
Huddleston was reported to have promised collector William Sherman
that he would give £5 towards the mission's debt. A month later, on 19
June 1850, when this promised £5 failed to materialize promptly,
Thomas Quinlivan wrote to Edward Huddleston at Sawston Hall,
reminding him of the oversight, going in to great detail as to what
extra amount he might be owed for deputizing for the chaplain. Glad
that he was now released from the duties and responsibilities of the
Sawston congregation, he presented a statement of the 'little money
transactions' and what he considered due for his services. The Canon
was concerned that his goodwill was being compromised at expense of
the mission's finances. 'To do business in a businesslike way', he wrote,
was 'always a satisfaction'. Among the many bills that week were
£2.4s.6d. due for coals to the poor and their delivery, and £1.10s.0d.
for bus and train fares.

You have 'placed me in a delicate position between yourself and my
flock', wrote Quinlivan. 'You will', he continued, 'pardon me for
setting the matter plainly before you for personally it is no affair of
mine'. Having consulted 'one or two confrères of long missionary
experience' as to what he ought to get for his services, Quinlivan
suggested that he was fairly within reasonable limits in setting down
the labourer's hire at one half what would be due to Mr Scott for the
same period. 'Poor as he was', he didn't object himself giving 30s. in
expenses to priests doing duty, and he expected a reciprocal courtesy.
The correspondence illustrates that the following up of every promise
or pledge was critical for the survival the missions, and an all-important occupation of so many Catholic priests at that time.

## Memories of St Andrew's Catholic Church

Despite the many financial hardships encountered, belonging to the church during Quinlivan's time was a happy experience.

> Picture to yourself a cosmopolitan congregation united not only in faith, but, in real friendship with one another, attacked from every direction by missions held in every protestant church and chapel in Cambridge 'especially against Irish Catholics', as also by itinerant preachers and lecturers who thought no slander too base or statement too vile to bring against us.

Mr W. E. Fisher, looking back in 1931, recalled that 'the little Catholic Church of Saint Andrew, Union Road stands out as an oasis of rest and genuine pleasure when many other things were so hard and difficult to deal with'. There was a cast of colourful and faithful characters. There were assistants Father Pate, and Doctor Logan, 'very old and delicate in health'. The two disciplined and effective church vergers, Mr W. Kent and Mr G. Allen, were the strong rocks of the congregation, ready to deal with those who came to mock. The choir in the organ loft included Miss Ventris, who with such a sweet voice was known as the Cambridge Nightingale. And of course, Canon Thomas Quinlivan, not averse to pausing a moment before the Gospel to tell a small boy to behave better, and almost certainly responsible for the absurd rumour circulated every Palm Sunday that he was going to ride round the church on an ass!

## The Statue of the Blessed Virgin

One of the most important and prized relics at St Andrews was the elegant image of the Blessed Virgin bearing in her arms her Divine Child, the Infant Jesus (Pl. 22a). This statue was a gift to the Church from A. J. Wallace, a convert undergraduate from Emmanuel College, who was subsequently to be priest at Cambridge in about 1880. This statue of Our Lady was reputed to be the same one which before the Reformation was the centre of devotion to the Blessed Virgin Mary in Cambridge. It had been discovered buried in the grounds of, or in the walls of the College, saved for 300 years from Puritan vandalism. The figure was symbolically and reverently handed over to Canon Quinlivan, who then represented the pre-Reformation Church in Cambridge.

# Notable Persons

There were a number of important supporters of the mission during Canon Quinlivan's time at Cambridge that deserve briefly introducing. Mrs Esther Price, born near St Ives in 1784, was one such notable. At the time of the 1851 census, she was aged sixty-seven, and living at 40 Newmarket Road, Cambridge. It was in her house in 1841, that Mass was said in Cambridge for the first time since 1688. This event, in a small upper chamber in a cottage in the Barnwell suburb of Cambridge was a significant turning point, and the pillar on which the Mission was built. After the death of Mrs Price, Canon Quinlivan earnestly requested the attendance of all the congregation at the Requiem Mass, stressing that her benevolence was an important part of the Mission's heritage.

Mr William Sherman, a plasterer by trade, lived with his family in East Road, Barnwell. It was suggested that his family were the town's first converts. He was converted to the Catholic faith by Edward Green, an Irish carpenter, known to the congregation for years as 'Daddy Green'. Sherman was received into the Church at Sawston Hall by Father Huddleston.

Another great supporter and patron of the mission in Cambridge, second perhaps only to the Huddleston family at Sawston Hall, was Mr William Davey. He was born in 1782 in Dorchester, to an old Oxfordshire Recusant family. His wife, Amelia Davey, born in Limerick in 1801, was a benefactress of the mission. Sometime in 1843, Quinlivan moved from his first residence (probably one of the old cottages on Union Road) into the Davey residence at 3 Hills Road, enabling the cottages, which had served as a presbytery and chapel, to be converted into a school. Also resident in the hired house was twenty-nine-year old railway inspector William Collis and nine-year-old William Blackman, who would both later become priests in the Northampton diocese. William Davey was listed as 'blind' in the 1851 census, and died a few years later. Universal praise was lauded upon him after his death:

> Too much cannot be said in praise of the services rendered to religion in Cambridge by that excellent man; and what was true of him is true of his excellent widow, so far as her diminished means permit. The Rector and his flock are now engaged, in conjunction with the Lord Bishop of the Diocese, in putting up in the church a stained window in memory of her deceased husband's good deeds and benefactions.

By 1858, in return for all Mr and Mrs Davey had done for the Catholic religion at Cambridge, Canon Quinlivan had firmly taken upon himself to say one Mass a month for them. This loyal recognition was recorded on the lace of the missal, requesting that this practice be continued by his successors in the parish. On 1 June 1847 the Davey Trust was initiated, the Trustees being the Right Revd William Wareing, Amelia Davey, Thomas Quinlivan and Thomas Jend. By the late 1850s, the finances were looking in better shape, thanks in part to two large sums of money received – from this Davey Trust, and the Huddleston Trusts.

## The New Schools

As the Mission progressed, the two cottages in Union Road used as schools were becoming increasingly old, miserable, and 'wholly unsuited to the purposes for which they were used'. Indeed, the room used for schooling was described as just fourteen feet long by fourteen feet wide and eight feet in height. In 1867, after twenty-five years of constant use, the cramped and unhealthy school cottages in Union Road were condemned, as 'unfit and deficient in height', by the Council of Education. The funding body decided to refuse all further support except on the condition that a new school and teacher's house were to be built by 1 November of the next year. Faced with a possible lack of long-term Catholic education in the town, Canon Quinlivan did not hesitate in approving the building of a new school.

The new school house was listed as 'one of the most pressing wants of the Mission'. In 1865 Canon Quinlivan purchased Wanstead House, Hills Road, Cambridge, the grounds of which backed on to the church and school site. This purchase gave him land on which to rebuild the schools. The new school and house for the teachers were finished in 1868 at a cost of £1000, and were by all accounts much needed and 'much admired'. However, the mission had no funds at its disposal for such a building. Despite the help of a government grant, a heavy debt of £500 with high interest was incurred, which, if not paid off quickly, threatened to cripple the Mission's valiant efforts.

## The Crusade for the New Church

The Catholic church of St Andrew in Newtown was built with £1000 given to Bishop Wareing by Dr Walsh and Major Huddleston of Sawston Hall. The original church, was consecrated on 27 April 1843, a 'small but exceedingly neat edifice' of Early English style. The interior although 'very tasteful [in] appearance', was clearly not large enough to cope with the growing numbers of attendees, including the slowly increasing percentage of Catholic University students from rich families. In 1843, at the very start of his tenure, Quinlivan wrote to the public, mentioning that 'the Church itself will soon want enlarging'. The addition of a chancel would give a great increase in internal accommodation. More attractive, a church double the size of the present was needed. With the mission finances in a questionable state, the likelihood of an enlargement of the church, or a new building, was at best optimistic.

In 1879, under the eye of the Canon, 'valuable freehold property, adjoining the church' was secured (but not paid for) at a cost of £2000. This 'fine and excellent site', 'the best in all Cambridge', was the prestigious Lensfield estate adjacent to the church property. Many years before, the Wentworth family who occupied the site had refused Canon Quinlivan's offer to purchase some of the land. In 1879, when the estate passed in to other hands, Quinlivan 'seized the opportunity of obtaining an option to purchase the whole'. With no funds available for him to complete the contract, he looked for help outside the town. With a little mutual help from Canon Christopher Scott, then administrator of Northampton Cathedral, the Duke of Norfolk generously agreed to advance almost half the cost of securing the site. 'By mortgaging church property, Canon Quinlivan raised the remainder of the purchase price but was still faced with the task of finding a huge sum to pay off the debt.'

With the mission totally destitute of funds, the money to build a larger and better church more worthy of the *old* faith of Cambridge once again had to be gathered through gladly received, and thankfully acknowledged, contributions towards a building fund. The short-term aim was to pay off the debt on the freehold for the land, with the much prayed for and much needed church to be funded later. Despite securing the fine and excellent site in 1870, there was 'no money coming in from any quarter for the noble and needful work'. Appeals to Catholics at home and abroad were posted in the *Catholic Directory* as well as local and national newspapers, requesting 'a helping hand':

> The growth of the old faith here since 1843 has been like that of a mustard seed in the parable ... The time for throwing fresh vigour into our mission work is come. A new and imposing church, fully served, is the pressing want of the hour. Its position at Hyde Park Corner is known far and near as our great central thoroughfare. The mortgage with its interest, is a heavy burden; and it must be paid off before, on principles of finance, we can safely begin the new church. The Methodists and other bodies are sinking thousands in churches and colleges in Cambridge, in order to reap the benefits of the old and new foundations.

With the full sanction of my Bishop, I appeal to the Catholic body for cheques and post-office orders.

T. CANON QUINLIVAN, M.R

P.S. Our cause is a national one. I feel that this appeal, in the great interests of religion, should meet with a prompt and practical response from all Catholic hearts. After more than thirty-seven years in Cambridge, working my parish quietly, I now realize the sacred duty and dignity of becoming, for Christ's sake and His church, a *public beggar*.

Canon Quinlivan was determined that the urgently needed new church *would be built*, for the benefit of *all* Cambridge Catholics and their families. Gaining support for this 'noble object' became his personal project. He begged all Catholics to rally round him, which he heralded as the 'final crowning of his priestly life':

This great work, upon which the bishop and myself have set our hearts, will have to be put off for years, to the detriment of our holy religion, unless the Catholic body come generously to our assistance.

In 1871, the only sum in hand was £50, a gift of a 'kind friend at a distance', Generous donations such as this were the backbone of the building fund. However, the infrequency and unpredictability of such gifts left a question mark hanging over such a desirable work. In 1882 the debt was 'about £3000', a huge sum! By 1883, the mortgage on the Lensfield Estate was hardly dented. The interest rate at four and a half per cent started to become too heavy a burden on the resources of the mission. Sadly, Canon Quinlivan never saw this debt cleared, and his 'final crowning work' was not realized.

## Later Life

On 21 November 1883, after forty years of devoted service, Canon Quinlivan retired from his duties in Cambridge. 'Failing health and failing energies' forced him to place his resignation in the hands of Dr Riddell, the Bishop of the Diocese. The general infirmity of advanced years had not been kind to Canon Quinlivan, and he recognized that he was no longer capable of running the mission.

Eight months before his retirement, the Canon mentions that 'an attack of bronchitis' had kept him a prisoner indoors for a number of days. He writes, knowing that he is in his last years, but sounds content and peaceful. 'I am now old', he continues, 'and my old medical friends in London are dead or like myself nearly worn out. Sir Thomas

Watson – an old Cambridge man is gone, and so is another great friend – Sir Erasmus Wilson'. The larger part of his clerical life had been spent in Cambridge, establishing, then building on the success of the ever-growing Mission work. Canon Christopher Scott was to take over his position in Cambridge, being officially appointed as the second missionary rector of Cambridge in 1883.

Canon Quinlivan's 'friends (to whom he had endeared himself by his kindly disposition) felt it right that a testimonial should be presented to him on the occasion of his retiring from active life'. *The Cambridge Independent Press*, of 10 November 1883, announced that a 'Canon Quinlivan Testimonial Fund' had been opened at the London and County Bank, inviting subscriptions. *The Cambridge Chronicle* on 2 November 1883 paid him a fitting tribute:

> Mainly owing to the very great exertions of the Canon, his manly upright character and benevolence, the Catholic Church at the present day finds itself in a much improved condition, and its venerable pastor, beloved by his flock, and admired and respected by all. It is to be regretted that at the close of such a useful career, failing health should have rendered it necessary for him to retire from the discharge of duties faithfully performed for 40 years. We feel sure his many friends of every denomination will be only too pleased to contribute to the fund already inaugurated by his congregation for the purpose of presenting him with a befitting testimonial on his leaving Cambridge. We need scarcely say that the Rev. Canon takes with him our best wishes for his health and happiness.

He spent the last years of his life in Northampton. Indeed, he knew the city well, having become a Canon of the Cathedral Chapter at its erection in 1852. He spent his retired life at Nazareth House, Northampton. It was announced, a year into Canon Quinlivan's retirement, that funds for a new church in Cambridge had been acquired. After over forty years of hard work, the mission was finally to get a grand, imposing building, worthy of the valiant efforts endured. Sadly, Canon Quinlivan did not live to see the results of his labours – the church of Our Lady and the English Martyrs. However, I am sure that he would approve of the fine church that we have the pleasure of using to this day.

The Very Revd Canon Thomas Quinlivan died at his residence in Northampton on Tuesday, 12 May 1885. A Requiem Mass was sung at St Andrew's Catholic church in Cambridge on Friday 15 May at 11 o'clock by Revd Father Pate, who was associated with the late Canon in his last few years in Cambridge. The region's Catholic clergy were all present: The Very Revd Canon Collis of Shefford (deacon), the Revd

G. Wrigglesworth of Bedford (sub-deacon), the Revd M. Dwane of Lynford (master of ceremonies) and Revd Canon Scott and Revd Fr Blackman (cantors).

The Mass commenced with Matins and Lauds of the Office of the Dead. Throughout the service plain chant was sung. In the centre of the church, a catafalque was erected, covered with a pall and surrounded with lighted candelabra. On this was placed a biretta and a stole, emblems of the priestly office of the deceased. *The Cambridge Chronicle* of 29 May 1885 noted that the sanctuary and body of the church were draped in black, and the whole of the congregation, including the school children, were mourning. This was a sad occasion, but also a celebration of the great work done by the late Canon. After the Mass, the ceremonies at the catafalque were performed by the new missionary rector, Canon Scott. The following Sunday, at the invitation of Canon Scott, the congregation made a general communion, on behalf of the late Canon.

Later that day, a solemn Requiem Mass was sung by the Lord Bishop of the Diocese in the Cathedral at Northampton for the repose of the soul of the Very Revd Canon Thomas Quinlivan The clergy in attendance there was equally impressive, proof of the late Canon's widespread popularity. Among those present were the Very Revd Canons Collis, Duckett, Land and Hammond, and the Revd Fathers Allies, Stokes, Moser, Murray, Smith, Pate, Murphy, Middleton, Wrigglesworth and Wendling.

After the absolution, the coffin was borne to the cemetery, followed by many of the relations and friends of the deceased. Several of the late Canon's 'old flock' had travelled from Cambridge especially for the funeral. *The Tablet* of 23 May 1885 reported that the coffin was covered with floral crosses and wreaths 'which testified to the esteem in which the late Canon was held'.

## Conclusion

The Quinlivan era of Catholic Cambridge was one of great fortunes, both personally and for the progress of religion in Cambridge. Looking back with hindsight now, we can appreciate how fortunate we are to have in our possession everything Canon Thomas Quinlivan worked for, 'a good church, good schools, a well trained choir, a rectory for the Priest, and everything well appointed and in good keeping'. We have an immense amount to be thankful for.

# Chapter 7

# Canon Christopher Scott, 1838–1922

*Christine Branch*

## A Protestant Stronghold

Cambridge in the 1830s was staunchly Protestant. Despite Catholic worship being permitted from 1791, and the Catholic Emancipation Act of 1829, there were no English-born Catholics living in Cambridge. The private chapel of the Huddlestons at Sawston Hall provided the only place for Catholics to worship on Sundays. Irish families coming to work seasonally on Cambridge farms had to walk a fourteen-mile round trip to hear Mass. Cambridge, both town and University, had remained at the heartland of Protestant England.

Into this secure non-Catholic environment, on Christmas Day 1838, Christopher Scott (Pl. 5b) was born; the youngest son of David and Sarah Scott of Ram Yard, a narrow alley off Round Church Street. He was baptized on 20 January 1839 at the church of the Holy Sepulchre (Round Church) where his father, a cook at St John's College, was churchwarden. Early in his life he was thought to have the qualities for ordination and, with this in mind, he was sent as a boarder to study at St Peter's Collegiate School in London. At home for holidays he studied in the top room in the family house at Ram Yard and sang in the choir of Holy Sepulchre; later he occasionally read lessons during services there.

## An Early Conversion

Whilst still at school in London he made friends with some Catholics and accompanied them to their church services. An important meeting took place when he was sixteen. He became friendly with William

Collis, a convert to Catholicism, who worked as a railway inspector at Whittlesford, about six miles from Cambridge. Collis was later promoted to stationmaster at Peterborough and the deep friendship that had developed between him and Christopher Scott became closer. He introduced Scott to Canon Seed, the Catholic priest in charge at Peterborough. William's decision to go to Rome to study for the priesthood led Scott to feel 'a conviction ... [to] become a Catholic', so he placed himself under Canon Seed for instruction. This devastated his devoutly Anglican family as their son had been destined to become a clergyman in the Church of England. There was much prejudice and misunderstanding about Catholics at that time. Scott's mother was especially upset, as she had read in an 'expensive' book that Scott could now buy an indulgence for one shilling. This would allow him to commit any sin, even taking his mother's life!

Scott was received into the Catholic Church at about the age of nineteen, and, as he had a desire to enter the Catholic priesthood, Bishop Wareing of Northampton sent him to St Mary's College at Oscott to study philosophy. He then went to the Venerable English College in Rome, where he studied for his ordination. This took place in the church of St John Lateran on Holy Saturday 1862. On St Stephen's day, he had the honour of preaching before Pope Pius IX. The Pope presented him with a crucifix, which Scott used for many years when attending the sick, until the crucifix was accidentally buried with a parishioner.

Scott studied theology in Rome, obtaining his Doctorate of Divinity by public examination and viva voce. He was attached to the Church of S. Maria Sopra Minerva. In view of his later church building in Cambridge it is interesting to note that this church is the only example of Gothic architecture in Rome.

## Northampton Diocese

With his studies completed Scott returned to the Northampton Diocese which in those days stretched as far as the East Coast. His first appointment in 1862 was as chaplain to Lady Clifford at her private chapel at Coldham Hall in Suffolk. There were very few Catholic churches in the diocese at that time. One of Scott's predecessors at Coldham Hall had been Fr Bernard Shanley, the Irish priest who started the Cambridge Mission in 1841.

After nearly three years Scott was recalled to Northampton and was made a canon of Northampton Cathedral Chapter and Cathedral Administrator. He spent the next eighteen years there. Among the many duties he undertook was to be on the Northampton Board of Guardians and he gained great popularity and respect among 'all classes of the community', as *The Cambridge Chronicle* reported at the time of his death. At that time he also paid several visits to Mr and Mrs Valentine Carey-Elwes at their home, Billing Hall, near Northampton. He instructed them and their three children and received all five into the Catholic Church. One of the children, Dudley Charles Carey-Elwes, later became Bishop of Northampton.

In 1879 Bishop Amherst of Northampton appointed Scott Vicar General of the Diocese. Thus he had authority for diocesan administration. At the Bishop's retirement he became Vicar Capitular giving him responsibility for the running of the diocese until a new bishop was appointed. On Bishop Riddell's accession Canon Scott was re-appointed Vicar General. This procedure occurred with each succeeding bishop, so the Canon was Vicar General for forty-three years altogether.

## First Steps

The stage was set at this time for Christopher Scott to become more directly involved with the town of Cambridge. The hierarchy of the Catholic Church had strongly dissuaded Catholics from studying at Oxford and Cambridge, because of the staunchly Protestant attitudes of the universities. Following the abolition in 1856 of the religious tests that prevented Catholic students from proceeding to degrees, there was a small increase in Catholic students. Catholics still needed their bishop's permission to attend as it was felt to be dangerous to their faith to be in an atmosphere of liberalism and scepticism. The small mission church of St Andrew's in Union Road was viewed as being too modest to uphold the position of the Catholic faith in the town. Canon Scott became aware of the need to expand Catholic activity and build a larger church.

In 1865 Canon Thomas Quinlivan, who was parish priest at St Andrew's from 1843, had purchased with donations a property adjoining the mission church (Wanstead House on Hills Road). In 1879 the adjacent Lensfield Estate on Hyde Park Corner became available and the Canon obtained an option to purchase. The only problem was funds.

## From Vicar General to Mission Rector

In 1879 as Vicar General Canon Scott was consulted by Canon Duckett, the priest in charge of the secular mission in Norwich, concerning the difficulties in obtaining a site for a church there which the Duke of Norfolk wished to build. The outcome was that Scott undertook to discuss the problem with the Duke, who summoned Canon Scott by telegram to Arundel Castle. The Norwich negotiations were satisfactorily completed. Feeling that the Canon had more to discuss, the Duke prompted him to mention other matters, so the Canon raised the difficulties of purchasing the Lensfield Estate in Cambridge. The Duke generously provided half of the £6100 needed and Canon Quinlivan raised the rest by mortgaging church property. There still remained the daunting prospect of raising sufficient money to pay off the debt and build the church.

In his capacity as Vicar General Canon Scott had visited a potential Catholic benefactor, Mrs Lyne-Stephens of Lynford Hall, Norfolk. She wished to build an imposing church but, as she did not know where to place it, she sought to consult him. Canon Scott, as a native of Cambridge, was able to point out the need for a Catholic church there, worthy of the town's architecture and ancient University, which would become a centre for a resurgence of Catholicism in Cambridge.

By 1883 Canon Quinlivan was in failing health due to the heavy load involved in running the Cambridge mission for forty years. He retired to Northampton. Canon Scott, his great friend and fellow member of the Northampton Cathedral Chapter, was his natural successor as a native of the town who had always been closely involved in Cambridge matters. His earlier talks with Mrs Lyne-Stephens were resolved a year later when she came to the vicarage on the feast of the Assumption 1884 and promised her financial help. The Canon's 'heart was rejoicing with thankfulness' (*Cambridge Chronicle Reminiscences*). The building could now start in earnest.

For the next thirteen years the mission rector was fully occupied with building the new church and establishing a sound foundation for the Catholic community in Cambridge. There was much controversy in Cambridge over the building of the new church and inevitably Canon Scott was at the forefront in answering the critics. He was drawn into a lengthy newspaper correspondence. His gentle, charming manner in dealing with opponents courteously was one of the major influences in slowly refuting those criticisms. Canon Scott was well versed in matters of architecture and church doctrine so able to discuss the opponents' views; both those against the Romanist Religion – and those against the 'pseudo-Gothic style'. Critics felt that Catholics should not be so conspicuous as they had only lately been classed as criminals. The poplar tree at Hyde Park Corner was white with leaflets showing local opposition to the church building.

The problems faced by Canon Scott did not stop with the consecration of the new church in 1890. The addition of a peal of English bells to the tower was one cause for complaint. Local residents were quick to write round robins, petitions and even threats to Canon Scott, but eventually familiarity silenced the opposition.

## A Frustrated Ambition

Once the building had been completed the Canon had many other problems to face in the growing parish. The more prominent Catholic presence in the town gave a raised profile to the rector as he began to organize the pastoral needs of both town and University. Canon Scott had always seen the new church as serving both town and University as had members of the Cambridge University Catholic Association. The association provided finances for the parish, especially helping to support a curate. In 1895 Canon Scott was instrumental in inaugurating the Fisher Society. The membership was open to all Catholic members of the University as he wished to promote a closer social union among Catholic University members as well as following literary pursuits. At that time there were only fifteen Catholic undergraduates; by the time of the Canon's death there were 140. Despite the local view that the church of Our Lady and the English Martyrs was a joint 'town and gown' church, the English hierarchy (after sanctioning Catholic attendance at the University) decreed in 1895 that a separate chaplaincy be established. Canon Scott was greatly disappointed as this left him with a church far larger than his congregation required. Nevertheless, Catholics at the University helped to support the church for many years.

## Ideal Parish Priest

Once the parish had been defined as serving only the town Canon Scott had the challenge of maintaining a church whose size far exceeded its congregation. Despite the small numbers he developed the full range of ceremonial and supporting roles expected from a church of near cathedral size.

Canon Scott was a gifted musician. He not only played the piano and organ but also composed several musical pieces, although he was too modest to have them published. He took a great interest in the new church organ. The University Professor of Music, Sir Charles Villiers Stanford, was keen to advise and gave a specification. Once it was installed the organ builder, Mr Smith of Leeds, asked Canon Scott to try it out. The Canon discovered that it was similar to the Schulze organ built for the Great Exhibition of 1851 which had been removed to Northampton Town Hall. It was written in one obituary that few who heard Canon Scott at a sung Mass would ever forget the experience, thanks to the thrilling harmony of his voice, which seemed to gain rather than diminish with age. There were even occasions during the First World War when Canon Scott, then in his late seventies, had to deputize at the organ during Mass. Due to his talent, and expectations of high standards, it is not surprising that the choir established a high reputation for its singing of Gregorian chant at sung Masses and Benedictions. Canon Scott did admit that the choir did not compare to King's College, but 'it is better because it sings for nothing'.

Over the following years the Canon expanded his interests both within the parish and in secular affairs. His interest in education led him to offer accommodation at the rectory for men training for the priesthood, prior to the establishment of St Edmund House. He promoted Catholic higher education; keenly supporting plans for a Catholic Women's Residence and helping to start a committee to encourage women teachers in secondary schools. He was a wise and sympathetic counsellor to the Sisters of the Institute of the Blessed Virgin Mary when they set up a girls' school in the town in 1898, giving religious instruction to the pupils.

The profile of the Cambridge mission rector was inevitably raised by the new church and Canon Scott was eager to become involved in the wider aspects of Cambridge life. He served with kindness and sympathy on the board of Addenbrooke's Hospital, and gave warm co-operation in the administration of the local NSPCC committee. His desire to maintain his interest in history, new developments and current affairs shows in his involvement in the work of the Cambridge Antiquarian Society and, in the last year of his life, becoming a founder member of the Cambridge branch of the League of Nations. The people of Cambridge grew to respect the gentle and dignified manner with which the Canon promoted many acts of kindness. He is said to have had a charm which especially appealed to the young and also enabled him to be sympathetic to all who sought his help. These gifts gradually eroded much of the anti-Catholic feeling in the town and Christopher Scott's influence helped Catholics to play a fuller part in Cambridge life.

Pope Leo XIII created Christopher Scott a domestic prelate

(Monsignor) while he was on a visit to Rome in 1901. The event was marked on his return to Cambridge by a celebration in his honour at the Victoria Assembly Rooms. The wider acceptance of the Catholic community was evident from the many prominent people of both town and University who attended, as well as the Catholics from the Northampton Diocese. The presentation gift of the robes of a monsignor was accompanied by an address given by Lord Acton, Regius Professor of History, and a prominent member of Mgr Scott's congregation. A purse containing 100 guineas was presented by Mr D. Learne on behalf of parishioners and friends.

The year 1912 marked a milestone in Christopher Scott's life as he celebrated the fiftieth anniversary of his ordination. In the same year he received the title of Provost when he became Senior Canon of the Northampton Chapter. He also became President of the Old Brotherhood of the English Secular Clergy (Old Secular Brethren), a friendly society founded in 1623, originally for the mutual support of the English secular clergy, who at that time where outlawed and persecuted. The Provost's Golden Jubilee was celebrated at the Guildhall. Bishop Keating of Northampton presented him with a purse containing 140 gold sovereigns and an illuminated address from 450 subscribers, both Catholic and non-Catholic residents of Cambridge. Mgr Scott donated the money to the decoration of the Sacred Heart chapel.

## A Time for Support

By the time of his jubilee Mgr Scott was seventy-four years old and had been showing signs of ill-health for some time. Since the turn of the century he had formed a close friendship with his neighbour, Edward Conybeare, former vicar of Barrington, who had been drawn to the Catholic faith. The Canon received him into the Church on 10 December 1910 and he became closely involved in the affairs of the parish. From the early 1900s Canon Scott's poor health had resulted in a series of accidents involving collisions with bicycles; falls (one causing a broken arm); being hit in the face by a football at dusk on Parker's Piece; several bouts of lumbago and many chest infections. During these indispositions Edward Conybeare was a constant visitor to the rectory, helping the Provost with nursing, getting meals and encouraging him to get going again by taking walks – even to the Botanical Gardens on a cold February day when he lent him his Inverness cape. Conybeare also supported the Provost by taking on some parish duties.

In August 1921 Mgr Scott hosted an event for which the church provided a wonderful venue – the Catholic Bible Congress. This was held at the request of Pope Benedict XV to mark the fifteenth centenary of the death of St Jerome. The Provost must have been proud that his church could host the largest Catholic gathering in Cambridge since the Reformation. As Cardinal Bourne pointed out in his closing address 'Provost Scott . . . thanked God that he had seen this day'.

It was only a few months later that Mgr Scott was on a visit to London to attend the annual meeting of the Old Secular Brethren. While crossing Trafalgar Square on 12 October he was knocked down by a taxi and fractured his right leg. He was ill for some time, including a dangerous bout of bronchitis. It depressed him to learn that he would never walk again, but he recovered sufficiently to return to Cambridge by ambulance in December. He was initially frustrated at feeling inactive but, although forced to use a wheelchair, he was soon taking part in the life of the parish again.

A new bishop was appointed to the Northampton Diocese in 1921, Dudley Charles Carey-Elwes, whom Christopher Scott had instructed in the 1870s. Scott felt some apprehension about the new bishop, but he proved to be 'just the same Carey-Elwes' when he arrived at the rectory on 2 January 1922. On 3 January 1922 the Cambridge parish held a reception for the new bishop at the Lion Hotel and the Monsignor attended in his wheelchair. At the meeting he commented on his desire to resign after the accident, but the Bishop refused it as unthinkable. Mention was made by the Bishop that all his learning came from 'Scotti'. The parishioners presented an illuminated address to their parish priest as a mark of 'affection, gratitude, love and deep respect' and 'in joy at his recovery'.

Sadly it was only a month later that Christopher Scott caught a chill, which developed into bronchial pneumonia. His former curate, Fr Kay, and the Bishop were sent for and he seemed to rally, but on 9 February he relapsed. By 16 February he had slipped into a coma, and he died peacefully, Edward Conybeare at his bedside, at 9.30 a.m. on 17 February 1922. He was eighty-three years old.

The huge attendance at his funeral, spilling out from the church into the street, served as recognition of his achievements in the parish (Pl. 6b). He had come to a little mission church in a back street of Cambridge, with a small congregation, which had to submit to prejudice, ignorance and non-acceptance. When he died after thirty-eight years as rector he left a beautiful church as a conspicuous monument and place of worship for the town, and by his courtesy and saintliness provided a basis for Catholics to be accepted into local life. As Sir Arthur Shipley, master of Christ's College, said in a written tribute: 'Unlike Mr Gladstone, who was once described as a good man in the very worst sense of the word, Canon Scott was a good man in the very best sense of the word... [His] picturesque figure will be much missed in the streets of our town' (*The Cambridge Chronicle*, 22 February 1922). The range of tributes from Catholics and non-Catholics, from town and University, and large crowds at the funeral confirmed the debt that Cambridge Catholics owe to Christopher Scott.

He is buried in the presbytery garden at the east end of the church.

## Chapter 8

# Founding a Cambridge Cathedral: Yolande Lyne-Stephens, Canon Christopher Scott and the Church of Our Lady and the English Martyrs

*Philip S. Wilkins*

When Bishop Arthur Riddell of Northampton issued his pastoral letter of Advent 1894 to the clergy and faithful of his diocese, he commended especially to their prayers the soul of Mrs Lyne-Stephens, then recently deceased. Her generosity had contributed greatly to the considerable progress made in the diocese during the previous decade. This had included the provision, at her sole cost, of churches and priests' residences at Lynford and Cambridge, the Bishop's residence at Northampton, and a handsome donation to the church at Wellingborough. The terms of her will were equally generous and included a bequest for the maintenance of the Cambridge church in addition to numerous gifts to Catholic and other charities. At that time the Diocese of Northampton, founded in 1850 at the restoration of the Catholic hierarchy, was the largest of the English dioceses in area but contained the fewest Catholics. It was consequently continually short of funds for the development and maintenance of missions under its jurisdiction. Fortunately for the diocese, Mrs Lyne-Stephens had a large country residence within its confines at Lynford Hall in Norfolk and was prepared to use her wealth to benefit good causes and her religious interests in the region.

# A Popular Ballerina

A portrait of Yolande Marie Louise Lyne-Stephens, painted in her latter years by the eminent French artist Carolus-Duran, has hung in the dining-room of the Cambridge rectory for over the past one hundred years (Pl. 7a). It shows her dressed formally in black and wearing the traditional mantilla, a pearl necklace offering only slight relief to an otherwise austere and melancholy appearance. In great contrast are the several portraits of her which appeared in her younger days at the height of her fame as a bright, attractive and extremely popular dancer in the Romantic ballet of the 1830s (Pl. 7b).

Born in Paris in 1813, the daughter of Jean Louis Duvernay, she studied ballet at the Paris Opéra under such influential teachers as Filippo Taglioni and Auguste Vestris. Under the name of Pauline Duvernay she made her début at the Opéra at the age of eighteen and two years later at Drury Lane Theatre in London where her performance received rapturous reviews. Her talent and great beauty appealed to the critics, *The Times'* correspondent being captivated by her elegance and grace of movement. She became a firm favourite in both capitals and was especially famed for her performance of the Spanish dance the *cachuca* in the ballet *Le Diable boiteux* which she first introduced to Drury Lane in December 1836. Thackeray, writing some years later, was ecstatic at 'a vision of loveliness such as mortal eyes can't see nowadays ... There has never been anything like it, never. There never will be.' Duvernay's dancing was also much admired by the young Princess Victoria during her excursions to the theatre, and drawings of the ballerina featured in the future queen's sketch book. Her career though appears to have been somewhat erratic and reports in 1835 suggested she had attempted suicide after an unhappy love affair. That and subsequent liaisons were the subject of much publicity in the gossipy Parisian journals of the day leading to a minor scandal.

Duvernay's unexpected early retirement in 1837 at the height of her career caused a sensation. It followed her involvement with the extremely wealthy Stephen Lyne-Stephens, owner of the prestigious Grove House at Roehampton and a further large estate at Lynford Hall in Norfolk. At the time he was reckoned to be the wealthiest commoner in England, having inherited a huge fortune which his father Charles had accumulated in trading between Portugal and England. The couple did not marry until 14 July 1845 and she suffered some ostracism, her notoriety doing little to endear her to conventional Victorian society. There were no children of the marriage and in the years following her husband's premature death in 1860 Mrs

Lyne-Stephens devoted much of the fortune she had been left to charitable causes.

## The Cambridge Mission

By the 1870s Canon Quinlivan had laboured for some thirty years seeking to develop the Mission of St Andrew in Union Road, Cambridge in the face of considerable opposition from other religious bodies. He had been successful in opening a new school in 1868 and for much of the time had appealed for funds to build a larger church. Throughout those years his appeals for funds appeared almost annually in the *Catholic Directory*. The chain of events surrounding this project and the manner in which Canon Scott became involved in its progress are elaborated elsewhere. Unfortunately, Canon Quinlivan had to retire because of ill-health in 1883 but not before he had acquired the adjacent Lensfield Estate which offered a prime site for a new church at the busiest crossroads of the town.

## The Cause Prospers

The need to gather building funds then devolved on his successor, Canon Scott, who appealed to a wide and influential section of the Catholic public. Cardinal Newman was among those approached and he lent enthusiastic support to Scott in a letter marked 'for publication':

> Cambridge, as being the seat of a great university, has a hold on the hearts and minds of Catholics in all parts of England. This is why I feel a special satisfaction in hearing from you that, with your Bishop's sanction, you are receiving subscriptions with the view of building there a new Church on a new site, an undertaking which, though local in its purpose, is not local in the interest which attaches to it, nor in the call which it makes on our cooperation.
>
> I pray God to bless so important a work, and I beg of you to accept from me, in aid of it, the enclosed offering.

The Cardinal's letter, written from Mrs Lyne-Stephens' residence at Lynford, Norfolk, begs the question as to how much influence he may have had ultimately in her decision to pay for the new church. For it was only a matter of months later, on the feast of the Assumption in August 1884, that she visited Canon Scott at his rectory to confirm her willingness to pay for the building – hence the full dedication of the church to Our Lady of the Assumption and the English Martyrs. It had been obvious to Scott that to raise the necessary funds for such a project would have been quite beyond the limited means of his small congregation, especially for the large and imposing church he envisaged would be necessary. Though fully aware of the extent of her charitable gifts, he had yet hoped that the Cambridge venture would appeal to the further generosity of Mrs Lyne-Stephens.

> What hopes should we have had of utilising the site, obtained with such difficulty, unless we had looked to her who had already done so much, but who crowned her many deeds of munificence by erecting the church? ... There had been no need of repeated requests, of urgent appeals to persuade it, the work was as spontaneous as it was lavish in its generosity so soon as the opportunity for it was discerned.

## The University Influence

Canon Scott was keen for Catholics to have wider access to opportunities in higher education, and he recognized that the University held a prime attraction for those Catholics wishing that their sons might benefit from its higher studies. With no Catholic establishments available to satisfy that need, he was also aware that a majority of bishops were moving in favour of withdrawing their embargo against Catholics attending Oxford and Cambridge. He therefore used his considerable influence to support other prominent clergy and laity who were urging the hierarchy to reconsider its position, though in this respect he failed to convince his own bishop, Riddell, of the necessity for change. He was of the opinion, moreover, that when obstacles to entry were removed, the consequent increase in Catholics attending the University would create the need for a larger and more dignified church in the town.

During his years studying for the priesthood, Canon Scott had travelled widely and become well-versed in the finer aspects of traditional church architecture. He took pride in his Cambridge roots and had a high regard for the architecture of the town and University. Consequently he formed definite ideas as to the features of a church which might blend with the older colleges and make the most of the imposing site at the major crossroads of the town. Moreover, he envisaged the possibility of a church and rectory which, in addition to their parochial functions, might become the centre of a Catholic resurgence in the life of the University. Mrs Lyne-Stephens thus found in him the ideal churchman whose enthusiasm, knowledge and vision might fulfil her intention of providing a worthy building on a grand scale.

## Progress and Controversy

With a site secured and a generous donor now at hand, the frustrations of the past were at last over and work on the church foundations began in 1885. Plans were commissioned, those of Dunn and Hansom being accepted after some revisions. Though Joseph Hansom, the celebrated founder of the firm of architects, had died three years previously, the church incorporates a number of features reminiscent of some he had originally proposed in 1871 for Arundel Cathedral but which had been rejected for that scheme. These include the position and design of the north-western tower and spire, the west doorway and the baptistery. The new rectory, built of red brick traditional in some of the older colleges and designed in the form of an open court, was completed and occupied as St Andrew's Rectory in 1887. In the same year Mrs Lyne-Stephens attended the impressive ceremony of laying the foundation stone of the church by Bishop Riddell.

Whether or not, as some suggested, her generosity was born from a desire to expiate her earlier lifestyle, Mrs Lyne-Stephens insisted on bearing the entire cost of the church and its furnishings and likewise the rectory, totalling in all over £70,000. One exception only was made, that of a restored medieval processional cross given by Baron Anatole von Hügel, a faithful supporter of Canon Scott from the latter's earliest years in charge of the mission.

The delight with which local Catholics witnessed the gradual rise of their new church may well have been tempered by the adverse reactions of some local non-Catholics, particularly those with entrenched Protestant and Nonconformist views of the 'Romanist' religion. Though the University, for so long the foremost centre of education for Church of England clergy, had gradually adopted a more liberal attitude towards Catholics during the nineteenth century, there yet remained in both University and town a strong minority inveterately opposed to all things Catholic. Their antagonism to the building of a new Catholic church in the town initiated a scathing and often vitriolic correspondence in the local press into which Canon Scott and his supporters were inevitably drawn in defence of Catholic principles. The controversy was later recalled by Edward Conybeare, a former Anglican clergyman who converted to Catholicism and became a leading member of the congregation:

> Though a generation or more had passed since Catholic Emancipation, the penal laws ... were still remembered and some non-Catholics considered that a religion so recently ... outlawed ought to avoid making itself conspicuous. Yet the new church was the most outstanding landmark in

the whole town. Hostility was thus aroused; shoals of letters, of bigotry now almost unthinkable, were sent to the local Press, and the great poplar tree which then stood at Hyde Park Corner was white with ultra-Protestant posters and leaflets ...

The dedication of the church to Our Lady and the English Martyrs gave added cause for controversy: 'a temple is being built in Cambridge dedicated to the idolatrous worship of a creature'. This travesty of Catholic doctrine initiated a lampoon which persisted as a local folk-tale for many years and still resurfaces occasionally. It falsely asserted that the fortune of Mrs Lyne-Stephens's husband had been made from the invention of movable dolls' eyes and it typified the church as the 'eye-doll house' or 'idol house'.

The English martyrs, then recently beatified by Rome, were denounced as traitors to their country, a likely reaction in some entrenched Cambridge circles where Cranmer, Latimer, Ridley and companions were perceived as the only true martyrs of the English Reformation. Scott, however, had a strong regard for the Catholic martyrs of those turbulent times, many of whom had been educated at the University. He was especially concerned that the church should commemorate John Fisher, Bishop of Rochester, Chancellor of the University for over thirty years, fellow of Michaelhouse and president of Queens' College, who was martyred for his Catholic faith. Hence the church and rectory embrace numerous references to the saint, including a series of windows portraying his life and statues of him at the entrances to the church and rectory.

## The 'Cathedral'

After delays at various stages of the building, the church was eventually consecrated on 8 October 1890 and opened for public worship a week later (Fig. 5). The first public Mass was sung by Bishop Riddell in the presence of almost all the Catholic bishops of England and Wales, a large gathering of clergy, and prominent Catholic laity including the foundress. The imposing building on such a prominent site made an immediate impact on the townspeople and was generally welcomed as a worthy contribution to the architecture of the town. There were some who, understandably, criticised its neo-Gothic design as a mere reflection of a bygone age, though it is hard to imagine that a more modern style would have been acceptable in Victorian Cambridge. Dissenting voices were raised too among the Catholic public at large, most of whom were unaware of the ambitious idea behind the venture. They

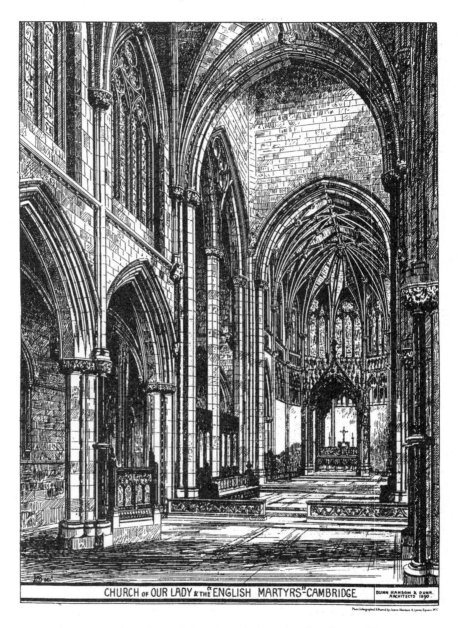

CHURCH of OUR LADY & the "ENGLISH MARTYRS" CAMBRIDGE

Fig. 5.    A drawing of the church interior by the architects
Dunn and Hansom.

questioned the need for such an expensive church to serve an area sparsely populated by their brethren; particularly when numbers of poor missions elsewhere were unable to provide even the most humble accommodation for their rapidly increasing congregations. Since the entire cost of the vast project was being met by a single donor, however, fears that such expense might seriously deplete existing funds for new Catholic churches were to a great extent allayed. Besides, others argued, the time was appropriate for Catholics 'to come out of the catacombs' and to raise the standard of their church architecture.

Until long after the turn of the century townspeople referred to the church as 'the cathedral' or 'the pro-cathedral'. In correspondence of March 1883 just previous to his retirement, Canon Quinlivan had referred to the intended demolition of the old Lensfield House in the 'Cathedral Precincts', a phrase he would scarcely have used unless it were authentic. It may well have been debated whether the church should become the cathedral of a new diocese embracing Cambridgeshire, Norfolk and Suffolk. Northampton Cathedral was small and far from ideally situated, being on the fringe of the Midlands, whereas the diocese extended as far as the East Anglian coast. Subsequently rumours of the Cambridge church becoming the cathedral of a new diocese recurred from time to time, including a suggestion in 1912 of a Cambridge bishopric under the celebrated preacher Monsignor Robert Hugh Benson. A permanent rearrangement of the diocese was delayed until ultimately in 1976 the counties of Cambridgeshire, Norfolk and Suffolk were hived off into a new Diocese of East Anglia with its cathedral at the church of St John the Evangelist in Norwich. The new diocese, which embraces one of the smallest Catholic populations in England, thus has two of the largest Catholic parish churches in the country, at Cambridge and Norwich.

## Last Bequests

The building of the Church of Our Lady and the English Martyrs was the culmination of Mrs Lyne-Stephens's charitable works, though she added a further act of generosity to the Cambridge Mission in the last year of her life. By the early 1890s the mission school in Union Road desperately lacked accommodation for infants who formed a large proportion of the pupils. Inspectors had strongly advocated the building of a separate classroom for them and, after an appeal from Canon Scott, the necessary funds for an infants' classroom were provided by Mrs Lyne-Stephens.

On 2 September 1894 she died at her Norfolk home and her body was brought to lie in state overnight in the great church she had founded. In the evening a funeral dirge was sung and the following morning a Pontifical Requiem celebrated by Bishop Riddell. The bishop's throne was hung overall in purple, the communion rails and pulpit draped in black, and the singing was performed by a choir from the London Oratory. Canon Scott preached on a text from Hebrews 6, 'God is not unjust that He should forget your work, and the love that you have shown in His name, you who have ministered to the saints'. In referring to the many charitable gifts given by the foundress within the Diocese of Northampton, he mentioned particularly the church in which her funeral Mass was then being celebrated:

> ... the church she erected on a scale of magnificence which testifies to her love of the beauty of God's House, and to her desire to render back to God something commensurate with all He had bestowed upon her. Greatly indeed was she indebted to God; richly had she been endowed with gifts of every kind; of natural character, of special intelligence, of winning attractiveness, which compelled homage from all who came under the charm of her influence; with the result of widespread renown and unbounded wealth ...

The Canon also recognized that, in spite of her vast wealth, Yolande Lyne-Stephens had experienced years of social exclusion:

> Therefore it was that the blessing of God came in another form – by the discipline of suffering and trial. There was the trial of loneliness. Soon bereft, as she was, of the husband, of whose affection we may judge by the way in which he laid all he possessed at her feet; French and Catholic, living amongst those who were not of her faith or nation, though enjoying their devoted friendship; deprived of the surroundings of Catholic sympathy, she was thrown entirely upon herself in all that which is of the deepest concern. With advancing years, deprived by death even of intimate friends, she was lonely in a sense throughout her life. These were her crosses, destined doubtless as a corrective to the fascination of wealth, and which led her to become, in addition to her contributions to general charities, the great benefactress of our large and poverty-stricken diocese.

Immediately after the Requiem Mass the cortège left for Grove House, Roehampton, where, after final rites had been conducted by the Bishop of Southwark in the presence of Bishop Riddell, Canon Scott and family relatives, the coffin was laid beside that of her husband in the mausoleum which Mrs Lyne-Stephens had erected in the grounds. In her will she left further money to the Bishop of Northampton for the development of missions and good causes within the Diocese, including a sum of £5000 for 'the sustenation' of the Cambridge church. This endowment, however, was to be restricted to structural maintenance of the church only, so that Canon Scott found himself struggling to meet the expenses of the mission and the huge church of which he was now rector.

## The Memorials

Small wonder then that the vexed question of funding a memorial to the foundress became a continuing problem for the rector. Many may have thought that the splendid church she had provided might be considered a sufficient memorial to her, but it was an era when a more personal representation would have been expected for so generous a gesture. Thus when the church had been designed, space had been allocated in the north transept for the eventual erection of a chantry chapel to commemorate her memory. Not surprisingly therefore, within a month of her death the architect Edward Hansom sought the go-ahead from Canon Scott: 'Can we put up the monument to Mrs Lyne-Stephens which was contemplated?'. Some parts of the church, however, were either still unfinished or in course of completion; the bells had only recently been installed, Westlake's large painting for the lantern tower wall was incomplete, and the rood at the entrance to the sanctuary had yet to be commissioned. It can be imagined how prudent the Canon would have needed to be with building funds remaining to him after Mrs Lyne-Stephens's death, being uncertain whether those funds would cover the work still to be completed.

A few years later, on the occasion of his appointment as a domestic prelate to the pope, the rector was presented by his parishioners with a purse of 100 guineas. He expressed an intention of devoting a portion as a subscription towards the erection of a monument 'in the confident hope that the Catholic public might complete it [the transept], and so remove the eyesore of its unfinished condition'. There was evidently insufficient response to this appeal and, since with the passing years of his rectorship a memorial to the foundress failed to materialize, the empty transept became a reproach to the Canon and his congregation. In due course, as recounted elsewhere, Baron Anatole von Hügel bequeathed money for the purpose and an altar, dedicated to St John Fisher and also commemorating the foundress, was erected in the north transept. The altar, unfortunately, had a comparatively brief existence, being dismantled in more recent years during alterations to the sanctuary and north transept. Only the commemorative stone plaque remains embedded in the transept wall, a forlorn reminder of frustrated intentions.

In striking contrast to this confused chapter of events, Scott's death in 1922 was immediately followed by a popular demand that his memory should be perpetuated in an appropriate form. The esteem and affection in which he had been held by his congregation and many beyond the bounds of Cambridge and the diocese was evidenced in the widespread support to a fund for that purpose. Several schemes were proposed and rejected; ironically, one from a former close friend of Scott that 'the derelict niche which was intended for a memorial to the foundress of the church might be used for a memorial to the Provost, as it would never be used now for the foundress'! Eventually a fine brass in traditional style, depicting the Canon in priestly vestments, was commissioned and placed inside the sanctuary rails (Fig. 6). Thereafter generations of clergy, choristers and altar servers would dutifully skirt it while proceeding to and from their appointed places until recent times when it was removed to a side chapel.

Yet other memorials do exist to both the priest who conceived and brought to fruition the impressive scheme of church building and also to the generous donor who made it possible, memorials less tangible perhaps but nevertheless more consonant with their Catholic faith, namely the foundation Masses offered in the church each year for the repose of their souls.

Fig. 6.    Brass of Canon Christopher Scott, d. 1922.

Account of the opening of Our Lady and the English Martyrs for public worship from C.E. Sayle's annotated copy of the 1890 edition of the church guide (CUL Adv.d.119.1).

The opening of the Church was fixed for 11.0. But it was 11.15 before the Procession entered the Church.

Thurifer

Acolyte [Cross] Acolyte

4 Dominicans

1 Carmelite

Franciscans

2 Passionists

Benedictines

60 Priests (including an Oratorian)

Mgr. Stanley

Bps. in the order of their consecration, q.v.

Bp. of Clifton [William Clifford]

Liverpool [Bernard O'Reilly]

Newport [John Cuthbert Hedley OSB]

Nottingham [Edward G. Bagshawe]

Shrewsbury [Edmund Knight]

Birmingham [Edward Ilsley] – was late

Middlesburgh [sic] [Richard Lacy]

Portsmouth [John Virtue]

Southwark [John Butt]

Emmaus [James Laird Patterson]

Northampton [Arthur Riddell]

T. Wingham organist of the London Oratory presided, & the Oratory choir sang. The Processional was the 'Cœlestes Urbs Jerusalem'. 'Ecce Sacerdos' W. Schultes (late Organist of the London Oratory). Mass, Gounod, No. 3. Offertory, Ave Verum, Gounod. Te Deum. Bp. Hedley preached. At Vespers. F. Rickaby S.J. 'Magnificat' Dr. F. E. Gladstone. At Benediction Motett 'Recordare' Walter Austin. 'O Salutaris' F. Westlake. Litany, Rev. C. Scott. 'Tantum ergo' W. Sewell (Organist of the B'ham Oratory).

# Chapter 9

# 1914–1918: A World in Turmoil

## Christopher Jackson

During the period of the First World War the Cambridge Catholic Mission continued under the care of Mgr Canon Christopher Scott, who had served as Mission Rector since 1883. He was assisted by his curate, Fr A. J. Kay, who had been appointed to Cambridge in 1909, and other clergy such as Fr Fellows and Fr Wainwright who served in the parish at various times during this period. The congregation at this time consisted of about 200 regular Mass-attenders (swollen to twice that number for Midnight Mass at Christmas); there were active branches of the Guild of the Blessed Sacrament, the Catholic Women's League and the Society of St Vincent de Paul, a Catholic Men's Club and a Catholic Scout Troop. By 1914 Canon Scott was seventy-six years old and in addition to the assistance he received from the other clergy he depended quite heavily on the support and friendship of his active and energetic next-door neighbour Edward Conybeare, then in his early seventies. Conybeare's diaries provide an invaluable source of information on the parish life of this period.

## Outbreak of War

The declaration of war against Germany on 4 August, the day after the hot Bank Holiday Monday of 1914, seemed to owe more to the inevitable than the unexpected. Long before the assassination of Archduke Franz Ferdinand at Sarajevo on 28 June, the naval race between Britain and Germany and the build-up of military strength by the main powers in Europe had pointed to the near certainty of some future conflict. Six years previously, in 1908, the county units of the Territorial Army, among them the Cambridgeshire Regiment, had been given modern organization and equipment to enable them to take their place in the front line in any future conflict. In January 1914 a recruiting week throughout Cambridgeshire had already brought the Cambridgeshire Regiment up to its full war strength of 960 with a waiting list of new recruits. The regiment had actually left for their two-week summer camp on 18 July, during the developing crisis, well prepared for the mobilization orders which came only two days after their return home. At least one parishioner was included among their number. On 8 August Conybeare wrote: 'Territorials off – town and varsity mixed. Did O.L. flowers by moonlight 11pm.'

## Troop Concentrations

If the departure of the local regiment left Cambridgeshire virtually empty of its soldiers, this situation lasted no more than a few days. Cambridge was designated as the assembly point for the 18,000 troops of the 6th Infantry Division, and an influx in such numbers between 14 August and 7 September 1914 had its impact on the local population and the Catholic community as the following diary entries show:

> 1914 August 15th Thousands of regulars poured into Cambridge, camping on Midsummer Common. Huge camps on Jesus Green (5000 Yorks and Durham reservists).
>
> 17th – Military flood pouring in all day – to 15000. Had to seat 300 soldiers at High Mass.
>
> 18th – Great camps formed on Coe Fen and Coldhams Common & Stourbridge Common.
>
> 22nd – In morn. Fr Kay & Baron [von Hügel] – who is trying to be naturalised- about getting 3000 soldiers in to Mass. Much artillery entering town, where we now have a complete Army Corps without a word in the Press.
>
> 23rd – Wonderful day. 5 successive Masses 8.30–1 for over 3000 soldiers (Mostly Leinster)[i.e. the 2nd Battalion The Prince of Wales's Leinster Regiment (Royal Canadians], newly arrived from their depot in Cork); church simply packed espec. 9.30 when over 1000; thrilling sight, even sanctuary full right up to altar. Confessions, Baptisms and Receptions all rest of day. At SVDP work all day seating soldiers and giving them prayerbooks, etc.
>
> 24th August – All day at SVDP work taking crucifixes, etc., to Catholic soldiers in camp along with RC chaplain, Baron, etc.
>
> 30th August – 6 Masses for troops 7–11.30. Church full at all and packed at 7 (Leinster)
>
> September 1st – Much shifting of troops, Leinsters gone and Artillery.

6th – 4 crowded Masses. Splendid singing at Benediction; 200 soldiers in front.

This was the last Cambridge was to see of the 6th Division. All had left for France by 8 September, eighty special trains being required to move them from Cambridge Station. By October 1914 the Leinster Regiment had been engaged in the first battle of Ypres and had to be replaced by other troops in the front line owing to their heavy losses.

Similar events marked the assembly training and departure of part of Kitchener's New Army, the 53rd (Welsh) Territorial Division, between January and May 1915, to be sent as reinforcements to the front, 'where we have lost 104,200 men'.

> 1914 December 19th – Billeting begun for 17000 troops – first in Cambridge since Civil War
> 26th – Getting library and school ready as recreation room for Catholic soldiers
> 28th – High Mass at which church packed with soldiers who also found School Recreation Room nice 3–9.
> 1915 January 27th – Barricades all round Cambridge to stop spy motors – none allowed through after 9 p.m.

The diary entries for 1 February, 'Soldiers to bath 5–7', and 16, 'back to bath soldiers', appear to denote pre-arranged bath facilities made available at 'Stokeslea' to billeted soldiers.

> February 11th – King here to inspect troops on (Parker's) Piece. An impressive sight. Saw with Convent Boarders from Tower.
> March 28 (Sun) – To 7.30 Mass, a new departure to relieve overwhelming pressure of communions at 8.30.

## Winter Quarters

Only one other influx of troops on a similar scale took place in Cambridge during the war, when a large contingent spent the winter of 1915–16 billeted in Cambridge, 'but they were in very inferior numbers to the Welsh Division' (*The Cambridge Chronicle*).

> 1915 December 29 – In to soldiers club at Rectory (10,000 more troops into town today).
> 1916 January 2nd – Many soldiers in church, Kents & Surreys having come into billets here last week.

## Our Boys in Blue

The Eastern General Hospital, Cambridge, had been planned in pre-war days as a support component of the Territorial Force, itself intended to be mobilized for home defence in the event of war. This explains its original character as a hospital for a theatre of operations (Eastern England), rather than the base hospital which it soon became. On mobilization its territorial and reservist staff assembled first at the Leys School in Cambridge, but within a short time the hospital moved to Trinity College in search of greater space (and under pressure from the school authorities anxious to reopen for the autumn term). The first cases admitted to the hospital, on 16 August 1914, were casualties from battle-training in England, but these were soon followed by ever-increasing numbers of wounded from the battlefields of France.

These wounded soldiers, soon to be seen on the streets of Cambridge, came to be known as 'Boys in Blue', from the distinctive light blue uniforms with red ties worn as their walking-out dress. Each soldier would also wear the headdress appropriate to his particular unit. Local residents and parishioners became deeply involved in relief work for the wounded. Conybeare's diary entries reflect these events:

> 1914 August 10th – Downing commandeered for Red Cross Nurses depot. 92 there headed by Misses Leach and Norton.
> 12th – Our house [Stokeslea, Lensfield Road] made Red Cross distributing centre so drawing room piled with shirting.
> 15th – Neviles Court turned into hospital. Took F. [Mrs Conybeare] in hansom to see Trinity cloisters being floored for hospital.

The Eastern General Hospital was originally established beneath the Wren Library in Trinity College, then expanded across Trinity Backs to an extensive area beyond Queens' Road, the site of the present-day University Library.

> 31st – In aft. first 150 wounded installed in Trin. cloisters.
> September 5th – 80 big hospital tents (8 beds) in Trinity Backs.

These tents brought the capacity of the hospital up to 500 beds.

> 23rd – 150 wounded brought to Trinity 3 a.m. from Aisne.
> 28th – In aft. to inspect Neviles Court Hospital – quite ideal. Nurses flitting from Downing to King's.
> 30th – Walking down Burrells [Walk] to see wonderful new hospital range rising like magic in King's Cricket Ground.

The single-storey hutted accommodation in Burrell's Walk was completed on 14 October 1914 by local builders Arthur Negus and Sons, providing 1470 beds.

> December 3rd – In aft, round Military Hospital. Gave out 70 packets of Woodbine cigs and as many cakes, choc, she giving postcards and pencils. A marvellous place but bitter cold, all wards being merely verandahs.
> 5th – 250 wounded come in and brought from station to hospital in single hour.

> 1916 May 28th – Had to escort Addenbrookes soldiers to High Mass.
> June 5th – Sent teachers and children to see Ambulance Train at station.
> 30th – Long prepared day of British advance on Somme ...
> July 2nd – Advance wounded coming in.
> 19th – Multitudes of wounded coming in.

After this harrowing episode Conybeare's diary is empty of references to the wounded in Cambridge save to record various occasions when the Catholic Women's League and the Society of St Vincent de Paul would entertain parties of wounded soldiers, such as:

> 1918 August 15th – Wounded soldiers (60) in Rectory & our garden 2.30–6.30. Some 20 helpers to tea in dining room.

During the First World War a total of 62,664 wounded soldiers passed through the Eastern General Hospital and its later sections at Barnwell Hospital, Newmarket Road, Cambridge (with 850 beds from 16th August 1915) and Cherry Hinton Hospital, Cherry Hinton Road, Cambridge. Of these, 351 were Belgians. A total of twenty convalescent homes run by the Red Cross were set up in surrounding villages (in manor houses, rectories and the like), to which wounded soldiers were moved for recovery. Dr Apthorpe-Webb (a parishioner) served as registrar of the hospital (Major F. E. Apthorpe-Webb RAMC) and was responsible for setting up the Bath Ward, a pioneering medical development in the use of baths for the relief of severely wounded patients. A young military policeman from Ireland, Patrick (Paddy) Harris served on the gate of the Barnwell Hospital and later settled in Cambridge, becoming a parishioner and founder of Camtax and International Progressive Coaches. Mgr Barnes, the University Catholic Chaplain, served until 1916 as one of the hospital chaplains and his successor Capt. (later Canon) James Marshall served as chaplain to the Red Cross convalescent home in Great Shelford when he first arrived in Cambridge.

## The Refugees in our Midst

Refugees arrived in Cambridge in plentiful numbers during the war, giving both the town (through the likes of the Belgian Hospitality Committee) and the Catholic community much opportunity for relief work among these fugitives. Most of the refugees were Belgians, a stream of whom, after the German invasion on 4 August, had turned into a flood when the fall of Antwerp on 11 October led to the German occupation of the whole of Belgium. They were willingly received, as in every part of Britain, as living proof of German aggression and atrocities. According to Conybeare's diaries, he, and the Catholic parish, were kept extremely busy during the period of their first arrival, in the autumn of 1914, though the crisis gradually resolved as appropriate arrangements were made for the refugees to settle into the local community. Furthermore, in response to an invitation from the University, a number of Belgian professors and students settled in Cambridge and university facilities were placed at their disposal. Edward Conybeare was well placed through his university connections to act as a go-between in these arrangements, as some of the following diary entries indicate. The earliest refugee reference occurs on 20 September 1914 and gives a hint of possible language misunderstandings ahead.

> Sheppard to lunch with tale of Belgian 'Professor' (of Music). Really a wheelwright, quite plebian with wife and children to match speaking only Flemish. But nice people from Malines. Went down with rosaries and holy water.
>
> 27th – Sad Belgian Refugee muddle disclosed by Baron at SVP.
> October 10th – called Fr Van Donacker, Canon of Bruges and Old Testament Prof. at Louvain, the one professor so far to accept inter-university invitation to come here *ad eundem*. Then to Belgian refugee family in Croftown, with whom he chatted in Flemish, to touching joy of children.
> 15th – Introduced Canon Van Donaker to E. Clark and Union. Then took him to station to greet trainload of wounded Belgians from Antwerp.
> 17th – Belgian errands all day. In morning getting Van Donaker to translate notice of service into French and Flemish, in aft. to Newnham with mugs for refugees (100 of whom arrived today, 14 hrs late).
> 18th – SVP Conference. Head of Liege Conference, Prof. Dejace of Liege University. Many Belgians in garden after High Mass.
> 19th – Running about on Belgian errands all day. Introduced Prof Dejace at Union.

25th – Prof Breithoff of Louvain Univ. (engineering) to tea with nice bright wife.

27th – Professors of Ghent, Liege and Louvain meet to organise lectures for Refugee Students (P Dejace President).

29th – Made acquaintance of nice Prof. Coloon (science) of Liege.

250 more wounded brought in.

31st – With F. to Belgian Refugees 11 Brookside to take pencils and paper. 22 in house (of single family) incl. lovely mother who teaches Belgian class at Convent.

November 8th – Interesting SVP (how to pay for Belgian soldiers burials).

9th – F. got wounded Belgians (for whom Cintra Terrace [now Cintra House, Hills Road] is convalescent hospital) into garden where they played swans like children ...

14th – Belgian flag up on church scaffolding.

15th – King Albert of Belgium 39, so Belgian Te Deum 10 a.m. attended in state by Mayor and Vice-Chancellor.

17th – All aft. Belgian convalescents in garden and to tea in Library.

December 2nd – With F. to crowded Belgian fete at Guildhall.

14th – Funeral of Prof Van Hooten. All Senate in residence at Requiem.

18th – Junior Paston House Concert mostly by Belgian children (in English).

1915 April 14th – Professor Deschamps is to arrange for starting Belgian SVP Conference.

18th – Badly worshipless Sunday, only 8.30 Mass & Communion. Belgian-ridden day. SVP President for all Belgium coming 12–5 to help establish Belgian Committee of Conference to work for country's refugees. Had him to lunch + Dejace & Deschamps, then presided at Meeting & made my first French speech. 30 Belgians joined, 8 coming to tea afterwards. Then Van Hoonaker till 6.30.

From this time onwards the picture of emergency conditions expressed in Conybeare's diaries quickly subsided as the Belgian refugees settled into their temporary homes and the children and university students carried on with their education in new surroundings. Even so, there are occasional reminders of their presence in a strange land, and of the causes of their flight.

1915 – August 4th – In eve attended carrying into church of Belgian girl dead in Convent thro' German outrages.

16th – Met Van Hoonaker returning from vain attempt to get into Holland 'which is on eve of war'.

22nd – Dejace to breakfast with tales of country visiting. At Wimpole Hall he was shown into the Servant's Hall by Miss Roberts.

From then on happier diary entries appear:

1916 March 6th – Belgian children's Carnival at Paston House 2–4.
July 23rd – After High Mass Te Deum for Belgian Independence, Canon
    V.Hoonaker officiating, then Belgian children in our garden.
1917 June 28th – Convent bazaar 2.30-8. Entertainment by Day Sch
    Belgians and Boarders. Belgian Portia excellent ('Who wrote it' says
    Canon Scott).

Once the war was over, most of the Belgian refugees returned home,
though there would have been some instances of individuals staying on
in Cambridge, possibly as a result of marriage. A notable example was
Mrs Holmes, the long-serving housekeeper at the rectory under Canon
Marshall, herself the Belgian widow of a British officer.

## Parish Life in Wartime

The impact of wartime conditions on civilian life in Britain during the
First World War only developed slowly, certainly when contrasted with
the immediate introduction of most emergency measures from the very
start of the Second World War. Much had by then been learned from
the experiences of the earlier conflict, which itself had no fund of
earlier experiences to draw on. Conscription was not introduced until
March 1916, then made inevitable by the huge manpower losses
among the regular and volunteer forces; dimming of lights, an earlier
version of the blackout, not until January 1915 when Zeppelins were
already ranging freely over the countryside; rationing not until
February 1917, by which time it was realised that the U-boat blockade
was bringing the country uncomfortably close to starvation. The
concept of a total war, involving British civilians in a 'Home Front'
would not emerge until 1939.

Even though much was happening in Cambridge at the outbreak of
war in terms of military activity, reception of wounded soldiers and
arrivals of refugees, time could still be devoted to parochial matters.
One of the main preoccupations which the parish could allow itself in
1914 involved the installation of the Rood Beam and figures of Our
Lady, St John and Christ in Majesty (or 'Majestas') over the Sanctuary
arch, a unique finishing touch to a Church completed in all other
respects twenty-five years previously. As in many other spheres of
parish life, Edward Conybeare was closely involved in the arrangements and recorded the proceedings in his diary.

1914 February 9th – Canon came to tea with lovely sketches for Rood by
    Leach [the local artist Mr B. Maclean Leach]
May 12th – ... fixed up Our Lady on Rectory plane *Exaltata sum quasi*

*platanus*. Then up tower helping Leach to measure height of rood arch (50 ft). Clay models for Rood beam. Beautiful but Canon has made Our Lord Bishop instead of Priest.

November 19th – Rood beam got up.

25th – Helped to erect Majestas for Roodbeam. Glorious.

30th – Roodbeam lowering began.

December 5th – Roodbeam at lower level, a vast improvement.

18th – Rood completed and scaffolding down.

20th – Rood glorious.

27th – Blessing of Rood at High Mass at which ch. packed with soldiers . . .

1915 July 22nd – Lovely effect of sun on Majestas, Our Lord crowned with glory.

1916 December 26th – Rood crown lovely at High Mass.

Inevitably wartime preoccupations influenced religious observances. The first Sunday of 1915 was designated by King George V as a National Day of Intercession, recorded by the following diary entry:

1915 January 3rd – Intercession Day for War. Gt. experience. 4 crowded Masses, 3 or 4 hundred Communions. Exposition 12.30–7 on High Altar, never less than 50 present, about ¼ of them soldiers.

This call to prayer was repeated three more times before the war ended.

1916 2nd January – National Intercession Day with Lenten vestments and no touch of Xmastide except Preface. Litany after instead of carols. Exposition all aft. Miserere after Benediction. Many soldiers in Church.

1918 6th January – New Year Sunday- King's Day of Intercession. Litany before High Mass. Veni Creator at Bened. for 1918.

Occasionally a similar directive would emerge from the Vatican, such as

1916 July 30th – In charge of children. All Cath. children thro'out world to Communion for Peace by order of Pope.

As the war dragged on, and especially after conscription was introduced on 1 March 1916, manpower shortages started to have their effect on parish life:

1916 February 21st – First lesson in winding church clock as Clarence [Mills] is called up.

December 25th – No Mdnt Mass for first time since 1845. But 400 Communions at 8.30 (+ 250 yesterday). High Mass and Carols wonderful considering depletion of choir.

> 1917 September 9th – Services at last for first time really touched by War.
> Provost [Canon Scott] at organ. No proper singing at High Mass. Had
> to lead choir at Benediction myself.

Sometimes good news from the front gave rise to rejoicing:

> 1917 November 22nd – Joy peal for wonderful victory at Cambrai, tanks
> smashed Hindenburg line. Cavalry through.
> 22nd – More Cambrai peals.

Military obsequies at the church called for additional ceremony:

> 1916 5th November – Glorious requiem for the dead in war; 30 soldiers
> holding candles before catafalque & Cadet Guard of Honour (fixing
> bayonets at Gospel) (Pl. 8).
> 1917 September 28th – brought in corpse of French Officer with full
> military pomp.
> 29th – Great military High Requiem 10 a.m. with full pomp and church
> crowded mostly with cadets.
> December 13th – Great military funeral of Australian cadet – ch. packed
> with 500 cadets.

The cadets referred to in these entries were members of the Officer
Cadet Corps, formed, according to *The Cambridge Chronicle* 'for the
training of rankers as officers.' Three battalions of the Corps were
accommodated in Cambridge from late 1915 onwards, 'occupying
space in the University whilst the ordinary students had all but
disappeared.'

A shortage of priests in the Northampton Diocese would have been
the cause of the following entry:

> **1918** August 2nd – Sudden news of Fr Kay going next Thurs to sole
> charge of Slough. Poor dear old Canon. [Canon Scott was by this time
> eighty years old.]
> 9th – Fr Kay's last Cambridge mass. His 11 years ended here in eve with
> his departure to Slough. He came to bid farewell 3 p.m. In to Rectory
> supper to help Provost with his first meal with his new curate, Fr
> Wainwright, a pleasing youth near 30.

Behind the scenes preparations for a presentation to Fr Kay were
momentarily overshadowed by news of the Armistice.

> November 11th – Armistice signed. Ran up tower and got first chime.
> Meanwhile Gt St Mary's belfry wrecked by overzealous cadets who went
> mad tearing about streets all day. 18th – Running about all day various
> Fr.Kay testimonials. Sch. gave him a clock in aft. Congregation £91 in eve
> at Convent Gymnasium.

According to *The Cambridge Chronicle*, 20 November 1918, speeches at the farewell ceremony were made by Mgr Scott, Mr Conybeare and Fr Kay.

Edward Conybeare's diary entries for the Treaty of Versailles in 1919 and the dedication of the Parish war memorial bring the story of Catholic Cambridge in the First World War to a conclusion:

> 1919 June 28th – Peace signed 3 p.m. at Versailles in same room where German Empire proclaimed 1871. So mighty rag at night, stalls, telephones, handcarts, boats, canoes, punts bonfired on Market Hill.
> 29th – Te Deum for Peace at High Mass.
> 1920 December 2nd – War memorial, very ideal, unveiled by Bishop in miraculous ideal service (at which he preached powerfully) 7–8, beginning with Veni Sancti Spiritus & ending with Last Post (first time of hearing it). Not a hitch all through. A session to have lived for.

The war memorial commemorates twenty parishioners killed in the First World War. Their sacrifice was not in vain, though hopes that they might have died in a 'War to end all Wars' were dashed by the outbreak of the Second World War less than twenty years later.

# Chapter 10

# The Catholic Bible Congress, 1921

*Christopher Jackson*

## Commemoration of St Jerome

The year 1920 saw the fifteenth centenary of the death of St Jerome, long venerated as the author of the first translation of the Bible into Latin, which has been known ever since as the Vulgate. Thanks to the labours of St Jerome, the various parts of the Bible, which had previously been written in different languages, appeared for the first time in a single tongue and became accessible to the civilized world of the later Roman Empire. The Vulgate was to become the accepted source from which further translations would be made into other vernacular tongues, among them the various English translations.

Pope Benedict XV called for three days' supplication, throughout the Catholic Church, in honour of the fifteenth centenary of the death of St Jerome. In response to this call, the bishops of England and Wales adopted the proposal of the Bishop of Northampton to hold a National Catholic Bible Congress in Cambridge on 17, 18 and 19 July 1921. The Congress would include solemn liturgical offices, with prayers for the purposes proposed by the Holy Father, popular addresses for the benefit of the faithful at large, and conferences designed to help and encourage those who had made some progress in these sacred studies, or who desired to do so, and to explain the Catholic standpoint for the benefit of their fellow-countrymen.

## Preparations for the Congress

Less than four years after the Bolsheviks seized power in Russia and in an atmosphere charged with talk of threatened coal and rail strikes and the 'Red Peril', Fr Cuthbert Lattey, SJ wrote about the spirit of the Bible Congress in *The Tablet* ( 21 May 1921):

> The Christianity of the nation is notoriously shaken; it is a choice between the Church and anarchy.
>
> If religion is to be saved at all, it must be the religion of the New Testament ... not modified, as appears to be suggested, by borrowings from the Old Testament, into a creature of the critics' own fancy.
>
> In the face of such a crisis it has been an act of no small wisdom on the part of our Catholic Hierarchy to take the bold and decisive step of summoning a Bible Congress, to call upon priests and people to declare publicly that faith in the truth of Holy Writ which is an essential part of the faith in God and the Church. To learn a little more, then, of all that Our Heavenly Father has to tell us ... And the whole spirit of the Congress will be the spirit of St Jerome, the great translator of the Scriptures into the vernacular of his day; a spirit of profound veneration for Holy Writ and a desire to make it a living force in the lives of all.

A number of letters appeared in the correspondence columns of *The Tablet* in the following weeks, prompted by an anonymous plea for the adaptation of the Authorized Version of the Bible for Catholic use, so forging a sympathetic link between Catholics and their separated brethren. There seemed to be an emerging body of opinion that the Douay Version then used by Catholics compared unfavourably on grounds of literary merit with the Authorized (or King James) Version, owing to its strong dependence on Latinisms, even though it was considered to be a more accurate translation from the Vulgate. The debate was brought to a constructive head by a letter from Fr Bernard Marshall, the chairman of the Congress Executive Committee, then serving as chaplain to Cambridge University and soon to become rector of the Cambridge Catholic parish:

> Sir, It would be a great pity – if not a reproach – if this question of the English Version of the Bible were not discussed at the Congress at Cambridge. So many considerations of far reaching importance have been brought forward in this correspondence that the Committee of the Bible Congress has decided to arrange a special meeting on this question. It will be held in the early afternoon of Tuesday 19 July, and Canon Barry has very kindly consented to initiate a discussion. It is hoped that those who have participated in this correspondence and the many who have been stirred by it will congregate at this meeting, so that every 'pro' and every 'con' concerning the Catholicization of the Authorized Version may be ventilated and recorded.
>
> Yours &c, (*The Tablet*, 2 July 1921).

## Four Crowded July Days

The Congress began on Saturday 16 July with scenes unprecedented in Cambridge since the Reformation. Such was the formal entry into the west door of the church from Lensfield Road of two cardinals, each in separate processions as befitted their rank as princes of the Church. The first to enter was Cardinal Francis Gasquet, an English Benedictine and head of the Pontifical Commission for the Revision of the Vulgate, who had travelled from Rome, followed by Cardinal Bourne, Archbishop of Westminster (Pl. 9b). They were to join the Archbishops of Birmingham and Liverpool and six other bishops, already robed and mitred in the sanctuary, for a short service to open the Congress. The occasion was described in *The Tablet*:

> For the first ecclesiastical function of the Congress, the reception of Cardinal Bourne and Cardinal Gasquet on Saturday afternoon at the Church of Our Lady and the English Martyrs, that magnificent building supplied a fitting and impressive setting. Not so large as to make the congregation seem a sparse one, the church is yet on a scale proportionate to the needs of a big ceremony, and the scene in the sanctuary was strikingly impressive when all the prelates and clergy had assembled with two princes of the Church kneeling side by side in their midst.

The short and simple service consisted of *Veni Creator Spiritus* in plainsong, Pontifical Benediction given by the Bishop of Leeds, and the hymn *Faith of Our Fathers*.

In the evening the delegates were welcomed at a combined civic and University reception at Cambridge Guildhall. Speeches were made by the Archbishop of Liverpool, the Most Revd Mgr Francis Keating (only recently advanced from the Diocese of Northampton), the Deputy Vice-Chancellor of the University, the Mayor of Cambridge and Cardinal Bourne.

On Sunday 17 July all available altars in the church and in the chapels at St Mary's Convent, St Edmund's House, and the University Chaplaincy were taken up for the many Low Masses said by the bishops and other clergy. At 11 a.m. Archbishop Keating of Liverpool celebrated an impressive pontifical High Mass in the presence of the two Cardinals, the Archbishop of Birmingham, the Bishops of Brentwood, Leeds, Salford, Shrewsbury, and Southwark, many clergy, regular and secular, and a large congregation. The sermon was preached by the Bishop of Clifton.

In the afternoon the first business session of the Congress took place in the large Examination Hall off Free School Lane, with Cardinal Bourne presiding. Papers were delivered by Revd Dr R. Downey on

'Catholic Exegesis' and by Revd Dr J. P. Arendzen on 'The Church and the Bible'. Afterwards there was the first of several contributions from the floor by Dr G. G. Coulton, at that time University Lecturer in English, a noted opponent of the Catholic Church and author of a printed tract which he had circulated prior to the opening of the Congress 'of a very contentious character' (*The Tablet*).

The day's proceedings concluded with Vespers and Benediction at the church, with a sermon preached by the Archbishop of Birmingham from the text: 'Heaven and Earth shall pass away but My Word shall not pass away'.

Three papers were presented to the Congress on Monday morning: 'Inspiration' by Fr Hugh Pope, 'The Mosaic Law' by Dr T. E. Bird and 'The Organized Church in the New Testament' by Fr Ronald Knox. The Cambridge University Catholic Association then entertained the Cardinals and other prelates to a private lunch at Christ's College.

In the afternoon, a reception and garden party was given by the Vice-Chancellor of the University, Dr Peter Giles, in the grounds of Emmanuel College.

On Monday evening, Cardinal Gasquet delivered a lecture, illustrated by numerous lantern slides, on 'The Revision of the Vulgate' and was received by an enthusiastic audience when he appeared accompanied by Cardinal Bourne and other members of the hierarchy.

On Tuesday 19 July there was a large attendance for a crowded programme, though the inclusion of several important papers in a single morning ruled out the possibility of much discussion. The speakers were: Canon William Barry, DD, on 'St Jerome the Interpreter', Fr C. C. Martindale, SJ, on 'The Prophets', and Fr Cuthbert Lattey, SJ on 'The Genesis of a Myth – the Book of Tobias'.

The afternoon was devoted to the promised additional session in which a paper was read by Canon William Barry, putting the arguments in favour of a Catholic adaptation of the Authorized Version. Among these, according to Canon Barry, was the likelihood of effecting 'the reconcilement of many English-speaking non-Catholics to the ancient religion'. However, these arguments were at least equalled in authority and weight by the views of other speakers who extolled the virtues of the Douay Version. As Fr Hugh Pope put it, 'the Douay was the primest fruit of Tudor scholarship written by the pick of Oxford and Cambridge scholars'. It was claimed that the Latinisms of the Authorized Version outweighed the much criticised Latinisms of the Douay, and that the borrowings from the Douay which appeared in the Authorized Version were sufficient acknowledgement that they originated from a superior source. Even expressions which had passed into common use in the English language ('whited sepulchre' and 'holocaust' among them), were shown to have come *via*, not *from* the Authorised Version, as was generally supposed.

The Archbishop of Liverpool proposed a vote of thanks to Canon Barry for his address and the delegates then moved on to the second afternoon garden party of the Congress, hosted by Canon Scott in the Rectory grounds and overflowing into Mr and Mrs Conybeare's adjoining garden at 'Stokeslea', where the guests, including the Cardinal and other prelates, spent a pleasant hour.

The final general meeting of the Congress took place on Tuesday evening, at which Fr Hugh Pope gave a lecture on 'A Canaanite City', illustrated by lantern slides. So the Congress came to an end, and it only remained for Cardinal Bourne to bring the proceedings to a close with words of thanks to the organizers.

## Postscript

More than seventy-five years later, it has to be said that some of the hopes and aspirations ventilated at the Congress would eventually be realized, but not during the lifetime of many of the delegates. After years of delays, alternative projects (such as Monsignor Ronald Knox's versions of the New Testament, which appeared in 1945, and of the Old Testament, which appeared in 1949) and prolonged negotiations between the different English-speaking denominations, a Revised Standard Version of the Bible eventually made its appearance in an Ecumenical Edition, acceptable to and welcomed by both Catholic and Protestant traditions in the English-speaking world. What had started merely as an expression of a wish at Cambridge in 1921 had by 1973 turned into a reality, with daily readings in Catholic churches throughout the English-speaking world taken from the Revised Standard Version (RSV), an adapted, but nevertheless direct, descendant of the King James Bible. The Douay Version had served its turn and gained the love and devotion of the Catholic community in its day, but its everyday use is now confined only to those 'borrowed passages' which still survive in the RSV, of which the following is one of the more noteworthy:

'For to me, to live is Christ: and to die is gain'

(Phillipians 1.21).

# Chapter 11

# Baron Anatole von Hügel (1854–1928)

*Michael de Wolff*

It is appropriate to include a profile of Baron von Hügel in recognition of the vital part he played in many aspects of Catholic life in Cambridge. To him must go the credit for leading the moves to persuade the Catholic hierarchy, and even the Holy See, to allow Catholic undergraduates to enter the University, for assisting in the foundation of St Edmund's House as a Catholic house of studies and for encouraging the emergence of the University Catholic Chaplaincy. Alongside these activities he was, during his forty-five year residence in Cambridge, an active and loyal supporter of the Catholic mission and deserving of lasting gratitude for outstanding services to the Catholic community in Cambridge.

## Arrival in Cambridge

Baron Anatole Andreas Aloys von Hügel (Pl. 10a) was born in Florence on 29 September 1854, the son of Baron Carl Alexander Anselm von Hügel and Elizabeth, the daughter of General Francis Farquharson. His brother Friedrich, two years his senior, was to rise to prominence as a leading Catholic theologian in England. Baron Carl was an Austrian diplomat, then serving as Minister to the court of the Grand Duke of Tuscany, and also distinguished as a soldier, botanist, traveller and collector. The young Anatole was educated by the Jesuits partly in Austria, at Kalksburg, Vienna, and partly in England, at Stonyhurst. Like his father, he was well travelled and acquired a fine collection of birds and of valuable ethnological items, mainly from Australasia and the Fiji Islands where he had spent three years with the natives between 1875 and 1877. His collection of South Sea Island artefacts, along with other collections presented by his friends and fellow-collectors Sir Arthur Gordon and Mr Arthur Maudsley, became the nucleus of the collections in the Museum of Ethnology at Cambridge. This museum opened in 1883 with von Hügel as its first Curator and in 1913 became the Museum of Archaeology and Ethnology. The problem of von Hügel's non-graduate status in this university post was overcome when he was granted an honorary MA degree and membership of Trinity College in 1889. It appears debatable whether von Hügel ever aspired to a university education in his youth, though this would in theory have been denied him by the Papal Decree of 1865, which remained in force until 1895.

In 1880 Baron von Hügel married Eliza Margaret Froude; they came to Cambridge in 1883 at the time of his appointment as Curator. They took up residence at 53 Chesterton Road for five years, then, after a spell in lodgings in Lensfield Road, moved to their permanent home at Croft Cottage, Barton Road, Cambridge in 1890. While von Hügel was preoccupied with the Museum and University matters, his wife, the Baroness, became involved with Canon Scott in holding catechism classes for the Catholic children on the Chesterton side of the river, at first in a little chapel established near the School of Pythagoras, off Northampton Street; this would be taken over by the IBVM sisters when they arrived in Cambridge in 1898. Another chapel for catechism classes was established in the basement of 53 Chesterton Road but was closed when the von Hügels moved away in 1888.

## A Centre of Catholic Life

Once established at Croft Cottage, the von Hügels' home became, for the next thirty-eight years, an important meeting-place for Catholic academics in the University and for visiting Catholic dignitaries to Cambridge. As an alternative to the rectory it was particularly appropriate in the earlier years if, as was often the case, the business of these visitors concerned the important University developments which were beginning to unfold. A chapel was established as well, first in the house and later in a specially built extension, where visiting priests and prelates alike could say Mass, the attendance of local parishioners was welcomed and the Baroness could carry on her catechism classes.

## Bringing Catholicism to the University

Once established in Cambridge, Baron von Hügel embarked on a single-minded mission to reverse the Papal Decree and Rescript of

1865, so as to permit the attendance of Catholic undergraduates at the University. He became a close collaborator of Canon Scott in these efforts, he entertained the eminent Benedictine Bishop Hedley at Croft Cottage to discuss the spiritual dangers to undergraduates at Cambridge and how to counter them, and later received Cardinal Vaughan, head of the English hierarchy, there to discuss the removal of the papal prohibition (see also Chapter 28).

The terms of the Decree of Propaganda in 1895 led directly to the appointment of a university chaplain, and it was again thanks to von Hügel's efforts that the support of the Catholic Maintenance Association in Cambridge (itself founded on his own initiative in 1887) was turned towards the infant chaplaincy in Cambridge and became the Cambridge University Catholic Association in 1899 with Baron von Hügel as its first President.

Prompted by the changes of 1895, von Hügel was approached in the same year by Fr. Edmund Nolan, then Vice-President of St Edmund's College, Ware, about the possibility of sending seminary students to Cambridge for a university education. Unknown to Fr Nolan, von Hügel had already been negotiating with the then Prior of Downside with the aim of establishing a Benedictine house of studies in Cambridge. This plan rapidly collapsed when it emerged that Benedictine opinion preferred the establishment of a parish presence in Cambridge, apparently to be achieved by taking over the existing mission, much to the annoyance of Canon Scott and Bishop Riddell of Northampton.

Although this crisis left the way clear for the further development of Fr Nolan's own proposal, it found significantly little support from most of the English diocesan bishops, who lacked enthusiasm for sending their seminary students to either of the ancient universities. Bishop Riddell, for his part, was reluctant to tolerate this unwelcome intrusion into his diocese, but relented in return for a promise of support for Canon Scott's pastoral work in Cambridge from the new complement of secular priests. With von Hügel's involvement, and after further anxious discussions at Croft Cottage, the Duke of Norfolk was persuaded to provide funds for the purchase of a property for St Edmund's House which opened at its present site in Mount Pleasant, Cambridge in November 1896, Fr Nolan being its first Master. Baron von Hügel's close and continuing support for this venture was recognized by his election as President of St Edmund's House for the years 1917–20.

## Von Hügel Benefactions

Throughout Baron von Hügel's residence in Cambridge he was unhesitatingly generous in the provision of funds from his private means for the needs of Catholic activity in the town, whether these originated from the mission or the University. Always motivated by a highly practical streak, it was typical of von Hügel's approach to make sure that the separation of chaplaincy from the mission in 1896 did not leave the latter without the financial support that Canon Scott had anticipated from a combined venture.

The Catholic Men's Club had petered out in the late 1870s owing to lack of financial support, but when Canon Scott attempted to revive the club in 1907 much greater success was achieved thanks to backing from von Hügel and his active participation as first president. During the First World War the social activities of the Club had to take second place to the needs of visiting soldiers and refugees, and plans to raise funds for a parish hall and club, started in 1913 had to be shelved 'for the duration'. By the end of the war the opportunity arose to purchase a surplus hut from one of the military hospitals then being disbanded in Cambridge. Von Hügel generously paid the cost of the hut, which was re-erected on part of the rectory garden (now the site of St Alban's School) in the summer of 1920 and named the Houghton Hall. One section served as the men's clubroom and the remainder as a hall for the school and parish organizations. It is recorded that the cost of the Houghton Hall hut was £250, though Conybeare in his diary mentions a figure of £150. Either way, this was an extremely generous gift by the Baron.

Baron von Hügel's final gesture to the parish was a legacy in his will for the provision of a memorial to Mrs Lyne-Stephens, the benefactress of Our Lady and the English Martyrs church, but stipulating that an equivalent amount should be raised by the parishioners. The funds were forthcoming, in recognition by the parishioners of the debt they owed to the Baron as well as to their benefactress.

## Pillars of the Congregation

No profile of Baron von Hügel can be complete without a reference to the friendly co-operation that developed between the Baron and his close friend Edward Conybeare. These twin pillars of the laity in Cambridge gave unhesitating support to the Catholic mission and its rector, Canon Scott, often in close collaboration with each other. Starting in 1911, when Conybeare was sixty-three and von Hügel was fifty-seven, there are many entries in Conybeare's diaries that record the attendance of both at the Annual Meetings of the Catholic Men's Club, at meetings of the Council of the Cambridge University Catholic Association at Croft Cottage (one of these 'hideously long'), and at the Cambridge SVP Conference. There is mention, too, of the Conybeares going to dinner at Croft Cottage and returning the hospitality at Stokeslea, and encounters with eminent Catholic figures (generally also at Croft Cottage). Conybeare even entrusted his prized collection of archaeological remains from Barrington to the care of von Hügel as museum curator in 1914. Although Conybeare was the senior in age, it seems that von Hügel's seniority as a Catholic layman (Conybeare had only been received into the Church in 1910), ensured his presidency of most local Catholic organizations. Conybeare seemed content with the supporting role of vice-president, sometimes taking the chair if ill-health prevented the Baron attending meetings himself. Their involvement in the work of the SVP led them both, during the First World War, into active relief work for visiting soldiers, war wounded and Belgian refugees.

## The War Years and Beyond

The period of the First World War was a time of great personal sadness and strain for Baron von Hügel, and his health suffered as a consequence. He was committed in every way to the British way of life, but when Britain and Austria entered the conflict on opposing sides he suddenly found himself an enemy alien by birth and nationality. Deeply distressed at having to register as an alien, he made every effort to obtain naturalization as a British subject, the painful episode brought happily to a conclusion thanks to intervention by sympathetic fellows of Trinity College. The Baron's activities for war relief were mainly centred on the Catholic Men's Club, and his work, and that of the Baroness, for Belgian refugees earned them decorations from the King of the Belgians after the war.

Baron von Hügel retired as curator of the Museum of Archaeology and Ethnology in 1921 and by then, moreover, his active life in support of Catholicism in Cambridge was drawing to a close. In 1922 he was given the Sc.D. *honoris causa* for his eminent work as an ethnologist. One more honour was to come his way when, in 1924, he was created a Papal Knight of St Gregory in recognition of his efforts in securing the entry of Catholic undergraduates into Cambridge; Baroness von Hügel also received an award.

Baron von Hügel died at Croft Cottage on 15 August 1928, aged 73.

His Requiem Mass was symbolic of the part he had played in the Catholic life of Cambridge; it was celebrated at Our Lady and the English Martyrs by the rector, Canon Marshall, and appropriately supported by the Master of St Edmund's House (Fr J. McNulty), as deacon and the University Catholic chaplain (Fr John Lopes), as sub-deacon. Baroness von Hügel died in 1931 and after her death the Baron's personal papers were deposited in the museum which he had helped to found and to which he had devoted the greater part of his active career.

## A Fitting Memorial

In 1987, fifty-nine years after his death, the Von Hügel Institute was founded at St Edmund's College (the former St Edmund's House) to perpetuate the memory of Baron Anatole von Hügel and to promote studies in the relationship between Christianity and society.

# Chapter 12

# A Doyen of the Parish: Edward Conybeare and his Diaries

*Philip S. Wilkins*

In the early 1900s the white-haired figure of Edward Conybeare (Pl. 10b), wrapped in a black clerical cloak, could often be seen either in the church of Our Lady and the English Martyrs or at the various parochial functions. He became exceptionally prominent in the Catholic community, constantly supportive of his rector in the latter's pastoral role and a member of several guilds, societies and organizations. The wide extent of his activities becomes clear from diaries which he kept continuously from boyhood, hardly missing a day until failing eyesight in his eighties caused him to abandon writing altogether. Throughout his life he maintained a keen interest in people and topics of the day, his journal providing a fascinating picture of personalities and events both local and national. Many relatives, friends and acquaintances of his earlier years connected with Cambridge and its University continued to visit him after he converted to Catholicism. Thereafter he was closely involved with the Catholic clergy and laity in the town, in due course becoming a particular friend and adviser to Canon Christopher Scott, rector of the Cambridge church. The later diaries reflect his life and endeavours among the Catholic community, thus making a unique contribution to the 'living' history of the Catholic parish during the first quarter of the twentieth century.

## A Distinguished Family

John William Edward Conybeare, born at Liverpool on 29 September 1843, came from a distinguished succession of Anglican clergymen, including a former Bishop of Bristol, whose Huguenot forebears had fled from persecution in France and had originally settled in the West Country where they joined the Church of England. His father, William John Conybeare, was educated at Westminster School and at Trinity College, Cambridge, eventually becoming a fellow. He was ordained to the Church of England in 1841 and married Eliza Rose, daughter of a Leicestershire vicar who was related through marriage to the prominent Macaulay family. The Conybeares were thus joined in kinship with distinguished intellectuals and gifted literary figures, an impressive dynasty which, in addition to the Macaulay family, also included those of Trevelyan, Arnold, Huxley and Vaughan. Instead of taking up a clerical career immediately after graduation, William John Conybeare went into education and became the first principal of the newly-founded Liverpool Collegiate Institute. His health was not good, however, and, though he moved to the less arduous duties of a country parson, he died in 1857 at the early age of forty-two. William's father, the Very Revd William Daniel Conybeare, who was Dean of Llandaff and also an eminent geologist and palaeontologist, died within a short time of his son. Thus by the time Edward, as he was generally known in the family, was fourteen both his father and grandfather had died leaving him with responsibilities as head of a family and the need to prove himself worthy of its traditions. After education at Eton College and Trinity College, Cambridge, he proceeded to Anglican orders in 1869, economic need and family tradition substituting for the certainty of a true vocation to the priesthood. Though he aspired to follow his father as a Cambridge don, he was bitterly disappointed when a similar position failed to mature.

After curacies first in Staines and then East Molesey, Edward Conybeare was appointed in 1871 to the Trinity College living of Barrington in Cambridgeshire. Though it was far from the rewarding life of a college fellow for which he had hoped, he was an intensely lively and active character and threw himself wholeheartedly into his clerical duties. He found Barrington parish in a deplorable state after years of neglect by predecessors whose lack of pastoral care had allowed a strong spirit of Dissent to take root in the village. By dint of sheer effort, he gradually won people back into church and restored order to the parish and its school. Involving himself closely in village life, he was soon recognized by his parishioners and the chapel-goers as a devoted pastor always ready to guide and help them whenever possible. He took pride in the title by which he became known, 'Father of the village' and later, after moving from Barrington, he often returned to renew friendships there, his diaries always referring to the village as his 'home'.

## A Difficult Decision

When at Cambridge University, Edward Conybeare, like an uncle before him, had joined the English Church Union and become inclined to the ecumenical position of that organization, longing for the reunion of the Christian Churches. That position had probably done him no favours with Cambridge circles of the day which were predominantly Low Church Evangelical and may well have cost him the fellowship he had so ardently desired, but nonetheless over the years he leaned progressively closer to the teachings of the Catholic Church.

On one occasion he attended a service in St Andrew's Catholic church in Union Road as a silent protest against fellow undergraduates who often disrupted services there with their unseemly conduct. He could be extremely sensitive when others attempted to disadvantage Catholic bodies or persons. 'Wild No Popery orgie against St Edmund's Hall, the low churchmen following the atheists blind, and lying like devils ...' is the outburst in his diary for May 1898 when, after fierce debate in the University Senate, an application from the Catholic house of studies for recognition as a public hostel was voted down. Again, when the church of Our Lady and the English Martyrs was being built in the late 1880s, he had publicly voiced his sentiments against the anti-Catholic slander which the dedication of that church engendered and had attended its consecration in October 1890 as a minister of the Church of England. Though such action by a present-day minister of the established church would receive but slight attention, in the often hostile religious atmosphere of late Victorian Cambridge it would have been strongly deplored by many Anglicans and Nonconformists.

Over the years Conybeare had held the firm belief, with many of his Anglican colleagues, that from its earliest days the Christian Church in England had always been autonomous and independent of the Papacy, though nevertheless subscribing to Catholic beliefs in general. In 1897 he circulated a broadsheet reiterating this position, but possibly Pope Leo XIII's encyclical *Apostolicae Curae* of 1896, which declared Anglican orders to be invalid, had raised doubts in Conybeare's mind. At all events, a year later he made the hardest decision of his life when after twenty-six successful years as vicar of Barrington he decided with utmost reluctance to resign the living where he had become greatly respected and a friend of so many villagers. He explained later: 'I must needs give up my ministry and therefore all that life worth living held for me. I did not act on any hasty impulse ... I went forth into the abyss a naked soul to abide God's pleasure concerning me.'

It is not apparent from his diaries whether Conybeare faced

ostracism as did many fellow Anglican clergymen who changed to
Rome, but his conversion could not have come as a complete surprise
to those who knew him well. He was of an outspoken disposition and
consequently his family and friends would have been aware of his
deeply felt sentiments and not unduly surprised when he indicated an
intention to change from Anglicanism. When at Barrington vicarage,
the Conybeares had encouraged provocative religious and social
discussion at the frequent gatherings of relatives, friends and academics from the University. Those attending included three Macaulay
brothers then undergraduates of whom the eldest, George, subsequently became a fellow of Trinity and married Grace Conybeare, his
distant cousin and Edward's sister. Edward's wife, Frances, came from
the Northumberland Quaker family of Cropper; her grandfather had
campaigned against slavery and her father had become a Member of
Parliament. She too kept a journal but there is no indication whether
or not she was averse to her husband's change of allegiance. It might
be remembered, however, that families such as hers, with their special
backgrounds, were in the main liberal-minded. In general they practised tolerance and intellectual freedom and, though critical of one
another, were not unduly concerned by their relatives' turns of
conscience.

## A Change of Direction

In 1898 Edward Conybeare moved with his family to 'Stokeslea',
formerly known as Lensfield Cottage, a large house off Union Road,
Cambridge, where he planned to make a living writing books and articles. Like many of his literary-minded relatives, he had already had a
number of books published on archaeological and historical themes
and just a year previously his *History of Cambridgeshire* in Elliot Stock's
series of 'County Histories' had been well received. A month before he
moved house he was further encouraged by the interest of another
publisher in his work: 'Macmillans have bought up my History and
wish me to make a map for it'. This probably refers to his topographi-
cal work on Cambridgeshire which was ultimately printed in the
'Highways and Byways' series.
    The 'Stokeslea' property had access from Union Road with large
grounds extending to Lensfield Road and adjoining the rectory garden
of the new Catholic church which stood at Hyde Park Corner.
Conybeare at once began attending daily Mass at the church when fit
to do so. He was still plagued though by doubts and impediments,
some of the latter concerning his eldest son who was pursuing a career

in the Church of England. He had delayed his resignation from Barrington until his son had been ordained. It was, he wrote later, a dreary time of hope deferred and loneliness of spirit. While debating his future religious life, he became a close friend of his neighbour, Canon Christopher Scott, whose influence drew him gradually into involvement in the parish, though it was not until twelve years after his departure from Barrington that he was received formally into the Catholic Church. For so long convinced of his Catholic faith, his diary entry for 10 December 1910 merited merely the terse comment: 'Received at last by the Canon in the morning'. By then both Edward and his wife Frances had built up bonds of warm friendship with many of their Catholic co-parishioners and welcomed them cordially into their home, Frances also occasionally attending services in the Catholic church and events in the parish.

## Devoted to Children

Conybeare's connection with the Catholic School in Union Road became paramount among his associations with the parish community. When the need arose due to teacher shortage, he taught in the school and forged a strong bond with the staff and generations of children, eventually becoming a school manager in 1913. Though his experiences in the classroom went largely unrecorded, being a school manager and the only male teacher in the school, he found he was able to resolve awkward situations and disputes between members of staff: 'School ructions, old & faded teachers jealous of young & attractive supply. Poured oil on waters.' In contrast, out-of-school activities of every kind were noted down in profusion: 'Gathered 38 children, parents and teachers after 7 a.m. Mass for run to Hunstanton; ... Took teachers in boat about Backs: ... took 7 children to Anatomical Museum ... took 2 teachers to Magdalene, Sidney Sussex, S.Clement's, Round Church and S.John's.' Over the years he was accustomed to give prizes to the schoolchildren and delighted in receiving presents from them on his birthday or at Christmastime: 'Notable birthday. 14 children to Communion with me. ... 33 birthday letters. Flowers from Rector; ... 75 [birthday] D.G. Avalanche of presents and letters (32); ... presented by school with electric bicycle lamp ... back to school for Prizegiving & Xmas tree bright with coruscating safety fireworks'.

He had a deep love for children and young people and opened the ample grounds of his house for school sports and pastimes, as he had been accustomed to do for village children at Barrington vicarage. In inclement weather, children living at a distance from the school were allowed to use the summerhouse at 'Stokeslea' in which to eat their sandwich lunches, or at other times to play games in the garden and have the use of two swinging boats for their added amusement. In those days when fasting from midnight before Holy Communion was the practice of the Church, he would regularly provide a meal for large numbers of children: 'Had 15 children to breakfast during Prophecies (i.e. Holy Saturday); ... First Communion. Had 20 to breakfast; ... .40 children to breakfast; ... 25 children to breakfast.'

Former pupils remember his flowing white beard and skull-cap, creating for them the impression of a kind of patriarchal figure or Old Testament character. Though he was kind and generous to children, he was to some extent a martinet and insisted that they should be well-mannered and remember their place. Misbehaviour by one child, whether in school or church, could bring sanctions on a whole group: 'Garden closed for wrongdoing of Lanham. Complained of him at Rectory.' The antics of altar-boys in church did not escape his notice either: 'Misbehaviour of wretched boy on altar at Benediction, so in to denounce him at Rectory.' In contrast, if children kept to accepted rules all would be sweetness and light: 'School treat, children having unlimited tea under Rectory sycamore & then coming to our garden for games till 7.30 ... behaviour perfect!'

Conybeare was equally generous with the time he gave to the senior girls and boarders at St Mary's Convent. 'Took Convent pupils to Ely; ... Took Convent girls to races [i.e. University boat races] in brake; ... Gave Tennyson lecture at Convent taking teachers with me; Xmas tea & games at Convent; ... Tea Convent to show them microscope; ... Took Conventuals to museum; ... Took Rev. Mother for her first sight of Queens.'

## Conybeare's Wartime Service

Conybeare clearly delighted in worshipping in the church of Our Lady and the English Martyrs. The sanctuary of the church occupies a third of the large building and provided an ideal setting for the dignified liturgies of the Roman rite which were traditionally carried out in full rubrical detail. The spiritual and ceremonial aspects of those services, particularly on special occasions, appealed greatly to him and none more so than during the 1914–18 War when large numbers of military were present. 'Wonderful day. 5 successive Masses for over 3000 soldiers ... church simply packed ... thrilling sight, even Sanctuary full right up to altar; ... Thrilling sight of masses of troops at church services; ... Great military High Requiem with full pomp & church crowded; ... Glorious requiem for dead in war – Cadet Guard of Honour fixing bayonets at Gospel.'

Being an intensely loyal subject himself, he sought to instil the virtue among the children in school where he ensured that Empire Day was duly celebrated each year. After the War when Bishop Keating preached strongly on the virtue of loyalty to one's country after blessing the church's war memorial, Conybeare immediately approved: 'War Memorial unveiling by Bp in miraculous ideal service (at which he preached powerfully), beginning with "Veni S.S." & ending with Last Post – a session to have lived for.'

Wounded soldiers from the front received much sympathetic attention from Conybeare and his wife Frances: 'Our house made Red Cross distributing centre so drawingroom piled with shirting ... All day SVDP [St Vincent de Paul] work taking crucifixes &c to Catholic soldiers in camp; ... In to soldiers club at Rectory ... played billiards with men; ... Preparing for 60 wounded + 20 helpers who spent aft in garden with tea under Rectory plane.'

After the German invasion of Belgium, refugees flooded into the Cambridge area and the Conybeares were at the forefront welcoming them and helping them to settle into a useful life here: 'Belgian-ridden day SVDP President of all Belgium coming to help establish Belgian Cmtee of Conference to work country refugees. Had him to lunch ... then presided at mtg and made my first French speech. 30 Belgians joined, 8 coming to tea afterwards; ... in eve attending carrying into church of Belgian girl dead in Convent thro' German outrages; Yvonne Requiem 9.30.' The principal Belgians including their chaplains were often present at the Conybeares' table or making social calls at 'Stokeslea'.

## The Foremost among Parishioners

While at Barrington Edward Conybeare had become the firm friend of many villagers, and as his association with the Catholic mission developed so did his involvement with its people. Over the years he assumed a leading role in the life of the Catholic community, being elected to parochial committees and joining the various church societies and organizations which came into being as the mission developed. He remained a practising member of the Guild of the Blessed Sacrament and the Society of St Vincent de Paul as long as he was fit enough to attend their meetings, and at his funeral the then rector paid special tribute to his devotion to the latter organization and his many unobtrusive acts of charity to the poor. He made a special access from his grounds leading directly through the rectory garden to the church, and 'Stokeslea' became open house to all who wished to visit him for advice or hospitality. His intense interest in people and their activities may well have been considered intrusive by some in the parish and certainly his relatives, including his niece the authoress Rose Macaulay, felt themselves vulnerable to his analytical criticism. But without doubt he revelled in receiving the stream of visiting clergy, laity, friends and acquaintances at his house and being at the centre of parochial life. The grounds of his house were often used to accommodate the overflow from parish gatherings in the Rectory garden: 'All day at work for Rectory Garden Party which swarmed into ours as usual.'

He could be extremely tetchy and disapproving when inconvenienced, so it is not surprising to find him expressing irritation when in 1920 the parish wished to erect a community hall in the Rectory garden adjacent to his boundary: 'Had to ride Croft Cottage for wretched Parish Hall mtg.' Nevertheless he joined in manfully with labouring work to clear the site and help erect the prefabricated building which had become surplus accommodation at the wartime Eastern General Hospital: 'Pegging out Parish Hut site; ... Strenuous P.H. & sch. work. Flattened out.' The building obviously impeded his accustomed way through the rectory garden but he soon rectified that: 'Opened new gate into Rectory.' Far from it being the 'white elephant' he predicted, the building – named Houghton Hall after the first martyr of the English Reformation, St John Houghton – provided much needed accommodation for the expanding organizations of the parish. The men's club occupied one section while the remainder proved invaluable to school and parish organizations for entertainments and meetings until in 1936 the structure was demolished to make room for the new combined school building and parish hall. The utilitarian structure almost certainly impinged on Conybeare's view from his garden towards the church and rectory but in the autumn of 1920 he found at least a partial solution: 'Started on new fence to block out P[arish] H[all].'

His earlier experiences as a conscientious country parson fitted him well for assisting the parish clergy with pastoral work in the field of sick calls, hospital visiting and counselling those in difficulties: 'Having to spend morn over dear little boy run over by taxi dying in Tipperary Ward – summoning his parents, &c.; ... Rush to Newnham for priest, sick call coming from hospital; ... Rode to see poor Mrs Dickerson (Eddy has now been missing 10 weeks [during the war]); ... Telephone sick call 7.10. Rush to Convent for Fr Davidson'. As the rectory was not equipped with a telephone until after Canon Scott's death, it is more than likely that Conybeare bore much of the brunt of enquiries to the clergy.

With his considerable literary ability and University connections, he was able to provide invaluable support to his rector during a period when priestly assistance was in short supply. Scott himself was for many years Provost of Northampton Cathedral Chapter and either Vicar General or Vicar Capitular and consequently much occupied with diocesan affairs: 'Working out Justinian's marriage law with Canon for Diocesan Conference; Chastising Editor of Cambridge Review for blasphemous ribaldry; ... correcting CDN letter for Provost on Guilds & Masses; ... Helping Provost with Income Tax returns, &c.' When the important Cambridge Bible Congress of 1921 was being arranged Conybeare became deeply involved as a member of the committee: 'Bp sent his Triduum prayer for correction; ... Began work on Bible Congress Handbook – historical Cambridge in 2000 words!' After Scott's death, Conybeare was a natural choice to compose a memorial inscription to him: 'Making out inscription for St Andrew memorial to Provost'. The plaque still stands in the north transept of the church under the figure of St Andrew. A former parish curate also remembered Conybeare's expertise: 'Fr Davidson in to approve Latin inscription I have made for foundation of his new church.'

On wider issues his advice was sought by clergy and laity alike and he had considerable influence with succeeding bishops of the diocese who often consulted him when they were in Cambridge. Cardinal Bourne, too, visited him on more than one occasion. His close involvement in parish and diocesan affairs brought him an unusual and possibly unique honour for a member of the laity, recorded in his diary for 4 May 1919: 'Monsignor Christopher Scott Bright day for Confirmation DG; children with my badges. Then had 22 choirboys to tea in Libr. Bp [Keating] also to tea after reviewing Scouts on lawn also Provost and Fr Davidson. Given privilege of Hon. Canon.'

Once he had gained prominence in the parish, Conybeare inevitably found himself at the forefront of such parish gatherings as the celebration of Canon Scott's Golden Jubilee in September 1912: 'High Mass "coram espiscopo" with 16 priests. Lunch at Univ. Arms after giving mementoes to all children ... Presentation to Canon in Guildhall where had to take first speech ...' Likewise he was present on major occasions such as welcoming and looking after prominent visitors: 'Prince Joseph of Uganda & Stanislaus his Regent about all day [June 1914] in gorgeous native robes. Lunched Rectory with them & their Bp Hanlon – just like St Paul. Again met them in aft with F. at Baron's...' (Pl. 6a).

The church tower held an almost obsessive attraction for him and he never ceased to delight in escorting individuals or groups of school-children, teachers, convent boarders and parishioners to climb the long winding stairway and show them views over the colleges, town and surrounding countryside: 'Took Convent borders up church tower; Took 15 of congregation up tower after Benediction; ... up tower to see Mercury, a mere glimpse thro' cloud; ... King here 9-11 [February 1915] to inspect troops on Piece. An impressive sight. Saw with Convent Boarders from Tower.' On Armistice Day 1918 he ran up the tower and got the first chime, [i.e. 11 a.m. of the church clock marking the first two-minute silence]. Often he climbed the tower alone, no doubt appreciating its solitude and possibly a respite from the very activities he so relished. On one occasion he composed up there part of a text he was writing for publication: 'All day at Bible Congress Handbk. Did 1000 words up tower.'

To Canon Scott he was a most loyal and trusted friend and adviser and during the Canon's later years especially was a frequent companion when the former suffered a series of accidents and illnesses. Living so close to the rectory, he was invariably at hand to give practical help, even bedside attention. Scott's last days in February 1922 are faithfully recorded by Conybeare who was at his bedside at the last: 'Called over to see the dear Provost die – quite peacefully. My first death! Arrangements all rest of day. Bishop came over to sleep ... Writing memoirs of Provost for C. Chronicle ... Rushing about all day on Provost's burial matters.'

## Health Problems

Concern over his health was a constant worry for Conybeare who suffered most of his life from neuralgia and headaches. While at University the severe strain of examinations had caused him to collapse and he had been awarded an aegrotat degree. His hypochondria is reflected throughout the diaries: 'S.O. [stayed out] ... Got to Mass, but barely, more dead than alive all day; ... Had to ride to Croft Cottage ... overwhelmingly cold & throat came on as a flash. Collapse at once on return. S.O. after miserable night of phlegm and toothache; Head desperate after 3 sleepless nights of relentless cough. Stroke imminent; Cruel night of shattering cough. Brain shaken up to a jelly; ... horrible influenza attack in eve. Third bad night. ... Rotting away faster than ever.'

The reaction of his wife and family to these foibles may be imagined but nevertheless he had been gifted with strength and stamina from his early years and when young had enjoyed mountaineering with his father and by night climbing of buildings when at University. It may be surprising for a person of such intellectual and literary ability that from his early days in the Catholic parish he concerned himself with so much manual work. But he had been accustomed to much physical effort during his years at Barrington and possibly it helped to counteract self-doubts about his general health. There was a very practical side to his achievements as he regularly undertook manual work in and around the rectory garden. Year after year he prepared the garden and outside altar for the celebration of Corpus Christi: 'Clearing in Rectory garden all day for Sunday procession ... Got all ready for Corpus Christi Procession; ... Continued nice O.L. shrine in Rectory garden; Hard all day at Mens' Club Treat held in both gardens 4–9.30 ... provided bowls, quoits, &c ... Strenuous tree lopping in Rectory all day; ... very strenuous work all day at local wreckage with two men tackling cedar fall at Rectory. With a serious shortage of manpower in the parish during the 1914–18 war and the mobilization of the church sacristan, Conybeare became the rector's right-hand man and general factotum assisting with most aspects of work in and around the church: 'First lesson on winding church clock as Clarence is called up; ... Got small scythe & made first try at mowing; ... cruelly heavy job helping to move catafalque for funeral, all labour lacking; ... mending latch at Rectory yard ... mending church door weight ... shirt sleeves in Rectory garden with labour brigade of 5; Black job getting 2 tons of coal in here & at Rectory 7.15 a.m. – then Rectory wood cutting.'

By May 1925 Edward Conybeare was eighty-two but still playing some part in the life of the parish: 'Confirmation. Acted Patrinus after lunch Rectory with Bp & 6 priests.' His eyes were deteriorating, however, and by the end of that month a specialist confirmed incurable degeneration of the retina, his diary recording this with the added words 'Laus Deo.' Over the following months he prepared to give up many of his customary activities: 'Farewell visit to King's; found the windows quite invisible, even best known ones; ... After tea farewell visit to Hope Lucas, making eyes much worse by sunlight; ... Bright evening shining upon lovely CX Procession in garden. Could not take part for first time.' At the end of July he attended a Pontifical High Mass at the commencement of the annual Catholic Summer School Lectures and managed to speak with Cardinal Bourne. In early August he had a talk with the Bishop, no doubt acquainting him with news of his enforced retirement from many parish functions, and a few days later reported: 'In aft taken to Ely for farewell sight of Minster.' At length on 15 August, after keeping diaries for about seventy consecutive years, he scribbled a last pathetic entry: 'Bad day of pain & eyes much worse ...'

During his last years Conybeare became increasingly infirm and almost blind and found difficulty in managing daily attendance at Mass. He eventually died on 14 February 1931, his body being brought in procession from his house to the church over paths, then snow-covered, which he had trodden almost daily for over thirty years. At his Requiem amid a large congregation of family, parishioners, University representatives, townspeople and villagers from his beloved Barrington, the rector, Mgr Marshall, paid tribute to the pre-eminent part Edward Conybeare had played in the life of the parish. With the passage of time it is from his diaries that we are still able to appreciate the remarkable service of dedication and loyalty he gave to the parish and his fellow Catholics.

# Chapter 13

# Robert Hugh Benson (1871–1914): A Heart of Fire

*Christopher Jackson*

A literary figure and preacher of the eminence of Robert Hugh Benson (Pl. 11a) deserves a profile in these pages even though his stay in Cambridge formed all too short a part of his meteoric career, cut short by his untimely death at the age of forty-three. His claim to fame as a leading Catholic writer of the early twentieth century is reflected by entries in many works of reference. Typically, he is described in *The Oxford Companion to English Literature* (5th edition, 1985) as:

> An extremely prolific writer, like his elder brothers A. C. Benson and E. F. Benson; ordained (in the Church of England) in 1895 but converting to Catholicism in 1903; most of his work consisting of Catholic apologia; having written sensational apocalyptic novels (such as *The Lord of the World*, 1907), melodramatic historical novels (such as *Come Rack! Come Rope!*, 1912); modern novels usually involving an impossible moral conundrum (such as *The Average Man*, 1913); also publishing sermons poems and plays.

## Anglican Ascendancy

Hugh Benson arrived in Cambridge as a newly-ordained Catholic priest in June 1904, aged thirty-three. His arrival marked the culmination of a six-year-long journey in faith which had led him from a conventional and privileged Anglican upbringing to an eventual acceptance of Papal supremacy and a decision to 'go over to Rome'. As the fourth son of the eminent educationalist and divine Dr Edward White Benson, his childhood homes reflected the steady advancement of his father, from Headmaster of Wellington College, to Chancellor of Lincoln Cathedral, then Bishop of Truro and ultimately, in 1882, Archbishop of Canterbury. His education, too, was conventionally privileged, first at Eton and then at Trinity College, Cambridge, where he read classics. He changed to theology in his final year, having by then determined to prepare for ordination in the Church of England. His first years after ordination in 1895 were unsettled, but after realizing that his vocation lay closer to preaching than to parochial ministry he decided to seek a contemplative life, under a vow of celibacy. This brought him to a consideration of the validity of Catholic claims but at first he dismissed these thoughts as temptations. Instead, in 1898, he joined the Community of the Resurrection at Mirfield, an Anglo-Catholic religious house devoted partly to studies and partly to preaching at parish missions. After some initial uncertainty, he involved himself enthusiastically in the heavy mission workload of the Community and, over the next four years, earned a reputation as one of the best preachers in the Church of England. In 1902, after four years with the Community and with the consent of his Superior, Hugh Benson began to correspond with a number of well-known members of the Catholic clergy, among them a Dominican, Fr Vincent McNabb, and a Jesuit, the Modernist Fr George Tyrrell. His beliefs were already in most respects indistinguishable from those of a Catholic while his inclination towards Catholic liturgy could have been accommodated in any Anglo-Catholic setting. What appears to have swayed his decision, at Easter 1903, to leave the Church of England was the realization that his Anglican orders were not recognized by the Catholic Church and high among his priorities was to see himself, and be accepted, as a validly ordained priest. On Friday 11 September 1903, he was received into the Church at the Dominican Priory at Woodchester and, his Anglican baptism being recognized as valid, Hugh Benson made his first Confession and Holy Communion on the following Sunday.

## To Cambridge by Way of Rome

Hugh Benson's next priority was to seek ordination as a Catholic priest. In the absence of any seminary courses in England for late vocations, still less for former Anglican clergy, the ecclesiastical authorities directed him to undertake a course of study in Rome, where he took up residence in the house of studies annexed to the English-owned Church of San Silvestro in Capite for seven months. This was a significant and concessionary curtailment of the full three-year course generally required for the ordination of former Anglican clergy. He was overwhelmingly impressed during his stay by the all-pervading atmosphere of history, tradition and ceremonial in the Eternal City, and this became apparent later on in some of his novels, where both characters and settings bear the stamp of the eyewitness, notably his fictional Pope John XXIV in *The Lord of the World* (1908), modelled on Pope St Pius X.

On Sunday 12 June 1904, barely nine months after being received into the Church, Hugh Benson was ordained into the priesthood at the Church of San Silvestro. By the following Thursday he was on his way back to England, where it was arranged that he would pursue a one-year course in theology under the supervision of Mgr Arthur Barnes, the Catholic Chaplain to the University of Cambridge, and would reside in the Chaplaincy, then at Llandaff House in Regent Street. It was deemed essential for him to gain this deeper theological knowledge before embarking on any kind of pastoral ministry. He is said to have worked hard at his theological studies during the daytime, but he spent his evenings in developing a literary career. This had begun with the publication of a volume of short stories with religious themes, *The Light Invisible*, written in 1902, and earnings from his writing were starting to supplement his modest private income. By the end of his twelve-month residence at Llandaff House he had completed his second historical novel, *The King's Achievement* (1905) about Henry VIII, and had made a start on his third, *The Queen's Tragedy* (1906) about Mary Tudor. Another work of historical fiction, *The History of Richard Raynall, Solitary* (1906) dates from this time as well. Hugh Benson's contacts with the ill-starred writer Frederick William Rolfe, author of *Hadrian the Seventh*, also began during his time at Llandaff House.

## The Cambridge Rectory

When Hugh Benson's theological studies at Llandaff House came to an end in June 1905 he offered his services as curate to Canon Christopher Scott, the sixty-seven year old Mission Rector of Cambridge, to fill the vacancy left by the departure of the previous curate, Fr W. H. Reade. It has been said that Canon Scott's acceptance of Fr Benson's offer displayed great perception, opening, as it did, the door to his public ministry. To the Canon, too, is due the credit for seeing that Hugh Benson's value, both to the Cambridge Mission and to academic Cambridge, lay primarily in apostolic work as a preacher and a missioner. Thus he was allowed to devote more time and energy to these fields than to pastoral care. The necessary faculties to preach and to hear confessions having been given by the Bishop of Northampton, Hugh Benson moved to the Cambridge rectory and preached for the first time as a Catholic priest on 4 July 1905, a sermon he had preached many times in his Anglican days, 'This is the Will of God, Your Sanctification'.

> 'It is HEAVENLY', he wrote to his friend Fr G. W. Hart, 'I have nice rooms ... in the red clergy house next the church. Three windows look into a big garden all overgrown with trees and flowers, and one on to the east end of the church, with angels and griffins grinning at me (the angels do not grin) and the heavenly chimes every quarter-hour day and night. (They play the Alleluia out of the 'Exultet' of Easter Eve, and continual plain-song hymns.) I bathe every afternoon, and write books every morning and evening. Mass 7.20 in convent or church; dinner 1 p.m. Bathe. Tea 4.30 p.m. (generally with an undergraduate or a don) write again until 9 – supper – bed.'

As well as his bedroom, Hugh Benson was given an adjoining sitting room which he soon started to furnish and decorate in a manner best described as retro-medieval, resulting in some turned heads, raised eyebrows and critical comment, even among his closest friends. 'I have hung it with green 'arras-cloth' with panels – polished boards with (leopard) skins down and one large rug – an oak chest, bureau, carved chairs ... all old furniture I have had for years. For the first time in my life I am content with my rooms.' This description stops short of mentioning other items placed in the room, rumoured to have included 'enormous oaken candlesticks, ancient Madonnas smothered in rosaries, pictures of art-nouveau, and innumerable photographs of friends' according to Fr C. C. Martindale's biography. A certain degree of eccentricity must account for a further comment in the same work, 'When actually on his knees before the (altar), he found he disliked the baldachino, and was quite sure that his prayers caught in the corners and could not mount beyond its roof.'

## The Trials of Pastoral Care

Hugh Benson never shrank from the work of an assistant priest while in Cambridge, but he was always first to admit that his talents lay specifically in preaching and writing, and not in the other areas of pastoral ministry, as some of the following quotations from his letters reveal:

I have started visiting, hard, and go round on a bicycle in the afternoons. Rather dreary work. I <u>cannot</u> do it; but I suppose it is necessary to make everyone's acquaintance, at any rate.

We have a horrible day tomorrow – a water-party with the choir. I am shirking most of it – by unselfishly offering to take the 9.15 Mass, so that I can't possibly start with them ...

I have just come from singing High Mass for the first time [Corpus Christi, 22 June 1905]. I suppose that some day one will be able to be devout during that action.

At last I have started in the Box [the confessional]; and next Sunday start in the pulpit. I am very much frightened ...

Preaching ... I hate it and love it, like a deep pool. It is terrifying and ecstatic ...

Yesterday [Palm Sunday 1906] was perfectly lovely – all except my sermon. We went outside with palms, for the first time in the history of this church, and had a large congregation to see the donkey,we suppose, in the evening [evidently a widely held supposition in non-Catholic circles in Cambridge that a donkey was an essential component of the Catholic Palm Sunday ritual]. And there was none, except myself, who brayed for half an hour.

However, later on during this first participation by Hugh Benson in a Holy Week at the Cambridge Mission, Edward Conybeare's diary contains nothing to suggest anything untoward: '1906 April 14 – Ceremonies 8–11 (Holy Sat.). Hugh Benson took blessing of candle and Prophecies (his first attempt).'

## Preacher, Lecturer, Writer

It was in the areas of preaching, lecturing and writing that Hugh Benson's status as a celebrity was steadily enhanced during his time at Cambridge, more than outweighing any shortcomings in the pastoral field:

Very rapidly he became one of the most regarded personalities in the town. The decoration of his rooms caused much admiration (in the theological sense); so did his eloquent sermons; while his volatility, artistic temperament, and unusual attitudes of mind made him a centre among undergraduates – easily attracted by faith and by extremes. Certain

Heads of Colleges feared his entry, as a walk with him was regarded as a
step to Rome

(A. J. A. Symons, *The Quest for Corvo*, London, 1934, p. 191).

Hugh Benson's legacy of works written during his three years at the
Cambridge Rectory is impressive even if considered as the only
evidence of his restless activity: two novels of modern life, *The
Sentimentalists* (1906), and *The Conventionalists* (1908); two studies of
abnormal temperaments, *A Mirror of Shallott* (1907) and *The Papers of a
Pariah* (1907); studies of Catholic ritual as if seen by an outsider; and
*The Lord of the World* (1907), a sensational description of the coming of
Anti-Christ. In reality there was much more. Handicapped by a stutter
in normal conversation, Hugh Benson became a powerful and flowing
orator in the pulpit, often perspiring and exhausted at the end of one
of his sermons. Although his reputation as a Catholic preacher soon
spread far beyond Cambridge, it was at the Church of Our Lady and
the English Martyrs that this reputation was first acquired, specifically
with a series of Sunday evening sermons on the theme of 'Plain Man
John'. These attracted much attention and a considerable following
among Cambridge undergraduates, not all of them Catholics. Later
published as *The Religion of the Plain Man* (1906), they probably stand
as Hugh Benson's best-regarded legacy to Cambridge, the first and
only town in which he assumed the pastoral duties of a Catholic priest.
Hugh Benson responded to calls to preach in Catholic pulpits all over
the country, to lecture to learned Catholic societies, to visit leading
Catholic families in their stately homes, to write articles in Catholic
journals and book reviews by the score. In July 1907 he felt obliged to
decline the high honour, offered to him by the American Cardinal
Gibbons, of the Chair of English Literature in the Catholic University
in Washington DC. Yet amidst all, Hugh Benson was sometimes left in
sole charge of the Cambridge Mission when Canon Scott was called
away to administer the Diocese of Northampton in his role as Vicar
General, though perhaps less so once Fr A. Wilson was appointed as
second curate in June 1906.

A further aspect of Hugh Benson's pastoral work in Cambridge must
be mentioned, by which many would choose to recall his time there.
His duties as chaplain to the nuns of St Mary's Convent brought him
into close contact with the pupils of their school. He enjoyed his
frequent visits to the school immensely, 'little hours of paradise', as he
described them, and the response he received in return was more than
enough reward. One of his greatest joys was to write and direct
mystery plays and little dramatic scenes for the children, most notably
among these *A Mystery Play in honour of the Nativity of Our Lord*, first

staged by the pupils of St Mary's in December 1907 and published in 1908. This still stands as a monument to his genius and as an outstanding labour of love, though the conspicuous simplicity of the verse is designed more to assist the children to learn their lines than to gain a place in any serious anthology:

> We therefore pray you of your grace
> To hear in silence and good face.
> Mock not, if here or there we fail
> To set out well this holy tale.
> Keep silence, too, except ye sing,
> As we shall do, before our King.

Hugh Benson's three-year stay at the Cambridge rectory had nearly run its course when Conybeare wrote in his diary: '1908 June 14th – Leaving present to Hugh Benson (a Spanish monstrance) given in Rectory after Benediction.'

## Hare Street Epilogue

For some time prior to June 1908, when his appointment at the rectory expired, Hugh Benson had been planning a more appropriate setting for his apostolic work, separated from the pastoral cares of a parish. He found and converted the dilapidated Hare Street House at Hare Street, near Buntingford, Herts., and from there, for the remaining six years of his life, he obtained ecclesiastical permission to conduct what was in effect a one-man apostolate, devoted to writing, lecturing and preaching, heedless of ever-increasing demands on his energies and the effects of overwork on his health. Among his written work during this time were two more historical novels, seven other novels, six religious works, three plays, two children's books and various fragments, essays, poems and other items which were to be published after his death. When he first moved to Hare Street in June 1908 he already had preaching engagements booked for a whole year ahead. These were followed by lecture tours in America, Ireland and around England, and a number of return visits to Rome to fulfil preaching engagements at the Church of San Silvestro. If critics found the financial success of these activities distasteful, he preferred to see this as a measure of the success of his religious mission. Hugh Benson's appointment as Monsignor dates from 1911, and it was possibly this ecclesiastical preferment which prompted a rumour, noted in Conybeare's diary: '1912 March 22 Persistent tidings that Cambridge is to be made a Bishopric! under H. Benson!!'

Hugh Benson's health began to suffer from 1913 onwards and by the autumn of 1914 he had little resistance left when overtaken by a bout of pneumonia from which he died at Bishop's House, Salford, on 19 October 1914, aged 43.

'I like best of all', Hugh Benson once wrote, 'saying Mass, and then, perhaps, writing my novels'.

> What then does anything else matter?
> Sorrow can be no more than a prick, death
> no more than a passing swoon; for to live
> is CHRIST, and to die is gain . . .
> (concluding lines of *The Religion of the Plain Man*).

# Chapter 14

# The Ministry of Monsignor Canon J. Bernard Marshall

*Christopher Jackson*
*with assistance from Canon Marshall's niece, Miss Molly Marshall*

### The Sidesman's Tale

I was pottering about the Church one fine sunny Sunday morning getting ready for the High Mass. Being a warm morning I had the west door open when in strode a tall distinguished looking man in uniform, nodding pleasantly to me. He marched up the centre aisle; as I watched him I thought you may be an officer, but you have not bought the Church, you may not sit where you like – that of course was in the old seat-rent days. However, he did not take a seat but wended his way towards the sacristy, and I forgot all about him.

Imagine my surprise, as the clock struck eleven, and the procession wended from the sacristy – there was my tall officer, vested in chasuble, alb and stole, attended by deacon and sub-deacon to sing the High Mass. I had not noticed he was a priest, and that was how I first met the Very Reverend Monsignor Canon Marshall.

Richard Ryan, 1946.

### The Rector's Tale

When I first came to Cambridge fourteen years ago, I was given hospitality for a fortnight at St Edmund's House. The first weekend, Canon Scott was ill in bed and a request came for a priest to come and sing High Mass on Sunday. As I was just back from my three years at the War, I was delighted to sing Mass in this beautiful parish church. And when I got here on the Sunday morning I found that the festival of the Dedication was being solemnized. So it fell out that on my first Sunday in Cambridge [13 October 1918], I was able to sing the Dedication Mass and carry the Blessed Sacrament in procession in the church of which I was afterwards the Rector.

J. Bernard Marshall, 1932.

## Early Career, Late Vocation

James Bernard Marshall (Pl. 11b) was born in 1879, the son of Sir James Marshall, a distinguished lawyer and Colonial judge. Sir James Marshall had been baptized an Anglican but had later converted to Catholicism. A vocation to the Catholic priesthood was, however, frustrated owing to a shooting accident at the age of seventeen when he had lost an arm. Instead, he pursued a distinguished alternative career in the law, eventually holding the position of Chief Justice of the Gold Coast. He was noted for his involvement, as a prominent layman, in a variety of Catholic causes, including extensive support for missioners in the colony and, after his return to England, the work of the Catholic Truth Society.

James Bernard, the son, was educated at Stonyhurst College and then went up to Oxford to read law at Brasenose College. He became a successful barrister, practising for eight years on the Midland Circuit from chambers in Birmingham and then, in 1911, entering the Beda College in Rome to study for the priesthood. At that time the Beda College admitted late vocations, lay converts and converts from the Anglican ministry and, by contrast with other English seminary students in Rome, their lectures were given in English, not Latin. It was said, with humour perhaps aimed at their maturity, that the only rule at the Beda was that the students were not permitted to light their cigars at the sanctuary lamp. Marshall's ordination as a priest of the Northampton Diocese took place in the Lateran Basilica in Rome on 27 February 1915. His bishop then recalled him to England for service with the Army Chaplain's Department and he spent three years on the Western Front with the 21st Division during the First World War, being appointed Senior Divisional Chaplain in 1917, receiving the Military Cross and a mention in dispatches. In 1918 he was invalided home and posted to Cambridge as the joint Catholic Chaplain to the Military Hospitals, the Officer Cadet Corps battalions in Cambridge, and the remaining undergraduates in the University. Marshall was demobilized in 1920 with the rank of Honorary Chaplain to the Forces. After his four-year service as University Chaplain during the years

1918–1922 and following the death of Canon Scott, Marshall was appointed rector of the church of Our Lady and the English Martyrs on 1 March 1922 and held this position for twenty-four years until obliged by ill-health to tender his resignation to the Bishop in the summer of 1946. The continuing success of his ministry was given recognition in 1926, when he became a Canon of the Cathedral Chapter of Northampton and in 1937, when he was appointed a Privy Chamberlain by the Holy See, with the title of Monsignor.

## Aspects of a Parish Priest

For his parishioners, Canon Marshall was recognized and remembered by two distinguishing features, his pipe and his dog. His pipe, seen often in informal photographs, was sometimes a potential hazard, which would set his pocket alight if not properly extinguished. His Airedale terriers, at first Gipsy, and later Billy her puppy, were each in turn to be his constant companion at many a parish function or on pastoral visits. Billy filled this role for eleven years until his death during the war, even gaining a mention from the Mayor of Cambridge at the laying of the foundation stone for the new school on 1 August 1935, when he opened his speech with the words 'My Lord Bishop, Canon Marshall and Canon Marshall's dog', addressing Billy stretched out full-length on the official platform.

If hospital and sick visiting were the duties which Canon Marshall liked least of all, this was quite possibly a reaction from his traumatic experiences as an army chaplain. Even so, this dislike was never allowed to show and never affected the diligence with which he performed those duties. Parish visits would be undertaken on foot, bicycle or bus for he never learned to drive.

## A Lively Inheritance

Canon Marshall succeeded to a busy and uniquely placed parish which, under the guidance and encouragement of his predecessor, Canon Scott, had become accustomed to high expectations in liturgy and sacred music. If performance in these fields was at a level higher than could have been expected on a basis of numbers alone, this reflected the nature of the church with which the congregation had been endowed. There was too an active parish life, operating through a number of organizations among which the Guild of the Blessed Sacrament, the Society of St Vincent de Paul and the Catholic Women's

League were prominent, along with a men's club and a scout troop. If these parish activities pointed to a degree of self-containment there was nothing unusual about this in the Church before Vatican II, and it was the congregation itself which had to be chided by Canon Marshall for rather negative reactions in 1934, following an address he gave to a meeting of the Cambridge Brotherhood in the Wesley Church. As he felt obliged to explain, 'I have had a number of requests lately to speak to non-Catholic audiences of men who want to hear about the Catholic Church. It should all help to remove some of the many misunderstandings which give rise to the prejudices against Catholicism' (*Cambridge Catholic Magazine*, 1934).

Like many Catholic congregations before or since, Canon Marshall's flock needed regular exhortation and encouragement, particularly on such familiar subjects as church collections, attendance at devotions other than Sunday Mass, or involvement in parish activities. Their collective enthusiasm or piety could, however, rise to the major occasion, and this was never demonstrated better than at the time of the canonization of St John Fisher, in effect Cambridge's own martyr-saint, and the restoration of the pilgrimage shrine at Walsingham.

Pilgrimages from the parish to the Catholic shrine of Our Lady of Walsingham took place every year during the 1920s and 30s, although until 1934 the pilgrims were obliged to visit a substitute shrine at King's Lynn. In 1934 pilgrims from Cambridge joined the first National Pilgrimage of Reparation, led by Cardinal Bourne to the Slipper Chapel, marking the first step in the restoration of Walsingham to its former role as a major national pilgrimage centre. Further national pilgrimages, with Cambridge representation, followed each year until 1939. The processional route, at that time, ran from the Slipper Chapel to the grounds of the ruined Abbey.

The feast of Blessed John Fisher and his companion martyrs, beatified in 1886, had been commemorated in Cambridge on 4 May each year, usually with a High Mass celebrated by the Bishop of Northampton and at which a Fisher sermon was, at least in later years, delivered by a specially invited preacher. Blessed John Fisher was given a special place in the Cambridge liturgical calendar as he had held the position of Chancellor of the University at the time of his martyrdom in 1535, and this devotion continued during Canon Marshall's time as rector, gaining increased significance as the cause of John Fisher and Thomas More gathered momentum during the early 1930s. This culminated in the canonization of the two saints at a joint ceremony in St Peter's in Rome on 19 May 1935, the fourth centenary of their martyrdom, at which Canon Marshall was present. Once St John Fisher had been canonized, it was permissible for an altar to be erected in the Cambridge church in his honour. Assisted by a legacy from the late Baron von Hügel and donations from parishioners, an altar dedicated to St John Fisher was constructed in the north transept and consecrated by Bishop Laurence Youens of Northampton on 9 July 1938, to honour the saint and to serve as a memorial to the founding benefactress of the church, Mrs Lyne-Stephens. With the re-ordering of the church in the 1970s, it was considered necessary to remove the altar and to transfer its dedication to the new central altar which Bishop Charles Grant of Northampton consecrated in 1973 (Pl. 20b).

## Hospitality at the Rectory

Judging by the number and frequency of their visits, many ecclesiastical dignitaries and academic theologians of high standing must have found the Cambridge rectory a convenient and attractive stopping-off point in the 1920s and 30s, whether their business lay in the further reaches of the Northampton Diocese or in academic Cambridge. Distinguished guest preachers formed another category which seemed more than ready to accept invitations to address the Cambridge congregation. As a member of the Cathedral Chapter on the one hand and as an incorporated MA, member of Trinity College and former University Chaplain on the other, Canon Marshall could claim to be appropriately well-connected in either role and the renowned hospitality of his housekeeper, Mrs Holmes, must have done much to enhance the reputation of the establishment. Bishop Cary-Elwes, until his death in 1932, and Bishop Youens, until his death in 1939, both paid at least three visits to Cambridge each year, one for confirmations, one for the Cambridge Summer School and one to celebrate the commemoration of Bl. John Fisher or, after his canonization in 1935, his feast day. The garden parties at the rectory at the conclusion of each Summer School between 1922 and 1939 became just as much a fixture in the calendar as the events themselves. Cardinal Bourne was present in 1932 and paid visits on three other occasions; other prominent visitors during this period included Mgr Ronald Knox, Dr Fulton Sheen, Archbishop Goodier of Bombay, Fr Martin D'Arcy, SJ, Archbishop Williams of Birmingham, Fr Martindale, SJ (Pl. 12a) and the Apostolic Delegate Mgr Godfrey.

Family and parishioners were not overlooked either in Canon Marshall's social programme. His sister Mary and niece Molly stayed at the rectory each Holy Week until Holy Saturday when they joined the special guests whom Canon Marshall would entertain to lunch (such as the Eyre Huddlestons of Sawston Hall). Mary and Molly returned to the rectory for the garden party at the conclusion of each Summer School at the end of July, and would stay at the rectory again during Christmas Week. Canon Marshall stayed with his sister and niece for two or three days during each Easter Week to recover from the heavy liturgical activities of Holy Week. This break, and another after Christmas, were necessary as he suffered increasingly from the effects of an enlarged heart as the years went by. Lastly in the seasonal cycle came the rector's Christmas party for parishioners, held in the Houghton Hall and generally regarded as a very jolly affair. But aside from these social activities, his involvement with the parish amateur dramatic group, later to be known as the Houghton Hall Players, was Canon Marshall's favourite of all.

## University Connections

It is no criticism of his predecessor or of his successors to say that relations between the Catholic parish and the Catholic chaplaincy were never stronger than during Canon Marshall's time as mission rector. He had after all transferred directly from the chaplaincy to the rectory in 1922, and while some links with the University were of his own making, others had been forged even before his arrival in Cambridge. Thus, when Mgr Barnes left in 1916 and the chaplaincy at Llandaff House had to be closed, the Catholic church and rectory became, for the next three years, the new meeting-place for Catholic undergraduates. Even when, under Canon Marshall, the chaplaincy had re-opened in 1919 at Round Church Street House, the undergraduate members of the chaplaincy (forming the Fisher Society) had continued to meet at the rectory and did so for another five years until the converted Black Swan Inn re-opened as Fisher House in 1924. This connection typified the links in sentiment and spirit between the parish and the chaplaincy which continued throughout the 1920s and 30s and grew ever stronger once the former Fisher House undergraduate Alfred Gilbey returned to Fisher House as chaplain in 1932. This does much to explain how Canon Marshall was chosen as the celebrant at the solemn High Mass held in the chapel of Fisher House to mark the canonization of John Fisher in May 1935.

## Support from the Clergy

Help was always at hand for Canon Marshall during his time in the Cambridge parish. At least one curate was always based with him at the rectory, more frequently two and sometimes even three. They stayed for varying periods before moving on, generally to the charge of other parishes in the diocese, and priests such as Fathers Davidson, Webb, Ketterer, Moir, Mullett, Phillips, Watkis and Grant gained an affection from the congregation which would be demonstrated at farewell presentations and whenever return visits occurred later on. In the case of Fr Charles Grant, who in his youth had been received as a convert by Canon Marshall and in 1935 was ordained in the church, his return visits between the years 1961 and 1982 would be as Bishop of Northampton.

Outside help, too, was always available. Fr McNulty, Master of St Edmund's House (1921–9), and his successor Fr Cuthbert Waring (1929–34) provided regular assistance at the High Mass on Sundays. The extremely precise and meticulous arrangements for the Holy Week liturgy were ensured by Canon Marshall's invitation, extended year by year, to a Jesuit priest chosen for his experience and preaching abilities to take the central role in the celebrations. Frs Doyle, Turner and Boyle were among those Jesuits who came in response to these invitations. Nevertheless, Canon Marshall himself sang the High Mass on Easter Sunday 1932, thankful to have recovered from throat surgery the previous year.

## Support from the Laity

Among the many lay people who worked devotedly in the parish over many years, the service of Clarence Mills as choirmaster, organist and sacristan and of Mrs Holmes as housekeeper can be deservedly picked out for special mention.

Clarence Mills served the church in a variety of roles, including sacristan, assistant organist and choirmaster during the years 1890–1946, so spanning most of his adult life. Having been reared in an orphanage and then befriended by Canon Scott, Clarence's life had an almost Dickensian flavour to it. Initially the young protégé of Canon Scott, he was given employment as sacristan of the new church and his benefactor saw to it that he received a musical training. By the time that Canon Scott died, it can be fairly said that Clarence's talents had developed to the point of indispensability. Certainly Canon Marshall depended heavily on his support throughout his ministry in Cambridge.

Clarence's service at the church was interrupted by direction into war industry in 1916 (his eyesight was too poor for active service) but after his return to civilian life his musical talents found their true vocation.

Thanks to his early orphanage years, he had an unrivalled knowledge of Anglican hymn tunes which he could put to good use, not least in the many melodies he would play on the church bells after his daily ringing of the Angelus. With the retirement of the organist, Mr Otto Wehrle, in 1919 Clarence was given the responsibilities of choirmaster and deputy organist, to be added to those of sacristan. From then on, Clarence Mills found himself in constant pursuit of musical and liturgical perfection, ruling the choir with quick temper, iron discipline and acid wit. Choirboys who remembered his training with gratitude would admit that they were often a great trial to him. As sacristan he saw to it that every sacred article and vestment was in place, no matter how involved the liturgical requirements. Few could understand his arrangement of the men's sacristy and some who came to help after the bombing of the church in 1941 were upset to see the disorder there, not realizing that the room had escaped bomb damage. It was as sacristan, too, that he unlocked the church doors before each service and often stood guard in the porch in his cassock, preventing it from becoming a playground for noisy children and a parking place for bicycles.

> The children – how he put the fear of God into them! (Or was it only fear of Clarence?). I have seen them scatter like the wind when he came in sight, and heard noisy voices stilled at the sound of his.
>
> *Cambridge Catholic Magazine*

Among their many other commitments, Canon Marshall and Clarence Mills conducted a Monday morning ritual of counting the Sunday collections in Canon Marshall's study with Clarence, the noted expert, listening intently to the hymns broadcast in the BBC's Morning Service. The collection was taken by Canon Marshall to Lloyds Bank in Sidney Street later on a Monday morning in his Gladstone bag, accompanied by his Airedale terrier.

Clarence's service to the parish ended soon after Canon Marshall's death in 1946, and his deep qualities of devotion beneath a forbidding exterior and volatile temperament were recalled with genuine affection when he died two years later:

> He never recovered from the shock and grief of Canon Marshall's death – it was then that he began to leave us in spirit, and all will rejoice that after two years of mental darkness he has gone to the realm of perpetual light.
>
> *Cambridge Catholic Magazine*

Canon Marshall inherited Mrs Hubbard from Canon Scott as housekeeper when he arrived at the rectory in 1922 but she moved to

Southport in 1924 and her place was taken by Mrs Holmes, a Belgian war widow with a heart as generous as her accent was pronounced. Mrs Holmes came with her eight-year-old daughter Madeleine and the rectory was home for both until Madeleine married and left in 1939. Mrs Holmes carried on as housekeeper at the rectory until she moved with Canon Marshall to Ely in 1946, having gained a reputation for generosity among tramps, itinerant farm workers, altar servers, members of the choir and visiting servicemen alike.

## Foreign Travel

Canon Marshall undertook many journeys abroad during the 1920s and 30s, some of these being of an official nature, others pilgrimages, and the remainder his annual summer holidays. Into the official category came his visits to the biennial Eucharistic Congresses held in Malta, Vienna, Dublin (1932) and Budapest (1938), and at least three visits to Rome, in 1929 for a papal audience, in 1935 for the canonization of John Fisher and in 1937, possibly connected with his appointment as Privy Chamberlain.

Pilgrimages with other parishioners took place in September every year to Lourdes, from 1923 until 1938, with the exception of 1935. Mrs Holmes was a devoted participant in these pilgrimages and while at Lourdes in September 1931 she was invested with the 'Sept Douleurs' medal of the Hospital of the Seven Sorrows for her invaluable work on behalf of the sick, her fluency in the French language having naturally placed her in charge of the voluntary lady helpers from the parish for a number of years. In 1939 Canon Marshall planned to move on from his holiday in Spain to join the parish pilgrimage and wrote of his intention to meet the party from Cambridge on the station platform at Lourdes, 'I shall eagerly look for a good group of Cambridge pilgrims stepping from the train.' Unfortunately these plans had to be cancelled owing to the outbreak of war.

As for his annual holidays, Canon Marshall went away for the best part of six weeks (but only four Sundays) each summer, and would travel extensively on the continent, generally to destinations in France, Italy, Spain or Portugal where he would visit ecclesiastical acquaintances, such as the Master of the English College in Lisbon, his counterpart in Valladolid, or the Master of the Beda College in Rome. He visited Spain while the Civil War was in progress and was in Rome in January 1937 to celebrate Molly Marshall's twenty-first birthday on 18 January 1937. His holiday absence abroad in 1939 when war broke out was not a conscious act of defiance or bravado; he probably failed to notice the gathering war clouds. He was delayed by at least two weeks in his return to Cambridge owing to disruption of train and ferry services on his journey home.

From 1927 until 1938, Fr Brodeur, a lecturer in English at the Sorbonne, came to stay at the rectory from June to September and acted as supply priest while the rector and each of the curates took their summer holidays in turn. Fr Brodeur was obliged to take twelve months sick leave from his university post in 1935–6 and chose to spend the entire convalescent period at the Cambridge rectory, providing clerical support to the parish clergy. Fr Brodeur loved nothing better than provoking laughter from the congregation, a sure sign, he felt, that they were paying attention. His favourite trick was a deliberate misuse of English, thus 'Please collect a leaflet as you leave the church' would become 'Please collect a leaflet as you pass away'.

Canon Marshall took his last holiday abroad in 1946 when he flew for the first time for his first holiday in Ireland, perhaps wishing he had not left either experience so late in his life.

## Building a Hall, Building a School

The sustained efforts of Canon Marshall and his parishioners during the nine-year period 1927–36 were to result in a fitting monument to his determination and to the faith shown in his leadership: the combined St Andrew's School and Houghton Hall, completed in 1936.

Apart from the church, which owed its monumental scale to the lavish gift of a single benefactor, the other parish buildings which Canon Marshall took over in 1922 gave a more accurate impression of the modest size of the Catholic community in Cambridge and of the limited financial resources at its command. The earlier St Andrew's School (the present-day parish hall), completed in 1868, was by the 1920s starting to suffer from problems of overcrowding and looked increasingly outmoded by comparison with more up-to-date school building standards. The then parish hall, given the title 'Houghton Hall' in honour of St John Houghton, the protomartyr of the English Reformation, had originated from the opportunistic purchase of a prefabricated war-surplus building which had served during the First World War as part of the First Eastern General Hospital in Newmarket Road, and was largely the gift of a generous parishioner, Baron von Hügel. Modest in appearance and of temporary construction, it served the parish well for fifteen years, accommodating the Catholic Men's Club at one end, and constantly in demand for every kind of social activity and meeting in the remainder, from concerts, dances, bazaars, lectures, teas, lunches, whist drives and school plays to wedding receptions, presentations to departing curates and even a weekly rheumatic clinic.

By 1927, the Houghton Hall no longer complied with Borough building and public health by-laws. The threat of forced closure or demolition was considered sufficiently serious for a parish meeting to be held on 31 July 1927 at which Canon Marshall called for the establishment of a Parish Hall Building Fund, aiming to raise £2000 over a five year period, after which a permanent replacement could be considered. By 1932 this target had been achieved and the noted Catholic architect Mr J. Arnold Crush of Birmingham was then engaged to make preliminary proposals. Among many Catholic building projects around the country with which Mr Crush was associated, those in or near Cambridge included the Paston House extension (Crush's Building) at St Mary's School in Bateman Street, the conversion of 'The Black Swan', Guildhall Street, into the University Chaplaincy and St Francis of Assisi church, Papworth.

Another factor came into the reckoning in 1932. At national level plans were being made to raise the school-leaving age from fourteen to fifteen, and for the first time to provide separate senior (or secondary) schools for the eleven to fifteen age group. The Catholics of Cambridge were faced with the somewhat bleak prospect of St Andrew's School being reduced to a junior school for the under-elevens, with no Catholic school available for the senior children. The Borough Education Committee was insistent that separate school provision should be made for the senior pupils and rejected a proposal that the Parish Hall Building project should be combined with a new school, putting seniors and juniors in a single building with the hall partitioned into three classrooms during school hours. Eventually, after an appeal to the Board of Education in London and prolonged negotiations, consent was given for the construction of a school for 220 pupils for all ages up to fifteen.

The old Houghton Hall was removed from the site to make way for the new Hall and, to allow adequate playground space for 220 pupils, the two cottages on the Union Road frontage, survivors from the property first acquired for the Cambridge mission in the 1840s, were demolished. Thanks to its pre-fabricated nature, it was possible to save the old Hall for further use, part of it being re-erected two years later to serve as St Laurence's, High Street, Chesterton. The salvaged section still survives as St Vincent de Paul's Chapel in Ditton Lane, Cambridge.

When the foundation stone for this novel set of 'Siamese twins', Parish Hall and St Andrew's School, was laid on 1 August 1935, it was announced that £5000 had so far been raised towards total building costs of £13,000. Inevitably the parishioners were faced with the prospect of more house-to-house collections, summer fairs, theatrical performances and concerts, and invitations to subscribe to interest-free loans in order to repay a building debt of £8000. Few could have forecast then that the building debt would be paid off entirely in another nine years time.

At least the building work was finished by August 1936; term started in the new school on 31 August with 127 pupils, the infants class remaining in an improved classroom in the old school building. A ceremonial opening of the school took place on 24 September which included speeches by the Bishop of Nottingham, Mr Francis Blundell (Chairman of the Catholic Education Council), the Mayor of Cambridge, the Bishop of Northampton and Canon Marshall. The builders, Kidman and Sons, were represented by Mr William Kidman (himself a parishioner) but unfortunately the architect Mr Crush had died before the ceremony took place. A performance of the play 'St Thomas More', presented by a visiting Catholic theatre company, took place in the evening to inaugurate the Houghton Hall and a Grand Inaugural Ball followed on 2 October.

If the school took time to make its expected impact (127 pupils in 1936, 143 in 1937, 177 in 1938 and only fully functioning with the practical room in operation and cooked dinners available at the start of the 1937 school year), quite the opposite was the case with the Houghton Hall. Its impact on parish activities, and even on the wider Cambridge community, was immediate. Before long parish organizations, even when planning fund-raising events, had to be warned to book well ahead to avoid clashing with outside organizations who discovered in the Houghton Hall accommodation well-suited to their needs for plays, socials, dances, lectures and dinners.

While some parish organizations were able to expand their activities in the newly-available space, others too were encouraged to make their appearance in the years following the opening of the hall, notably the newly-styled Houghton Hall Players (the parish amateur dramatic group), the Squires of St Columba (junior branch of the Knights), and a revived branch of the Catholic Women's League Juniors. Even when war broke out in 1939, after an initial reluctance to hold functions of any description anywhere, the Hall soon regained its popularity for events and entertainments of all descriptions, whether parochial or external.

Surplus assets could not be allowed to go to waste. The Catholic Men's Club, displaced by the removal of the old hall, found a new home in the redundant parts of the old school building, which were specially renovated and adapted for their needs.

## The Cambridge Summer School of Catholic Studies

The Catholic Bible Congress of 1921 was no isolated event, destined to be forgotten by those involved. As Secretary of the Organising Committee in 1921, Canon Marshall saw to it, when transferred to the parish in 1922, that Cambridge continued to host the remarkable eighteen-year sequence of Summer Schools of Catholic Studies which followed between 1922 and 1940. These were events of national significance, at first organized by the scholars involved in the Bible Congress and attracting noteworthy speakers and numerous students and other participators. In his foreword to the printed volume of learned papers which appeared after the first Summer School in 1922 the organizing secretary, Fr Cuthbert Lattey, SJ, wrote: 'It is nothing more than a repetition upon a more modest scale of the Catholic Bible Congress held at Cambridge in July, 1921. The success of that Congress naturally led to the suggestion that something similar should be established permanently.' He went on to explain that the Catholic Conference of Higher Studies had undertaken responsibility for organizing the lectures and securing the best available lecturers, while a local committee consisting of the Cambridge clergy and certain laymen made all the arrangements on the spot. Each Summer School had its own theme, such as 'Catholic Faith in the Holy Eucharist' (1922), 'The Papacy' (1923), 'St Thomas Aquinas' (1924), 'English Martyrs of the Reformation' (1928), 'Church and State' (1935), 'Man and Eternity' (1936). Interest at the highest level was demonstrated by the visit paid by Cardinal Bourne to the 1932 Summer School, on the theme of 'Moral Principles of Life'.

In 1939, as noted in the *Cambridge Catholic Magazine*, a more ambitious and conspicuously successful programme was adopted for the first time. By holding three summer schools in conjunction with one another, an attendance of 250 was attracted to the component sections, Scientific, Psychological and Russian (including church liturgy). Sadly, the onset of the Second War prevented the high expectations for future combined summer schools from being realized.

The final Cambridge Summer School proved to be that held in 1940, already curtailed by emergency conditions to the Whitsun weekend (11–12 May), when a course of lectures was held on the subject matter of the 1939 encyclical *Summi pontificatus*, issued by the newly-elected Pope Pius XII, on the role of the Church in a world of conflict.

So ended this annual series, its high scholarly significance deriving from the distinction of the long list of visiting lecturers who made their contributions year by year, men of the calibre of Knox, Chapman, Myers, Jaggar, Reeves, de la Taille, Cabrol, Lattey himself, and many others. The organizational problems for the parish and its rector in running these Summer Schools year by year were immense. Taking only one example of this, arrangements had to be made for a multitude of Masses to be said each day between 6 a.m. and 10 a.m. at every altar in the church by those clergy attending, whether as lecturers or delegates. The success of this unbroken sequence stands as a major achievement of Canon Marshall's ministry in Cambridge.

## The Further Reaches

Serving the scattered Catholic population of Cambridge and the surrounding countryside from a single parish church was always a problem. Even within the borough boundaries, distances could be considerable, and chapels-of-ease were therefore made available for parishioners at St Edmund's House, Mount Pleasant, and at the Carmelite Convent in Chesterton Road. Further afield, the chapel at Sawston Hall was a long-established but occasional Mass centre served from Cambridge, and another had been created at Papworth after the First World War, in response to the foundation of the Papworth Settlement for the treatment of tuberculosis. As Cambridgeshire was somewhere near the bottom of any league table of Catholics per head of the population, this ratio was bound to be disturbed if a sizeable migration from industrial areas took place, as happened when patients and staff started to arrive at Papworth. The care of Catholics there was given initially to the Huntingdon mission, but was passed to Cambridge in 1926. The Papworth Scout Hut served for the fortnightly visits of one of the priests from the rectory for six years, involving a twelve-mile drive each way. Canon Marshall never learned to drive, even though the car became increasingly influential during his time in Cambridge, until suddenly halted in 1939 by the emergency conditions of wartime. One of the curates, Fr Webb, was a motorist and drove out to Papworth for Masses and sick calls to the patients, until he was appointed to Thetford in 1929. His place was taken by Fr Ketterer, a non-driver, for whom a rota of lifts had to be organized by Mr Hussey and some fellow members of the Cambridge Catenian Circle. By 1932, the small congregation at Papworth was sufficiently well-established to justify the purchase of a freehold plot and a modest chapel dedicated to St Francis of Assisi was built as a goodwill project by Papworth Industries, to the design of the architect, Mr Crush. An inaugural Mass was celebrated on Thursday 16 June 1932 in the presence of visiting church and civic dignitaries and a choir from the Cambridge church. Afterwards a celebratory lunch was held for eighty persons at the Village Hall, for which 'all the cooking had been carried out by Mrs Holmes of the Cambridge Rectory' (*Cambridge Catholic Magazine*).

The revival of Sawston Hall chapel as a regular Mass centre, also in 1932, took place by a different route. The owner, Cdr Eyre-Huddleston RN, was a prominent parishioner and benefactor of the parish in whose chapel Mass was said on an occasional basis. To establish regular Masses for the benefit of local residents, Cdr Eyre-Huddleston provided a subsidy for the support of a third curate at Cambridge to allow for Mass to be said fortnightly at the Hall. To overcome travel problems he even presented a Ford Eight saloon car to the parish, along with a garage at the rectory, for the journeys to and from Sawston.

Another influx of Catholics to a country location took place in 1937 when the establishment of the Land Settlement Association colony at Great Abington brought 50 families (12% of them Catholics) from areas of high unemployment in the north-east of England, and created a need for Mass-hearing facilities and Catholic schooling. A Mass centre was soon established in the Abington Village Institute, while the schoolchildren found their way to St Andrew's School in Cambridge by bus, their fares being provided by the parish with assistance from Cdr Eyre-Huddleston and the Society of St Vincent de Paul.

With the transfer of the Carmelite Convent from Chesterton Road to premises in Waterbeach in September 1937, Catholics in Chesterton were left without a Mass centre. This gap was filled by hiring a room adjoining the Co-operative Stores in High Street, Chesterton, from November 1938 until a temporary building, part of the former Houghton Hall, was opened in October 1939 on a site specially purchased by the parish in the High Street and dedicated to St Laurence.

## Vicar Capitular

One of the responsibilities which fell to Canon Marshall during the early years of the war was that of Vicar Capitular of the Northampton Diocese, which he held for the unusually long period of sixteen months between the death of Bishop Laurence Youens in November 1939 and the appointment of his successor, Bishop Leo Parker in February 1941. In exercising all the powers and duties of a bishop *ad interim*, Canon Marshall was obliged to preside at every monthly meeting of the diocesan chapter in Northampton, travelling by rail between Cambridge and Northampton. Even in peacetime this journey involved changing trains at Bedford and Bletchley and, with railway services disrupted by emergency conditions or enemy action, Canon Marshall was frequently obliged to wait on draughty station platforms in inclement weather, thanks to missed connections or trains long delayed or even cancelled. This had serious effects on the state of his health, which had already started to deteriorate in pre-war days. It may be supposed, though not officially confirmed, that the long delay in finding a successor to Bishop Youens may have had something to do with Canon Marshall's own inability, or unwillingness, to accept the position himself.

## The Closing Chapter

When the Second World War ended in 1945 Canon Marshall had served as rector of the Cambridge parish for more than twenty-three years, the last six made more stressful by the wartime conditions, his additional service as Vicar Capitular in 1939-40, and a possible legacy of long-term health problems from his earlier war service. At all events, his deteriorating health was no secret, and when Fr Guy Pritchard was appointed to the position of first curate early in 1946 there was more than an implication that a successor was already in place. By the middle of that year, Canon Marshall felt compelled to tender his resignation of the parish to the Bishop, 'the one and only reason being that physically I have become unequal to carrying the burden and responsibility entailed. I was medically advised to give it up some time ago.' Predictably, Fr Pritchard was appointed parish priest in his place.

Canon Marshall was given the opportunity to make his farewell to his parishioners in the pages of the *Cambridge Catholic Magazine*, a quarterly publication which he had inaugurated in February 1931 and then edited for the following fifteen years, so leaving an invaluable source of information for individuals seeking to discover the history of the parish years later. He wrote:

> It is a tremendous satisfaction to me that the Bishop has chosen Father Guy Pritchard to succeed me. In him I see a priest after my own heart, one who will assuredly serve you well and add lustre to the records of the Parish of Our Lady and the English Martyrs.

Canon Marshall moved to Ely, taking Mrs Holmes with him as housekeeper. His intention, to undertake the lighter duties required of a parish priest there, was not to be realized and it fell to Mrs Holmes, only six months later, to make the sad discovery of Canon Marshall's death in the Ely presbytery on New Year's Eve 1946. He was sixty-seven years old.

# Chapter 15

# There's A War On: Catholic Cambridge, 1939–1945

*Christopher Jackson*

This chapter describes how the Second World War affected the Catholic community in Cambridge. It is the story of what happened in and around the Church of Our Lady and the English Martyrs and to its parishioners, yet inevitably it echoes what would become familiar in varying ways to many other denominations and communities throughout the country. The 'Home Front' became the description given to the wartime conditions under which the civilian population of the British Isles was obliged to live and to play a part in the war effort. Sometimes the dangers and hardships became as serious for civilians as they were for members of the armed forces, particularly on account of enemy attacks from the air. The trials visited upon the parishioners during the Second World War put them to a severe test, but one which they were to survive with credit and some justifiable pride.

Unless otherwise stated, all quotations in this chapter are taken from the 'What I Have to Say' feature contributed to the quarterly *Cambridge Catholic Magazine* by the rector, Monsignor James Bernard Marshall, during the years 1939–45.

## Cambridge and County Well Prepared

From headlines in the local press during the last week of August 1939 it was evident that the outbreak of war was regarded as a certainty, only the date still had to be announced:

'Evacuation Test: Orders for Children' – *Cambridge Daily News (CDN)*, 26 August.
'Public Air Raid Warning Signals ... will be sounded on Saturday morning, 2nd September' – *CDN*, 30 August.
'Evacuation Starts Tomorrow' – *CDN*, 31 August.

But less pessimistically:

'Holidays As Usual – departures from Drummer Street Coach Station today for holidays on the East Coast' – *CDN*, 26 August.
'Robert Sayle's invite you to see Television' – Advertisement, *CDN*, 1 September, proving to be the last opportunity for Cambridge residents for another seven years.

The rector of the parish, Mgr Bernard Marshall, had served in the First World War as a front-line chaplain and had perhaps acquired some measure of imperturbability from those experiences twenty years before. Even so, the signs of clearly gathering war clouds seemed to have escaped him as he arranged to take a summer holiday on the Continent in 1939, first visiting France and then moving on to Spain, where he was staying when war was declared. Fr Watkis, the senior curate of the parish, had to deputize for him in this sudden emergency, until Canon Marshall arrived back in Cambridge, his journey unavoidably disrupted by delays and cancellations to train and ferry services.

Cambridgeshire was designated as a 'safe' area to which children from the large cities, much likelier targets for air raids, could be evacuated. The problem faced by the parish clergy in September 1939 was the sudden arrival from London of many hundreds of Catholic children scattered over a score of villages with very limited chances of attending Catholic churches or schools, or even of being placed with Catholic families; bus services on Sunday mornings had been suspended for the duration of the war as a fuel-saving measure. The rector wrote of the many problems and much labour which this gave rise to, with 'many other Catholics arriving in Cambridge in one capacity or another: the front door bell and telephone bell were in constant action . . .'.

Air raid precautions were swiftly introduced. The blackout had begun in earnest on 1 September 1939 and one press photograph had shown a gang of workmen painting the kerbs of Cambridge streets with white paint even before the outbreak of war. By November 1939 a photo caption showed 'Workmen preparing foundations for a series of ARP shelters on Parkers Piece beside Regent Terrace' (*CDN*, 29 November).

Canon Marshall evidently felt some irritation over the absolute nature of the prohibitions against the display of lights during the hours of darkness. Perhaps one can understand his point of view, given his responsibility for a church in which most of the windows were far too high and large to be covered with blinds or curtains, a rectory with many more windows to cover than it had occupants, and a front door working overtime by night and day. At one point he referred to the 'blackout demands of the "air-wardens" to be faced and dealt with', but it was to be 'business as usual' so far as church services were concerned. Few changes were made to the times of services, morning or evening, and if it was 'black-out time' they continued in an unlit church by the light of a bare minimum of candles, never enough to cast light through the stained glass windows and hardly enough to read by. These arrangements continued with the common consent of a congregation who were more than once asked if they would prefer church times to be kept within the hours of daylight. But soon, after only four months of war, a major problem had to be faced and solved.

## Midnight Mass at the Proper Hour

Newspapers reported the patriotic determination of King's College to continue their Christmas Eve arrangements undeterred by the war:

> War could not 'black-out' the Christmas Eve Festival of nine lessons and carols in King's College Chapel ... (broadcast) ... all over Britain [and] to France Italy and Switzerland. Candles continued to burn after blackout. ... no dangerous amount of light could be seen from the outside – *CDN*, 27 December 1939, reporting a venturesome excursion into the early twilight.

Although 'Midnight Mass Cancelled In All Catholic Churches' was a headline in the same newspaper this proved to be premature in its application to Cambridge whether in 1939 or in any subsequent year of the war. 'Our great triumph was that we celebrated the Christmas midnight Mass at the proper hour each year ... when the Bishops everywhere were discountenancing it', wrote Canon Marshall, who had become Vicar Capitular of the Northampton Diocese in November 1939. One of the Bishops told him that the Civil Defence would never give approval, but the Chief Constable of the Cambridge Borough Constabulary saw differently. He told the Canon that if people went out in the blackout to amuse themselves he did not see why they should not go out to pray. Canon Marshall therefore ruled that Midnight Mass could take place throughout the Northampton Diocese if the lighting restrictions were observed. While banned in virtually every other diocese no less than five Midnight Masses were said in Cambridge at Christmas 1939, including those at the various religious houses. Inside the church, Fr Charles Grant (one of the curates and himself later Bishop of Northampton) took on the task of devising candle shields which prevented the escape of light through the windows and at least allowed the congregation to find their places in the near darkness. 'The dim glimmer of light in the Church has been devised and contrived by Fr Grant. Since conquering the irritation [which] everything connected with air raid precautions is apt to cause me I have been lost in admiration for his handiwork', wrote Canon Marshall.

The unique atmosphere was greatly appreciated by the large numbers who attended each year, especially one family who happened to be present on the first occasion and liked it so much that they booked rooms for Christmas each succeeding year at the University Arms Hotel. None of this made the newspaper headlines, but Canon Marshall felt justifiable pride in the unbroken record at his church, at a time when even Westminster Cathedral was closed for Midnight Masses.

## On Active Service

There had been no hesitation among the men of the parish to enlist for active service when the war started and of these one hundred names were listed in the *Cambridge Catholic Magazine* in August 1940 as an interim record of those who were by then serving in the forces. Some were already members of the Territorial Army and were immediately called up for service or were already serving in the regular forces. Some chose to volunteer early for the service of their choice (such as the more glamorous RAF) lest conscription denied them that choice. Others were to serve in emergency services such as the National Fire Service on the Home Front in conditions just as demanding as in other theatres of war and others again were obliged to wait several years until old enough to join up. From May 1940 the Local Defence Volunteers (soon to be re-named the Home Guard) attracted recruits from older age categories or reserved occupations. Originally manned by volunteers, by February 1942 the nation's manpower requirements made it necessary to direct men into the Home Guard, and by 1943, (contrary to their 'Dad's Army' image), their value as a defensive force came to be realised. Gradually they began to replace troops manning static anti-aircraft and coastal defence installations on night-time rotas, somehow keeping up their 'day jobs' as well. Many a parishioner put in part-time service with the Home Guard until imminent danger to the nation was deemed to have passed and the force was stood down on 14 November 1944. Their contribution was in no way diminished by the caustic comment made by Canon Marshall in May 1942, following a General Communion of the adults on Sunday, 17 May:

> This was ... impressive – but not so big as I had expected. This was to some extent due to the fact that Cambridge was engaged on an 'invasion practice.' This meant that the military, the Home Guard and all members of Civil Defence units were on duty through the night until 11 a.m. on Sunday. It was somewhat cynical in appearance that this exercise should be timed so as just to prevent great numbers of people being able to attend any Sunday morning service.
>
> Of course that was not anybody's express object. It is just that our authorities do not consider the service of God in making their plans. A military exercise that interfered with business, as for instance necessitating the closing of banks and shops for half a day, would be considered impracticable – but not so the interference with Church services. It is a pity.

The calls of war service resulted inevitably in a shortage of menfolk trained and experienced in the various tasks of the parish. These included the Master of Ceremonies, called away to Home Guard parades on Sunday mornings, the clock-winder, and organizers of social functions and entertainment, all away on active service. Apart from Canon Marshall, the other two members of the Finance Committee became involved, one in the Home Guard and the other in Civil Defence, to an extent that sometimes delayed the appearance of the school and hall building fund accounts. Younger members of the parish, below the age for call-up, were drawn into activities hitherto regarded as the preserve of their seniors, one took on the role of Master of Ceremonies, another became the clock-winder, and the Squires of St Columba organized the parish social events in the Houghton Hall.

## They Came in Great Numbers

Departures for war service were heavily outnumbered by arrivals during the war years, swelling the congregations to unprecedented levels. 'The accommodation of the Church was sorely tested. For most of the period many people had to stand, especially during the later Sunday Masses.'

As already mentioned, the evacuee children were the first to arrive in

Cambridge and the surrounding districts, contributing to some crowding in a school built for 220 pupils but with never less than 260 on the roll, 60 of these being evacuees. 'We should have had more if the evacuation authorities had been considerate in arranging the billeting of Catholic children so that they could be near a Catholic school.' As it was, an extra class had to be formed and for five years a London teacher, Miss Ethel Grady, was supplied by the London County Council to help with the extra numbers.

Members of the forces, predominantly RAF but also army units, including some from the 1st Polish Armoured Division, and representatives from many other nations looked to the church in Cambridge as a centre for religious observance, friendship and social contacts. French, Belgians, Czechs, Canadians, Australians and Poles were to be followed by great numbers of Americans as the air bases of East Anglia proliferated in the surrounding countryside and Cambridge became their chosen centre for rest and recreation. The larger contingents brought Catholic chaplains with them and Masses were mostly said in their military camps. Sometimes the pull of a central place of worship was overwhelming, and on special occasions the church was filled with members of the forces attending Masses for their national days (Poles on 11 November, French on 14 July) or, at Christmas, anticipatory Midnight Masses in the early afternoon, for forces only.

During the Anglo-Polish Week promoted by the Ministry of Information in Cambridge in 1943 the Polish President-in-exile M. Ladislas Raczkiewicz attended the 9.45 a.m. Mass on Sunday, 2 May which was offered for Poland. The President heard Mass at a prie-dieu in the Sanctuary and afterwards a group of Polish officers and dignitaries sang the Polish national hymn. Not long after this, in July 1943, the tragic death of the Polish Commander-in-Chief, General Sikorski, in an air crash, was marked with a sung Requiem Mass at which Canon Marshall officiated, assisted by two Polish priests as deacon and subdeacon, in the presence of high ranking British and Polish officers and civic dignitaries. For the second time, the Polish national hymn was sung most impressively. Only a few days later it was the turn of the French to mark their national day with a Mass in the church celebrated by a French army chaplain who had escaped from German captivity. His sermon in French was heard by another distinguished congregation.

Another cause for the crowded wartime congregations was the designation of Cambridge as a 'reception area', not only for evacuated children and refuges, but for whole institutions (including a large part of London University), Ministries, an RAF Initial Training Wing and shadow factories undertaking a variety of wartime production from aircraft to radios, with an imported labour force, including a large contingent from Ireland. It was a plea from Dublin to help keep the Irish workers together that spurred on the formation of the Sunday Social, held every week in the Houghton Hall and strictly limited to Catholics, whether civilians or members of the armed forces of many different countries. The entertainment, which was mainly dancing, started immediately after the evening service and stopped promptly at 10 p.m. with prayers for peace. A total of 3500 admission cards were issued to military and civilian visitors to Cambridge during the war years. These Sunday gatherings were supplemented by a weekly 'Forces Party' organized by the Catholic Women's League. The Catholic Men's Club, after anxious times at the start of the war, discovered a new and prosperous role when it started to admit men from the forces and over 1270 servicemen were to sign the special Forces Register. Much less formally organized, but highly valued for all that, was the simple informality of the rectory kitchen where the housekeeper, Mrs Holmes, was always ready to welcome servicemen and women to a homely atmosphere which to many became a regular club. Problems over rationing and other shortages were eased for her by the generosity of parishioners and visiting servicemen alike. Mrs Holmes was to receive a special commendation after the war from Mgr Beauchamp, the Senior RAF Chaplain, for her hospitality.

There was even something of a silver lining, at least for the parish finances, behind the war clouds. The school and hall debt had hung somewhat uneasily over the parish since the new school had been opened in 1936, amounting at the start of the war to £6500. Thanks largely to the generosity of visiting American forces, this debt was entirely cleared by the time that hostilities ceased in 1945. Although the universality of the Church was fittingly demonstrated by their presence, there were others in Cambridge during the war less willing to be there. German and Austrian refugees were grateful to have escaped from their homelands to safety in England but the language of a hostile enemy set them somewhat apart from their hosts and the Canonesses of St Augustine made special efforts to provide care for them both spiritually and socially. The fortunes of war also placed a large contingent of Italian prisoners of war in a camp just outside Trumpington. Although by the end of 1943 Italy was no longer a belligerent and they were allowed a certain amount of freedom outside the camp, they were treated with much caution by the majority of the civilian population, some still regarding them as enemies and the language barrier creating formidable difficulties. At last, as the war drew to a close, their situation in Cambridge slowly improved, largely due to the efforts of Canon Marshall's niece Molly Marshall, a fluent Italian speaker. Social gatherings for them were held in the Houghton Hall on Sunday afternoons at which music and refreshments were provided by a group of ladies with some knowledge of Italian. Classes in English language and literature were organized in the POW camp with the approval and assistance of the English Commandant until the time came when the camp could close and the former prisoners be repatriated to Italy.

It was certainly of immense benefit to the priests and their congregations that Latin was then the sole language in which the Mass was said. Nothing stood in the way of a French priest saying mass for a Polish congregation or an Italian priest saying mass for an American congregation. Even Canon Marshall singing a High Mass with two Polish priests in support created no logistical problems or the need to book English speakers in advance. There was however an example of unity in diversity which caused some surprise, if not consternation, when it first occurred. This related to the observance of the eucharistic fast, in those days from midnight. Anyone intending to receive Holy Communion naturally aimed to do so reasonably early in the morning, i.e. before breakfast. It was therefore quite unknown for Holy Communion to be required at the Sung Masses later on a Sunday morning, and no provision was made for it in the proceedings. However, among our allies, American servicemen engaged in overnight flying duties had been given a dispensation from the eucharistic fast while in war theatres (such as Britain) and even our Italian enemies had been given a general dispensation for the duration of the war. This stood uneasily alongside the strict rule which continued to apply to the civilian population in Britain and was brought to an embarrassing head when a lone American serviceman approached the altar rail one Sunday morning while the rest of the congregation remained in their seats. The relaxations of the rules for eucharistic fasting would not be introduced until the late 1950s.

## Enemy Action

The effect of enemy activity in the air over Cambridge cannot be belittled, because lives were lost and some serious damage was caused. It was, however, Cambridge's extreme good fortune to escape from enemy air attacks far more lightly than other towns and cities. Even taking for comparison such similar-sized towns in East Anglia as Great Yarmouth Norwich and Lowestoft, all three suffered roughly ten times as many raids and ten times the tonnage of bombs inflicted on Cambridge, with Ipswich and Chelmsford not much far behind in this league table of suffering and destruction. This is no place to discuss the relative merits of the theories that there was an unspoken bargain that Cambridge would not be bombed so long as Heidelberg was spared, or simply that Cambridge was hard to find among the surrounding miles of arable farmland.

Bombing attacks on Cambridge, along with the rest of Britain, started during the second phase of the Battle of Britain. Daylight raids were changed to less risky night-time sorties, and so began the Blitz. In the first of these raids on Cambridge, on the night of 23–24 September 1940, bombs were dropped on the Fenner's side of Hills Road between Gonville Place and Tenison Road, supposedly falling short of their intended target at the railway station. This was a close call too for the Catholic church but, 'when a few bombs did considerable damage in the neighbourhood and a large number of windows on either side of the church were shattered its beautiful glass was unharmed'.

Three minor raids occurred in the southern outskirts of Cambridge on 15–16 October, 21 October and 8 November but nothing close to the church until the night of 16th January 1941 when 250 incendiary bombs were dropped in a close pattern appearing to be centred on the Hyde Park Corner junction (or possibly the prominent church spire). Some of these bombs slithered down the southern roof slope of the church causing some impact damage but not any fire. The main destruction was caused to the hall of the Perse School, then located on the opposite side of Hills Road; the fire took hold and the fire services found the blaze impossible to extinguish. By next morning schoolboys on their way to the rival Cambridge Grammar School had a grand-stand view from the top of a double deck bus as the timbered roof of the hall collapsed. The other casualty of this fire-bombing was Flinders' electrical wholesale store at 91 Regent St, next to The Prince Regent. Opinion seems to favour the theory that this raid too was intended for the railway installations little more than half a mile away.

> We must thank God that twice our church has narrowly escaped damage from blitzes. On the more recent occasion when our neighbours of the Perse School – to whom we offer all sympathy – suffered so badly, an incendiary bomb struck the roof of the church and blazed up but fizzled out innocuously. May we be protected to the end. At the same time if we do have to suffer as others have done let us be ready to bear it bravely as part of the cost of victory over the evil enemy we are fighting.

Further raids on 30 January and 15 February 1941 caused damage respectively to the railway and to a more distant area near to the present-day St Philip Howard Church in Cherry Hinton Road. The real trial for the Church and its congregation came on the night of

24 February (Shrove Tuesday) 1941 when German bombers flew in very low at intervals making a concentrated attack on the section of Hills Road between the church and the war memorial, leaving ten dead, mainly at The Globe and Bull's Dairy opposite, and the whole strip terribly battered. Again one can only assume that the intended target had been the railway sidings where, under cover of darkness, an important consignment of tanks was being unloaded that night. The extreme precision of this attack, even though rather off-target, has fuelled rumours and suspicions ever since that some assistance was given to the bombers from the ground, and the episode has come to be linked with the notorious German agent Jan Ter Braak who is known to have been operating in Cambridge at that time, before ending his life in an air raid shelter on Christ's Pieces on 1 April 1941. At 11 p.m. on 24 February a 50 kg high-explosive bomb, the smallest then in use on bombing raids, exploded on the roof of the sacristy. The explosion was sufficient to blow a hole six feet in diameter in the roof and a hole of similar size in the wall of the Sacred Heart Chapel, bringing down masonry from its groined ceiling and from the organ loft and elsewhere. All the windows of the apse, at the rear of the sanctuary, were blown out and most other windows round the church were damaged to a greater or lesser extent. The roof of the rectory was damaged and a large number of its windows blown out. What followed is best left to Canon Marshall's own words:

> We who have learned to love our beautiful church were deeply grieved to see it in its dilapidated condition, so many windows showing nothing more than scraps of coloured glass hanging on to twisted bits of lead, lumps of broken masonry and general debris strewn over the sanctuary, dust and broken glass everywhere.
>
> The note was set first thing in the morning after the calamity when people all unsuspecting arrived for early Mass. Amongst them were the Sisters of Hope. At once nuns and others armed themselves with brooms and dustpans and the like and cleared up in the Holy Souls Chapel for Mass. And the usual Masses were celebrated. Later in the morning a whole army of people commissioned themselves to clean things up and deal so far as they could with the disorder. Some were friends we knew and others were friends we did not know. They penetrated unasked into the Rectory and in an astonishing short time what seemed a hopeless mess of broken glass had been largely disposed of.
>
> The curates rigged up a temporary altar and a makeshift sanctuary all of a quite pleasing effect in front of the communion rail. And the services of the Church went on weekday and Sunday with only very slight curtailment.
>
> The weather was bitterly cold all the time that we were without windows or substitutes for them and it was no use attempting to heat the

church. But people just wrapped themselves up and endured it. A suggestion on the first Sunday morning that we should not have a sung Mass was indignantly rejected by the choir as savouring of defeatism.

Since then the builders have been occupied with "first aid" repairs and by Holy Week all was in reasonable order. On Maundy Thursday the organ which had been silenced because of injury to the electric power plant was enabled to burst forth with more than usual dramatic effect for the Gloria in Excelsis* and on Easter Sunday morning (13th April) the sanctuary in spite of the blocked-up window spaces above presented its wonted festal appearance.

*(thanks to the organist Mr Frederick Apthorpe)

Molly Marshall has provided a reminiscence of this event:

> Whenever the alert sounded at night Canon Marshall would get up, put on his steel helmet and walk the streets of Cambridge with his dog Billy, hoping to be on hand if any of his parishioners suffered in an air raid. It was fortunate for him that he was out on the streets when the church was hit by the bomb on Shrove Tuesday 1941. Judging from the blast damage and the amount of shattered glass in his bedroom it is doubtful if he would have survived had he been there. He went straight round to the Convent to see if all was well with the sisters and their boarders. Billy the dog was gun shy and took badly to air raids, it disappeared through the front door of the Convent and refused to come out, having to be retrieved next day. Canon Marshall had no idea at the time of the amount of damage to the church because no lights could be turned on, and he had to wait until daylight to see what had happened. Once all the church windows had been boarded up that put an end to any need for blackout precautions; inevitably the lights had to be put on whenever the church was in use.

No permanent repairs could be attempted until the war was over, then after long drawn-out negotiations between the War Damage Commission and Canon Marshall's successor, Canon Stokes, all the damage was made good, most of the stained glass windows being replaced to the original designs by the original makers. Those windows repaired with obscured tinted glass in diamond pattern still show where stained glass was lost but some additional daylight gained.

## Fire-watching

One important lesson learned during the Blitz and quickly put into effect was that incendiary bombs, if tackled swiftly enough, could be stopped from setting fire to buildings as had happened so frequently in the early stages of the bombing. A bucketful of sand was often sufficient to extinguish a 1 kg incendiary bomb, which was more akin to a power-ful firework and had no high explosive content. Individuals watching in every building could see to this, with little danger to themselves, far sooner than the hard-pressed fire services. From 7 February 1941 Cambridge was declared a compulsory area for fire-watching, and all business and private premises were required to provide fire-watchers. Inevitably the Catholic church, rectory and school were brought into the scheme.

> I must make acknowledgement to our fire-watchers. Under the leader-ship of Father Phillips a goodly company have been most faithful in keeping up a regular attendance night by night. We all owe them deep gratitude. I shall be glad if some more volunteers can be found. If raids are more serious again we ought to have a larger number on duty each night. The protection of our church is surely a war service that those who can will be glad to give (August 1941).

Sister Ursula, IBVM was a student during the war years, enrolled at Bedford College, a part of the University of London, which had been evacuated to Cambridge. She joined a student fire-watching rota, the members of which were paid 1s. 3d. per night (6p in decimal currency) to stay in one of the public buildings for which fire-watch-ing cover was required, including churches, schools, the Fitzwilliam Museum and the Observatory. Their duty was to be up and dressed either from midnight to 3 a.m. or 3 a.m. to 6 a.m. and they were equipped with stirrup pumps and buckets to tackle incendiary bombs. When fire-watching at the Catholic church or school they would sleep on straw mattresses in the church basement or in the Houghton Hall at the school. A priest from the rectory would make a point of visit-ing them before they settled down for the night. These visits were much appreciated, especially by students of other denominations. Luckily the members of the student rota never had to tackle an incen-diary bomb while the fire-watching requirement lasted; any incendiary bombs dropped on Cambridge during that time fell on other buildings.

Although Cambridge was not to be free from further air raids until the autumn of 1942, and none of these put the church at risk, no-one could be sure of this at the time, and the devoted vigil of the fire-watch-ers continued night by night until the scheme started to be phased out in September 1944.

# The Sword of the Spirit

In a broadcast on 10 December 1939 which attracted much public attention, Cardinal Hinsley spoke of his conviction that 'Britain has engaged in this war in the main for the defence of the things of the spirit', and urged his listeners, in the words of St Paul, to 'take with you the helmet of salvation, and the sword of the Spirit (which is the word of God)' (Eph. 6.17). The call of the Nation's leaders to arms had been echoed by this call, addressed to all who held Christian values dear, to engage in a spiritual struggle against the forces of evil and tyranny. Even without encouragement of this kind, the Catholics of Cambridge responded readily whenever acts of prayer and devotion were called for as part of a spiritual 'war effort'. The first of these calls, for a Day of National Intercession, was made by HM the King for Thursday, 23 May 1940, soon after the phoney war had been ended by the German invasion of France and the Low Countries, when an evacuation from Dunkirk appeared imminent. At the Cambridge church this coincided with the celebration of the feast of Corpus Christi, marked by a procession along Lensfield Road, Panton Street and Union Road (Pl. 17), 'the first Corpus Christi procession in the streets of Cambridge since the processions of Corpus Christi College 400 years ago', wrote Canon Marshall.

On each anniversary of the outbreak of the war, between 1940 and 1944, the King called for further Days of National Intercession, marked at the church by special Masses and other devotions; on Tuesday, 3 September 1940, for example, 'the Catholics of Cambridge once again did make a splendid response. Again there was a large communion; all the Masses were crowded; you filled the Church for a "Holy Hour" in the afternoon; you did it again for the evening service.' The following year the Day of National Intercession was moved to the nearest Sunday, 7 September, possibly to avoid disruption to the war effort on a working day, but in 1942 and 1943 it was moved back to the weekdays on which 3 September fell, Thursday and Friday respectively. On both occasions early Masses were put at the times appropriate to a holiday of obligation, with a Holy Hour in the evening. By 1944 all was well again as 3 September fell on a Sunday. 'This gave the opportunity for many more to share in the National Intercession which once again the King happily called for. And you came in very good numbers to pray before the Blessed Sacrament exposed upon the altar during the afternoon.'

By early 1945, with the end of the war in sight, but troubled by the plans of the 'Big Three' (i.e. USA, Great Britain and USSR, or Roosevelt, Churchill and Stalin) emerging from the Yalta Conference, the Catholic Hierarchy directed that in every parish church a weekday Benediction should be offered to secure a peace founded on the principles of justice and charity. 'The plans do not offer much reassurance of either justice or charity being recognised as basic principles. ... It is to be hoped that everyone who can will make an effort to attend these Benedictions. The situation is very grave.' Fifty or more years later one can only admire Canon Marshall's foresight, and his outspokenness while hostilities were still in progress. It was Canon Marshall's wider vision, too, which prompted him to invite to the rectory servicemen returning to the parish from overseas theatres to tell him about their exploits and the conditions they had seen.

When VE Day came, on 8 May 1945:

> The Catholics of Cambridge lost no time in coming to offer their thanks. The Church on Tuesday, May 8th, from morning Mass till evening saw numbers of you on your knees throughout the day. The congregation for the Te Deum resembled a midnight Mass crowd.
>
> Again on 'Thanksgiving Sunday' your piety was evident throughout the day. The early Masses saw large numbers of communicants. The Votive High Mass of Thanksgiving saw many standing for want of seats. Adorers were watching in good numbers during the hours of exposition. And another big crowd came to sing a second Te Deum in the evening.

In Cambridge, as in the rest of East Anglia, the war could only be regarded as truly ended with victory over Japan and the liberation of the men of the 18th (East Anglian) Division from captivity in the Far East. These joyful tidings came on Wednesday, 15 August 1945, the Feast of the Assumption and all the more reason to make a public holiday memorable. The Church was once more crowded with parishioners, as it was too on the following Sunday, 19 August, a National Day of Thanksgiving.

More than fifty years on, members of the present congregation continue to pray, as their predecessors did, for justice, peace and charity. The Second World War may have rearranged some of the factors giving rise to strife but from it no long-term solution to the sufferings and conflicts in the world had emerged.

# The Night Chimes of the Catholic Clock

From 'Letters to the Editor'
*Cambridge Daily News*
10 August 1940

Sir, – Last Saturday you kindly published a letter from me concerning the protest made by a few people to the Mayor against what were described as the "thunderous tunes" of the chimes of the clock of the Catholic Church. It was urged that the "unnecessary noise" during the night was seriously disturbing the neighbourhood. In order to test how extensive the discomfort might be I visited all who had views about the chimes to let me know how they felt about them.

Your readers may be interested to know the result. Precisely four individuals have written to support the original five who wrote to complain to the Mayor. One of these lives in City Road, another in Rock Road; so a very wide area is represented in which there must be many thousand residents. And no word has come to me of any other objection.

On the other hand I have received 47 letters speaking for over 80 people, very few of them Catholics or personally known to me, in appreciation of the night chiming with a fervour that surpassed my expectation; and I have been constantly stopped in the street, often by complete strangers to me, who have expressed their hope that there would be no interference with the chiming.

Can you give me space for some quotations from the letters which come from people in big houses and little houses, from people who have lived in sound of the chimes since the bells were erected and from others who have only come here in the last months, from people living all round about and nearer to the bells than anyone of the objectors, from good sleepers and bad sleepers, from sick people and old people and chronic invalids.

Here are a few of the remarks:

"I appreciate the chiming of the hour from a holy place during the night."

"I am a bad sleeper and not strong and I just love to hear the chimes at night."

"In the silence of the night, when unable to sleep, the sweet sounds have brought comfort and joy."

A lady of 84, who has lived very near the clock since it was erected, says "It is a comfort when lying awake at night."

The chimes in the night are described by others as "friendly," "the one normal thing in an otherwise mad world," "almost the only pre-war music left us," "most beautiful," "in illness comforting and in health cheery."

Others say how they missed them when for a short time they were stopped at the beginning of the war.

Several recommend the few who suffer from the chimes to plug their ears. – Yours etc.,

J.BERNARD MARSHALL
Catholic Rectory, August 9th.

# Chapter 16

# The Clock Winder's Tale

*Tony Brotchie*

By 1941, owing to the number of able-bodied parishioners involved in war work or away from Cambridge on military service, younger members of the parish had to undertake duties previously the responsibility of their elders. So it was that Canon Marshall approached Tony Brotchie, then a strong healthy lad of seventeen, awaiting call-up for military service and just starting his career in the Fire Service. The canon needed a replacement winder for the church clock, a Cambridge landmark prominently placed on the Hyde Park Corner junction of Hills Road and Lensfield Road. The clock and its chimes were weight-driven with a 24-hour power reserve and at that time required manual winding every day. Tony accepted this duty, though it was clear that his other responsibilities meant that he might not be able to attend to the clock at the same time each day.

It proved to be a rewarding but exhausting experience. I was briefly shown how to wind up the huge weights which operated the chimes and the clock itself. The problem was that the chimes lasted only twenty-four hours before they had to be rewound. I am happy to relate that only on a few occasions did disaster overtake my efforts. If the chimes ran down, the bells just did not ring until I started to rewind the weights. Then the bells started to catch up on each quarter of an hour that had been missed. Not only did the citizens of Cambridge complain about the missing chimes, they went berserk when on one occasion there was a continuous ringing of bells (the national warning that the Germans had landed). Most people took to their shelters. There was a clamp to stop the problem occurring but I had forgotten to apply this, which resulted in the clergy and three policemen climbing up the tower. I had visions of spending the duration of the war in the cells, but got away with a telling-off.

1  St Benet's church, Cambridge, showing the pre-Conquest
west tower.

2a St Michael's church, Cambridge, exterior of the chantry chapel of Hervey de Stanton.

2b Corpus Christi College, Cambridge, the gallery.

3a    Master's lodge and chapel, Sidney Sussex College.

3b    The Huddleston miniature chalice and paten, *c*. 1660.

4a    The chapel, Sawston Hall.

4b    Sawston Hall, a drawing by R. Relhan.

5a    Canon Thomas Quinlivan (1816–1885).

5b    Canon Christopher Scott (1838–1922).

6a    The visit of Ugandan dignitaries to Cambridge, 7 June 1914.

6b    The funeral of Canon Scott, February 1922.

7a    Mrs Yolande Marie Louise Lyne-Stephens (1813–1894).

7b    Mrs Lyne-Stephens, shown in her earlier career as the ballet
dancer Pauline Duvernay.

8   A 'War Requiem' held on 5 November 1916.

9b   Cardinal Bourne, Archbishop of Westminster, arriving at the west door for the inauguration of the Catholic Bible Congress, Saturday 16 July 1921.

9a   Catholic Bible Congress Committee, 1921.

10a    Baron Anatole von Hügel (1854–1928).

10b    John William Edward Conybeare, (1843–1931).

11a    Robert Hugh Benson (1871–1914).

11b    Canon James Bernard Marshall (1879–1946).

12a    Men's Retreat, Spring 1937, given by Fr Cyril Martindale, SJ.

12b    Corpus Christi Procession, Sawston Hall, *c.* 1937.

13a    A wartime wedding: Corporal Gene Mazzini USAAF to Miss
       Vera Kester, 2 June 1945, Canon Marshall officiating.

13b    Canon Stokes with St Andrew's School first Holy Communion
       group, Corpus Christi, Thursday 16 June 1949.

14a    Canon Edmund Harold Stokes (1888–1961).

14b    Canon Diamond with first Holy Communion group,
30 April 1967.

15a    Passion tableau in St Laurence's church, Chesterton,
Good Friday, 1951.

15b    Opening of the new church of St Laurence, Milton Road,
24 August 1958.

16　Enclosure of the Carmelite convent at Waterbeach, 14 September 1937.

17　Corpus Christi procession, Lensfield Road, Cambridge, 23 May 1940.

18a   Margaret Plumb in Paston
House uniform, 1943.

18b   Fr Gilbey opening
St Laurence's fete, Saturday,
19 June 1954.

18c   Sports Day, St Mary's
School, 28 June 1951.

18d   St. Laurence's May
procession, 1954.

19a    The interior of St Andrew's church, Union Road.

19b    Dismantling the redundant St Andrew's church, 1902.

20a　The sanctuary, Our Lady and the English Martyrs, April 1954.

20b　'The Canon's playpen'.

21a   St Jerome and the
Lion. A carving on the pulpit
by Ralph Hedley of
Newcastle.

21b   Display of roof bosses in Rattee and Kett's workshop prior to
installation.

22a    Ancient statue of the Virgin
and Child.

22b    South aisle window,
showing St John Fisher
receiving the
deed of foundation of
St John's College from
Lady Margaret Beaufort.

23    Figure of St Andrew crucified.

24   The Abbott & Smith organ.

25    The opening of the chapel at St Edmund's House,
16 October 1916.

26a   Fr Sebastian Bullough OP.

26b   St Michael's Priory, Cambridge, autumn 1939.

27a    Altar of the lower chapel, Blackfriars, May 1939.

27b    Mass in the Dominican rite celebrated by Fr Thomas Gilby in
the upper chapel, Michaelmas 1962.

28b   The girls and mixed infants of the Union Road School, unknown date (1890s).

28a   The boys of the Union Road School, unknown date (1890s).

29   The Union Road School (St Andrew's), completed 1936.

30a   St Bede's School, laying the foundation stone, 26 July 1961.

30b   St Bede's School: a technical drawing class in progress.

31a    The chapel,
St Mary's Convent
School.

31b   Senior class room,
St Mary's Convent
School.

31c    Junior class
room, St Mary's
Convent School.

31d    A bedroom,
St Mary's Convent
School.

32a    17th Cambridge (Catholic) Scout Troop: Holy Year Pilgrimage
to Rome, 1925.

32b    16th Cambridge Girl Guides 1921.

The fact that there were no lights in the tower caused another incident when I used a torch to wind the mechanism. Someone must have thought that 'those Catholics' were signalling to the enemy, because I was investigated by some men in long, black mackintosh-type coats – MI5 no doubt. After this I had to do the job in the dark or during daylight.

Because of security and fire precautions, it was necessary to have a central point for the keeping of the various keys of the church and the rectory. I had to collect the keys from Canon Marshall's study and return them after use. Well, one day I left the keys in the door in the porch and proceeded to the tower. Someone saw the keys, locked the door and returned them to the canon. When I came back down the spiral staircase I was locked in. What happened next was to give a very devout lady parishioner a nasty shock. At first-floor level in the tower is the bell-ringers' chamber which is open to the interior of the church and I stood there hoping that someone would come to my aid. I called down to her just as she had blessed herself with holy water and the result was dramatic. 'Excuse me, could you tell someone that I am locked in?', I said. She looked up to heaven but in my direction, blessed herself and disappeared. I escaped by climbing down a broken bell-rope. Next time you are in the church have a look at the bell-ringers' chamber to appreciate the effect I had on that good lady.

Many other things happened to me and the chimes, which sound the music of the Easter Alleluia. The church suffered bomb damage on Shrove Tuesday 1941 but the clock was not affected. My duties continued until my call-up papers arrived and I was to serve the rest of the war in the Royal Signals.

# Chapter 17

# Parish Priests, 1946–1968

*Christopher Jackson*

## Canon Edmund Harold Stokes, 1946–1961

Canon Stokes (Pl. 14a) was appointed parish priest of Our Lady and the English Martyrs in 1946, following the short-lived appointment of Fr Guy Pritchard. Fr Pritchard was intended to be the replacement for the elderly and ailing Canon Marshall who had been transferred to lighter duties at Ely, but his own health failed as a result of his experiences in the Japanese prisoner-of-war camps from which he had only recently been released. His replacement, Canon Stokes, was then aged fifty-eight and he served in Cambridge for the next fifteen years until his death in 1961. He presided over the parish during the years of post-war reconstruction and economic recovery which were reflected in the fortunes and expansion of the parish.

Edmund Harold Stokes was born in New Chesterton, Cambridge on 29 June 1888 into an Anglican family, his father being a Canon of Ely Cathedral and a Diocesan Inspector of Schools. He was educated at Wisbech Grammar School (1898–1905) and in Leeds, and at first he worked for the Great Northern Railway Company in Doncaster. He converted to Catholicism in 1908 and after training for the priesthood was ordained at Northampton Cathedral by Bishop Cary-Elwes on 13 July 1924.

The newly-ordained Fr Stokes served at St John's church in Norwich (the present-day cathedral) for two years before being appointed parish priest of King's Lynn in 1926, and he remained there for the next twenty years. During that time he was appointed Rural Dean of King's Lynn in 1938, Canon of the Cathedral Chapter of Northampton in 1945 and became a member of the Diocesan Finance Board.

Canon Stokes arrived in Cambridge to find a parish church sorely in need of repair and cleaning after the air raid damage in 1941 but with only temporary patching and most windows still boarded up. Nothing else had been attempted while wartime conditions and emergency restrictions lasted. It is to his enduring credit, and thanks to his prolonged negotiations with the War Damage Commission, that the church was restored to its pre-war state, damaged stained glass replaced and the organ cleaned and rebuilt. Even before this, Canon Stokes saw to it, as a matter of first priority, that the present heating system was installed in the church, to the lasting gratitude of his parishioners.

Increasing numbers of Catholics, in the country districts as well as in Cambridge itself, led to the birth of two daughter parishes out of the main Cambridge parish during Canon Stokes's time there, both in the year 1958. One of these was St Laurence's, in Cambridge, and the other was Our Lady of Lourdes, at Sawston. That part of the parish lying on the Chesterton side of the River Cam, including Canon Stokes's own birthplace, was allocated to St Laurence's parish. The inauguration of Our Lady of Lourdes parish at Sawston had some sentimental as well as historical significance. It marked the conclusion of a century of dependence on the Cambridge mission but also recalled the earlier times when the chaplains at Sawston Hall had, by serving the few Catholics in Cambridge, provided the first stepping stone towards a restored Catholic presence there. At the same time Sawston parish took over responsibility for the Catholics in many of the rural parishes in southern Cambridgeshire and with them the scattered Mass centres previously served from Our Lady and the English Martyrs.

Many parish and other Catholic organizations in Cambridge benefitted from the leading part played by Canon Stokes in their affairs. These included his service as first chairman of the Board of Governors of St Mary's School from 1951 until his death and as chaplain to the Knights of St Columba in Cambridge for many years.

The culmination of Canon Stokes's ministry in Cambridge was the planning, construction and inauguration of St Bede's, the first voluntary-aided Catholic secondary school in Cambridge. With accommodation for 300 pupils from eleven upwards, this provided much-needed relief for St Andrew's (now St Alban's) School in Union Road which at that time was taking children of all ages up to school leavers of fifteen, the last school to do so in Cambridge. The joyful occasion anticipated when Bishop Leo Parker of Northampton attended to bless and lay the foundation stone at St Bede's School on 26 July 1961 was unexpectedly marred by the news of Canon Stokes's death that same day. *The Cambridge Daily News*, reporting this sad event, wrote that he would be sadly missed by his parishioners, not least by the children of St Andrew's School. It went on to mention the arrangements for a lying-in-state in the sacristy of his church on the day before a Solemn Pontifical Requiem Mass. This was sung by the Bishop at 12 noon on Monday, 31 July 1961 and was followed by a committal at the vault in the rectory grounds, Canon Stokes being the third parish priest of Our Lady and the English Martyrs to be honoured in this way, alongside Canon Scott and Canon Marshall.

The following appreciation of Canon Stokes has been compiled from the memories of parishioners. A large heavily-built man, with glasses and a deep loud voice, he found it easier to lend support and encouragement to the men's organizations in the parish (Knights of St Columba, the Men's Club, Guild of the Blessed Sacrament), than those catering for the ladies of the parish (Children of Mary, Catholic Women's League, Ladies' Needlework Guild), with whom he tended to be shy and awkward. Truly appreciative of their work as he was, many of the womenfolk of the parish never got to know him well and some could be upset by his bluntness, especially from the pulpit. Nor was it only the women who could be intimidated by long pauses during his sermons, as he waited for latecomers to find their seats. His was a regime which contrasted with the wider, more intellectual vision of Canon Marshall, with its natural affinity with the academic world of the University. Instead, he concentrated on a programme of church and rectory renovation, sound parish finances and scrupulous adherence to diocesan financial commitments. Certainly there was little if any sense of continuity with his two long-serving predecessors, little reference to them in conversation, and little preservation of records relevant to their service. He may even have felt some regret at having left his long-established post at King's Lynn for the higher profile responsibilities entrusted to him at Cambridge. To identify this contrast in no way belittles the value of Canon Stokes's service to the parish, his positive encouragement of parish social activities, and his love of children, never more apparent than when they surrounded him in the school playground. He was strongly devoted to the Latin liturgy of the Church which, like his predecessor, he followed in the closest detail. As an advocate of plainsong, he saw the church choir flourish in numbers and excellence under the expert direction of Fr Christopher Roberts, whose curacy at the church extended to the unusual term of ten years but came to an end with his appointment as first parish priest at Sawston. Perhaps it was just as well that, as the last parish priest before the Second Vatican Council, Canon Stokes was never faced with the liturgical and vernacular changes which followed. His was the characteristically strong faith of a convert, and it is no more critical of the man than it is of his time to say that he had little sympathy for the

Anglican position or for ecumenical contacts with other denominations.

'Be like a lion in the pulpit but a lamb in the confessional' was Canon Stokes's exhortation both to himself and his curates.

## Canon Frank Diamond, 1961–1968

At the time of Canon Stokes's death in July 1961, Fr Harry Wace was serving as senior curate at the church of Our Lady and the English Martyrs. He had been there since 1959 and, with nearly three years experience of the parish behind him, Fr Wace was asked by Bishop Leo Parker to stay in charge until a permanent replacement could be found. By the late autumn of 1961 the choice had been made, and Canon Frank Diamond, then parish priest at Princes Risborough, Buckinghamshire, was appointed to succeed Canon Stokes. His arrival in Cambridge was something of a unique reappearance, seeing that Frank Diamond had been ordained in the Cambridge church, and by Bishop Parker too. No other parish priest before or since has been able to claim that connection through the circumstance of his ordination.

Frank Diamond (Pl. 14b) was born in Swindon on 18 February 1910, one of four brothers of whom two were to become priests. The Diamond family moved to Ipswich, where their house backed on to the grounds of the Convent of the Sisters of Jesus and Mary. There all four boys received their early education, Frank being remembered by a contemporary as a 'quiet, shy little boy'. A path in the convent garden is still called 'the Diamond Walk'. For his secondary education, Frank attended the Municipal Secondary School at Ipswich, where he proved to be something of a model pupil, passing his Higher School Certificate with flying colours, much to the satisfaction of his French master Dr W. M. Kerby (father of Fr Raymond Kerby).

After leaving school, and aiming for a career in banking, Frank joined Lloyds Bank in Ipswich. He moved from there to the Lloyds Head Office in the City, where he became part of the 'bowler and brolly' brigade during the 1930s. It was here that Frank Diamond's vocation for the priesthood became apparent and, as a 'late vocation' he was sent for training to the Beda College, which had been transferred during the Second World War from Rome to Upholland. He was ordained at the church of Our Lady and the English Martyrs on 20 March 1943, something of a pioneering occasion, as Canon Marshall pointed out in the *Cambridge Catholic Magazine* (May 1943):

The occasion that had brought the Bishop to Cambridge was the ordination which he had arranged to hold here on the Ember Saturday of Lent. His Lordship thinks it is well that members of his flock in different parts of the diocese should have the opportunity of assisting at the liturgy of the making of priests. He feels that it will help them to value the priesthood and increase their devotion to the Mass. He hopes also that it will stimulate vocations to the priesthood amongst our boys. And surely the Bishop is right. At all events a large number of people assisted at the long ceremony on Saturday, March 20th, and many were the expressions of edification to be heard afterwards.

There were eight priests ordained, also one deacon and two sub-deacons. Two of the priests were for this diocese, Father Diamond and Father Throckmorton; also Mr. Fagan the deacon. My curates put in a lot of hard work in making the extensive preparations necessary for the elaborate ritual. Everything on the day went off very well. The proper was admirably sung by a choir of priests and Mr. Mills. Boys newly trained for the choir by Miss Whatmough of Paston House School also showed up well in the little opportunity they had.

Like his predecessor Canon Stokes, Frank Diamond served first at St John's, Norwich, where he stayed for seven years, followed by his appointment as parish priest at St Teresa's, Princes Risborough (1950–1961). This was a quiet country parish in the heart of the Chilterns, and he described his time there as very much like Heaven. This may not have been the best preparation for the work required of a parish priest in the large and busy Cambridge parish, but what seems to have stood him in good stead was his earlier experience of banking, especially from his time spent in a large head office in the City. Financial aspects aside, Frank Diamond had clearly learned the need for good communications, and of the advantages to be gained from handling people with tact and diplomacy.

It is possible that Frank Diamond's greatest initial challenge was the need to come to terms with the somewhat disparate group of curates serving at the Cambridge rectory and to give them the leadership which had not so far been required of him during his priestly career. Fr Harry Wace conceded, with a degree of humour, that he might have been the cause of some difficulty through his three years prior experience of the Cambridge parish, including his brief spell at the helm, perhaps giving the new parish priest the impression that he 'knew it all'. Fr Kerby, soon to arrive at the rectory and well known for his academic past, even for a degree of otherworldliness, would have conveyed a different, though entirely commendable, message. Fr Berrell, with long service in a religious order behind him, may have seen himself as somewhat above the direction of a newcomer manifestly close to him in years. Good communicator though he was, Frank Diamond's natural shyness meant that his best form of communication was the written word. Mealtimes still took place in the rectory dining room (thanks to Miss Gunns the house-keeper, one of Canon Stokes's converts) and it was here that Canon Diamond handed out written messages to his curates, whether addressed specifically to an individual or to all of them collectively. Even with this degree of reserve, Frank Diamond showed a characteristic care for good relations by taking his curates out for an occasional lunch together, typically to the Bridge Hotel at Clayhithe.

Change soon manifested itself in the Cambridge parish. For the first time weekly newsletters were duplicated and distributed to the congregation, and their parish priest stationed himself at the back of the church after Mass as a point of contact with his parishioners. One old-time practice to be abandoned was the placing of white cloths at the altar rail, beneath which the kneeling communicants would place their hands receptively while Communion was distributed. The Catholic Marriage Advisory Council made its first, quite necessary, appearance in Cambridge. As Fr Kerby remarked later, 'This was all very hush hush. I was deemed to be too junior to be involved.'

Major changes were to come, too, in the aftermath of Vatican II. It fell to Frank Diamond to introduce all the innovative concepts of the Council, including the changes in the liturgy from Latin to English, to the English Martyrs parish. Much had to be absorbed by their parish priest before he could venture to introduce such matters to his flock. Fr Kerby, freshly arrived in 1962 from his seminary training at the Beda College in Rome, remembers having to explain the meaning of the vogue expression 'aggiornomento' (i.e. 'bringing up to date') to his parish priest, but that 'he grasped it in a flash'. Although he personally welcomed these modernizing trends, Frank Diamond's caring nature and gentle approach to his flock ensured that nothing was done without the fullest explanation and only when he was satisfied that he was carrying the congregation, or at least a majority of them, with him. It was noteworthy, too, that the utmost care was taken to ensure that the new-style liturgy was introduced meticulously and without loss of dignity. Inevitably some reactions to these changes were mixed, and Fr Wace recalls that his own choice of a traditionalist to lead the Latin choir could not have anticipated the degree of strain which resulted later on, once the liturgical changes had made their appearance.

Beyond the confines of his parish, Canon Diamond was active in his support of the Diocesan Pilgrimages to Walsingham, but this commitment or enthusiasm did not extend to any personal involvement with pilgrimages to Lourdes. On the other hand, he liked nothing better than being driven by his long-standing friend and diocesan contemporary, Canon McBride, on holiday trips to Rome most summers and, nearer to home, to visit office equipment exhibitions for fresh ideas, or the annual Motor Shows at Earls Court, as an enthusiastic follower of technical advances.

In his pastoral work, Canon Diamond refused to let his shyness or reserve get in the way of his visiting, and, in Fr Wace's words, 'he would do his stuff at the Hospital' (then Old Addenbrooke's in Trumpington Street). There was much more openness with ecumenical contacts than previously, and consequently the Week of Prayer for Christian Unity took a greater hold in the parish. The first of these ecumenical events, held in Cambridge in 1963, was opened with a meeting, attended by Frank Diamond and his three curates. Bishop Charles Grant and the Anglican and Methodist observers at Vatican II were the platform speakers. The deliberations of the Council were still highly confidential and Fr Kerby recalls that all three speakers only succeeded in adding suspense to the meeting by trying not to divulge what had been said. 'It was a very moving moment', added Fr Kerby, 'when we all said the Our Father together. Fancy praying together with non-Catholics! How times have changed!'

At that time it was still not possible for Catholics to attend even the service of Nine Lessons and Carols at King's College Chapel without permission, because prayers and readings were included as well as the carols.

Canon Diamond showed his influence, too, in the field of education. Parents sending their children to non-Catholic schools were no longer made to feel like outcasts. As Chairman of the Governors of St Bede's School, Canon Diamond established a successful rapport with the first Head, George Kent, which did much to assist the progress of the school in its early years. This explains why, according to George Kent, the School's sixteen-plus youth football team was named 'The Diamonds' after his departure from Cambridge.

In 1968, at the age of fifty-eight, Canon Diamond took leave of Cambridge for the next stage of his priestly career, being appointed Administrator of Northampton Cathedral and Vicar General of the Diocese. He served in these roles, and subsequently as Diocesan Administrator, elder statesman and father figure of the Northampton Diocese until ill-health overtook him, shortly before his death on 24 October 1992 at the age of eighty-two. Northampton's gain was Cambridge's loss, but sufficient testimony of his impact still survives, particularly in the recollections of Fr Harry Wace: 'He was a good man, and I learned a lot from him; how to run a parish, how to be caring and gentle; he listened to his curates and his congregation; he had humility, tact and a studied care of people.'

# Chapter 18

# Modern Times, 1960–1990

*Mgr Anthony Rogers*

## Canon Frank Diamond, 1962–1968

The death of Canon Edmund Stokes in 1961 marked the end of an era in more ways than one. The Second Vatican Council opened shortly after his death, and it would be the task of his successor, Canon Frank Diamond, to help people understand and implement the changes, the most obvious of which were in the field of liturgy. Frank Diamond had been parish priest of Princes Risborough before coming to Cambridge. After a career in banking he was a 'late vocation' and studied at the Beda College in Rome. A gentleman to his fingertips, somewhat reserved in manner, it was said by some that he even kept secrets from himself. Small talk did not come easily, yet in serious matters he was a wise, patient and gentle counsellor. He was only at English Martyrs for six years, and during that time the liturgical changes were neither completed nor settled. Those few years were characterized by ever-changing texts and responses. Hasty and well-meant efforts to translate from the Latin were often quite unsatisfactory, and a kind of weariness came over people when successive First Sundays of Advent marked yet another change. It is an era that is probably best forgotten. English Martyrs parish was fortunate enough to have a parish priest of tact and diplomacy who could steer the parishioners calmly through quite stormy waters. But there were yet stormier times ahead in a parish which, not surprisingly, had more than its fair share of articulate and well educated laity.

## Canon Paul Taylor, 1968–1980

The late Canon Paul Taylor became parish priest at Our Lady and the English Martyrs in 1968, following Frank Diamond's appointment as administrator of Northampton Cathedral. After ten years as assistant priest at Northampton Cathedral and thirteen as parish priest of All Souls, Peterborough, Paul Taylor returned to a city he had known well as a student in the 1930s. He read for the Natural Sciences Tripos at St John's College. He was proud of the fact that he was the first of many vocations to emerge from Fisher House during Alfred Gilbey's 100-term incumbency. Paul Taylor studied for the priesthood in Fribourg, Switzerland, but because of the war, he was unable to leave the country and so remained to complete his Doctorate in Divinity. As a man of considerable intellect, with a profound love of the Church and understanding of its mission, he was anxious to implement the liturgical changes that followed the Second Vatican Council.

It was hardly surprising that the liturgical changes following the end of the Council should have quite serious repercussions at Our Lady and the English Martyrs. There was a strong musical tradition with a robed choir of men and boys that flourished in the 1950s under the enthusiastic and skilled encouragement of assistant priests, of whom Fr Chris Roberts is the best remembered.

As well as providing music for the High Mass in the morning, the choir would be back again for Vespers, sermon and Benediction at 6.30 p.m. The impressive and spacious sanctuary with its rows of choir stalls was something of a rarity in a Catholic church, at least in this part of England. Although the Divine Office was sung in many churches in the nineteenth century, this practice was replaced by 'popular devotions' in all but a few parishes, of which English Martyrs was one.

Dr Dick Richens was choir master at the time when controversies raged in the Church about the abandonment of the Tridentine Mass of St Pius V. He was keen to preserve the Latin tongue and the sacred chant in the Church's liturgy. In 1969 he founded the Association for Latin Liturgy, which sought to promote both the traditional language and music of the Church, without demanding the retention of the 'old Mass'. He was able to be fully supportive of the *Novus Ordo*, and thus, with the help of Canon Taylor, avoided the kind of head-on collisions that characterized the life of parishes up and down the country.

Many parishes in this country retain a modicum of Latin chant, or celebrate the occasional Mass in Latin, either in the traditional rite or the new. Some of the great London churches, like the Oratory or Farm Street, maintain a fine choral tradition with the support of semi-professional choirs. But it is said that Our Lady and the English Martyrs is the only parish church in England which, week in and week out, has the unbroken tradition of a full sung Latin Mass with music provided by a voluntary choir.

If a satisfactory solution had been reached for safeguarding the sung Latin Mass, there were more serious battles to be fought over the re-ordering of the sanctuary at English Martyrs. A temporary free-standing altar had been placed towards the front of the vast sanctuary space. It was clearly an interim measure and Paul Taylor had a vision of something of a permanent nature. But the plans for the altar which was finally installed, together with a surrounding flight of steps, a space for the presiding priest's chair (referred to in its early days rather scathingly as 'the Canon's Playpen') (Pl. 20b), and a re-sited and trimmed-down pulpit which was to serve as a lectern, brought more opposition from a vociferous body of those who were unhappy with the proposals. Press coverage of the affair was quite extensive, but eventually the plans were implemented, despite a persistent resentment among a minority about the design of the new altar. Some of those who were opposed to these changes and to the failure to retain the traditional Roman rite became part of a breakaway group which began to attend Mass in a house in Blossom Street, subsequently moving to Mill Road. It was a difficult time, and though determined to see the plans through as part of a programme of authorized reform, the opposition which Paul Taylor faced and weathered took its toll on him.

But this was not only a period of controversy. It was also a time of great activity, particularly in the field of adult- and child-centred education. Acronyms ruled the day, with groups such as CRESE (Catholic Religious Education and Study Evenings) meeting in Blackfriars. Theologians and other distinguished speakers would be invited to address packed gatherings in the library, and Dominicans and diocesan priests (notably Gerard Meath, OP, Robert Pollock, OP, Paul Hypher and Anthony Foreman), together with committees of very able and proactive lay people, ensured that the intellectual life of the Cambridge parishes was well served. Catholic Family Days found a focus at the De La Salle Brothers' house on Brookside (now home to the IBVM community), providing a venue for faith, fun and friendship for families with young children.

Paul Taylor was always a man of integrity. Passionate in his love for the Church of the past, present and future, he was never afraid to defend his corner and stand by his principles. In other areas of liturgical reform he met with a greater measure of support. English Martyrs was one of the first parishes to commission special ministers of the Eucharist, and to introduce Communion under both kinds at all weekday Masses. Paul had a great gift for speaking about these developments clearly and simply in a way that enabled everyone to realize, above all, that he cared deeply about what he was doing. A woman who was very concerned about the impropriety of lay people receiving communion in the hand because only a priest's hands were consecrated, was met by a typical Taylor riposte: 'And who, may I ask, consecrated your tongue?' He was proud of his associations with the Diocese of Northampton, particularly after the East Anglia Diocese had been established on 13 March 1976 by the decree 'Quod Ecumenicum'. Paul had been a member of the Northampton Cathedral Chapter and he was delighted to accept an honorary canonry of that diocese from Bishop Charles Grant, himself a product of English Martyrs parish.

## Monsignor Anthony Philpot, 1980–1994

Paul Taylor was a wise enough man to ask for a move while he was still able to take on the demands of another, albeit smaller parish. Bishop Alan Clark appointed him to Ely where he stayed until his retirement in 1995. He was succeeded by Tony Philpot, parish priest of Newmarket, who stayed for fourteen years at English Martyrs, before returning to Ipswich, where he had been a parish priest before, and then to be the director of Palazzola – the villa of the English College, on the shores of Lake Albano, opposite Castelgandolfo. Tony Philpot will be remembered as a gentle and very gifted preacher and writer. His was not an era of liturgical controversy or innovation. Other tasks lay ahead for him in the city and the parish, with the reorganization of St Bede's School, and a major and much-needed refurbishment of the rectory. Tony adopted a professional approach to parish management, employing Janet Mancuso, first as secretary and later as parish administrator. The days of resident housekeepers were almost over. Cooks and cleaners came in, but clergy were much more used to fending for themselves, and the rectory kitchen, once forbidden territory, became a focal point for much that was going on in the house. Tony also made the rectory a place of welcome for priests of the diocese and further afield. Many of the strong international contacts were forged while he was parish priest, not least because of his particular ministry as the world-wide *responsable* for priests of the Jesus Caritas Fraternity. His role as one of the vicars-general of the diocese brought him into frequent contact with the East Anglian clergy.

St Vincent de Paul in Ditton Lane had a previous incarnation as the original church for St Laurence's parish. When the new church on Milton Road was completed in 1959, the tin tabernacle was taken over the river and re-erected on Ditton Lane. For many years it was in such precarious condition that planning permission was simply renewed on an annual basis. One survey of the building suggested that, like a house of cards, a hefty push on one side wall would probably cause everything else to collapse as well. Though much loved and cared for it had a down-at-heel, tired feel and needed more than a lick of paint to remedy the situation. Tony Philpot invited Julian Limentani, the parish architect and surveyor, to come up with a design for re-ordering. The result was a dramatic and wonderful transformation. By turning everything round ninety degrees a quite different ambience for worship was created, and far from heralding the death of a community it signalled a significant revival in that community's life. Around the same time the Mass centre at St Michael's parish church in Trumpington was closed. Trumpington was by far the nearest of the 'outstations' and neither distance nor access to English Martyrs was a great problem.

This was a period in many ways of numerical decline. Baptismal, marriage and conversion figures, and Mass attendance too, had peaked in about 1962. Pundits were only too ready to lay the blame at the door of anything from Vatican II to sixties culture. But a phoenix sometimes arises from the ashes. RCIA – the Rite of Christian Initiation of Adults – was a process of liturgical and spiritual initiation into Catholic Christianity. With a strong emphasis on a 'phased' or gradual process of initiation, enquirers were welcomed in stages into the life of the parish, the diocese and the whole Church. Designed primarily for the unbaptized, it was quickly adapted for the majority of those wanting to become Catholic, who had, more often than not, been baptized in another Christian tradition. Each year since its inception at English Martyrs in the late 1980s considerable numbers have journeyed together, supported by a team of parish catechists and sponsors. Many of those who have joined the Church in recent years have become actively involved in the life of the parish, and have benefited from being part of a group seeking to discover God's way for them. In this, and in many others spheres of parish life, lay people have discovered gifts and talents given to them by God which may have been untapped or unknown for many years. They have assumed a rightful place in the life of the Church, not as clergy helpers but as members of the baptismal priesthood, each with a service to offer.

It was also during Tony Philpot's incumbency that a parish justice and peace group was established, and the great work of regular support for CAFOD undertaken by the indefatigable and dedicated Catherine Green. Her success has always lain in never missing an opportunity to bring the work of CAFOD to the forefront of any parish venture. The response over the years has been magnificent. If some ventures were starting up and growing, others were coming to the end of their natural life. The Catholic Men's Club, in Cambridge Place, off Hills Road, in existence since 1907, had been limping along with a declining membership and finally closed in the 1980s.

## Assistant Priests

Current parishioners take a high turnover of clergy for granted. It is rare nowadays for an assistant priest to be in a parish for more than three or four years, at the end of which they are likely to have pastoral charge of their own elsewhere in the diocese. But in past years the picture was very different. A man would probably not become a parish priest until he had been ordained about fifteen years or more, and so some assistants spent more time at English Martyrs than their parish priests. Anthony Foreman, for example, was in the parish for nine years, from his ordination in 1965 until his appointment to St George's, Norwich in 1974. During that period, Paul Taylor was quite seriously ill, and so Tony was at the helm for several months. Before him, Harry Wace was effectively 'regent' during Canon Stokes's last illness. These men, as much as their parish priests, left their mark and are well remembered. Through sheer force of circumstances, they were often closer to the people, working in school and hospital chaplaincies, and accessible in times of real need.

## Come Follow Me

During the sixties, seventies and eighties a number of men and women from English Martyrs parish entered religious life, and several men were ordained either as religious or diocesan priests. Frank Bullivant, Frank Shanahan and Peter Wijnekus, all members of the choir, went in different directions. Frank Bullivant, an adult convert to Catholicism, joined the Oblates of Mary Immaculate; Frank Shanahan joined the Blessed Sacrament Fathers; and Peter Wynekus, a Dutchman who had worked in Cambridge for many years, went first to St Edmund's, Ware, and then to Oscott as a student for the Northampton Diocese. When the Diocese divided, Peter was incardinated into East Anglia. David Bagstaff was the first priest to be ordained for the Diocese of East Anglia. Cambridge born and bred, he studied at Oscott, as did Tom Murray, another product of St Bede's School, who was ordained within a year of David.

Pope Paul VI had restored the permanent diaconate, a ministry open to married and unmarried men. Dr Geoff Cook from St Laurence's parish and St Edmund's College was the first to be ordained for this diocese, and no fewer than five men from English Martyrs parish were ordained to this ministry in 1989. Tony Sutton, Tony Northrop, Robert Joyce, Martin Franks and Len Matthews were, at one time, all members of the parish pastoral team.

## That They All May Be One

The Cambridge city parishes have always served local communities in the suburbs and surrounding villages. Before the establishment of St Philip Howard parish in 1978 Mass was said in eight different places within English Martyrs' parish boundary, not including convents and other religious houses. Generations of local Catholics will have grown up with 'suitcase liturgy' because one priest was quite likely to celebrate Mass in three different places on a Sunday morning and would bring everything needed for the celebration with him. The contents of a large case would be emptied in village halls, village colleges, welding institutes and the like. Many of these Mass centres had begun in the 1950s as venues for the Northampton Diocesan Travelling Mission, an almost forgotten missionary venture which functioned in rural areas. It was the brainchild of Bishop Leo Parker, who started it as an experiment in 1948. Bishop Parker appointed a priest not to a parish, but to an itinerant ministry, perhaps Catholicism's nearest equivalent to John Wesley's travelling preachers. The travelling missioner's task was to provide Mass in outlying areas of the diocese which had no church or provision for weekly Mass. In the Northampton Diocese the Travelling Mission was staffed by Fr (later Canon) Anthony Hulme and Fr Bob McCormick, and many villages within the confines of English Martyrs parish feature in its annals. Mass was celebrated for fifty-one people 'near the spot where Our Blessed Lady gave the scapular to St Simon Stock.' At Lode, there were thirteen in the congregation for Mass that was celebrated in the Gun and Hare pub.

A small van was converted for use as a sort of outdoor chapel, with provision for an altar at the back. Mass was celebrated in villages like Bottisham and Caldecote, usually on a quarterly basis. Over the years, as some of these small Catholic communities grew and came under the umbrella of the local parish, they moved to whatever premises were available, often schools or village halls. From quarterly celebrations they moved to monthly or even weekly Mass, and in some parts of the diocese eventually became parishes in their own right.

In the Cambridge area some interesting developments took place in the 1970s. Practical ecumenism was still in its infancy, but thanks to the generosity and vision of successive bishops of Ely from Ted Roberts onwards and forward-thinking incumbents and PCCs, offers were made to the Catholic communities of Linton, Trumpington, Comberton, Bottisham and Fulbourn to use the parish churches for Mass on an agreed rental basis and at an mutually acceptable time. Certain conditions were rightly attached to the use of these parish churches, the most important of which was that the Catholics could not come in and re-order the church by moving the furniture around. In no case did this prove to be a problem, and although the Trumpington Mass Centre closed some years ago, the others continue to be used in fruitful partnership with the local Anglican communities to this day.

The knock-on effect of this could never have been envisaged. Apart from Saturday evening Mass in Fulbourn, the others are all used by the Catholic community on a Sunday morning, either between two Anglican celebrations or after their morning service. This has resulted in an overlap of congregations which have gradually, over the years, through almost accidental circumstances, been brought into growing and closer relationships. To be able to use, on a regular basis, buildings which have been the focus of Christian worship for as much as 800 years has been a privilege and a joy.

Over the years Catholic priests have played their part in working together with Christians of others traditions. Fr Tony Philpot served as chairman of the Central Cambridge Council of Churches for some years. But there have been outstanding examples of Anglican clergy who have laid down foundations for a real commitment to local ecumenism, taking on board the significance of the Lund Principle which states that 'Christians should do everything together, other than what conscience prevents them from doing'. Many will remember with great affection the Venerable David Walser, Archdeacon of Ely, and one time vicar of Linton, for the real hope he inspired in the hearts and minds of those who sought to answer Christ's prayer for unity.

Bar Hill was an interesting and innovative venture. Begun in 1965, it was designed as a new village, rather than a new town. With a maximum population of some 5000 people, virtually all of whom were housed within an outer ring, Bar Hill has some light industry, shopping facilities, a pub, a primary school and a church centre. From the outset the plan was that there should be but one church centre in the village, and that all the participating churches should contribute to its cost and its upkeep. A full time minister was appointed to care for the pastoral and worshipping needs of all the major Christian denominations apart from the Catholics who would need to make separate provision for pastoral and sacramental care.

Bar Hill is an LEP – a local ecumenical project – in which all the participating churches are committed to working together in their community. The original church centre, now called the Octagon, proved inadequate for the needs of the churches, and so a larger, more flexible church centre was built, retaining the smaller Octagon building for other church uses. Bar Hill has never been a separate Catholic parish, but continues to be served by one of the priests from Our Lady and the English Martyrs.

## A Centenary Celebration

Our story concludes with great celebrations in honour of a great church. Cardinal Basil Hume came to English Martyrs to preside at the Centenary Mass in 1990. The church, which was originally provided with nave seating for about a hundred and eighty people, but a great deal of space for movement, had over the years more than doubled its seating capacity, with chairs in side aisles and transepts. What was built as something on a rather grand scale for a relatively small community, was, on occasions such as this, to prove too small for the number of worshippers present.

The acronym OLEM – only used in the last twenty years or so, to the best of my knowledge – seems to be our own affectionate way of referring to a familiar friend and landmark, no longer on the very edge of the city, but still, arguably, Cambridge's most prominent landmark from distant views of the city.

# Chapter 19

# St Laurence's Parish

*Margaret Plumb*

The parish of St Laurence's, in north Cambridge, covers the area north of the river Cam, taking in Arbury, Kings Hedges, and North Chesterton, Histon, Impington, Girton, Cottenham, Milton and Waterbeach.

In the 1920s and 30s the church of Our Lady of the Assumption and the English Martyrs was the only parish church in Cambridge. The Carmelite Convent established in Chesterton Road in 1923 served as a Mass centre for Catholics living in the Chesterton area with daily Mass at 8 a.m. and Benediction at 5 p.m. on Sundays. On some of the Greater Feasts there was Exposition until 5 p.m. Benediction. On all days visits could be made to the chapel and the Blessed Sacrament was reserved. In Holy Week there were the Holy Week services and there was also Midnight Mass at Christmas. In 1937 the nuns moved from the Chesterton Road Convent, which had become too noisy, to Waterbeach. There is still a link between the Carmelites and St Laurence's; the painting of St Laurence which presently hangs on the right-hand side of the door as you go out of the church was painted by Sister Rosario and was a copy of one she had previously painted in oils for Bishop Youens.

In 1938 a parishioner of the English Martyrs gave a cheque 'for the magnificent sum' of £250, this sum to be used, if possible in some way to establish a Mass centre in Chesterton. This money enabled the purchase of a site with frontage on to the High Street. The street frontage was occupied by cottages, the rent from which helped to pay the interest on the borrowed money. Behind these cottages was a quarter of an acre of land. It was visualized that a church, presbytery and perhaps a small school be built. As the parish of the English Martyrs still owed thousands of pounds on their school it was 'intended that a hut be erected on one corner of the property and that it would be decently equipped and provide an attractive chapel for some 140 people, and still be of service when a permanent church is eventually built'. In 1939 the then Catholic Men's Club, a hut which was first used as part of the First Eastern General Hospital during the First World War, was moved to the site in High Street, Chesterton.

The *Cambridge Catholic Magazine* for November 1939 records:

> October the 8th is the date on which in 1890 our glorious Church of Our Lady and the English Martyrs was consecrated. On this same date in this year 1939 the new Chapel at Chesterton was blessed and used for the first time. October the 8th therefore becomes a 'dies mirabilis' in this parish.

The first Mass was said by Fr Edward Watkis. This Mass Centre, called St Laurence's because of the great devotion the then Bishop, Bishop Youens of Northampton Diocese, had to the Roman deacon-martyr St Laurence, was served firstly by priests from the English Martyrs and later from Waterbeach by Fr Flannery (the chaplain at the Carmel). Sunday Mass was at 9 a.m. The hut is now situated in Ditton Lane and known as St Vincent's. Prior to this, Mass had been celebrated in a room attached to the Co-operative Stores in High Street, Chesterton. This room formerly belonged to an inn known as The Bleeding Hart.

In August 1944 the *Cambridge Catholic Magazine* recorded:

> The feast of St. Laurence was observed by a special Mass in his chapel at Chesterton. It gives me the opportunity to say something of the good work that is going on in that section of the parish under the care of Fr. Flannery. The debt on the purchase of the land and the building of the temporary Chapel has been discharged this year. Moreover, the appointments of the Chapel have been improved. These things have been at least partly made possible by the support of the people of the district. Any special mention should be made of a number of services and benefactions rendered by Mr. O'Hannan.
>
> But more important-still is the ever-growing number of mass attendances and the fine number of communions each Sunday. As things are the Chapel is all too small; certainly this is considerably accounted for by war visitors. But there is no doubt that Fr. Flannery is building up what is going to be a flourishing parish on its own account.

A number of German prisoners of war attended Midnight Mass one year and sang the carol 'Silent Night', which was remembered by all those present for years to come.

At the end of the Second World War steps were taken to create St Laurence's parish. For a time the Mass centre was served from the

English Martyrs by such priests as Fr Oates who was later to become the second parish priest of St Laurence's and Fr Lyons. The parish came into being in the autumn of 1947. The first parish priest was Fr (later Canon) Gerard Hulme. Fr Hulme had great devotion to Our Lady and every year on the second Sunday of May St Laurence's had a procession in honour of Our Lady from the church, down the High Street round Water Street and Ferry Lane back to the grounds of the church, where the May Queen crowned the statue of Our Lady (Pl. 18d). Fr Hulme left St Laurence's for Walsingham, where he was placed in charge of the shrine.

The presbytery was 1 Ferry Lane, a very old, damp house where meetings, whist drives and social evenings were held in a large room at the back. Parish meetings, dances (like the St Patrick's Night dance), and children's Christmas parties were held in the parish hall of St Andrew's Church in Chapel Street, Chesterton and, on occasions, in Overstream House or the Haymakers public house in the High Street.

As the parish grew, so it became necessary to provide a larger church and facilities for a parish hall and presbytery. In the 1950s land was purchased on Milton Road, in part due to the efforts of Paddy Harris and Fr Patrick Oates, who became parish priest in 1951. The area of land was large enough to build a church, parish hall and presbytery. On 8 March 1958 Bishop Parker of Northampton laid the foundation stone of the new church of St Laurence the Martyr to serve the parish.

The *Cambridge Daily News* reported:

> Much of the credit for the erection of the new building must go to the Rev. Father P. Oates, who since he was appointed in 1951 has worked to form the organisation which made the building possible. So far £4000 has already been contributed from the efforts of the parishioners since 1954, but there is still a long way to go before the target is reached.

Later in the same year, on 24 August 1958, the church was dedicated and blessed by the Bishop of Northampton (Pl. 15b). On this occasion the *Cambridge Daily News* reported:

> The building is one of the most modern Catholic buildings in the diocese, and is intended as a replacement for the existing building in Chesterton High Street. Father Oates told the 'C.D.N.' reporter that it will be able to accommodate about 300 people. The brick walls are constructed in the 'British traditional' style. Heating is of the under-floor electrical type and lighting is also by electricity. The interior of the building is finished in brick with plaster decorations and all the wooden fittings are constructed from cedar. Pews are of polished mahogany and the altar is made from stone.

The ultimate cost of the building cannot yet be given with any degree of certainty, but is expected to be in the region of about £18,000. Much of the money has still to be raised, but the eventual target is well on the way to being reached by way of public subscriptions and a local football pool run between the parishioners.

Up until this time the services at St Laurence's had been Mass at 8 a.m. and 11 a.m. on Sunday, with Benediction at 6.30 p.m. on Sunday and 7.30 p.m. on Friday (preceded by choir practice); daily Mass was at 8 a.m. On moving to Milton Road the times of Sunday Masses changed to 8 a.m., 9.30 a.m. and 11 a.m., with Benediction still at 6.30 p.m. on Sunday but 8 p.m. on Friday. With the advent of Evening Mass on the First Friday of the month there was Mass at 8 p.m.

Many changes have taken place over the years. Following the building of the church the next step was to build the presbytery, joined to the church, with a large entrance-way to allow access to the parish hall which was to be built at the back. The church itself was built in such a way that it could be enlarged by extending eastwards from the altar into the garden. Owing to houses having been built on land behind the church it was no longer possible to build a hall as noise from it would disturb the residents. In later years what was the original house-keeper's room was enlarged and changed into a parish room, where meetings and small social gatherings could take place. A few years after the church and presbytery were built, work was started on the parish school – St Laurence's – on land at the end of Arbury Road.

The parish is no longer the small community which took two coaches of parishioners to Walsingham in the Marian Year of 1953. The boundaries have been changed; at one time the parish extended from Ditton along the north side of Newmarket Road to Milton Road. Now the boundary extends from the river Cam along the East side of Huntingdon Road, taking in the villages of Girton, Histon, Impington, Cottenham and Waterbeach.

There have been many priests who have been attached to the parish (see Appendix 2). It has been served by Fr Cunningham and Fr Waligo from Uganda, both of whom were at the time students at St Edmund's House. Fr Christopher Cunningham was choirmaster and helped the parish in many ways, especially during the time of Fr Brady's illness, and similarly, Fr Waligo 'lived in' to assist Fr Russ while Fr Drury was on a course in Dublin.

St Laurence's can be proud of the fact that it has had the privilege of producing several young men who have entered the priesthood, all of whom were former altar boys: Fathers Damien Walne, now in the Northampton Diocese, Peter Brown (a convert), parish priest at

Wymondham, Richard Conrad, OP, who entered the Dominican Order after obtaining his Ph.D. at Trinity College, and Paul Maddison. Two others whose homes were in the Chesterton area prior to the founding of the parish, entered the priesthood after being received into the Church. They are Fr Jakes, SJ, who lived in Belvoir Road, and Bishop Charles Grant, who lived in De Freville Avenue and was educated at the Perse School and Christ's College, Cambridge. Bishop Grant, who died in April 1989, served the English Martyrs parish as a curate.

# Chapter 20

# The Carmelite Convent

*by one of the Founder Sisters
with an appendix on St Joseph's Chapel, Waterbeach,
by Tony Brotchie, with help from Bill Scott*

## From Chesterton to Waterbeach

Among the many foundations made by Mother Mary of Jesus from the Notting Hill Carmel was one in Cambridge. In November 1923 the Carmelite nuns opened a convent at 104–106 Chesterton Road; their chapel served as a Mass centre for Catholics in the Chesterton area. The Chesterton Road property (now the site of St Regis flats) became too noisy for the nuns so they moved in 1937 to Waterbeach to 'a fine commodious house which adapted itself much more easily into a suitable convent than the two villas on Chesterton Road'. A chapel and extern quarters were built on to it. On 24 August Mgr Marshall said the last Mass in the little chapel at Chesterton Road and at midday the same day he said the *Itinerarium* with the nuns and accompanied them in a procession of cars to their new home at Waterbeach. During the morning the altar which was given by Mrs Thorneley in 1923 had been moved and was already in position when the rector led the community in procession into their new chapel. A crucifix given to the Prioress some years earlier by Major Pillow already stood erected as a Calvary at the end of a glade in the grounds.

The first Mass to be celebrated in the new chapel was offered two days later by Bishop Taylor, Vicar Apostolic for Nigeria. The Ceremony of Enclosure of the new convent was on 14 September, the Feast of the Exaltation of the Holy Cross. The nuns had three weeks prior to this for cleaning and arranging everything. This period of freedom from enclosure was an opportunity for special friends and relatives of the sisters to come and see them again without intervening veils and grills. The number of visitors increased until the last days before the enclosure when, according to the practice always observed, the public at large was invited to come and inspect everything they wished to see. Large numbers came both from Cambridge and Waterbeach – Catholics and non-Catholics alike.

The Corpus Christi altar belonging to the church of Our Lady and the English Martyrs was lent by Mgr Marshall and was erected under a plane tree. There was Benediction after a sermon preached by Fr Martindale, SJ. There were about a thousand people, although it was a working day afternoon. Cars and busloads of people came from Cambridge and the greater part of the men, women and children of Waterbeach 'must have come in though there is not a Catholic amongst them.' The Anglican vicar, Revd Mr Davies, set the lead. He apparently gave the Carmelite community a very warm welcome to Waterbeach. The Bishop of Northampton performed the Ceremony of the Enclosure (Pl. 16). He was attended by some fifty clergy, including the Right Revd Abbot Smith, CRL, Apostolic Visitor to the Carmelite nuns, and the Very Revd Canons Peacock and Garnett.

## The Waterbeach Carmel

It is recorded in the *Cambridge Catholic Magazine*: 'And so there has come back to Waterbeach a Catholic community of cloistered nuns. The Poor Clares had had a convent in the neighbourhood for some 200 years before the Reformation. The ruins of their church and refectory laid waste by the devastators can still be seen. Thanks to the Carmelites there is a priest in the village again, and Daily Mass.' This priest was Dom Ildephonsus Flannery, OSB who also said Mass at St Laurence's in the High Street in Chesterton at 9 a.m. on Sundays.

Due to the lack of vocations, the Waterbeach nuns amalgamated with the Chichester Carmel on 24 April 1973, so ending fifty years of the Foundation in Cambridge. The nuns left on Easter Tuesday. On the Sunday previous Bishop Grant, who served Mass in the chapel as a boy, visited and gave his blessing. While there he confirmed the mother of Sr Mary Clare – Mrs Trolley – whom Fr Drury, parish priest of St Laurence's, had baptized and received into the Church the day before in the chapel at Waterbeach. In 1994 the Chichester Carmel amalgamated with the convent at Looe in Cornwall.

One of the nuns, Mother Rosario of Christ, who before entering had been a professional artist, did an oil painting of St Laurence the martyr to hang in St Laurence's church. It was a copy of one she had painted for Bishop Laurence Youens who had helped her in a time of great suffering.

# Appendix: St Joseph's, Waterbeach

*RAF Waterbeach*

Following the outbreak of the Second World War, a start was made, though not without local opposition, on the construction of an airfield which became the RAF Station at Waterbeach. It occupied valuable fen farmland alongside the A10 trunk road, six miles north-east of Cambridge, and was opened for flying operations in January 1941. The original Catholic chapel provided there, in a hut among the extensive hangars and living quarters, fell within the jurisdiction of the Bishopric of HM Forces, as did St Joseph's, its later replacement. The base would have had enough Catholic service personnel and civilian staff to justify the services of a chaplain, probably shared with other bases. Certainly there are records of honorary RAF chaplains saying Masses there during the war and after. In 1941 Dom Ildephonsus Flannery, OSB was appointed as chaplain to the Carmelite Convent at Waterbeach and he also served the RAF base; in 1957 Fr Michael Halton, SMA was there and later still the octogenarian Jesuit priest, Fr George Bayliss, who acted as officiating chaplain alongside his appointment as chaplain to the Carmelite Convent.

During the post-war period the front-line role of the airfield began to diminish as various transport, fighter and training squadrons came and went. Eventually, in August 1963, the base passed to RAF Maintenance Command. It became the headquarters and depot for the Airfield Construction Branch of the RAF, housing a training centre and three operational squadrons, two of which were generally at work elsewhere in the United Kingdom. A change, too, in the provision for the Catholic airmen came about with the arrival of the new Station Commander, Group Captain Bernshaw, and his Station Accountant Officer, Flight Lieutenant Bill Scott. Bernshaw soon realized that the existing Catholic chapel was unsuitably placed for the new requirements of the base. Knowing that Bill Scott was a Catholic he consulted him as to the provision and conversion of an alternative building. The choice fell on a redundant shed, described by some as an old parachute store, by others as a dinghy servicing shed. Neither purpose had any place in airfield construction, and with sympathetic generosity Bernshaw saw to it that the basic refurbishment of the building was performed by the many tradesmen and apprentices under his command, mainly as trade testing exercises for individual craftsmen. It then fell to Bill Scott to invite the Senior RAF Chaplain, Mgr Roche, to discuss appropriate internal fittings to transform the converted shed into a chapel and, following this approach, an altar, floor coverings, statues and other religious items were provided by the Church authorities. The chapel was blessed and opened for use in February 1965. The following day, recalls Bill Scott, the Airfield Construction Branch moved in with a bulldozer to demolish the earlier chapel and by the end of their day's work nothing was to be seen on the site but newly laid turf.

In addition to the Masses said in the new chapel, Fr Bayliss would provide retreats for the service personnel and their families, often on a weekly basis, and civilians from the vicinity were also invited to attend. When Fr Bayliss retired his dual role, as chaplain to the convent and to the base, was taken over by Mgr Davidson, by then approaching the end of a priestly career in the Northampton Diocese which had begun in the Cambridge parish in 1919.

### St Joseph's, Waterbeach Barracks

In 1966 responsibility for airfield construction passed from the RAF to the Royal Engineers as part of a rationalization of service functions. The Waterbeach base was renamed 'Waterbeach Barracks', becoming the headquarters of 12 Engineer Brigade Royal Engineers and the home of 39 Engineer Regiment (Airfields). Under this new management, St Joseph's Chapel continued to be served by visiting clergy for the benefit of the newly installed Army personnel as well as for local residents.

When Mgr Davidson retired in the early 1970s, both his responsibilities at Waterbeach were assumed by Fr John Drury, at first a curate, then the parish priest, at St Laurence's church in Cambridge. By the early summer of 1973 the Carmelite Convent at Waterbeach had closed, leaving the barracks as Fr Drury's only responsibility in Waterbeach. It was he who first started to call the chapel 'St Joseph's', and Mass was celebrated there at 10.15 every Sunday morning by Fr Drury and successor clergy from St Laurence's. Later this became an anticipatory Mass on a Saturday evening. Eventually even this Mass was moved to St Laurence's Church with the result that Masses were said at St Joseph's on an occasional basis only.

As a result of reduced military requirements, Waterbeach Barracks closed in the year 2000, bringing with it the closure of St Joseph's Chapel and the end of forty-nine years of continuous Catholic presence at the base.

# Chapter 21

# Memories of a Parishioner

*Margaret Plumb*

I was born on 5 January 1936 and baptized in the baptistery (as was everyone in those days) at the church of Our Lady of the Assumption and the English Martyrs on 30 January by Fr Mullett. Canon Marshall was supposed to baptize me but he forgot and took his dog for a walk (I say the story of my life – 'Oh we forgot about you' or 'Oh didn't you know!'). My godparents were Francis Leach, Eleanora McLean Leach and Jean McLean Leach.

My mother, one of a family of seven, of whom six were baptized at the English Martyrs, was herself baptized there on 30 January 1898, Fr Page conducting the service. My father was received into the Church by Fr Ketterer on 26 March 1932 (Holy Saturday). They were married in August 1933, Fr MacGregor officiating.

My mother and her brother and sisters all went to St Andrew's School and I remember my mother telling me that her youngest sister came home with a 'burn' on her hand where Miss Ormerod had hit her with the cane. My grandmother went to the school and told the teacher off. As this sister was only seven when her mother died, a year after her father, you can see she was very young indeed when this happened. All seven of the family were married in the English Martyrs and all their children were baptized there. Two at least were members of the Scouts.

My parents used to go on their bicycles to the English Martyrs for Mass on Sundays – my father to the 7 a.m., passing on the way home on Midsummer Common my mother going to the 8 a.m. I was not left alone for long! Mass was also held at the Carmelite Convent on Chesterton Road before it moved to Waterbeach because Chesterton Road had become too noisy with the area being built up. The site is now occupied by St Regis Flats. When the Convent was closed in 1937 it is said I was allowed the run of the chapel. One of my cousins remembers that the nuns were given a special dispensation to come out for the day and relations came from far and wide to see them. The enclosure ceremony (Pl. 16) took place on the feast of the Exaltation of the Holy Cross, 14 September 1937. I still (July 1997) visit two of these nuns. One of them, Sr Bernadette, was the extern who used to call at our house collecting alms to enable the nuns to live. My father called her 'Rosy cheek Margaret'; she still has rosy cheeks today. Her sister, Mother St John of the Cross, was one of the nuns who moved to Waterbeach and Sr Bernadette entered there, but because they were full she went to the Convent at Chichester. When, because of falling vocations, Waterbeach closed in 1973, ending fifty years of the Carmelite Foundation in Cambridge, the nuns amalgamated with Chichester and so the two sisters were together. Because of falling vocations and the closure of the Chichester Carmel they are now in Looe, Cornwall.

In January 1941 I started school in the Kindergarten of Paston House School in Bateman Street, run by the IBVM (Institute of the Blessed Virgin Mary) nuns (sometimes known as the Mary Ward nuns). The IBVM opened a house and started a school in Cambridge on 1 September 1898 in Furness Lodge in Park Terrace. They later moved to the Elms in Bateman Street where a boarding school was started in the Convent. Classes for day pupils were held in a hut which was divided into two with nine or ten in each room. Later Paston House was bought and became the day school – the boarders were educated separately until the 1940s.

Mother Salome started a Girls' Guild at the Convent to which my mother and some of her sisters (who all went to St Andrew's School) belonged. Sometimes they were invited to be entertained by the boarders, some of whom were foreign princesses, in order that they could learn how to entertain guests.

In 1943 I, with other Catholics in my form, made my First Communion on Corpus Christi Sunday. Sr Xavier prepared us and Canon Marshall examined us on our understanding of the sacrament in his room (now the parish office). It was a dark room, I remember.

We used to take part (as a school) in the Corpus Christi Processions held on Corpus Christi Sunday (Pl. 17). The church would be beautifully decorated with many flowers. The procession would leave the church via Lensfield Road going towards Trumpington Road and then turning left into Bateman Street where we would enter the convent garden where a beautiful High Altar had been erected. Here we sat on the grass for the sermon and Benediction. I remember people used to comment that I never moved or fidgeted. The procession would then reassemble and return to the church via Panton Street, Union Road and Hills Road, entering the Church by the Lensfield Road entrance where there would be Benediction again. The Blessed Sacrament would be accompanied by the Guild of the Blessed Sacrament and preceded by small children (who had just made their First Communion) throwing flower petals and there would be many Children of Mary walking in their blue cloaks and veils. People along the streets would show reverence to the Blessed Sacrament; men used to stand and take their caps or hats off.

In 1950 some of us were enrolled in the Children of Mary. This took place in the small Convent chapel at the top of the house (Pl. 31a). When I left school I joined the parish Children of Mary. We used to meet once a month on the First Monday. My mother had been a member some years before me, together with Miss Rigg, Miss Ellen Ward, Miss Ward and Miss Russell – who were still members when I joined them. Unfortunately the Children of Mary in Cambridge folded in the or early 1970s, being taken over by the Sodality which did not last for long.

I also took part, behind the scenes, in the choir when Hugh Benson's Nativity Play was performed at Houghton Hall. This play had been specially written for Paston House.

My mother used to borrow books from the parish library which was situated in the rectory (the room next to the stairs). This was run by Miss Deagon and Miss Buckingham. Later Maureen McNamee who joined the La Sainte Union Nuns also helped to run the library.

My father was in the Guild of the Blessed Sacrament and I remember very clearly an outing to King's Lynn where we visited the Red Mount Chapel and the shrine of Our Lady of Walsingham in the church. On the way home a stop was made at a pub to buy bottles of beer which were consumed by the gentlemen on the coach. I remember in particular 'Tiny' Dargen was one of the party.

When the Mass centre in Chesterton was opened in 1939, Sunday Mass was at 9 a.m. and served from the Carmelite Convent at Waterbeach by their chaplain, Fr Flannery. Fr Flannery stayed with the nuns until the early 1950s when he became parish priest at Lynford in Norfolk until he retired to his monastery at Belmont, where he died in 1984. Mass was then said by priests from the English Martyrs, one of whom was Fr Oates, who was later to become parish priest. I remember very vividly coming out of Benediction at the English Martyrs one Sunday evening and Mrs Gifford saying 'Have you heard who your new parish priest is? You poor things!' He had quite a reputation. This was in 1951. On one occasion when he came to say Mass we thought there was a mouse on the altar as while he was preaching his head would be going from side to side. I remember one particular Sunday when we came out of church Daphne Spencer (née Asquith) remarked, 'Well you know why I have all this make up on!' Fr Oates had given a sermon in which he remarked that women who wore heavy make-up did so to cover up their sins. Daphne was always, and still is, very well made up. Fr Gerard Hulme was our first 'proper' parish priest. During his time we used to have May processions on the second Sunday in May. These would start in the grounds of the church with the crowning of the May Queen and the statue of Our Lady, carried by Children of Mary (usually parishioners), would then be processed down the High Street to Ferry Lane and round the streets of Chesterton back to the church for Benediction (Pl. 18d). Fr Hulme always said that it would not rain on that Sunday – and he was right!

In my late teens I joined the choir of St Laurence's. At that time Mrs Dunnington was the 'organist' – we only had an harmonium then – and Brian Lewis the choirmaster and the Lewis family made up the majority of the choir, together with Joyce Abbott, Edwina Cracknell and myself. Later Diane Dunnington took over as organist and I remember very well one Christmas in the 1960s when the members of the choir – not being local – all went home and Diane, Edwina and myself sung a full Latin Midnight Mass. In the 1950s the choirmaster was Tony Bristow who had been in the chorus of the D'Oyly Carte. His wife Joyce, who had been a principal soprano, was also a member of the choir. At this time we sang four-part Latin Masses. On one occasion we did a concert in Houghton Hall, singing Gilbert and Sullivan and other songs.

In the mid 1950s Fr Oates asked Edwina and myself (having been recommended by Sister Christopher) to take catechism classes for children who did not go to Catholic schools. Sometimes Sally Anne Goodman would come along and help and later Tony Brotchie. I remember the first lesson; we had to teach the children to make the sign of the cross and say the Our Father. Only one little girl knew the Hail Mary. These classes were held on Sunday afternoons and continued when we moved to Milton Road. We always finished with Benediction and on one occasion just before Christmas we were teaching the children Christmas Carols and I was playing the harmonium and Fr Oates said 'Why don't you play for Benediction?' That is how I started playing the organ and later became the organist and then in charge of the choir at St Laurence's. I was in the Choir for over thirty years. At one time, when Fr Hypher was the curate, we had about a hundred children as he used to go round the parish, particularly in Arbury, and persuade parents to send their children on Sunday afternoons.

Then there was the church cleaning. In the 1940s and early 1950s I used to go with my mother, two of her sisters and Mrs Povey to help clean the church in the High Street. My mother turned up one day to clean the church to find Mrs Dunnington and someone else already there. They had made a rota and had not thought of including my mother, who I think was the only one cleaning at the time. I later came back to cleaning the church when I left school and used to do it with Norah Callaghan who was a teacher at Paston House. When Norah left Cambridge Edwina Cracknell did it with me and we continued in the new church with Anne Haslop until, again, a rota was devised and everyone was doing it during the daytime. We did for a while do it in the evening but eventually had to give up.

In the 1950s there was a Sports and Social Club attached to the English Martyrs and many of us joined, playing tennis and badminton. On one occasion a mixed team went to Newmarket to play that parish in a hockey match on the Sunday afternoon. I seem to remember I played in goal. In the evening we went to the parish social which was held in their parish hall – the church was then in All Saints Road. It was the last social of the season and had 'live' music provided by Roger Osborne and his band. The small hall was packed with stable lads. Everyone just jived to all the music, except when a waltz was played. You try dancing with a stable lad who is much shorter than you!

Of course there was the Catholic Women's League. My mother had been a member for many years and as soon as I was old enough I also became a member. I used to attend the meetings prior to becoming a member, particularly during the war when my father was in the army. Meetings used to held in Houghton Hall on a Sunday afternoon. Later on I was elected to the committee and strangely enough was allocated similar duties as my mother had in early years, namely to go hospital visiting. I was to share this with Mrs Margaret Brown who was tragically killed in a motor car accident on Madingley Hill in the 1970s. Hospital visiting is not my scene! My mother used to go to Chesterton Hospital. In fact I think she probably only went once as she was to visit the men's ward where people like 'Gin' Barber were. She did not think it right that women should be going to those wards.

The Catholic Women's League formed a drama group. We performed a play called 'A bicycle made for two' at the annual dinner at the Goldsborough Hotel off Hills Road, which was owned by the Bristows. Barbara Elgar and John Curtin were in it and on this occasion I understudied Norah Callaghan. We later became the Catholic Drama Group and performed such plays as 'Red Sky at Night' by Philip Johnson, 'The Walrus and the Carpenter' by R. G. Boswell, 'The Bride' by Gertrude Jennings, 'Anti-Clockwise' by Muriel and Sydney Box, 'A Question of Fact' by Wynyard Browne, 'Home is the Hunted' by R. F. Delderfield, and 'Dark Brown' by Philip Johnson. I remember being terrified when reading this last play and got the main part as a result!

We used to perform Passion Plays in the 'Little Church'. One year we did a mime of the Stations of the Cross (Pl. 15a). Later I also took part in Fr Bull's Passion Play in Houghton Hall.

I remember on one occasion the representative on the group which arranged the Women's World Day of Prayer reported back that the service that year was to be held at Our Lady and the English Martyrs, but the ladies from St Paul's Church had come back to the next meeting and reported that St Paul's ladies could not possibly go to the Catholic church. When I told my father this he remarked 'Oh they are not still like that!' When he mentioned it to one of his brothers who was a sidesman at St Paul's he confirmed this. My father had left St Paul's because of the attitude of the Revd Mr Ainsley who said the devil was in the parish. He finished up in Fulbourn! The Women's World Day of Prayer has never been held in the English Martyrs.

# Chapter 22

# St Philip Howard Parish, 1978–1990

*Sean Lang*

It may not look particularly prepossessing from the road, but the church of St Philip Howard is the result of a remarkable example of the initiative in creating a new parish being taken by the parishioners themselves.

Before the church opened in 1978, Catholics on the southern side of Cambridge were to be found at Mass centres in a wide variety of different venues, including St Bede's School, Linton Village College, Townley Hall in Fulbourn, the hall of the Land Settlement Association at Abington, the infants' school in Fulbourn, and even occasionally in the Black Bull at Balsham. A site for a possible church building had been acquired at the corner of Walpole Road and Cherry Hinton Road in the 1950s, but by the early 1970s there had still been no decision about how best to use it.

On 14 December 1971 Canon Paul Taylor presided over a public meeting at St Bede's School to consider the issue, to which some fifty people came. After general discussion of the issues involved, ranging from whether or not a church building was needed at all, down to specifics, such as how big the car park would need to be, a committee was set up to go into the matter in greater detail. The committee met frequently in the months that followed, usually at the home of one or other of the members. At this stage it was by no means settled that the Walpole Road site should be used for a church. There were proposals to continue using St Bede's School as a Mass centre, perhaps by financing a new building on the school site which could double up as a music block. Then there was the question of the Polish community. Canon Taylor was keen for them to be involved in the plans, and in the spring of 1972 the committee met with Fr Trochim and other Polish representatives to see whether the two groups' requirements could be reconciled. Although, even at this early stage the idea of a dual-purpose building was more or less generally accepted, the practicalities were much more problematic. Should the building be essentially a church with a social role, or a social building which could also be used as a church? With other churches in the area extending their own social facilities, was there, in fact, enough need for another church-cum-social centre? In the end it was clear that the two groups' needs and visions were too different and the idea of a joint venture lapsed. But so too, or so it appeared, had the idea for having a church building at all.

Money, of course, was a problem. Would it be cheaper simply to sell the site? It had been bought from the Council for no more than £600 (or £750 including acquisition costs), but the terms of the sale gave the Council first option to buy if it were ever to be resold, and to buy, moreover, at the same price. In the inflation-afflicted 1970s this did not make financial sense. On the other hand building a new church would require a heavy financial outlay, and neither the parish nor the diocese could afford it without a major fund-raising effort. However, a church is its people, not the building they use, and as the building plans began to look stymied, the people of the parish began in effect to set up a church independently of a building. In November 1973 the first meeting was held to discuss the setting up of a series of house groups, and the first group met the following January, hosted by Peter and Josie Mountain. Soon there were nine groups, all in the southern area of the city, stretching out to Linton and Fulbourn and including one led by Fr Anthony Foreman at the Hills Road rectory. The groups discussed parish matters, such as forming a young people's music group, and also issues of more general concern, like the meaning of Baptism or the existence of Limbo. The groups sometimes gathered together for larger discussion meetings held at Blackfriars. In 1975 the Laity Commission pamphlet on *The Bishop as Leader* provided particularly challenging food for thought, and it was discussed at a whole series of meetings. Since it mentioned that under the new regulations bishops 'may invite the clergy and laity to give their suggestions', some of the parishioners decided to take the Commission at its word. In April 1975, in the absence of a parish council, fourteen house group leaders wrote to Bishop Grant of Northampton laying out the problem of a church community operating without a church building and asking him to address the question as a matter of urgency. From this letter can be dated the final phase in the pre-building story of the parish. The bishop responded positively and the matter was raised at the following meeting of the Diocesan Finance Board. Things were finally under way.

There was much to do. The St Bede's School idea was raised, but the headmaster felt unable to support this combined venture; the future of the school was in doubt at the time in any case, so a new church building it would have to be. The next three years saw all the familiar features of a Catholic parish raising a lot of money – dances, bingo nights, a subscription fund and so on – but the bulk of the money came from an unexpected source. The offices at 2 Hills Road next to Our Lady and the English Martyrs were owned by the church but let out at a rent well below their market worth. When this was adjusted it brought in enough money to make the building project viable. Designs were commissioned from the architect John Newton of the Burles Newton partnership in London and building work started. A completion date was set at September 1978 and, although it looked a close-run thing at times, the church was ready for the opening by Bishop Alan Clark on 25 October 1978.

The committee had taken great care in considering the church's design. A dual-purpose building fitted both the outlook of the parishioners and the diocesan budget, and committee members went to look at churches at Weedon and Rickmansworth to see what this might mean in practice. They also visited the neighbouring Anglican church of St James, Wulfstan Way, where the vicar, Fr David Ford, explained how the church had been designed and ruefully stressed the need to remember to provide for enough storage space. Opinions differed on the best arrangement for the church interior: should it be in traditional style or 'in the round'? In the end the solution was a compromise: the sanctuary was placed in a corner where it could be easily screened off. This layout was changed in the 1990s to place the sanctuary facing the congregation full-square. Some very fine lime wood carvings of St Philip Howard and of Our Lady, and a striking crucifix with the risen Christ, were commissioned from Anton Wagner. The priest's house also had to be designed. There was some debate as to whether it was still appropriate to plan it with a live-in housekeeper in mind; in the end the decision was taken to let the clergy experience the joys of washing up for themselves.

As the practical issues advanced, the more spiritual and pastoral aspects of planning had to be addressed. To general delight, Fr Tony Rogers, then an assistant priest at Our Lady and the English Martyrs, who had taken a keen interest in the project, was confirmed as the first parish priest. Then there was the issue of the patron for the new church. The parishioners were balloted for their suggestions, and in the end the bishop decided on St Philip Howard, one of those English martyrs to whom, collectively, the 'parent' parish church is dedicated. Philip, Earl of Arundel, of the same house of Howard as the dukes of

Norfolk, was born in 1557 and studied at St John's College, Cambridge before taking up his place at the court of Elizabeth I. Although brought up a Protestant, in 1584, at the height of anti-Catholic persecution in England, he took the brave decision to be reconciled to Catholicism after having witnessed a disputation between St Edmund Campion and Protestant ministers. The following year he tried to flee to the continent, but was arrested and imprisoned in the Tower of London. There he was held for three years until he was tried and condemned to death for treason in 1589, but the sentence was not carried out and he was left instead to rot in the Tower, where he died on 19 October 1595. He was included as one of the forty English and Welsh martyrs canonized by Pope Paul VI on 25 October 1970, so the official opening and blessing of the church dedicated to him took place on the eighth anniversary of his canonization. The guest list included the Master of St John's, the Mayor and Mayoress of Cambridge, and Lady Miriam Hubbard, representing the Howard family. The consecration was followed by a celebration at St Bede's School, a fitting way for the old venue to hand over to the new.

Fr Rogers wrote in the first newsletter of the new parish: 'If our new church is not properly aligned or bonded together – if its foundations are shaky – then it will not stand. Likewise the living church can only survive if our foundations are sound and we are working together for the right goal.' In physical terms, these were prophetic words, for within a year of the church's opening a number of defects in the building had come to light, most alarmingly in the block flooring. But in spiritual terms, the church was well founded. The years of working towards the church's opening had created a strong bond of common purpose amongst the parishioners, which carried over into the life of the new parish. As well as a parish priest, St Philip Howard had the services of four Sisters of Our Lady based at Howard House, Rotherwick Way. It would need them, for the new parish was extensive, and although the church building was well placed for Catholics in Cherry Hinton and the southern part of the city, there were still the outlying villages to consider, not to mention the heavy Catholic chaplaincy duties at Addenbrooke's Hospital, which the new parish was to share with Our Lady and the English Martyrs, dividing the wards between them. As well as providing the weekly Mass in the hospital chapel and attending to emergencies, this involved touring the wards on a Friday to see which of the Catholics admitted to the hospital would require Communion the following Sunday. It could be a heavy task until a rota system allowed the work to be shared out efficiently.

A noticeable and very welcome feature of the history of the parish is the part played by ecumenical contacts in getting the parish up and running. Catholics in Fulbourn had been having Mass in the village hall until in 1979, in a generous gesture, the Anglican rector of Fulbourn, Revd Brian Kerley, offered them the use of the parish church on Saturday evenings, an arrangement which continues to this day. At Linton the arrangement went even further. Not only did the vicar, Revd David Walser, offer the use of Linton parish church on Sunday mornings, sandwiched between the two services for his own congregation, but a joint committee of Catholics and Anglicans was set up to plan activities which the two congregations could undertake together. As a result, the Catholic, Anglican and United Reformed Churches in Linton come together for major festivals like harvest suppers or the Women's World Day of Prayer in a remarkable example of harmonious ecumenism which is as strong now as it was when it started. The building of the Walpole Road church took the ecumenical outreach of the parish still further. Two of the meetings held to discuss the formation of the parish were hosted by Fr Ford at St James's, Wulfstan Way, and he proved a good friend to the parish once the building was opened. From February 1979 the St James's parish magazine *Focus* was issued as a joint magazine for St James's and St Philip Howard, and the first joint issue had a foreword by Fr Ford and Fr Rogers. Articles specifically aimed at Anglicans or Catholics were labelled 'A' or 'RC' respectively, but on wider themes *Focus* lived up to its name, with whole issues devoted to particular problems like race, death (which raised the ecumenically delicate issue of the Holy Souls) and ministry. The January 1980 issue looked, appropriately enough, at Christian unity, and did so in a refreshingly frank way, with no attempt to pretend that the issue is easy or that difficulties or divisions do not exist. Having said that, however, the examples of Linton, Fulbourn and St Philip Howard show what can be achieved if ecumenical co-operation is approached with goodwill and a eye firmly set on practicalities.

Times change; people move on. In 1979 an Italian priest moved on from St Philip Howard to missionary work in Kenya, taking with him a tin of Heinz spaghetti to show his friends and family in Italy on the way: 'They'll never believe it', he explained, 'it's impossible to can spaghetti'. The next year Eugene Harkness from Nova Scotia arrived as a student for the summer, en route for the English College in Rome; his would become a very familiar face in the years to come. In 1983 Fr Tony Rogers moved to St George's, Norwich, and his place was taken for two years by Fr Michael Edwards. In 1985 Fr Michael Vulliamy came to St Philip Howard; it was he who presided over the church's tenth anniversary celebrations in 1988. The leaflet for the anniversary Mass summed up the varied uses to which the church had been put over its first ten years: 'Mass, Christian Unity services, Missions, Senior Citizens meetings (Corner Club), Scouts, Parish Meetings, Parish Council, Weddings and receptions, baptisms, Youth Club, CAFOD, Beer and Wine club, dancing classes, language school, Life, blind, Catechists' classes, playgroup, Garden Fetes, Christmas Bazaars, jumble sales, music evenings, discos, Inner Circle, Whist drives, retreats, Clinics, etc'. Ten years later a similar list would include dinner dances to mark St Andrew's, St Patrick's and St George's days, an Italian evening for San' Antonio, a parish drama club, as well as children's communion classes, Traidcraft stalls and quiz nights. Small wonder that, when the church was consecrated, Bishop Clark said, 'This has not been built as a conventional church' (*Cambridge Evening News*, 26 October 1978). He was right.

# Chapter 23

# The Polish Community in Cambridge

*Christopher Jackson with assistance from Mr T. Kubiakowski*
*and Mrs Anna-Maria Norman*

At a solemn High Mass in the church of Our Lady and the English
Martyrs on 4 October 1998, the Polish community celebrated the fiftieth anniversary of their presence in Cambridge. The purpose of this
chapter is to trace the development of that community from its first
beginnings in 1948, and to show how far it has managed to travel from
those austere post-war days to the position it now enjoys as an integral
and well-respected part of the wider Catholic community in
Cambridge, yet successfully preserving its own cultural identity and
traditions.

## A Debt Never to be Forgotten

In paying tribute to the Polish servicemen who had fought for the
Allied cause during the Second World War, Sir Winston Churchill
urged his fellow countrymen never to forget the debt they owed to
these faithful and valiant soldiers. He believed it to be an honour to see
them amongst ourselves and deserving to be treated in such a way as if
they were persons of our own kin.

Official policy in the early post-war years reflected this attitude in its
dealings with the many thousands of Polish servicemen who found
themselves under British command at the conclusion of hostilities.
Some had served as sailors or airmen from bases in Britain, others as
soldiers in the North African, Middle Eastern and Italian campaigns or
in the invasion of Europe. What was common to them all was that their
Polish homeland no longer existed in the form they had left it; large
parts were now incorporated in the Soviet Union and the rest subject

to Soviet domination. Few, if any, Polish servicemen were willing to return there. The British government had little choice but to recognize the newly-installed Communist regime in Poland and to withdraw its recognition from the Polish government in exile which had operated in London throughout the war years. This event, which took place on 5 July 1945, was however balanced by a choice, offered to all Poles, to return to Poland or to stay on in Britain. Virtually the entire body of servicemen elected to stay. They were then incorporated in the Polish Resettlement Corps, a semi-military organization whose members were accommodated in military camps, given pay books and civilian clothes, and arrangements made to give them education and vocational training, all-important language instruction, and eventual employment.

For the most part, the location of Poles when they joined the Resettlement Corps was random and fortuitous, but determined where individuals would remain while resettlement progressed. In the Cambridge area, former military camps at Trumpington, Fowlmere and Chippenham were already occupied by Polish servicemen, Trumpington being a transit camp and Fowlmere a school of business studies for about 200 Poles transferred with their families from Italy and preparing there for civilian life. Unless moved to other specialist education or training centres elsewhere in the country, most of the Poles at Trumpington or Fowlmere, when they were demobilized from the Resettlement Corps in 1948, stayed on at those centres and were gradually assimilated into local communities in Cambridgeshire.

## First Steps to Assimilation

Coming from a European nation with one of the highest proportions of practising Catholics to its population, it was only to be expected that the Poles settling in Cambridgeshire would be drawn to the Catholic church in Cambridge as a focal point for their religious observances. Needless to say, the Polish armed forces had provided their own Catholic chaplains and, as soon as Poles moved into the Fowlmere camp, provision was made for Sunday Masses there, celebrated initially by a Polish military chaplain, Mgr Herr. Similar arrangements followed at the Trumpington camp. On the social front, it was not long before Polish servicemen found their way to the Sunday evening social at the Houghton Hall, nowadays the hall of St Alban's School, joining with other servicemen awaiting demobilization or repatriation. The latter category even included German and Italian ex- prisoners of war, mingling amicably with their former adversaries and dancing to gramophone records with local Catholic girls.

Poles from the Fowlmere camp joined with Polish students at Cambridge University and members of the Anglo-Polish Society, led by Miss Susan Bale, to form a Polish Catholic community with Fr F. Brzóska as its first priest. Miss Bale, who later became Sr Susan of the Child Jesus, was awarded the Gold Cross of Merit by the Polish authorities in London for her services to the Polish community. Canon Stokes, parish priest from 1946 to 1961, willingly gave the infant community leave to have Polish Masses celebrated in Cambridge on Sundays and holidays, at first in the Houghton Hall, then, when the Hall passed into local authority control, in the church itself. Weddings and baptisms soon took their place as part of the developing pattern of Polish religious observance at the Cambridge church. Gradually the centres of population for the demobilized Poles shifted away from the camps towards more promising centres of employment, and individuals moved at first into rented housing and council houses, then, from the 1960s, into their own homes. Trumpington Camp was finally closed in 1953 and, as at Fowlmere, the army huts were demolished and the land returned to agriculture.

## 'Exsul Familia': The Exiled Communities

It is a matter for speculation whether the Polish Catholic community in Cambridge would have preserved so much of its national and cultural identity during its fifty years' existence had it not been for an apostolic constitution, *Exsul Familia*, promulgated by Pope Pius XII in 1952. This acknowledged the existence, and the needs, of 'exiled communities' resulting from displacements brought about by the Second World War. It urged that pastoral care should be provided so as to avoid any loss of identity for these communities in their new surroundings. In particular, it sanctioned the establishment of 'national' parishes and 'national' priests to minister to these communities in their own languages, alongside the existing parish and diocesan structure of the host country. These privileges were intended for all expatriate communities but in the United Kingdom only the Poles, along with a smaller Ukrainian community, existed in sufficient numbers to take advantage of them. In the case of expatriate Poles this led the Polish Primate, Cardinal Wyszynski, to appoint Cardinal Władisław Rubin, based in Rome, to serve as spiritual protector of the Polish emigrés throughout the world. On Cardinal Rubin's death in 1983, he was succeeded by the present spiritual protector, Archbishop Szczepan Wesoły. A Vicar Delegate for Poles in England and Wales (otherwise known as the Rector of the Polish Catholic Mission for England and Wales), based in

London, was appointed to supervise what has become a network of seventy-eight Polish parishes, each with a Polish parish priest, some even with their own parish churches, while others, like Cambridge, share a church with the local English congregation. Another Vicar Delegate (or Rector) supervises a similar Scottish network from Edinburgh. Even at the height of the Cold War, and during the worst days of Communist oppression, Polish-trained priests from Polish seminaries came to serve the expatriate parishes. Although these priests might be permitted to leave Poland to serve abroad, any return to their homeland was considered out of the question until conditions eased after 1989.

## The Bateman Street Connection

Sr Ursula, IBVM, then a teaching sister at St Mary's Convent, Bateman Street, Cambridge, recalls the early post-war years when a Polish priest, Fr Brzóska, then chaplain to the Poles, eased the duties of the parish clergy by celebrating the daily Mass for the nuns in their convent chapel: 'We never had our own resident chaplain. We were just lucky to get the Polish priest, and that saved the Parish clergy . . .'. Fr Brzóska was succeeded by Fr Zawidzki in the celebration of these daily Masses between 1952 and 1969.

Sr Gregory, IBVM, superior of the convent between 1964 and 1970, recalled 'a tremendous number of children with Polish names because there was a great Polish colony round here and the children were sent to school here. That increased the number of Catholics [in St Mary's School] enormously in the 1960s. By 1982 the Polish names had nearly all disappeared, and that, of course, because being girls they had mostly married English people so they had English names.'

## Friendly Co-existence in Walpole Road

In the spring of 1972, writes Sean Lang, Canon Taylor was keen for the Polish community to be involved in plans for a new church in the south of Cambridge, possibly using the Walpole Road site. Fr Trochim and other Polish representatives met the planning committee to see whether the requirements of the English and Polish groups could be reconciled. How should the local parishioners and the Polish community actually sort out the sharing of the facilities? At one point the idea was mooted of Fr Trochim serving as the parish priest, and a possible plan for an 'Anglo-Polish Community Centre/Church' was drawn up, with particular rooms designated as 'Polish Committee Room', 'Polish Society Room', 'English Committee Room' and so on. In the end the proposed scheme collapsed, and another six years passed before the idea of a new Catholic parish in the south of Cambridge came to fruition, with the consecration of St Philip Howard Church on 25 October 1978. Meanwhile, however, the Polish community were ready to implement alternative plans of their own.

## Polonia House

The purchase of 231 Chesterton Road, Cambridge in 1972 was an event of the highest importance for the development of the Polish community in Cambridge. Here, for the first time, a chapel, social club and community centre were brought together under the same roof, together with residential accommodation for the Polish parish priest. The Polish parish centred on Polonia House was given the proudly evocative dedication 'Our Lady Queen of Poland'. Although the chapel is on a scale which can accommodate no more than twenty-five worshippers, and is therefore better suited to weekday Masses, the hall can be called into use if the size of the congregation and the particular occasion requires greater space, such as the Holy Week triduum. Meanwhile, at 12.15 p.m. every Sunday, the Church of Our Lady and the English Martyrs continues to provide the Polish community with an appropriate setting for their Sunday Mass.

The hall at Polonia House is used for religious and social functions including theatrical performances and various receptions, and the house provides a meeting place for various religious, charitable and cultural organisations which include the Polish Saturday School, the Ex-Combatants Association and the Polish Women's Charitable Association.

Many distinguished religious and civic leaders, British and Polish, have paid visits to Polonia House during the quarter-century since it opened, including Bishop Alan Clark of East Anglia, the late Cardinal Władisław Rubin, the Polish spiritual protector, and his successor Archbishop Szczepan Wesoły, Archbishop Nowak of Częstochowa, and Rectors of the Polish Mission in London, Mgr W. Staniszewski and Mgr S. Świerczyński.

## A Mission Realized

If one of the main objectives of the Polish community in Cambridge is to meet the spiritual needs of its members in a form familiar to them, for long there existed another, wider purpose, shared with all other Polish expatriate communities throughout the world. This was, during the Cold War years, to keep alive a Polish culture free from communist influence and to promote sympathy for the concept of a free and independent Poland among their host countries. At last, in 1989, all hopes and prayers in this direction were realized, when Poland emerged from its long twilight under Communist domination and normal contacts could be established between the expatriate communities and their homeland, and between those families long separated by artificial political divisions. Freed from these darker preoccupations, the Polish community in Cambridge nevertheless continues with its spiritual and cultural purposes, a welcome neighbour in the midst of the wider community of Catholic Cambridge. Never is this more true than in those occasions of shared worship and celebration which bring the two communities together and serve to strengthen the bonds between them. On 4 October 1998 the Polish Catholic community in Cambridge presented the Church of Our Lady and the English Martyrs with the icon of Our Lady of Częstochowa as a mark of gratitude for the shared church facilities enjoyed by the community over the previous fifty years.

## The Polish Priests, 1947–1999

Mgr F. Herr (1947–48), former Polish Army chaplain at Fowlmere Camp
Dr F. Brzóska (1948–51)
Mgr W. Cieński (1951–52), Major, Polish Army, former Chief Chaplain of the 2nd Polish Corps
Dr J. Zawidzki (1952–69), W/Cdr, Polish Air Force, Pallottine Father
*Fr H. Posłuszny (1969–71)
*Fr J. Trochim (1971–93)
*Fr H. Pilak (1993–96)
*Fr. E. Stachurski (1996–97)
*Fr K. Bidziński 1997–)

* Denotes trained in Polish seminary

# Chapter 24

# Italians Come to Cambridge

*John Rowgotzow and Enikö Regös*

## The Immigrants

Italians migrated to England in three groups. Some came over before the Second World War. They settled down and started small ice cream and sweet shop businesses, one of the first in Cambridge being Mr Silvester. The second group, who came after the War, were former prisoners of war who had served in Africa. These men worked on farms helping on the land, and earned much respect from the farmers for their hard work. After a time these men returned to Italy and married. They then brought back their wives and resumed agricultural work as their jobs had been left open. In 1949 there were 30,000 Italians in England.

The third group arrived after this; between 1949 and 1952 20,000 Italians came over as a result of a request from the British to the Italian government. A four-year work programme was drawn up. Men went to work on the railways and in the brick works, mostly in London and Peterborough. In Cambridge many went to work at the Co-op bakery and dairy, or for the Health Service at Addenbrookes or other Cambridge hospitals. The ladies worked as housekeepers and domestics. Each year their ID cards had to be signed at the police station. At the end of this four-year period many stayed with their employers. Some moved on and started up small businesses, such as building firms, roofing firms, ice cream and coffee bars, restaurants and continental shops, and hairdressers. Many are still in business today.

## The Mission

In 1954 the Scalabrini Missionary Fathers, an Italian congregation originally devoted devoted to the Apostleship of the Sea, started a mission in Bedford to assist the Italians, many of whom were living in Bedford and Peterborough. In 1957 another mission was started in Peterborough and in 1966 one was set up in London. At this time there would have been about 60,000 Italians in England. At this stage here were ten Scalabrini Fathers and fifteen Sisters split over the three missions helping with the schooling of small children.

The Italian Mass in Cambridge was celebrated each first Sunday of the month from 1956. Later this changed to celebration every Sunday; priests from Peterborough and Bedford take it in turns to celebrate the Mass, with much-appreciated help from Italian-speaking priests at Our Lady and the English Martyrs and Mgr Harkness at St Philip Howard. By now there are only four Scalabrini Fathers and five Sisters of the Working Sisters of the Holy House of Nazareth.

# Chapter 25

# Pugin's Church in Cambridge: Architectural Sources and Influences

*Roderick O'Donnell*

## A Local Prototype

A. W. N. Pugin (1812–52), a Catholic convert from 1835, was the acknowledged leader of the Gothic Revival. By 1842 he had not only many controversial publications but also over thirty Catholic churches to his credit, including the future Catholic cathedrals at Birmingham (1839–41) and Southwark (1840–8). He was a friend of Bishop Wareing and was known to other 'subscribers' to Fr Shanley's building fund, and he may perhaps have discussed a Cambridge church with Fr Scott, the chaplain at Sawston Hall, in 1839. Pugin was often at his best in simple buildings of local materials, whether brick or stone. Occasionally he used a specific model or source, in this case the thirteenth-century church of St Michael's, Longstanton, seven miles north-west of Cambridge. The buttressed west gable and bellcote, and the relationship of the aisles to the clerestory-less nave are, however, modelled on, not 'quoted' from the original. Because of the restricted site in Union Road, Pugin had to omit the chancel, although the triple lancets of the model are used in the east end. It is unclear how Pugin chose his source, but significantly Longstanton was noticed in *The Ecclesiologist*, in June 1843, and later proposed 'to serve as a model for the Colonies'.

The design was published in March 1842. Phoebe Stanton, in *Pugin*, lists 'drawings 1840, estimates 1841', but this does not accord with the internal progress of the Cambridge Mission. The first references in Pugin's diary, 21 July 1841, 'Left London for Cambridge' and 22 July 'Cambridge for London' do not necessarily refer to the church, but the

# THE NEW CATHOLIC CHURCH
### OF
## CAMBRIDGE.

On MONDAY, April the 4th, a MEETING will be held at Mr. ALDRIDGE's, Gate Street, Lincoln's Inn Fields, to raise Subscriptions for purchasing an ALTAR PIECE for the above New Church. The co-operation of every sincere Christian is earnestly requested in this meritorious work. The Chair will be taken at Six o'clock precisely by

### MR. BURNS.

N. B.—The Rev. Mr. SHANLEY, Pastor of the New Church, will address the Meeting, and explain the object of his mission. He is the first Catholic Pastor that attempted to preach Catholicity during the last three hundred years in the University Town of Cambridge.

Fig. 7.    The new Catholic church of Cambridge. Leaflet published by Fr Bernard Shanley, April 1842.

entry for 2 May 1842 'Left London for Cambridge began church' is specific. The rapid progress made in 1842 suggests that the threatened attack of 5 November 1841 would have been aimed at the foundations rather than a mere site.

It was usual for Pugin to be concerned with the furnishing and ritual arrangement of his churches and accounts for furniture occur in the 1842 diary. The sum of £35. 11s. 0d. charged to his account by Hardmans, the Birmingham church furnishers, was presumably for the furnishings and vestments required for the consecration. Later decorations included the stained glass by William Wailes in the three east lancets. The most original furnishing to Pugin's design survives in the Church of Our Lady and the English Martyrs: a saltire cross with a vested figure of St Andrew crucified, all set within a roundel with seated angels and stiff leaf foliage of Early English pattern (Pl. 23). The label in Gothic lettering reads 'The gift of A. Welby Pugin A.D. 1843 St. Andrew Pray for us'. Traditionally this gift was the result of a vow to St Andrew when Pugin was threatened with shipwreck off the Scottish coast and Bishop Wareing referred to it as such at his funeral.

## The Rival Neighbour

The Cambridge Camden Society, lately described by D. J. Watkin as 'the most influential undergraduate society of all time' began its journal *The Ecclesiologist* (1841–68) with an anonymous review of St Paul's Church, Hills Road, Cambridge, then under construction by the architect Ambrose Poynter, little more than 200 yards from the site of the future St Andrew's Church in Union Road. The review was withdrawn after protest, but Pugin reprinted it in *The Dublin Review* in February 1842. Following Pugin's *Contrasts*, 1836, the Society tested contemporary churches against ethical rather that stylistic criteria, condemning the classical style as 'pagan' and the perpendicular as 'debased'. The ironic tone of *The Ecclesiologist* followed the style of Pugin's own journalism, and was complimented by him. To Pugin and his followers everything about St Paul's was wrong, the materials 'very red brick indeed ... relieved by nice little white quoins [and] black bricks ... intended we presume for a pied variety of Great St Mary's', the stone tracery 'meagre in detail, the brick piers and arches plastered to imitate stone, the roof ceiled in with applied wood principals'. But even more damning than these architectural 'lies' was the inadequate ritual plan and liturgical arrangement: the church was 'all gallery' with 'no chancel whatever'.

By contrast Pugin's church across Hills Road (Pl. 19) defined the new architectural faith; here for the first time Cambridge architectural 'reality' and 'correct' style and planning were combined with Gothic antiquarianism. St Andrew's was in the 'correct' Early English style, unlike the 'something between the Elizabethan and debased perpendicular' of St Paul's. *The Cambridge Independent Press* described St Andrew's as 'a correct specimen of a beautiful English parish church of the Middle Ages; though plain, elegant, chaste and devotional', using Pugin's own language, save for 'elegant and chaste'. It was stated that 'every feature is real, genuine and natural' and the furnishings [screen, altar, and open seats] all 'so beautifully carved'. The plan and elevation were congruent, the interior correctly planned with distinct nave and aisles, the roofs open-trussed not ceiled, the porch and sacristy distinct on plan. Although, Pugin explained 'the space being exceedingly limited, the chancel is taken out of the east compartment [of the nave] enclosed by open screen work with the aisles on either side', it was nevertheless dignified with a rood and figures and provided with an altar with stone benches and holy water stoups, the baptistery screened off with a stone font and two aumbries for chrism and holy oil for the sick. All these stone furnishings, like the St Andrew crucifix, had Early English details.

## Pugin and the Camden Society

The day after he began the church, Pugin recorded in his diary, 3 May 1842, 'Ely with the Camden men'. Benjamin Webb, the Camden Society's Secretary, recorded three days of meetings, but did not refer to the new church. *The Ecclesiologist*, for political reasons, resolutely ignored it. Despite Pugin's warm support, the 'Camden men' were coy in acknowledging his influence. Distinctions between the advanced architectural and religious views of the Society and those of the contemporary Catholic revival, represented by Pugin, were too nice for general consumption. A series of conversions to Catholicism triggered by that of the future Cardinal Newman in November 1845 included two Camden Society committee members, Frederick Apthorpe Paley and Scott Nasmyth Stokes, both of whom had met Pugin in May 1842. These losses were to be countered by an anonymous attack, 'The artistic merit of Mr Pugin', in *The Ecclesiologist*, January 1846, which was commissioned from A. J. B. Beresford-Hope. Despite the early good relations and the fact that Pugin had designed the seal of the Society in 1843, no church of his had been noticed before the 1846 attack apart from one Anglican restoration. Thereafter Pugin's Anglican commissions in Cambridge, the restoration of Jesus College Chapel from 1845 and the east window at Magdalene in 1850 were noticed almost in spite of the further criticism by *The Ecclesiologist*. Pugin's church was avoided not on account of ignorance, but of fear.

## Undergraduate Fascination – 1863 Style

If *The Ecclesiologist* ignored the church, undergraduates, fascinated by the religious implications of the Gothic revival, clearly visited it in significant numbers, regardless of their sympathies. Of the first hostile demonstration, on 5 November 1841, Fr Shanley wrote of 'astonished hundreds that witnessed our unhappy position' and of those who 'now the danger is over ... make long speeches and a great noise about their sincere attachment of the ancient faith but [who] at the hour of danger ... were in their happy homes and comfortable beds, [but] I do not stand in the need of such feather-bed soldiers'.

Fr Shanley was writing in 1843, two years after this episode, which was not reported in the local press. However, twenty years later, in 1863, a full-scale riot led to the arrest and imprisonment of two undergraduates, and to full, if conflicting, reports of the events and of the motives of those involved.

Undergraduates wearing gowns had, for several weeks, attended the evening service and, 'evidently acting in concert ... interrupting the priest by laughing derisively, smoking long clay pipes and other unseemly conduct' according to *The Tablet*, 9 May 1863. A policeman stationed in the congregation attempted an arrest which began 'a general melée ... in which policemen, congregation and students all participated.' Although the original culprit escaped, two others were held in custody overnight. Seven undergraduates appeared before the Borough Magistrates, who included the Master of Christ's. Two Pembroke undergraduates, both cousins called Watson, were sent to prison without hard labour for one week. 'A stentorian sympathetic cheer from their brother undergraduates' greeted the prisoners on their way to the Borough Gaol, where 'the inmates ... also cheered lustily but this was because they saw two gownsmen going to prison'. A Trinity undergraduate was fined £4; charges against another were withdrawn and those against further three dismissed. According to a policeman, one of the Watsons said 'I should not have struck you, only I thought you were a Roman Catholic.' Others objected to the suggestion of sectarian rowdyism where perhaps mere Town versus Gown rivalry was involved. According to R. G. Glenn of Magdalene, one of those against whom charges were dismissed, the 'smoking clay pipes' were 'long pipes (not clay) protruding from an upper pocket' and 'no religious motives' were involved. His testimony was accepted by Canon Quinlivan, who also asked that a Parliamentary question be dropped. Glenn described himself as 'a constant attender ... for more than three terms ... for the sake of the music' and sent to the newspaper the cards of '50 undergraduates who have been occasional attenders'. Few of these can have been Catholics as no more than twelve are estimated as resident at this time.

One convert undergraduate who later became an priest, T. E. Bridgett, associated his conversion with two specific events, reading Kenelm Digby and visiting the 'Catholic Chapel': 'It was a very small building in an obscure street in the suburbs of the town, and we had some difficulty in finding it. We got the keys from a poor Catholic man, who lived near, and after we had looked at the Church, my friend .... began to banter the poor Irishman. "Why Paddy", he said, "do you think you've got the truth all to yourselves down this little back street, and all our learned doctors and divines in the University are in error?" The answer that Paddy gave was this, "Well, sir, I suppose they're very learned but they can't agree together, while we are all one."'

Despite such moving evidence, the next priest, Canon Scott, wrote to Cardinal Newman: 'the present church is small and dark, almost suffocating in summer, and so badly situated that many who come to the University go away ignorant of its existence, and others who come ... are so greatly inconvenienced by the crowd and heated atmosphere, that it is a matter of astonishment that they ever pay a second visit'.

## Moved to St Ives

Except for the St Andrew crucifix, nothing of the earlier church was incorporated in its successor. Having stood disused since the opening of the new church in 1890, Pugin's church was in 1902 dismantled and moved to St Ives, Huntingdonshire, at the expense of a convert, George Pauling (Pl. 19b). The surviving brick and stone building (albeit with red bricks replacing the original Cambridge whites) is recognizably Pugin's, although its architectural impact and liturgical arrangement were altered both at the time when the screens were sold on and in the more recent re-ordering. A dedication to the Sacred Heart has also replaced that to St Andrew. The screens were sold to the Liverpool Catholic architect, Edmund Kirby, and re-erected in his private chapel at Birkenhead.

The church is still of five bays with no chancel but a clerestory has been added, and a two-storey sacristy changed from liturgical north at Cambridge to south. The east and west elevations are the same. Cut stone details such as the bell-cote and dressings to the porch are re-used but most window reveals are replacements. The porch door with its Early English foliate hinges and elaborately over-structured joinery is clearly Pugin's. The elaborately carved altar with bas-relief front of three quatrefoils, the outer two with seated angels, the centre with a cross and Agnus Dei, similar to those on the St Andrew crucifix.

The first and second bay nave piers have round Early English drums with capitals and one octagonal decorated type to the sanctuary with semi-octagonal responds at both ends, as Pugin varies his sources to suggest historical development. The stone niches from the baptistery are re-used in the south aisle and the chancel; the font is now re-positioned at the east end. The most important survival are the three lancet east windows by William Wailes, the centre a Virgin and Child, the two outer lancets with St Andrew and St Felix, installed in the Cambridge church in 1845 to Pugin's design at a cost of £20.

# Chapter 26

# Dunn and Hansom's Church in Cambridge

*Roderick O'Donnell*

## Introduction

The Church of Our Lady and the English Martyrs in Cambridge (1885–90) (Frontispiece) represents a major statement of the Catholic Revival of the mid- to late-nineteenth century in East Anglia, an area not noted for its Catholic presence. It was designed by the Newcastle-based Catholic architects, Dunn and Hansom, paid for by a millionaire French widow and was said by an unsympathetic donnish wit to be built with 'money derived from dolls' eyes ... to be devoted to the cult of idols'. Although built a mere ten years before Westminster Cathedral and decorated by the first rank of specialist Catholic designers of the day, it has been regarded as old-fashioned. The University and the town, which had already employed the leading Gothic Revival architects and designers Pugin, Morris, Bodley, and Scott, and was soon to see the work of the Catholic Leonard Stokes at nearby Emmanuel College, was by then moving on to a refined, 'late' style, based on English Perpendicular and on vernacular references, evolving into a freer, less 'historicist' Gothic than that used by Dunn and Hansom.

Catholic architects, however, drew on quite different ecclesiological and stylistic sources, favouring a certain literalness and eclecticism in sources and forms, as well as a rightly asserted triumphalism, especially in the dedication to the English Martyrs. So the 'cult of idols' jibe exactly sums up the 'otherness' of the building compared with the Anglican and Nonconformist churches of the town. The church was provided with overwhelmingly rich furnishing and decoration, and filled with statues. A key to this taste must surely be its patron.

## Patron and Benefactor

Yolande Marie Louise Lyne-Stephens (1812–1894) was, as Pauline Duvernay, a star of the ballet at the Paris Opéra and at Drury Lane in the 1830s (Pl. 7). Despite the reputation of her profession, she retained her devotion and religion, and finally married an English millionaire, Stephen Lyne-Stephens, who left her a rich widow in 1860 with a house in Paris and another in London, Grove House, Roehampton. In 1851 she rebuilt Grove House, adding in 1862 a massive neo-Norman mausoleum for her husband in which she too is buried. Her country house, which she also rebuilt in 1867–74, was Lynford Hall, Norfolk. For all these she employed the highly successful Scottish country house architect William Burn. In London she probably went to Mass at Mortlake and in Norfolk she was content to travel seven miles to Mass at Thetford until a guest, the 13th Lord Lovat, prompted her to build in the grounds of Lynford Hall the church of Our Lady, Lynford (1878–79), by the architect Henry Clutton, which she endowed and opened to the public. Later she became a major benefactress of the poor Northampton diocese: the orphanage and church of St Francis, Shefford (1878–82), the bishop's house at Northampton (1884) and the church of Our Lady of the Sacred Heart, Wellingborough (1886). Her most lavish gift was the Cambridge church where she is commemorated by a portrait in the Rectory dining room, the Gothic letter inscription 'Pray for the good estate of Yolande Mar[ie-] L[oui]se Lyne-Stephens, foundress of this church' above the rose window of the north transept, and the label-stop carved head in the north porch. Finally, she paid for the tabernacle and massive candlesticks at the church of St Joseph, Roehampton.

## Competition Success

The replacement of Pugin's chapel in Union Road had long been an ambition of the missionary rector, Canon Scott, but in diocesan politics the provision of a new church in Norwich took priority once the Duke of Norfolk had announced his intention to fund it. However, it was the same Duke who offered to assist with the purchase of the site upon which the building funded by Mrs Lyne-Stephens could be erected. The public aspect of the scheme is probably shown in the decision to offer the new church to a limited competition of Catholic architects.

The commission was awarded to the Newcastle practice of Dunn and Hansom. Edward Joseph Hansom (1842–1900), the son of Charles Francis Hansom, was a pupil of his father and of A. E. Waterhouse.

Archibald Matthias Dunn (1833–1917) had been in practice since 1862, and was also a pupil of C. F. Hansom and possibly also of E. W. Pugin. He inherited the vast £70,000 fortune of his father, Matthias Dunn of Castle Hill, Wylam, Newcastle in 1871. He offered a partnership (1871–93) to E. J. Hansom and they began a successful practice in the north-east, largely based on a fruitful connection with the Benedictines, for whom they began Downside Abbey church in 1873 (now forming the transept and some east end chapels of the complete building), as well as monastic ranges at Downside (1878). The firm's domestic and collegiate work at Stonyhurst (1873) and at King's College, Newcastle (for the University of Durham) (1887–95) is reflected in the Tudor red brick rectory next to the church, also the gift of Mrs Lyne-Stephens. Dunn and Hansom are commemorated in the church as whiskered men of business in label-stops to the window in the first bay of the south aisle.

Others taking part in the competition, some of whom published their designs in the building press, included Goldie, Child and Goldie, responsible for the contemporary St James, Spanish Place, London (1887–90); Pugin and Pugin, the continuation of the family practice by Peter Paul Pugin; and W. Purdue, responsible for the elaborate English Martyrs, Streatham (1892–3). S. J. Nicholl, who was already working for Mrs Lyne-Stephens, was not mentioned among the competitors. As winners, Dunn and Hansom represented a conservative choice, following their successful work at Downside and Stonyhurst. In St Michael's, Newcastle (1889–91) they were to build to a very similar design but with a straight-ended sanctuary and an octagonal crossing. There was obvious appeal in the richness of their style, with its opportunity for the fullest decorative elaboration of narrative architectural and figurative sculpture externally and internally, following the Decorated style, by contrast with the more austere Perpendicular more characteristic of East Anglia. Dunn and Hansom had produced simple, austere Early Gothic designs for the new Downside Abbey church, but had been persuaded to adopt a rich Geometric and early Decorated style in the church as begun. Although the Cambridge church, too, was originally described as Early English, and indeed the drawing of the interior exhibited at the Royal Academy represents something much more hard-edged than the finished building, the design as it progressed became richer and richer. A set of nine drawings, dated November and December 1885, deposited at the Cambridgeshire County Record Office illustrates the process. A further drawing signed Dunn and Hansom in the rectory shows the church seen in three-quarter view from the corner of Hills Road and Lensfield Road, with the bracketed clock (of steel construction, plated to look like cast iron) prominent on the tower (Fig. 8). Another plate published in the building press shows some slight differences from the completed church.

The overall result is busy and mannered, far from the rustic simplicity of Pugin's earlier church (borrowed, it will be remembered, from St Michael's, Longstanton), or the sophistication brought to Cambridge in 1862 by the architect G. F. Bodley at All Saints church.

## External Structure

The church is remarkable for its rich Bath stone structure (on a brick core) transported to East Anglia ready-cut from the works of Mr Joseph Bladwell in Bath, with the architectural carving done on site by Mr Ovens of Preston (Pl. 21b), and figure sculpture by R. L. Boulton of Cheltenham. R. L. Boulton provides an interesting link with the previous generation of Catholic church builders, having trained in the workshop of Pugin's builder, George Myers.

Further richness is assured by the creamy, smooth Combedown stone of the walls, which originally were to be in the much harder Ancaster (still used for the plinth of the tower). The details of the church show a tendency towards Geometric Gothic in the nave and aisle windows, which are plate tracery or lancets, but are richer at the eastern end, where the higher windows have full Decorated tracery heads. With such subtleties, the architects suggested the elapse of historic time and progress within the design. The church has steeply pitched roofs covered with warm, red-orange plain tiles, an attractive and somewhat domestic effect, reminding us of the best late Victorian domestic architecture.

## Devotional Complexity

The plan of the church is very complex, both architecturally and liturgically, and attempts to provide for the many devotions of late Victorian Catholicism, particularly 'private' Masses at side chapel altars. There is a deep narthex or ante-chapel like that of college chapels, but here reached through a west front with an elaborate sculptural programme by R. L. Boulton. There is also a porch under the tower, with a ringing gallery above. The body of the church is cruciform, of nave and aisles with a crossing of transepts supporting a lantern tower, with a deep choir and sanctuary arranged as an apse following French, not English precedent; there are a baptistery and

side chapels on the north side, sacristies and other chapels on the
south. The nave has flying buttresses to support the vault.

## A Lavish Interior

The internal elevations are equally lavish, the walls also faced in Bath
stone (from Farleighdown), with much carved architectural and natu-
ralistic decoration. The piers have semi-detached colonnettes of
Plymouth marble in the nave and sanctuary, and a faded red
Newbiggin stone in the narthex; these run through the clerestory to
support a stone vault with elaborate tierceron divisions, with simpler
quadripartite divisions elsewhere. The order is a full double chamfer
moulded type, with beautifully carved capitals, especially to the
central pier of the crossing which has arches divided by a carved span-
drel, with another pier rising the full height to the vault in the north
transept. The height of the interior is striking, better understood in
the narthex than in the crowded nave, where the effect is heavy rather
than spacious. Even more vertiginous is the crossing, with its wooden
vault, shown as stone in the 1885 drawings. As so often in the
Victorian Gothic Revival, the smaller spaces are the most successful,
such as the Holy Souls chapel of the narthex, the baptistery and the
Sacred Heart chapel to the south of the sanctuary.  There are also
stone Stations of the Cross, specifically referred to (*Building News*,
1890) as Dunn and Hansom's design, above dado-like stone benches
in the aisles.

## Fittings and Works of Art

The church was completed both structurally and decoratively at its
opening with all its furniture installed; most Catholic churches were by
contrast opened with only temporary furniture, awaiting further piety
to finish them. To achieve this, the original estimate of £30,000 had
risen to £70,000. A series of metal screens by Hardman and Co. divide
the narthex from the church, and enclose chapels; they are some of the
best fittings in the church and some retain their original gas-bracket
fittings, a very rare survival. Richer still is the carved woodwork by
Ralph Hedley of Newcastle, who provided the pulpit (Pl. 21a) and four
screens originally under the crossing but now repositioned. Pews and
stalls were by Rattee and Kett, who furnished the two sacristies and
probably the fittings in the rectory.
    The organ in the south transept gallery is by Abbot and Smith of Leeds,

the case by Lewis and the specification by Sir Charles Villiers Stanford (Pl. 24).

A complete set of stained glass was installed in the narthex to an elaborate iconographic programme of the English Martyrs by Hardman and Co. of Birmingham. The figures are elegantly drawn and highly coloured, for example the blues and purples of the Seven Sorrows window in the narthex; their work can also be inspected in the lancets below the north rose window. Hardman's chief designer at the time was Pugin's son-in-law John Hardman Powell, leading to the confusing attribution of the main west window to 'Powell' *tout court* in early guides. As a result the glass has been mistakenly assigned to Powells of Whitefriars, the London stained glass artists.

The nave clerestory glass is by Lavers, Barraud and Westlake, depicting the saints of the English church and post-Reformation mission (including nearest to the crossing the founders of the Counter-Reformation and later orders such as the Jesuits and the Passionists). These are all by N. H. J. Westlake and are closer to modern taste, in particular the charming scenes of the seven sacraments in the baptistery, showing the administration of these sacraments, and complemented by the carved panels of 'the types of the seven sacraments' on the font. The overall effect of the stained glass in the church must have been overpoweringly solemn and gloomy before wartime damage led to replacement by glass on clear fields in the aisles and the north chapels, and by the unsuccessful big pictorial windows in the apse (all by Hardman and Co.).

The climax of all this decoration is in the furnishing and painted decoration of the sanctuary where the rood, the Doom, the baldacchino and high altar are all seen in sequence. The Doom painting by Westlake is above the chancel arch, and in the front arch of the crossing is a rood beam installed in 1914. The stone altar and oak baldacchino, based on the tomb of Robert the Wise at S. Chiara in Naples, also used as a model by Pugin, are both carved by Boulton and painted and gilded by Westlake (Pl. 20a). The series of carved figures of martyrs in niches in the piers of the baldacchino and the angels on the gables guarding the Blessed Sacrament are especially fine. The altar with its open arcaded mensa and simple dado-like reredos contrasts with the enormous 'benediction' altars of the period with their many gradine shelves and towering benediction thrones, so beloved of the clergy and the faithful, which were produced in great numbers by the Pugin and Pugin firm but became the butt of much liturgical criticism even before the Second Vatican Council. The Cambridge ensemble by contrast was for its date highly liturgical. It also closely follows medieval precedent as shown by Pugin in his *Present*

*State of Ecclesiastical Architecture in England* (1843), and as developed in the French Gothic Revival. The tabernacle and candlesticks and other altar furniture are said to be from Lyons, whence much expensive nineteenth-century church plate and vestments came. The fine brass and enamel candlesticks based on French thirteenth-century models have champlevé and incised enamel medallions of the English martyrs such as Blessed John Forest and St Edmund Campion, and are clearly commissioned pieces. Stencilled painting was formerly applied to the apse walls and elsewhere, and survives in the restored Blessed Sacrament chapel. In contrast to all this neo-medievalism, the deeply-carved reredos of the Holy Souls chapel, by Boulton, is based on a painting by the nineteenth-century Austrian 'Nazarene' painter Johann Gebhard Flatz (1800–1881).

The church has some fine works of art. The highly original carving of St Andrew crucified on a saltire cross, given by Pugin, was transferred from his earlier church (Pl. 23). The wooden statue of the Virgin and Child (Pl. 22a), presented in 1864, is an object of great devotion; it is probably of mid-sixteenth century date and German origin, suggesting that it cannot have come, as previously supposed, from the Dominican friary suppressed in 1538.

The painting of the Descent from the Cross by N. H. J. Westlake (1895) includes vignettes of the donor, H. G. Barnard, and of Canon Scott, who received him into the Church as an undergraduate in 1891. Barnard's benefaction serves as a reminder of the apocryphal story, told by the late Mgr Gilbey, of Canon Scott denying that such a splendid church was for the townsfolk of Cambridge, but rather for University men, anticipating the long-awaited lifting of the Catholic bishops' ban on Catholics attending in 1895 and the setting up of the chaplaincy, now at Fisher House.

The rectory furnishings and fittings include a distinctive suite of dining room chairs, following a pattern of A. W. Pugin's at the House of Lords, and as further evolved by E. W. Pugin, with monograms 'F' for Fisher and 'MR' for Mary, likely to be a design from Dunn and Hansom. There is a fine carved stone and marble fireplace in the dining room, and a portrait of Mrs Lyne-Stephens in widowhood (Pl. 7a).

## Critical assessments

The appreciative Cambridge congregation has treasured the building and its contents ever since 1890, as is demonstrated by the excellent series of guidebooks from that date onwards. Other twentieth-century opinion has been more quizzical. E. M. Forster noticed it in *The Longest Journey* (1907):

> 'Oh here comes the colleges', cries the Protestant parent, and then learns that it was built by a papist who made a fortune out of moveable eyes for dolls. 'Built with dolls' eyes to house idols' – that at all events is the legend and the joke. It watches the apostate city, taller by many a yard than anything within, and asserting, however wildly, that here is eternity, stability, and bubbles breaking upon a windless sea.

The first break with anti-Victorian prejudice was Sir Nikolaus Pevsner's entry in *Cambridgeshire* (1954) in 'The Buildings of England' series. Understanding the picturesque genius of Cambridge, he saw it almost as a Gothic folly in relation to the Greek Revival buildings and setting of Downing: 'A very big, ambitious building, appearing to greatest advantage from the lawns of Downing College'. Pevsner also remarked on the prolixity of a design which included as many features as possible of a great church; the western tower and spire, the narthex, the transepts, the crossing and apse; a prolixity closer to the Gothic Revival of the continent. Stefan Muthesius noted in *The High Victorian Movement in Architecture* (1972) that such Catholic churches are 'more like continental exemplars, for their decorative richness.' The importance of the church was recognized when it was listed at Grade II* in 1972.

With the exception of Pugin's church of St Giles, Cheadle, few Catholic churches in England could approach such a meeting of generosity, enthusiasm, scholarship and Gothic Revival workmanship as is to be found in this church, a wonderfully rich and generous coda to the Puginian and High Victorian phases of the Victorian Gothic Revival.

## Epilogue: 1972

Iconoclastic proposals for re-ordering the church in 1972–3 represented a grave threat to its interior, at a time when anti-Victorian prejudice, allying itself with a liturgical primitivism which many claimed to be authorized by the Second Vatican Council, wrought havoc in many churches, as at Pugin's St Chad's Cathedral in Birmingham. It was proposed to demolish the screens of the narthex, dispose of the pews and replace them with a raked platform and seating, and demolish the baldacchino and high altar so as to achieve a basilican plan, the priest then 'presiding' from an empty apse. However, members of the parish and of the University such as Professor J. A. W. Bennett, Professor Elizabeth Anscombe, Dr David Watkin, and Dr Richens, the founder of the Association for Latin

Liturgy, successfully resisted the scheme (which apparently had the blessing of the Victorian Society as communicated through the architect John Brandon-Jones). A less radical scheme was implemented by Gerald Goalen, the leading Catholic church architect of the post-war period working in the modern movement style (Pl. 20b).

Appropriately, Canon Scott's memorial brass, by Hardman, originally in the sanctuary, was carefully removed from the site of the new altar platform and relaid in the Blessed Sacrament chapel.

CHVRCH OF OVR LADY and THE ENGLISH MARTYRS, CAMBRIDGE.

Fig. 8.   Perspective drawing, dated 1887, by A. M. Dunn of Messrs
Dunn & Hansom, Architects.

# Chapter 27

# The Abbott and Smith Organ

*Andrew Johnson*

## Hidden origins

The newly built, lavishly furnished church of Our Lady and the
English Martyrs was given an organ to match, with its three manuals
(Great, Choir and Swell) and pedal organ and a total of 2018 pipes
(Pl. 24). Abbott and Smith of Leeds were chosen as builders and
Charles Villiers Stanford, the then organist of Trinity College,
Cambridge, drew up its specification and gave its inaugural recital in
1890. So much, but little more, survives of its history on record: gone is
any correspondence between the church authorities and the donor or
between either of them and the builders or Stanford; absent is any
record in Stanford's own papers; gone is any information as to how its
siting in the south transept gallery was decided; gone, even, is any
record of what Stanford actually played on the instrument. Gone, too,
is documentary evidence of modifications claimed to have been done
by, for example, Canon Bonavia-Hunt, an Anglican clergyman with a
reputation for tinkering, not always harmlessly, with the organs to
which he was allowed access. The absence of archive material in the
care of church authorities is a keen disappointment. Did such material
exist before records were consigned to salvage in the austerity years
during and after the Second World War?

## The known history

The history of the organ is based chiefly on recollection, speculation
and the evidence to be found in the instrument itself as it stood in the
spring of 2002, the time of its major renovation.

The builders were Messrs Abbott and Smith, a firm founded in Leeds in 1869. The 'Abbott' was Isaac Abbott who had worked with the eminent nineteenth-century builder, William Hill. They were responsible for building numerous small- and medium-sized instruments, some 200 in Yorkshire alone, and over the years were called in to work on large organs in St Alban's Abbey and Leeds Town Hall. In 1964 the firm ceased trading and their records have subsequently vanished. Many of their organs have not escaped radical alteration or replacement, but in 1984 Michael Sayer was able to write that 'an excellent example survives in the Church of Our Lady and the English Martyrs, Cambridge' (*The New Grove Dictionary of Musical Instruments*). Paul Hale, in his consultant's report on the organ (1999), quotes from a letter from Stanford to the builders (5 March 1890): 'The Organ seems to me a complete success, and is of beautiful balance and quality. The touch is excellent. I congratulate your firm sincerely on the work.' When the organ was dismantled for renovation in April 2002, torn strips of envelope were found stuck inside the Swell soundbox (to assist the airtight movement of the sliders) with a Leeds address and postmarked '6 Feb 1890'. The presumption is, therefore, that the organ was moved from the Leeds works and assembled in the church during February 1890, ready for Stanford to try out.

## Later Alterations

Mr Hale highlights the instrument's musical pedigree in his Report. Mgr Scott, rector at the time, wrote to the *Northampton Mercury* (21 April 1894) praising the virtues of the Schulze organ in Northampton Town Hall which was made for the 1851 Great Exhibition and saying how the tone of it resembles that of the organ procured 'for our new Church at Cambridge' in its 'lighter stops ... its magnificent diapasons'. Organists say these qualities are best heard from the organ gallery, and various attempts have been made to boost the sound to make it travel down the length of the nave as well as across the sanctuary and transepts. Exactly what was done, when and by who is unclear. Canon Bonavia-Hunt's involvement in the 1920s is marked by a plaque on the console, but experts are puzzled by the absence of any evidence from the pipework itself that much was actually done. The wind pressure was certainly put up to its maximum in order to increase the organ's volume, with long-term deleterious effects, but volume was not the problem. Why was the organ tucked away into the south transept rather than placed at the west end, for example? Was space the only consideration? At Trinity College, Stanford would have played on an instrument on a gallery at the western end of the chapel dividing the ante-chapel from chapel proper. A similar arrangement could have been contrived at Our Lady and the English Martyrs, or, as at Scott's St John's church (now cathedral), Norwich, a high gallery built for an organ over the west door. Was it that liturgically the emphasis in the building was very much on the sanctuary, the location and focus of the grand ceremonies the church was partly designed to host? The length of the sanctuary in fact equals that of the nave (excluding the fore-church, sometimes referred to as the 'ante-chapel', though the building itself is no 'chapel'). The size of the congregation of the time was very small and the liturgy of the day required little more than simple plain-song accompaniment and a few hymns. It certainly fits the emphasis in the building on providing Cambridge with a bold, even triumphalist, statement of Catholic presence directed towards the University as much as filling the needs of a poor, small, largely working class community.

For the first fifty years of its life the organ was spared alteration. An electric blower, installed in the cellar below the south transept, may have replaced Abbott and Smith's original hand-pumps (for the pedals) and blowing engines for the manuals. On Shrove Tuesday 1941, however, it suffered damage from the high-explosive bomb that pene-trated the roof of the adjacent sacristy. While escaping fire damage, the organ was showered with shattered glass and debris from the windows and stonework around, and in the post war period repairs focussed, necessarily, on the windows and stonework. The organ was cleaned, but it is not known how thoroughly or expertly this was done; no bills, accounts, contracts or descriptions of the cleaning up survive. The first post-war event to affect the organ was the installation of the central heating system in the church. This accelerated the splitting of the organ case and the sound boxes. More directly, the tracker action was replaced during the 1950s, 60s and 70s by an electro-pneumatic system which, by 2002, needed a major overhaul and replacement.

## The 2002 Renovation

The £110,000 renovation, carried out by Messrs Nicholson of Malvern, following advice from the consultant Paul Hale of Southwell Minster, marked a fresh start of life for the instrument in many ways. First, its financing did not rely on the generosity of a sole donor; the major part of the money came from parishioners themselves through donations, gifts and legacies. Secondly, the organ was provided with a new console, incorporating thumb pistons and up-to-date computer technology to make the instrument infinitely more manageable and attractive to leading instrumentalists. Thirdly, a brand new solo eight-foot tuba stop was added, filling what many believed to be a gap in Stanford's specification (there was space left for such a stop and pipework both on the console and in the organ chamber). The organ's and the church's link with the foremost church musicians of the day was maintained through this ambitious but necessary programme. Congregations at the Sunday 10.45 am Mass have been delighted to be accompanied by distinguished supporters such as Wayne Marshall, of Bridgwater Hall, Manchester, and Vincent Warnier (Maurice Durufle's successor at St Etienne-du-Mont, Paris) while Martin Baker has brought Westminster Cathedral Choir to sing in the church. It is planned to continue these connections over the coming years.

In May 2002, while the organ had been totally dismantled and the south transept and gallery were enclosed in scaffolding and metal caging, leaving the empty shell of the casework in place, Fr Rafael Esteban preached a moving sermon likening the exhausted breath of the old organ to the exhausted spirit all mankind labours under at times. In our dialogue with God, the organ voices our need for solace and expresses our sense of the glory of God. Its silence on Good Friday is overcome by the triumph of its music at the Easter Gloria. Generations of worshippers in Cambridge have reason to thank the generosity of Yolande Lyne-Stephens, the expertise of Sir Charles Villiers Stanford and subsequent musicians, the craftsmanship of Abbott and Smith and Messrs Nicholson, and the care and vision of those responsible for its continued stewardship.

SPECIFICATION (* = Nicholson 2002 additions)

| Great Organ | | | Swell Organ | | | Choir Organ | |
|---|---|---|---|---|---|---|---|
| Double diapaison | 16 | | Bourdon | 16 | | Open diapaison | 8 |
| Large open diapaison | 8 | | Open diapaison | 8 | | Violincello | 8 |
| Small open diapaison | 8 | | Lieblich gedacht | 8 | | Clarabella | 8 |
| Doppel flute | 8 | | Viola ga gamba | 8 | | Dulciana | 8 |
| Principal | 4 | | Voix celeste (tc) | 8 | | Lieblich flute | 4 |
| Harmonic flute | 4 | | Octave | 4 | | Piccolo | 2 |
| Fifteenth | 2 | | Fifteenth | 2 | | Contra fagotto (tc) | 16 |
| Mixture III | 15.19.22 | | Mixture II | 19.22 | | Clarionet | 8 |
| Trumpet | 8 | | Double trumpet | 16 | | Solo tuba | 8* |
| Clarion | 4 | | Horn | 8 | | Swell to Choir | |
| Swell to Great | | | Oboe | 8 | | | |
| Choir to Great | | | Clarion | 4 | | Pedal Organ | |
| | | | Tremulant | | | Open diapaison | 16 |
| | | | Super octave | | | Bourdon | 16 |
| | | | | | | Violincello | 8 |
| | | | | | | Trombone | 16 |

3 composition pedals to the Great and 3 to the Swell
Reversible pedal to Great to Pedal
8 thumb pistons to Great, Swell, Choir and Pedals*
6 reversible thumb pistons*
8 toe pistons each to Swell and Pedal*
2 reversible toe pistons for Great to Pedal*
8 general pistons*
Set and General Cancel pistons*

Electric blower and humidifier
Blower for solo tuba*

# Chapter 28

# Gown and Town, 1856–1965

*Michael de Wolff*

## An Uneasy Relationship

Relations between the Catholic Church and the University of Cambridge during the second half of the nineteenth century were uneasy to say the least. Bowing to years of political pressure and lobbying from various directions the University authorities had eventually agreed to allow persons other than communicant members of the Church of England to receive degrees from Cambridge. This concession was given legal effect by the Cambridge University Act of 1856. The decision had, however, been more pragmatic than sentimental and there were many individuals in the academic world who regarded this development with suspicion and little sympathy. Nonconformists, Jews and Catholics were all now permitted to graduate from the University and began to enrol for undergraduate courses of study. Perhaps not surprisingly the subject of theology was still barred to them.

If the University authorities had seen their gesture as a generous concession, any expectations of gratitude were rather short-lived, and might even have been followed by feelings of indignation at the response displayed by the Catholics. It soon became apparent that the suspicions and reservations of the traditionalist academics were more than equalled by those of the Catholic authorities of the day, whether the English hierarchy or the Vatican itself. There was a strong feeling that both Oxford and Cambridge were dangerously agnostic and entirely unsuitable for the further education of young Catholic Englishmen. The very fact that well-born and talented young men were prepared to run this risk in the years following 1856 forced the Church into countermeasures. At the instance of Cardinal Manning, the Congregation of Propaganda issued a Papal Decree in 1865 and a Rescript in the same year, forbidding English Catholics from attending the ancient universities of Oxford and Cambridge. This was not well received by the English laity and by the time of Cardinal Manning's death in 1892 opposition had risen to such levels that his successor, Cardinal Vaughan, felt obliged to reconsider the situation.

Vaughan's change of mind was largely brought about under pressure instigated by Baron Anatole von Hügel, the curator of the University Museum of Archaeology and Anthropology in Cambridge, an academic who claimed to speak on behalf of the Catholics in the University. In February 1893 von Hügel had joined 500 English Catholics led by Cardinal Vaughan in a pilgrimage to Rome to celebrate Pope Leo XIII's golden jubilee. Although he was uneasy about von Hügel's presence as an unofficial representative of a proscribed body, Vaughan allowed him to hand to the Pope an address, accompanied by a presentation set of Willis and Clark's *Architectural History of the University of Cambridge* in four volumes, the papal arms stamped on the front of each volume and the arms of the University on the back, purchased with donations from Catholic undergraduates. Von Hügel was forbidden from making any spoken address, and so handed over the gift in silence. He was at least reassured to hear, later that day, that the Pope was well satisfied with this silent gesture. Cardinal Vaughan was rather less pleased that Von Hügel had attired himself for the ceremony in the gown and hood of a Cambridge MA. Von Hügel's influence among the Catholic laity was such that by 1894 a petition with 436 signatures (including those of eighty Catholic clergy) was presented to the Cardinal by the Duke of Norfolk, seeking the abandonment of the 1865 Decree. One of the signatories was the rector of the Cambridge mission, Canon Scott, who added a supportive rider to the effect that none of the Catholics who had so far graduated from the University had abandoned their faith. The petition led to a further decree of Propaganda dated 1 April 1895 which permitted English Catholics to attend the Universities of Oxford and Cambridge, 'until such time as a suitable Catholic university could be established in England'. In the meantime regular courses of lectures were to be given by Catholic professors on philosophy, history and religion. The University Catholic Education Board (UCEB) was established by the English Hierarchy in order to implement these impractical conditions but the Board soon realised that the cost of setting up what would amount to a Catholic faculty in each of the two universities was entirely prohibitive. Worse still, the attendance of Catholic undergraduates at such extra-curricular lectures could not be guaranteed. What emerged instead was the appointment of a chaplain in each university, given the task of putting into effect the conditions from Rome so far as was deemed practicable. On 16 January 1896 Fr Edmund Nolan, then Vice-President of St Edmund's College, Ware, was appointed by the UCEB to be first Catholic chaplain in Cambridge.

## The First Catholic Chaplain

The six years of Fr Nolan's chaplaincy, 1896–1902, were troubled initially by problems of location and jurisdiction. Ever since plans had been prepared for the building of the new Catholic church in Cambridge, Canon Scott's hopes and expectations to establish a centre for undergraduate life and worship had been reflected in the spacious rectory building and the imposing church adjoining. If these hopes now appeared to be threatened by Fr Nolan's appointment as chaplain, the picture was further confused by the emerging plans, approved by the English hierarchy, to establish a Catholic house of studies in Cambridge, Fr Nolan being one of the principal protagonists. A choice was becoming inevitable. On the one hand, the Catholic house of studies (soon to be named St Edmund's House) might also serve as the chaplaincy, with the twin appointments of Master and University Chaplain held by Fr Nolan. The local claimant, on the other hand, was Canon Scott based at his rectory. The Bishop of Northampton, Dr Riddell, made his move in April 1896, seeking to assert his diocesan jurisdiction over Cambridge. He notified Fr Nolan that he had appointed Canon Scott to be University Chaplain, the chaplaincy to be located at his rectory in Hills Road. The English Hierarchy, led by Cardinal Vaughan, responded with an appeal to Rome. Couve de Murville and Jenkins wrote, in *Catholic Cambridge*, that it said much for the equanimity of the 'Chaplain' and the 'Anti-Chaplain' that, while awaiting the verdict, Fr Nolan went to live at the rectory under the same roof as Canon Scott. The reply from Rome in June 1896 ruled that the appointment of university chaplains fell within the collective jurisdiction of the English hierarchy; the only right vested exclusively in the local bishop was to grant a faculty to the appointed chaplain. Dr Riddell had lost, and Canon Scott's hopes for a chaplaincy based in his rectory were dashed.

On the opening of St Edmund's House the following November the separate nature of the chaplaincy was further underlined when the hierarchy designated the chapel to serve also for the undergraduates. The pattern of undergraduate provision which emerged allowed for a half-hour instruction period following the Sunday Mass in St Edmund's chapel, given by a visiting lecturer and on a higher level than could be attempted in a parish sermon. Undergraduates and their parents were severely cautioned that attendance at these instruction periods (or 'conferences' as they were called) was a condition of studying at Cambridge with episcopal approval (*Instruction to the Parents, Superiors and Directors of Catholic Laymen who desire to study in the Universities of Oxford and Cambridge*, August 1896).

In 1899 the number of Catholic undergraduates had increased to forty-five and, St Edmund's House having by then been found too remote, rooms were rented centrally in Green Street to accommodate a chapel and meeting place for the students. The chaplaincy continued at this location until 1902 when the link with St Edmund's was severed with the departure of Fr Nolan for two years to serve as President of Prior Park in Bath. He returned as Master of St Edmund's in 1904, and continued his close connection with the chaplaincy as a member of the UCEB until his death in 1931.

## Cambridge University Catholic Association

It can fairly be said that the moves to secure more tolerant attitudes in the Church towards Catholic undergraduates at Cambridge and the provision of the material resources needed for their spiritual care all originated within the University of Cambridge. As the original guiding spirit in these areas, Baron von Hügel had been joined by Canon Scott and a number of academics in the formation of the Church Maintenance Association in 1887. At first its support was given to the Cambridge parish, but after a change of name to the Cambridge University Catholic Association (CUCA) in 1899, it has directed its funds ever since to the provision of accommodation and upkeep for the university chaplaincy. In this role the CUCA had to work with little help from the English hierarchy at national level or from Canon Scott at local level. For their part the bishops had shown reluctance to encourage the attendance of Catholic youth at Oxford or Cambridge in their Instruction Document of 1896 and their active participation, through the UCEB, was limited to the appointment of chaplains. As for Canon Scott, an ardent supporter of higher education for Catholics, he nevertheless remained opposed to a separate chaplaincy in Cambridge which he saw as passing over the original purpose he had intended for the church and rectory. His church was large and beautiful; their numbers were few. As a result, any funding required for chaplaincy premises and upkeep had perforce to be raised by the committee of the CUCA (though a fortunate exception occurred on the appointment of Fr (later Mgr) Barnes to succeed Fr Nolan, as explained below).

# Four More Chaplains, 1902–1932

Fr Nolan's successor, appointed by the UCEB, was Fr Arthur Barnes, soon to be made a Monsignor and almost always referred to thereafter as 'Mugger Barnes' by a Cambridge populace unfamiliar with this ecclesiastical title or its abbreviated form. Mgr Barnes immediately saw the need for the chaplain to reside on the premises and his independent means permitted him to take a lease of Llandaff House, a large and rambling mansion in Regent Street (on a site opposite the University Arms Hotel but since demolished) for the combined purpose of chaplaincy and chaplain's residence. Llandaff House had belonged to the Anglican Bishop Watson of Llandaff in the 1780s and had served as his residence in Cambridge when he held chairs in the University, first as Professor of Chemistry, then of Divinity. It continued in use as the Catholic Chaplaincy until the lease expired soon after Mgr Barnes left Cambridge in 1916. Unimpeachable as a scholar and public speaker, Mgr Barnes somehow failed to impress the CUCA, who saw him as indolent and over- preoccupied with other interests. Even so, Barnes introduced the highly successful policy of the chaplain being available to his undergraduates at any hour without appointment (a practice followed by his successors ever since), and it can be said on his behalf that undergraduate membership of the chaplaincy had risen from fifty when he first arrived in Cambridge to eighty on the outbreak of the First World War in 1914. Numbers fell sharply with the wartime call to arms and even chaplains were hard to come by to replace Mgr Barnes when he left in 1916. However, these wartime exigencies gave some short-term consolation to Canon Scott. Without premises or chaplain, and with numbers reduced at times to as low as ten, the remaining undergraduates resorted to the parish church and rectory from October 1916 until October 1918. For the academic year 1917–18 Fr O'Connell was posted to the rectory to care for these students ('Spanish, Portuguese and Indians mainly', wrote Edward Conybeare).

To succeed Mgr Barnes after this wartime gap, the UCEB appointed Fr James Bernard Marshall (whose subsequent career as rector of the Cambridge church is described earlier). Fr Marshall had served as a military chaplain on the Western Front and had been posted to Cambridge in October 1918 to serve as chaplain to convalescent soldiers. He moved to a chaplaincy housed in temporary accommodation and with only fifteen undergraduate members. However, by the following January the numbers had recovered to fifty and by May 1919 the CUCA had managed to provide and furnish new premises in Round Church Street House. Here the chapel was consecrated by Bishop Keating of Northampton on 4 May, with an address given by the Bishop of Brentwood. By October 1919, with conditions returning to normal, the undergraduate membership had increased to 100, and for the first time the UCEB showed some financial responsibility for the chaplaincy by awarding Fr Marshall a grant of £50 per annum towards expenses which were at that time nearer to £500. Apparently he was expected to meet the difference from his own pocket.

'My Dear Catholic Undergraduate', wrote the new chaplain in a briefing to his young readers, reminding them to look to the special needs of their eternal souls 'amid the special dangers and temptations of your circumstances here', and insisting on their presence at the weekly conferences. The message was clear; each undergraduate individually was under obligation to seek his own salvation and not to forget the realities of sin and death. While the Church in its official liturgy celebrated Mass for the conversion of pagans and Protestants, individual Catholics were instructed in the virtues of bringing non-Catholics to the faith. He also emphasized the importance of personal acts of will, whereby Catholics repented of their sins and prayed for Almighty God's forgiveness and mercy from the Church which unashamedly claimed to be the sole successor of St Peter. For five terms Alfred Newman Gilbey (Trinity 1920–24), later to take over as chaplain himself in 1932,was under Marshall's chaplaincy. In 1922 Fr Marshall was unexpectedly moved from the chaplaincy to be rector of the Cambridge parish on the death of Canon Scott. His successor was the Revd Dr John Ludlow Lopes (pronounced 'Lopez').

Fr Lopes's over-sized personality (described as 'Johnsonian') and his extravagant style seem well-matched to the pinnacle in the fortunes of the chaplaincy achieved during his time in Cambridge, from 1922 to 1928. In 1925, after two years of negotiations and substantially aided by the tireless energy of the CUCA Treasurer, Professor Edward Bullough, the chaplaincy was given its permanent home at Fisher House in Guildhall Street, the former Black Swan public house. If Dr Lopes, through his success in creating a model for a University chaplaincy, was the principal actor on the Catholic stage in the Cambridge of the 1920s, then Bullough, fellow of Caius and University lecturer in Italian, was sponsor, director and producer.

The serious financial challenges involved in the purchase and conversion of these premises were eventually overcome thanks to the intervention of well-connected members of the UCEB and a substantial and timely legacy. The opening ceremony, on 4 May 1925, was performed on a grand scale, even described as 'basilican'. Mgr Canon Edmund Nolan, the first chaplain and by then serving for a second time as Master of St Edmunds House, returned to the chaplaincy to sing the mass of St John Fisher in the lavishly appointed chapel. Fr

Lopes, although an effective and well-liked chaplain, had no head for finance and the enthusiastic expenditure of his personal fortune on the embellishment of Fisher House led him into debt and forced him to resign in 1928. It has been fairly said that all succeeding chaplains followed the lines laid down by Fr Lopes for the running of the chaplaincy, while his material legacy still survives in the oak-panelled rooms and the bottle-green leaded panes inserted in the downstairs windows.

Lopes was succeeded by an altogether more conventional and less theatrical figure, Fr George MacGillivray, the first Cambridge graduate to serve as chaplain. He put in solid and effective work at the chaplaincy, though he seemed to have a penchant for engaging in heated and well-publicised debates with former clerical colleagues in the Anglican communion. During his years there, 1928–32, MacGillivray was the first chaplain to benefit from a restatement by the UCEB of the duties of the Oxford and Cambridge chaplains. This gave them a greater measure of independence from the CUCA and the local bishop than had been the case in Cambridge for some years previously. However, on the financial front, Fr MacGillivray fared little better than his predecessor, and was forced to resign 'for financial reasons' in 1932.

## The Gilbey Years, 1932–1965

A successor had to be found, one, as it turned out, who was to serve the Catholic chaplaincy for one hundred terms and, by so doing, equalled the combined service of his five predecessors. Alfred Newman Gilbey (Pl. 18b), whose undergraduate membership of the chaplaincy has already been mentioned, graduated BA from Trinity College in 1923, trained for the priesthood at the Beda College in Rome and was ordained in 1929. His ordination by the Bishop of Brentwood in the Gilbey family chapel at Mark Hall, Essex, 'in his own patrimony' (and thus outside the jurisdiction of any bishop), spoke much for the affluence of his family, well known as distillers and wine shippers. His private fortune made him highly suitable for the appointment, as did his strong and recent Cambridge connections. Only his youth caused some hesitation among the members of the appointing UCEB, and for his part the Bishop of Brentwood displayed some reluctance to release Gilbey from his position as Bishop's secretary. His move to Cambridge was eventually secured by the combined efforts of the Archbishop of Birmingham, the Chairman of the Fisher House trustees and Canon Marshall, parish priest in Cambridge. This marked the start of fourteen years of close and friendly co-operation between the parish priest and the University chaplain in Cambridge, an instant rapport born of their earlier roles respectively as chaplain and undergraduate president of the Fisher Society. Less easy for Fr Gilbey to establish was a working relationship between himself and the CUCA. It was to his advantage, unlike the earlier chaplains, that he was financially independent and needed to place no reliance on the Association to maintain the solvency of Fisher House. The major drawback, one unintended by the English hierarchy, was that an essentially ecclesiastical property had been vested in trustees for an exclusive lay association, a situation which appeared to question the authority of the chaplain. Even before his arrival in Cambridge, Fr Gilbey had been warned by Canon Marshall of the all-controlling hand of the CUCA. As Fr Gilbey later recalled, it soon became necessary for him to define his role, by virtue of his appointment by the UCEB, as chaplain to the Catholic undergraduates, not to the CUCA. From the sidelines, Fr Lopes commented 'I am most anxious that the CUCA problem is settled within the family, so to speak'. Happily, a working relationship based on understanding was to emerge between Fr Gilbey and Outram Evennett, a contemporary from Trinity, Secretary of CUCA from 1931 to 1942 and President from 1942 until his death in 1964. For thirty years these two played their respective parts in the harmonious running of the chaplaincy.

Meanwhile, any remaining domestic tensions in the early and mid-1930s were eclipsed by the major commemoration of the quatercentenary of the martyrdom of Blessed John Fisher, Chancellor of the University of Cambridge, in 1935. In Rome, John Fisher and Thomas More were canonized by Pope Pius XI on 19 May, and soon after his return from the ceremony, Canon Marshall celebrated a Sung Mass at Fisher House and attended the Fisher Dinner the same evening. Catholic Cambridge felt able to lay some claim to both new saints as St Thomas More, though an Oxford man, had when Lord Chancellor also held the position of High Steward of the University of Cambridge.

Fr Gilbey's pastoral approach was by example rather than exposition and he exerted a quiet but considerable influence. Notwithstanding numerous personal friendships, the links he maintained with the colleges as Catholic chaplain, while cordial, were unobtrusive. He desired no 'official recognition' from them or the University. His mode of introduction to deans of colleges at the start of the academic year typifies this approach:

> I am venturing to write and ask whether there are any members of my 'flock' among your freshmen. I enclose overleaf the names of such of

your undergraduates as I know to be Catholic. If you are aware of no others, I hope that you will not trouble to answer this note, for I appreciate how busy you must be at this time.

Peaceful co-operation with the parish and assistance from time to time with its pastoral work came to be a consistent feature of the pre-war and wartime years. Examples noted in the *Cambridge Catholic Magazine* included Fr Gilbey opening the parish Christmas fair in 1938; Fr Gilbey preaching the sermon at the Corpus Christi procession and observances in 1940 (his subject was 'Divorce and Commitment. He who brings you into this world also takes you away, – let nothing stand between you and Him'); Fr Gilbey preaching at the Feast of SS John Fisher and Thomas More in 1945. As Fr Gilbey was to point out later, 'There was no conflict between the Parish and the Chaplaincy neither bellicose nor interest.' Fisher House survived the wartime years unscathed, neither damaged by bombing nor requisitioned for emergency purposes, though in 1942 a plan to convert the Fisher Room into an RAF canteen, staffed by the Catholic Women's League, had fallen through.

Two threats, as each would have been perceived by Fr Gilbey, still remained to challenge the chaplaincy as he knew it during the post-war years. The first of these involved the Catholic women undergraduates of the University who since their first appearance in Cambridge in the late 1870s had enjoyed no equivalent chaplaincy provision to that offered to the men. Women had first been admitted to the Tripos examinations in 1881 but were not recognized as members of the University nor permitted to graduate until 1947. No recognition was at first afforded to this anomalous female status by the chaplaincy, the CUCA or the UCEB, all uniformly male preserves. At last, in 1937, the Canonesses of St Augustine (Les Oiseaux) established a small convent at Lady Margaret House in Grange Road, Newnham, and the following year it became a House of Studies. At this point the UCEB stepped in to appoint Fr Humphrey Johnson to act as chaplain to the Catholic women undergraduates of the (Lady) Margaret Beaufort Society. Sunday Mass was held for them at Lady Margaret House, followed in the afternoon by a conference. From this time onwards Cambridge had two separate Catholic chaplaincies. After 1947, with women now recognized as full members of the University, proposals were made with increasing frequency for the merger of the two chaplaincies under joint chaplains. Gilbey (by now a Monsignor) was opposed in principle to the admission of women to Fisher House. He saw such a move as contrary to all his traditionalist beliefs and outlook and a potential breach of his personal commitment to hand Fisher House over to his successor exactly as he had found it. Out of deference to the chaplain the CUCA agreed to postpone the admission of women until after Mgr Gilbey's retirement date in 1966. Gilbey felt some resentment that the proposal for a mixed chaplaincy had percolated upwards from a resolution of the undergraduate members of Fisher House (on 30 April 1965) when to him it should have come from above, perhaps as a directive from the English hierarchy to be implemented by the UCEB. Bowing to the inevitable and to avoid any confrontation on the issue, he tendered his resignation one year early, in 1965. Almost immediately Fisher House became a mixed chaplaincy in its present-day form and after twenty-seven years of separate existence the Margaret Beaufort Society was no more.

The other threat to the chaplaincy concerned the proposal, first mooted in 1948, for compulsory purchase and comprehensive redevelopment of the area of central Cambridge known as the Lion Yard site, which included Fisher House on its periphery. Refusing to admit any inevitability about this proposal, Mgr Gilbey, by use of his unrivalled network of friends in high places, ensured that a petition to save Fisher House reached the hands of the Minister of Housing and Local Government, Sir Keith Joseph. On 29 August 1964 the Minister announced that Fisher House would be excluded from the compulsory purchase order. No-one could doubt that the credit for saving Fisher House was due solely to Mgr Gilbey. The CUCA and the Fisher House membership were lastingly grateful for his achievement.

Such was the style of the man that little surprise was caused when Mgr Gilbey chose to take up permanent residence in a London club for the last thirty-three years of his life, remaining, as *The Times* put it, impressively active into his nineties and developing what became in effect a ministry to his legions of friends. Among the many obituaries and tributes which followed his death on 26 March 1998 the following excerpts may serve to illustrate the lasting impression that survives him:

> Monsignor Alfred Gilbey was the last Roman Catholic priest of his kind – and had been for a considerable time ... [his] attitudes ... were those of another era. He held his beliefs with an absolute conviction, and the result was a grand and magnetic serenity which attracted many from a more uncertain era. Alfred Gilbey was highly influential, particularly ... among a generation of Cambridge undergraduates. During his 33 years as chaplain to the university there he instructed around 170 converts. Gilbey loved Cambridge and the feeling was mutual for three decades (*The Times*, 27 March 1998).

> The English Catholic community is unlikely ever again to produce a priest quite like Mgr Alfred Gilbey, and his funeral marked the end of an era. Alfred Gilbey himself was a society priest, chronically politically

incorrect, his self-consciously old-fashioned lifestyle a world away from the ethos of preferential options for the poor. The real life of any priest is invisible, measured in secret by the lives he touches and helps heal. The hundreds who crowded to pay their last respects to Alfred Gilbey were the best possible testimony to the breadth and depth of his priestly life (Eamon Duffy, *The Tablet*, 11–13 April 1998).

# Chapter 29

# St Edmund's College, Cambridge

*Christopher Jackson*

No history of Catholic Cambridge would be complete without a reference to the story of St Edmund's, the only example of a Catholic academic institution existing within the University of Cambridge. If unique for its denominational affiliation, it may also be considered unique in the century-long path it was obliged to follow from its humble origins in 1896 through a prolonged process of acceptance which ended in its eventual recognition as one of the colleges of Cambridge University.

## Fr Edmund Nolan

It was only shortly after the Decree of Propaganda of 1 April 1895, which withdrew the prohibition against English Catholics enrolling as undergraduates in the University of Cambridge, that Fr Edmund Nolan began his campaign, prompted at the suggestion of Cardinal Ledochowski (of *Propaganda Fide*), to establish a Catholic house of studies in Cambridge. This was intended initially to be a branch of St Edmund's College, Ware. Fr Nolan was the charismatic Vice-Principal of St Edmund's College, which at that time admitted seminary students, and he must have seen the potential value to the teaching role of the Church to have graduates among its clergy. He also realized that, to make any such project viable, adequate numbers would have to be found, whether from seminary students or from laymen, and that substantial funding would be required. Fr Nolan approached the diocesan bishops in the hope that they would be willing to send seminary students to Cambridge for a university education. Surprisingly few of them were. The northern bishops had devoted hard-won resources to the establishment of their own seminary, at Ushaw College near Durham, and had no desire to have it drained of numbers or talent to support a venture in Cambridge. In any event, most bishops wished to see their candidates for the priesthood embark upon their much-needed pastoral role without too much delay in the pursuit of academic refinement. A particular opponent among the hierarchy proved to be the local bishop, Dr Riddell of Northampton, without whose consent priests could not come to live or work within his diocese. As to financial help, any thought that this might have been found from St Edmund's College was soon put aside. It would only have been sufficient to support their own Cambridge branch on an extremely modest scale. Seeking more broadly-based funding, Fr Nolan chose to approach Baron von Hügel in Cambridge.

## Ayherst Hostel

The Revd William Ayherst, a Low Church Anglican, had opened Ayherst Hostel, containing twenty-four sets of undergraduate rooms, in Mount Pleasant, Cambridge in 1895, in the hope of obtaining University recognition for his establishment as a Public Hostel. The project soon ran into financial difficulties and the premises were put up for sale in 1896. Following Fr Nolan's approach, Baron von Hügel succeeded in persuading Henry, 15th Duke of Norfolk, a noted Catholic benefactor, to provide in great secrecy the £6000 purchase price. The Duke was allowed to view the property from the security of a closed carriage as it drove past, lest his identity should provoke a change of mind on the part of the committed Low Church vendor.

The purchase was, however, completed without any such last-minute hitch and in spite of the Baron's anxiety the property was conveyed quite openly into the Duke's name. The Duke had been persuaded to part with his money on the understanding that the property was to be used as a seminary to which secular students for the priesthood could come at the direction of their bishop. As will be seen, this objective was never actually realized, but at a stroke the prospect of financial dependence on St Edmund's College had vanished, along with the concept of a 'branch college' status. Flushed with this triumph, von Hügel suggested to Fr Nolan that, with Cardinal Vaughan's consent (which was readily granted), he too should apply, as Revd Mr Ayherst had originally intended, for recognition of the new project as a Public Hostel. This would be the inviting first rung on the ladder towards an eventual incorporation within the University. To attain this status a formal constitution would have to be drawn up and approved, adequate funding would have to be shown, and the University authorities would require to be satisfied as to the purposes of the new institution. Only two other Public Hostels had ever been recognized before, Cavendish College (with its irritating complement of immature students) in 1882 and Selwyn College in 1883. A name was obviously needed too, and almost by default Fr Nolan carried on using the name 'St Edmund's', deriving from the original connection with his College. Even when no link remained after 1896, this name (adjusted to 'St Edmund's House') was included, with no debate and little logic, in the formal constitution of the new foundation which was signed by the Duke and the other members of the Governing Body in December 1897. By this time it was already evident that most English bishops were not prepared to use St Edmund's as an alternative diocesan seminary, though at least Bishop Riddell was persuaded to withdraw his own opposition, permitting other priests into his diocese on return for a promise of support for Canon Scott's pastoral work in Cambridge.

On the financial front, it soon emerged that the University authorities would not consider the registration as a Public Hostel without a minimum permanent endowment of £6000. An appeal was launched among Catholic well-wishers and a sum of £6330 was raised by February 1898, most of this coming from a further donation of £6000 from the Duke of Norfolk.

## The Senate Vote

With the conditions for recognition satisfied, the application was debated in the University Senate in March 1898 and a vote among the members was called for the following May. Much vigorous campaigning took place during the Easter vacation of 1898, from which it emerged that anti-Catholic feeling might have been more easily swayed in favour of an exclusively Catholic seminary than a more broadly based foundation. In the interests of attracting sufficient numbers, the founders of St Edmund's House had been obliged to allow for the admission of lay undergraduates, while naturally retaining a Catholic identity. The critics found it easy to allege that a limitation of academic freedom was inherent in the denominational affinity of St Edmund's, and in spite of the most active efforts of Baron von Hügel, the opponents of recognition won the day by 471 votes to 218. Writing eighty years later, the College historian Garrett Sweeney took the view that this was probably by far the best result for the infant foundation because, with such tiny numbers (never more than four students for the priesthood enrolled during the next twelve years), it would have been doomed to extinction as a Public Hostel.

## Sub-Collegiate Toleration

As a result of the Senate vote, St Edmund's carried on 'a species of sub-collegiate life', as Garrett Sweeney put it, for the next sixty-six years, solicitously welcomed and supported by Good Samaritans from the Lodging Houses syndicate, the Non-Collegiate Students Board and Fitzwilliam Hall, this last taking the undergraduates wholeheartedly under its wing. In terms of student numbers and the necessary expansion of buildings, progress was extremely slow during those sixty-six years. One factor served, however, to offset the otherwise rather humble status of St Edmund's in Cambridge during this time. This stemmed from the roughly contemporaneous foundation in France of Catholic Universities at Lille and Angers, and Catholic Institutes in Paris and Toulouse. Eminent French theologians and other academics from these institutions tended to make their contacts in Cambridge through St Edmund's, and certainly in the early years, 1896-1902, a number of such individuals paid visits either to Baron von Hügel's residence at Croft Cottage or to St Edmund's when in Cambridge.

## Improving Status

The application for recognition as a Public Hostel in 1898 was described above as the inviting first rung on the ladder towards eventual incorporation in the University. By the time the next (successful) application was made at the end of the First World War, the 'Public Hostel' designation had been replaced by that of 'Official House of Residence', and St Edmund's was granted this status in close relationship with Fitzwilliam House. It was not until 1964 that adjustments to its constitution brought admission to the next, still lowly, rank of Approved Society, while another eleven years of development and reorganization brought advancement to the more permanent status of Approved Foundation in 1975. St Edmund's could now stand alongside the rest of the older University institutions and it would surely have been most reassuring to its then complement of twenty-five undergraduates that this new status, once gained, could no longer be withdrawn arbitrarily and at any time by the University, at the expense of their own academic careers.

As if to offer reassurance to intending scholars, especially those from overseas, not to mention intending benefactors, the decision was made, with effect from the start of the academic year 1986-7, to change the name of St Edmund's House to St Edmund's College. The grant of a coat of arms by the College of Arms in October 1987 followed as an appropriate sequel to this confident step forward. With improved status came improved prospects, extended buildings which from 1993 could accommodate an expanded student enrolment of 225 men and women pursuing courses in every academic discipline, and a Tower Block, completed in 1992, which gave a prominent, almost landmark status to this newly emerging College.

## The Royal Charter, 1998

The final goal was now within reach. In February 1996 the University approved a report in support of recognition of full collegiate status for St Edmund's College. Important formalities then had to be implemented; the preparation of a draft charter, statutes and ordinances of the College for approval by the Privy Council, a petition to the Queen for a royal charter, the grant of that charter under the great seal to 'St Edmund's College, Cambridge' in 1998, followed by the recognition of full collegiate status in the University of Cambridge.

# Chapter 30

# The Priory of the Dominicans in Cambridge

*Fr Aidan Nichols, OP*

## Introducing the Dominican Order

The Order was founded by St Dominic (1216 is the official date of foundation) to be an 'Order of Preachers'. He was responding to the need he saw for people to be trained for the work of preaching (as most clergy then were not) who would lend weight to their words by the manner – derived from ancient Christian monasticism – of their life. From the beginning the Order took on both the work of popular preaching and the study and teaching of philosophy and theology, so as to harness the new intellectual developments of the time in the service of the Gospel.

At the date St Dominic established the Order, new orders had to adopt existing Rules, and St Dominic adopted the Rule of St Augustine, to which he had been used while a Canon at Osma in Spain. It is so basic and simple a Rule about living together in peace and mutual respect in a religious community dedicated to a committed Christian life and service, that the orders which adopted it could supplement and adapt it with their own constitutions. That fact allowed St Dominic to give the Order a set of Constitutions strikingly different from those of other orders then recently founded. The Constitutions were thoroughly revised in the period 1960–68, but preserving the emphases of St Dominic as they need to appear today, when the Order is much smaller in many areas than it was in the Middle Ages. Since the Order was founded for the good of souls, St Dominic allowed superiors to dispense members from the observances when they would impede preaching and study. He avoided having numerous detailed and fussy rules in the Constitutions. Rather, to promote personal responsibility and local initiatives to meet local needs, he made the Order democratic, with superiors elected and sharing their authority with chapters and councils, and had it stated in the Constitutions that disobeying the Constitutions did not make one automatically guilty of a sin of disobedience.

From the beginning the Order has included not only communities of friars but monasteries of enclosed nuns who contemplate the Word preached by the brethren and pray for the apostolic fruitfulness of their activities. Shortly after, it acquired chapters of lay members living in the world but committed to a life of penance, prayer and Christian good works. In the modern period, these were joined by sisterhoods living the 'mixed' life, combining community life with such active tasks as education and nursing. The first three groups constitute the Order proper; the last is associated with them in the wider 'Dominican family'.

## Medieval Cambridge

The foundation of a Dominican priory in medieval Cambridge constitutes an important chapter in that 'coming of the friars' which reinvigorated urban Catholicism in particular in early thirteenth-century England. The exact date at which the Order of Preachers reached the small University town on the edge of the Fens is unknown, but it cannot have been long before 1238, when Henry III made them a gift of timber for the building of their chapel. The priory, with its close University connections, would remain until the Reformation one of the foremost English houses of an order which, under the pre-Tudor dynasties, enjoyed the special patronage of the crown as well as maintaining a high profile in ecclesiastical society, congruent with its eminence in Western Christendom at large. Yet the life of a Religious house, like any household, is largely made up of routine events, and the chief scholarly study of the medieval Cambridge Blackfriars nicely combines the humdrum with the high-flying when, after duly noting the limitations in our evidence, it records:

> Hundreds of Cambridge Dominicans are known by name but few other features can be clearly discerned. We catch random glimpses of them around the town; one plays the organ in Great St Mary's; ... another goes to hear the confessions of the nuns at St Radegund's and a third receives alms from the fellows of Corpus Christi. The younger ones might receive ordination in churches such as St Clement's or All Saints. Most were English, but there were foreigners too within the priory walls.

A few of the friars became distinguished or famous, and the normal routine of the convent might be interrupted by the holding of a parliament, the preaching of a cardinal, or the prior being taken away to the Tower of London. In the eyes of many here and abroad the convent was a place of learning, but we should not forget that it was also a place of prayer and of pilgrimage.

Since 1990, when Dr Patrick Zutshi and Fr Robert Ombres wrote those words, the dedication of the medieval priory, which they confessed themselves unable to locate, has been found by Mr Nicholas Rogers in the obit-roll of Prior Robert Ebchester of Durham – thus proving that some yawning gaps in our factual information about the past can betimes be closed. But, despite the newly discovered title of the *collegium* – the Holy Trinity (the later and parvenu 'Trinity College, Cambridge' beware!) – it was an image of Our Lady of Grace which provided the devotional complement to the intellectual and pastoral efforts of the friars, and which continued to attract pilgrims and testators up to the very eve of the Reformation (indeed, the evidence for its prominence in the city of Cambridge and beyond is essentially sixteenth-century). It has been claimed that a statue of the Virgin and Child venerated in the modern Catholic parish church of Our Lady and the English Martyrs is the selfsame image; alas, the claim is more seductive than compelling.

The chief work of the Dominicans was, of course, to teach and to write – and both entailed above all, in the medieval Scholastic context, the production of commentaries on Scripture. The markedly metaphysical and ethical cast of the Order's philosophical tradition may be apparent, however, in the fact that Holcot, d'Eyncourt, Hopeman and de Ryngstede, all Cambridge friars whose works are extant, chose to write on the wisdom books of the Bible, where these features (metaphysics, ethics) are especially plain. The library facilities open to them – to judge by the cast-off books acquired at the Reformation for the Vatican Library by the future Pope Marcellus II – consisted largely of classical, patristic and later medieval authors, not least the prince of Dominican thinkers, St Thomas Aquinas, and this is wholly unsurprising since Latin Christian culture was built on just these bases. Dominican publications were intended for an international readership of an élite kind; to the city folk of Cambridge far more important would have been the preaching and sacramental ministrations offered in the priory church and, on frequent though irregular occasions, elsewhere. Vernacular preaching, and a liturgy which created around itself the kind of popular devotional penumbra described by Professor Eamon Duffy were stimulants to areas the austere liquid of Scholastic exegesis could not reach.

These services did not save the friars, however, from the vagaries of Tudor religious policy and the more predictable constant of hunger for revenue. What the English Crown had given – by way of repeated financial assistance, and the resolution of disputes in the predominant, if not exclusive, favour of the friars, it now – in 1538 – took away. The theological confusion of Henry VIII's reign divided minds among the Cambridge friars: Prior Robert Buckenham was doughty as an opponent of the reformer Hugh Latimer (both occupied the pulpit of St Edward, King and Martyr, off Market Hill); Prior Gregory Dodds became Anglican Dean of Exeter and would later subscribe the Thirty-Nine Articles. Sixteen names appear on the deed of surrender of the house (certainly not the full complement of brethren). They owned nothing save the property, parts of which (notably the church) would be re-cycled by the founder of Emmanuel College (for buttery, hall and fellows' parlour) under Elizabeth I. The gateposts (or at any rate the stumps thereof) were rediscovered in the 1770s when they were bought by Revd William Cole for the embellishment of his drive at Milton.

## Modern Cambridge

There matters rested until the advent, in the Cambridge of the 1930s, of a remarkable married pair of lay Dominicans, Edward Bullough, Caian and eventually, if briefly before his premature death, Serena Professor of Italian, and Enrichetta Bullough, only child of the celebrated Italian actress Eleonora Duse. It was through their vision, piety, and good planning that the Order of Preachers returned to Cambridge on the seventh centenary of its presumed date of arrival (1238) and the fourth of its perfectly definite date of dissolution (1538). The English Prior Provincial, Fr Bernard Delany, wrote on 20 September 1937

> Dear Mrs Bullough
> Hurray! I have just heard from Fr. General that he and his Council have approved of the Cambridge Foundation and they give the necessary permission to accept your generous gift and to make a start at Cambridge. Since we already had a foundation at Cambridge there will be no need to have recourse to the Holy See. So the official procedure will be simple.

The 'gift' in question was the handing over of the splendid Italianate house, complete with balconies, shutters and a stone and tile courtyard staircase, designed for the pleasure of the ultramontane Mrs Bullough and her cosmopolitan husband by the Cambridge architect H. C. Hughes (Pl. 26b). Edward Bullough, who was to play no less consequential a part, for Cambridge Catholicism, by his purchase, as treasurer of the Cambridge University Catholic Association, of the premises soon to be known as 'Fisher House', was a significant player in the University of the inter-War years.

## The Bulloughs

Edward Bullough was a Trinity man, though it is with Caius, the college of his fellowship and to which, in Professor Christopher Brooke's phrase, he 'brought a European culture', that his name should be associated. The son of wealthy industrialists (on his father's side Lancastrian, his mother's Swiss), he was born in the Bernese Oberland and educated in Germany, at the prestigious Leipziger Vizthum Gymnasium where he met the girl, well-connected in the world of literature and the theatre in Italy, who would be his wife. The fledgling Medieval and Modern Languages Faculty at Cambridge was to be his intellectual home for the future, though in keeping with the polyglot composition of the School (he was expected to lecture on not only German but also Russian and Italian language and texts), his own interests were ebulliently polymathic. Among them, aesthetics were chief. As a former pupil explains, Bullough approached aesthetics from the 'psychological and even physiological point of view', conducting experiments at the Cambridge Psychological Laboratory and producing distinguished papers on such matters as the perception and appreciation of colours and the role of 'psychic distance' in the enjoyment of objects of art. His approach anticipated that of the art historian Ernst Gombrich; it influenced the philosopher Michael Oakeshott; it was ground-breaking in a period when aesthetics had no university base in England save the recently founded Courtauld Institute in London; and it left a lasting mark on the mind of his son, the Dominican Halley Sebastian Bullough. Not till 1923 did Bullough become a Catholic, received into the Church by the celebrated Jesuit writer and preacher Cyril Martindale. He was a 'catch' of a magnitude (he had just served as assistant secretary of a Royal Commission on the ancient universities) that his co-religionists were not slow to exploit. Joint president of the British Federation of University Catholic Societies, and subsequently president of Pax Romana, the international umbrella for such national networks, his translation into English of a major product of the Thomist renaissance, Etienne Gilson's *Le Thomisme*, affected Catholic intellectual life in England more substantially than did his studies of Italian literature, though the latter prepared the way for the career as Dante expositor of another pupil, and future Dominican, Francis Kenelm Foster.

Edward Bullough's unexpected death from septicaemia occurred before the fine house he had planned with his wife was completed. With both their son and their daughter (Leonora) on their way into religious life (the latter as Sister Mark of the English Dominican Congregation of St Catherine of Siena), Mrs Bullough took steps to hand over in her lifetime a home now too large and, doubtless, lonely for her needs. The dedication of the house on Mount Pleasant to the archangel St Michael was the choice of the Bullough family, who remembered how shrines of the angels are usually on hill tops (such as Mont St Michel) and wanted a symbol of the struggle of intellectual good with evil – which archangels can fittingly furnish.

The size and discreet elegance of the building made it perfect for a small community of friars in a city where English Dominicans certainly wanted to be. The early history of their Order, after all, was inseparable from the growth of the European universities, and their mission of doctrinal teaching, study, writing could hardly find a more fitting environment. Unlike the medieval Blackfriars, however, its modern successor would not be a study house of the Province in the sense of a place where young Dominicans were trained. That slot was already filled – for philosophy by Hawkesyard Priory in Staffordshire, the gift of the Spode family of china fame; for theology by Blackfriars Oxford, the dream-come-true of the great Edwardian Provincial Fr Bede Jarrett. Some other description needed to be found for the revived house in Cambridge – and it was in the shape of *domus scriptorum*, a 'house of writers'. For not every one who likes to write likes to teach, while teaching at seminary level, like that in overstretched modern universities, can drive out research.

## The House of Writers

Most, but not all, of the 'writing' Dominicans in the English Province turn out to have spent years, many or few, at Blackfriars, Cambridge – profiting by the calm of its garden, the moderation of its small regular congregation's pastoral demands, the decent library, and the proximity of university and faculty libraries beyond. When researching for a book on the major figures of the pre- and immediately post-Conciliar Province, the author of this chapter found that six out of seven of his 'just men' fitted this description. Thus we have Victor White, acute dogmatician and pioneering critical student of C. G. Jung; the spiritual theologian Gerald Vann whose books still find new publishers in the United States; the Thomist philosopher and moral theologian Thomas Gilby, who combined flair and finesse in exegesis of St Thomas's texts, with a style that made Scholastic metaphysics acceptable to the most English of Englishmen; Sebastian Bullough (Pl. 26a), who, after an early thesis on the concept of aesthetic beauty, turned his hand to almost any plant in the Catholic garden; Kenelm Foster, Reader in Italian in the University, and fastidious student of Dante and Petrarch, St Catherine and St Thomas; Conrad Pepler, explorer of the English medieval mystical tradition and continuator of that wonderful experiment in counter-cultural Catholicism, the Guild of St Joseph and St Dominic at Ditchling, where art, craft, natural things and communal living were worked into a unity around the prayer of the Mass and the Divine Office.

The vocation to be a 'house of writers' was also realized in the form of corporate projects, above all, the editing of the massive multi-volume bilingual *Summa Theologiae*, with copious introductions, notes, appendices, which the publishing house Eyre and Spottiswoode undertook in the shadow of the Second Vatican Council, unaware that, all unintentionally, that Council would have the effect of temporarily eclipsing St Thomas's reputation in the eyes of many Catholics who, imperfectly instructed, blamed classical Christian Scholasticism for their Communion's real or supposed ills. Again, it could manifest itself in the editing of journals – first, *New Blackfriars*, until that peripatetic organ of English Dominicans and friends moved back to Oxford in 1970, and then, twenty years later, the erstwhile journal of the diocesan clergy in England, the *Clergy Review*, now rebaptized *Priests and People*, and with a wider, and more popular remit, until its editor, Fr David Sanders, went to Oxford in 1998 as master of students.

## Expansion and its Limits

Meanwhile, the material fortunes of Blackfriars fluctuated. Thomas Gilby, during thirty years of residence, risked much on expansion, envisaging the future along the lines of the medieval past, when a revived *studium generale*, or study-house for the whole Order of Preachers worldwide, would take shape around the nucleus of St Michael's, the Bullough property. In 1955 Fr Thomas was aided and abetted by the Province's other last great builder, Fr Kenneth Wykeham-George, then Superior of Blackfriars, who took the lead in acquiring Howfield, St Michael's elder neighbour, on the demise of its owner, A. S. Ramsey, president of Magdalene and father of Arthur

Michael Ramsey, the future Archbishop of Canterbury. Ramsey *père*, a former Congregationalist, had disapproved of the Dominicans; the ecumenism of Ramsey *fils*, at the time Bishop of Durham, was oriented more toward Constantinople than Rome. Nonetheless, a deal with another buyer was stopped so that the offer from Blackfriars might be accepted. Until such time as the two houses could be joined (Howfield now houses the refectory and common room of the priory, as well as the kitchens and seven bedrooms for the community), a married fellow of Clare – Timothy Smiley, later Professor of Logic – came as warden of a set of student tenants of the friars. Other initiatives of conventional empire-building were not so successful. Enquiries were made about St Giles's vicarage, across Buckingham Road, for the parish of St Giles's was failing (the last incumbent left in 1968), and the building would have a chequered history until in 1982 it became the rectory of a new combined Anglican parish of St Giles with St Luke's and St Augustine's. (In 1991, however, the Church Commissioners disposed of it to New Hall.) When the well-known Cambridge authoress Gwen Raverat died in 1957 the question was raised of entering a bid for The Granary, since it was not realized that the owner was Sir Charles Darwin, with Mrs Raverat as lessee. (That house too fell to New Hall, as the Darwins' gift at the new college's inception.) More successful, if only temporarily so, was the incorporation of Buckingham House, the Reddaway family home which had given its name to the street where Blackfriars stands, and, by 1964, a Magdalene College hostel superfluous to requirements. On a site much disturbed by nineteenth-century archaeologists eager for coprolite (fossilised dinosaur excreta), with consequent subsidence problems of a chronic kind, it was not perhaps a good buy, but hard financial necessity alone forced the community to consider its re-sale as early as 1970 and in 1981 to part with it (to the benefit – once again – of New Hall).

In compensation, Fr Thomas had at least been able to unite Howfield with St Michael's in 1961–2, by a piece of building by David Roberts which a 1964 guide, *Cambridge New Architecture*, deemed 'admirably direct and straightforward, ... the first high quality modern religious building in Cambridge'. The *aula* (lecture-room, but convertible for worship, since the original oratory is small) has generally been approved, its two faces – into nature, the primordial creation, and the city, the human continuation of the creation – suggesting the twofold orientation, to contemplation and action, of the Order. The new library, too, is a good, simple design, but the proposed 'instruction rooms' are in the main more reminiscent of the supervision offered by Her Majesty's Prison Service than of anything called by that name in the University. All this, however, was but a stage in a grandiose plan, which would have produced a convent covering numerous acres and rivalling in size its medieval forebear.

The *aula*'s iconographic austerity has been relieved in recent years by the acquisition of a copy of the Thornham Parva retable, the principal visual art work left by the Dominicans of the English Middle Ages (the original, made in the fourteenth century for an East Anglian priory, is now, by the gift of its last lay owners, the Barons Henniker, in a tiny Suffolk church).

The Blackfriars retable has since been complemented by a set of engraved windows of angels and archangels, based by their designer (the Icklingham stained glass artist and lay Dominican Bronwen Pulsford) on the late medieval panel-painting of St Michael in the Norfolk church of Ranworth; a Flemish Virgin and Child of *c.* 1700, and an early Gothic Revival wooden figure of St Dominic, of French provenance.

## Lay community, Congregation, University Chaplaincy

Financial over-optimism was not the only cause for the non-happening of the one-time grandiose scheme. There was also the little point of the vocations crisis which struck the English Dominicans (as all, or almost all, Orders and communities in England) after the Second Vatican Council. The reduction of the resident brethren to four led to a decision in 1980 to accept, on an annual basis, a variety of young lay-people – nearly all members of the University, and overwhelmingly graduate students, not as tenants simply (as previously in Howfield), but as associates or oblates, with the obligation to attend the choir offices and common meals. The friars offered in effect on a miniature-scale and in a less schoolmasterly way a formation in Christian wisdom and the liturgy of the Church previously given to larger groups in our 'apostolic schools'. A number of vocations to the Dominican priesthood, and one to a Dominican sisterhood, have come from this experience.

But if, in rational economics, buildings must be filled, an imaginatively conceived apostolate will not be confined to one's own building. The Sunday and weekday congregation at Blackfriars increased dramatically after the opening of the *aula* chapel (though the first, confined, chapel on the ground floor continues to house the Blessed Sacrament and be used for the majority of the Offices – its choirstalls were added to this end in 1997). This encouraged the Dominicans to provide Bible study sessions and programmes of talks, with speakers both external and internal, in the priory itself. But their apostolate had always been intended to *focus* on the University (which is not to say be exclusively directed thereto). Throughout the post-War years the 'Dominican Lectures' held annually in the Mill Lane lecture theatres were a high point of Catholic intellectual life in Cambridge. Unforgivably, they were permitted to lapse in 1970 – though Fr Maurice Couve de Murville, later Archbishop of Birmingham, considered himself to be reviving them 'under a slightly different guise' in 1979, when he proposed to have Dominicans alternate with others as holders of a 'Fisher Lecturership'). The idea was a tribute by a diocesan priest to what he had gained from attending the Dominican Lectures as an undergraduate. At Fisher House itself, the Dominicans were a more consistent presence, providing assistant chaplains with Fr Robert Ombres and Fr Aidan Nichols, and then a senior chaplain in the person of Fr Allan White who, however, retained a canonical assignation elsewhere (first to the Oxford priory, and then to the London one). For fifteen years Fr David Sanders animated the very successful Fisher House Bible Study, drawing on his considerable New Testament expertise from teaching in the University of the West Indies and the Cambridge Divinity Faculty, while friars too numerous to mention contributed to the 'Blackfriars Theology Group', originally founded by Fr Edward Booth, and were celebrants and preachers at College Masses.

## Present and Future Prospects

Though the resident Dominican community at Cambridge was for many years rather small, its identity remained well-defined in terms of the medieval and modern story I have traced. At Easter 2000, the English Dominican Province tacitly acknowledged this in electing to make Blackfriars the common noviciate for its priories and houses. The prior and community are engaged in a wide variety of intellectual and pastoral roles, lecturing in the University and elsewhere, and writing on theology, dogmatics, spirituality and canon law. Our novices come from a variety of academic and professional backgrounds, with diverse gifts to bring to the 'contemplative apostolate' of preaching and teaching in the Order. When space permits, the priory accepts Dominicans from elsewhere for periods of a year at a time: these can range from young friars improving their English-language skills to distinguished scholars seeking a sabbatical amid the Cambridge libraries.

# Chapter 31

# The Catholic School, Union Road, Cambridge

*Philip S. Wilkins*
*with a contribution by Stella Fox*

It may be helpful at the outset to note that during its existence the school has been known consecutively by three titles. From its foundation in 1843 it was referred to by the education authorities as the Union Road Roman Catholic School, though, being closely associated with the nearby Catholic church of St Andrew, it was soon known widely by that title. Not until 1936, however, when a new building was commissioned, did the school become officially entitled St Andrew's. Finally, in 1962 when the senior pupils were transferred to a new Catholic secondary school in the city, the resulting primary school changed its name to St Alban's to terminate a confusion which had occurred for years with St Andrew's Church of England School in the suburb of Chesterton.

## Foundation and Early Years

Fr Quinlivan, who was appointed in charge of the Cambridge mission in July 1843, held strong views on good secular and religious education for Catholic children living in an atmosphere antagonistic to their religion, and one of his first priorities was the provision of schooling for the children of his flock. By December 1843 he had opened a school in a pair of semi-detached cottages which served as the mission house and which stood on church property in Union Road (see Fig. 9 which shows the cottages as numbers 15 and 16 St Andrew's Place).

*THE CAMBRIDGE CATHOLIC MISSION IN 1880*

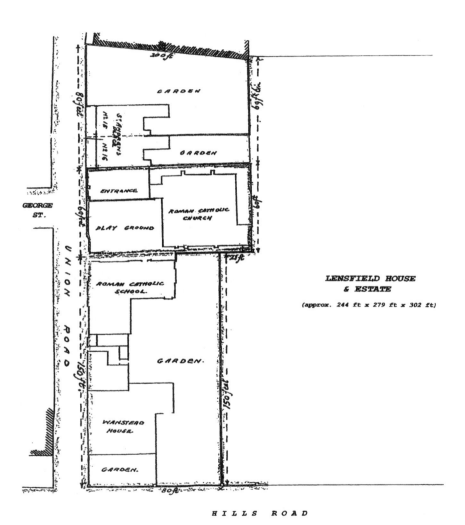

Fig. 9.    Site plan showing the location of the original church and
school buildings.

The Union Road area, then known as New Town, was the first sizeable housing development to be built south of the ancient town centre and included a mixture of cheap and modest houses. Much of the accommodation was intended to cope with an influx from the countryside of people who had been deprived of their traditional land rights by enclosures and who sought work and housing in an urban environment. A considerable expansion of the University at that period added to a demand for more employment and attracted other people to this area of new dwellings from which a majority of the few pupils at the Catholic School was drawn in its early years.

## The Struggle to Survive

The decade in which the Union Road School was started saw an impressive growth in Catholic elementary education in England and Wales, some 166 Catholic schools being founded between 1841 and 1851, more than the total previously in existence. The impetus for this increase arose through a government decision to award Catholics grants for erection and annual support of their schools on the basis previously enjoyed only by Anglican and Nonconformist establishments. This aid, channelled through the Catholic Poor Schools Committee, provided the Union Road school with a total of £169 in support grants during the years 1848 to 1865.

While welcoming this material aid for the purposes of secular education, the Catholic bishops strongly emphasized that schools should equally promote the importance of 'sound faith, virtue and piety, by far the most important elements in education'. Accordingly, ecclesiastical inspectors would be appointed to examine pupils in religious education and 'there should also be public catechetical instruction on every Sunday in church, at which the mysteries of the faith and the commandments of God and the Church and the doctrine of the sacraments shall be explained in a plain and clear manner in conjunction with the service of Benediction'. Thus 'Sunday School' was instituted in Catholic missions throughout England and Wales, a practice which was immediately adopted at the Union Road School and which continued until after the Second Vatican Council. Each Sunday afternoon during the school year the more senior children would be gathered in the church for instruction based on the Catechism of Christian Doctrine issued by the Catholic Bishops of England and Wales.

A return made to the Committee on Education in 1845 indicated that fourteen boys were then in attendance at the school though 'the number of children requiring gratuitous education' was stated to be forty. The Mission acknowledged that the accommodation was inadequate but funds for erecting a proper school building were non-existent. Among the first teachers at the school was a James O'Brian, who was in charge in 1847. He may well not have been specially qualified but was a member of the Catholic community with some education.

Like many other Catholic mission schools, it was a most humble beginning for such a venture, but one backed by intense faith. The majority of Fr Quinlivan's parishioners were of very limited means. To finance the school he had to rely mainly on help from one or two influential patrons with some contribution from his own stipend and collections in church and at social gatherings to make up the regular deficit, but for many years the existence of the school remained precarious. Nevertheless, though the school consequently lacked all but the barest facilities, it had the great advantage of being situated next to the church and thus enabling and encouraging the children's exercise of their religious duties.

An application submitted by Father Quinlivan to the Committee on Education in 1849 gave further details of the school. It includes a brief reference to the earlier years of Catholic deprivation, stating that 'the school belongs to Rev. Dr Wareing (Vicar Apostolic), Rev. T. Quinlivan and Major Huddleston in common but that the Penal Laws have prevented regular settlement in trust'. The cottages in which the school was conducted had been built about 1820, the classroom measuring 14 feet long by 14 feet wide and just 8 feet in height. The annual expense of running the school outstripped the income but the deficiency was supplied by the Priest. A master, Hugh McCormack, and a mistress, Martha Rice, were then in charge of the school with assistance from one boy and two girl monitors. In line with general practice in Catholic elementary schools of the day, a monitorial system of teaching based on that of Lancaster and Bell but modified by the Christian Brothers was most likely used in the school.

## 'No Schools, no abiding Catholicity'

Fr Quinlivan was delighted when, in 1850, he succeeded in obtaining the teaching services of two sisters of the Order of the Infant Jesus. He wrote enthusiastically to his patron, Edward Huddleston of Sawston Hall:

> The schools are flourishing under the holy direction of the good nuns.
> To get them here is the best, the wisest and most important step I have

taken since my appointment to the charge of souls ... without such Schools and without such training Catholicism, instead of flourishing as it is now sure to do, would gradually become sapless and ultimately disappear, as is the case in many, alas! instances. Missions that some twenty or thirty years ago were prosperous are now little better than the wretched lifeless wreck of Catholicism; and this because there were no efficient Schools to train up and carefully develop and mature the rising hope of the Church in these localities. No Schools, no abiding Catholicity.

But added to his enthusiasm were worries about debts then standing at £52: 'how shall I get rid of its pressure and the anxiety thereon? ... My principal object in going to Town [i.e. London] is to beg ... Do offer up a prayer for the success of a beggar who is woefully destitute of brass.'

It must have been a bitter disappointment to him when the nuns had to leave Cambridge after only a brief stay. It appears their departure may have been occasioned by difficulties with the security of accommodation in an area rife with anti-Catholic sentiment. A further reason may have been that their community in Northampton, depleted by a visitation of plague, had been forced to amalgamate with the Sisters of Namur. At all events, by 1852 a master and a mistress had taken charge of the twenty boys and twenty girls being taught in a classroom then stated to be twenty-two feet in length.

## More Financial Difficulties

That same year Quinlivan was created the first Canon of the newly-formed Northampton Cathedral Chapter which would have placed him in a more influential position with his bishop. That situation was reinforced in May 1859 with the erection of St Andrew's as a missionary rectorate which gave the Canon certain rights of tenure. Later that year Bishop Amherst conducted the first Episcopal Visitation of the Mission on the occasion of which Canon Quinlivan's return included a report on the school. The Bishop would no doubt have been gratified to learn that only two of the Catholic children in the community were known to be attending non-Catholic schools but certainly concerned that the financial state of the school remained insecure with expenditure (£48) for the previous year exceeding income (£38) yet again. There was little, if any, financial aid the Bishop could offer Canon Quinlivan since he had admitted earlier that his Diocese, the largest among those constituted at the restoration of the Catholic hierarchy but with the smallest Catholic population, was 'in a most destitute condition ... and in sad want of priests and money'. Nothing daunted, the Canon's response to continuing financial predicaments throughout his long rectorship was to issue appeals almost annually to the Catholic public at large through the medium of the *Catholic Directory*. One encouraging fact had emerged at the time, however; a benefactor, Mrs Dias Santos, had arranged to leave in her will the princely sum of £300 to the school fund.

Canon Quinlivan was determined to provide a purpose-built school for the increasing number of children at the mission and he continually sought extra land for development. A small portion of the Lensfield Estate which adjoined the mission property would have sufficed for the purpose but the resident Wentworth family refused to sell any land for use by Catholics. However, many years later when Lensfield fell into other hands Quinlivan was able to negotiate purchase of the whole estate, on which he had the grand idea of building a much larger church. In so doing he obtained sufficient land to build not only the church of Our Lady and the English Martyrs but also, in the following century, an extension to the school.

## Hopes for Development

A more stringent code for evaluating grants to schools was introduced by the Committee on Education in 1862, two important conditions being attendance and examination results in reading, writing and arithmetic. A grant might also be withheld if an inspector was dissatisfied with the condition of a school building, a significant point which the authorities would take into account when a few years later they considered the age and state of the cottages in which the school had been housed since its inception.

A statement for annual grant made to the Committee on Education in August 1863 presented a more optimistic view of possible development. By then Mrs Santos Dias had the opportunity of purchasing a property adjoining the mission and had agreed to convey it to the diocese. Wanstead House, a substantial Regency building with frontage on Hills Road and grounds extending along Union Road would provide an excellent site for a new school as near as possible to the Catholic church. Meanwhile there remained the usual deficiency between school income and expenditure which was met as previously from mission funds. Of the forty-five boys and girls then attending the school, only thirty-four paid a weekly contribution to the teacher's salary at rates varying between three pence and a penny. The application included for the first time a reference to a teacher with some qualification being in charge of the school; Mary Ann Maloney, then aged twenty-two, had attended the Roman Catholic Training College in Liverpool for just twelve months gaining 'the second degree of merit for first year's training'.

Small support grants from the Catholic Poor Schools Committee continued to be received into the 1860s but hopes of building a new school were continually frustrated. The situation changed dramatically, however, when in 1867 the educational authorities intervened to insist that the school accommodation must be improved without further delay. Canon Quinlivan was forced once again to make a public appeal for the necessary funds: 'The present schools have been condemned as unfit and deficient in height, by the Council on Education who have decided to refuse all further support except on condition that a new school and teacher's house be built by 1st of next November ... Valuable freehold property, adjoining the church, has been secured at a cost of 2000 pounds, though not yet paid for. Contributions towards the building fund will be gladly received and thankfully acknowledged'.

With the authorities exerting such decisive pressure, work in the grounds of Wanstead House commenced without delay to a design by the architects Kendal and Maw, the builders being Canham and Son of Newmarket Road, a local Catholic family. H. E. Kendal was one of the first architects to receive commissions from the Council on Education to build schools conforming to certain requirements, and he had produced an album of standard designs. Notable points were the ecclesiastical style of buildings and the inclusion of ventilation shafts in the roof, both of which features were incorporated in the new Union Road school.

## A Purpose-built School, at last

The opening of the new premises was reported in *The Cambridge Independent Press* of 18 January 1868:

> The Roman Catholic Schools – The new schools built in connection with the Roman Catholic Chapel were opened on Monday afternoon last, when about 80 of the schoolchildren were regaled with tea, &c. After the repast, various amusements were indulged in. The room was decorated with evergreen and there was also a large Christmas tree ...

The new building of brick and stone included a teacher's residence and was able to accommodate immediately almost double the number of pupils in the old school. The dimensions of the single classroom were stated to be 40 feet by 22 feet, the height of the bell turret 50 feet and the airshaft 17 feet higher than the roof. The whole structure cost about £1000 and Canon Quinlivan resorted to another appeal for a shortfall of about half that amount.

When the schoolroom was first opened, the one large classroom was not divided in any way with the infants occupying a gallery at one end and a monitorial system of teaching in use. Increasing numbers eventually brought the need for some division of the room, a semi-glazed folding screen being erected in 1903 to segregate the senior class from the remainder, followed in 1920 by additional portable screens for the separation of other classes.

Still remaining at the present time is the entrance porch with its sculpture of Our Lady and the Child Jesus which resembles the medallion of the Catholic Poor Schools Committee. Other carvings on each side of the porch represent the cross of St Andrew while a figure of Christ the Good Shepherd stands on the south side of the building facing Union Road.

With much improved accommodation, the school prospered during the following twenty-four years under the enlightened headship of Mary Trehearne, a certificated teacher trained at Notre Dame College in Liverpool. A firm disciplinarian, she nevertheless won the deep affection of her pupils and much respect from the mission community. During her headship numbers in the school trebled, governmental grants increased considerably, and her pupil teachers passed four times at the head of all others in the country – a unique distinction. The diocesan inspector had highly commended her work on religious instruction in the school just a year before Miss Trehearne tragically died in 1892, the victim of one of the periodical epidemics which swept through the school. Attendances then dropped under a succession of head teachers but regained their former averages and even rose to 141 by 1898.

A financial statement of 1882 reveals that a deficiency in school expenditure for that year was met yet again from mission funds. By then the school had become open to children of other denominations following the 1870 Education Act which set up Board Schools financed out of local rates. Keen competition for pupils then ensued between the various Board and Church schools, though the latter were disadvantaged by the withdrawal of building grants, the abolition of school pence and the effect of the school leaving age being raised to fourteen.

## New Infants' Accommodation and Extended Classes

With the number of infants in attendance approaching fifty by the early 1890s, the need for a separate classroom became urgent and inspectors' reports pressed for the provision of an additional building.

Mission funds for such development remained unavailable, though ironically many outside the Catholic community may have been given quite the opposite impression by the replacement of St Andrew's church in 1890 with the large and ambitious church of Our Lady and the English Martyrs Canon Scott now approached Mrs Lyne-Stephens with his predicament over the school, and almost the last of her many generous acts of charity was to provide the cost of a new infants' class-room which eventually opened in November 1894. In effect it amounted to an extension to the 1868 building, providing a classroom 22 feet by 20 feet to accommodate up to 55 infants.

In addition to the three Rs, other subjects being taught in the school at that period included poetry, geography, needlework, cookery, singing, physical training, drawing and elementary science. An Evening Continuation School was commenced in October 1896 with an attendance of fourteen boys and eighteen girls, the boys being taught bookkeeping and shorthand and the girls vocal music, needlework and domestic economy. Adults joined these classes in subsequent years when the range of subjects was extended to ambulance, drawing and home nursing, but the average attendance of twenty in 1899 had dwindled to just five by 1901 when the evening classes were finally closed.

## The Victorian School

Conditions in the late-nineteenth-century school are revealed in fascinating sidelights from the school log books which also reveal a constant obsession with recording daily attendances on which grants from the education authority largely depended.

School inspectors often indicated general satisfaction with most standards in the school:

> Taking into consideration the difficulties which have arisen here, the higher grant for attainments may this year be recommended. Tone and discipline are excellent. Singing and Drill deserve praise. The Infants class is well and kindly taught and disciplined (1897).

The Mission priests were regular visitors in support of the teachers:

> Canon Scott visited the school today and read the 'drawing report'. The excellent grant has been given for this subject.

Inclement weather caused large falls in attendance since at that period almost all children walked to school, public transport being either non-existent or very limited until the turn of the twentieth century:

> School reopened on Monday with very poor attendance. Holiday in afternoon on account of great storm ...

Outbreaks of infectious diseases such as smallpox, measles, influenza and lesser ailments would sometimes result in closure of the school for considerable periods. Children unfortunate to suffer skin complaints, ringworm and the like had to be excluded from school for a time, the only practical means then available of limiting the spread of such conditions:

> The school is closed by order of the Medical Officer of Health on account of an epidemic of measles.

On major church festivals the children attended Mass in St Andrew's church nearby, sometimes being given a day or half-day holiday for the occasion:

> The registers were not marked, the day being Ascension Day. Children attended Mass in the morning and the remainder of the day was devoted to Religious Instruction ... Holiday on Thursday being the feast of Corpus Christi.

Visits to the town by fairs and  circuses caused disruption because of the inevitable absenteeism:

> Holiday given yesterday owing to town being visited by Barnum and Bailey's Show ... a half-holiday is being given this afternoon on account of Annual Fair and the visit of Buffalo Bill's Show.

There were holidays, too, when royalty or public dignitaries visited the town, holidays which, with the limited media coverage then possible, were intended to increase children's awareness of important events and to stimulate public spirit; but all inevitably contributing to disruption of lessons:

> School was closed on June 21st 'Jubilee Day' of Her Most Gracious Majesty Queen Victoria. 89 of elder scholars went in procession to corn exchange to a 'Children's Dinner' to celebrate the joyous occasion ... A holiday was given for the children to view the State Procession of the Lord Mayor of London on his way to take LL.D. degree in the Senate House ... the visit of the Colonials to Cambridge ... the return of the Cambridge volunteers from South Africa ... A half-day holiday was given to celebrate the Queen's birthday ... Coronation Tea Party on Parker's Piece ... On account of the King's Coronation school closes for one week.

During the Boer War, Empire Day each May was kept strictly in line with the sentiments of the times, and this particular celebration continued on similar lines until after the 1914–18 War:

> Empire Day entertainment introducing national costumes of England, Ireland, Scotland and Wales accompanied by singing of National Songs, recitation of 'the Red, White and Blue', National Anthem, cheers for King, Queen, Empire and Union Jack ... lecture by Fr Kay, 'Extent of the British Empire' (May 1913).

In keeping with the strong religious tradition of the school, the mission priests conducted classes in religious instruction  and periodically the children were tested by diocesan inspectors:

> The Very Rev. Provost Blackman has issued the report in Religious Knowledge of the Diocesan School. The school is classed 'Excellent' and received special mention.

As was to be expected, the work achieved by an outstanding head teacher, Mary Trehearne, brought its rewards:

> A 'Grant of Honour' from the Catholic School Committee was presented to the Mistress for the 'Excellence' of Religious Teaching in the school ... The report of the Pupil Teachers Religious Examination has been received and Mary Canty has gained the first place on the Honours List of Great Britain of the 1st Year Pupil Teachers.

## Into the Twentieth Century

From the early 1900s the average attendance at the school appears to have stabilized at about 120, the teaching staff consisting of a head teacher and three assistants. In addition to the normal lessons, occasional talks and lectures were sometimes given by leading members of the local Catholic community such as Baron von Hügel  and Edward Conybeare. The children were given regular drill and marching lessons, often by a former serviceman, in accordance with the military awareness of the times, and the children's prowess in that respect was put to the test on Empire Day each year.

As a church school, St Andrew's would have obtained increased grants from the local education authority set up under the Balfour Act of 1902. This Act also abolished School Boards which had been instituted under the 1870 Education Act, thus in effect rectifying the unfair competition for pupils which followed the earlier legislation. At that point the management of St Andrew's Catholic School passed to the local authority which became responsible for teachers' salaries, equipment, books and some decoration of premises. The ensuing protests of 'Rome on the Rates' from Nonconformists did nothing to soothe the antipathy which had long existed between local Catholics and those of other denominations under which generations of children at St Andrew's School grew up. For many decades there remained a strained atmosphere often bordering on hostility between the Catholics and their counterparts in other local elementary schools.

## Schoolboy Memories of Wartime

It is curious that the school log book makes little mention of conditions in the school during the 1914–18 War. Clearly though, as the following account indicates, the pupils must have been much affected, particularly those whose relatives were away on active service and became casualties of the conflict:

> To us youngsters the dull, dark days of war seemed an eternity but Miss Webster helped to relieve the gloom by recounting fairy stories often of a bloodthirsty nature. ... Sometimes on a very hot day after dinner at home we were treated to a bus ride back to school, the fare being a half-penny.
>
> During the war motor-buses were few and far between and were liable to break down frequently, especially on any kind of rise. One or two single-deck buses ran on coal gas and carried their fuel in a bag-like container on the roof. ... During those winters the school was a very cold place with only one fireplace to heat what was known as 'the big room' which catered for several classes or 'standards'. When it was freezing cold and we were blowing on our hands and could see our breaths, the teacher instructed us to 'close up' on benches nearest to the fireplace.
>
> One always sensed the kindly presence of the parish priest, Canon Scott, presiding over the well-being of the school. I felt the countenances of the saints themselves must have been modelled on the Provost's benevolent features which were ever beaming with joy on us children. ... He seemed to be often visiting the school to gently tell us of the death in action on some member of the congregation and to ask our prayers ...
>
> There was a great feeling of patriotism abroad in the land and naturally much of this sentiment flowed through the school ... Empire Day was the occasion for much waving of Union Jacks handed out to the classes, and patriotic songs resounded throughout the 'big room'. Young as we were, we were ever aware at the back of our minds that the war was a long and bitter struggle with many reverses for our Forces. I never remember any of us thinking for a moment that our

country could possibly lose the war ... We often seemed to be running to Parker's Piece to see huge parades or reviews of troops by some brass hat or other. From there long columns of soldiers marched past the top of Union Road en route to the railway station and thence to the trenches in Flanders, etc., most of them, of course, never to return. ...

The Provost's birthday fell on Xmas Day and during the last afternoon of term he would visit the school to attend the customary Xmas concert and to receive the children's present. His progress through the rectory garden towards the school was closely monitored by some reliable scout or other so that by the time he entered the schoolroom we were upon our feet and fully primed to burst into a song of welcome, the words of which went something like this: 'Welcome, Monsignor dear, With hearts full of joy and in accents bright and clear, We wish you a Merry Xmas and a Happy New Year'. During the proceedings the Provost beamed beautifully and continuously and we tried to look as angelic as possible, doubtless a hopeless task for most of us. ...

Since few children went away for holidays in those days, the annual school treat was much looked forward to by us all, if only because sweets and little luxuries were usually distributed. Transport to the field of action was usually in one of the Arnold family's farm carts suitably lined with straw. We seemed to be praying for fine weather for this event a long time beforehand and we never embarked on the venture without previously attending Benediction in the church.

(A reminiscence by Hubert Charles Wilkins (1907–2001))

## Planning Ahead

By 1922 when Canon Marshall took charge of the parish it was already clear that the school buildings were inadequate to meet current standards. Pupil numbers then were about 100, just over half of whom were from Catholic families, but ten years later numbers had increased to 135 of whom only a handful were from other denominations. Parish finances were insufficient to shoulder the entire cost of a new voluntary church school for which state building grants were not at that time available. In the face of warnings from the local authority that the school accommodation must be improved, plans were made for the consolidation of an existing parish hall building fund to be used for the eventual construction of a combined school and parish hall.

This bold proposal would have required persuasion enough of its own, but it was allied to an insistence by the diocese and the parish that the new school should be allowed to continue as an 'all-age school' for pupils up to the new leaving age of fifteen, obviating the split then normally required of senior pupils from infants and juniors. After two years of intense negotiation with the local education authority and the

Ministry of Education, a compromise was reached which allowed all pupils to remain on the same site, though in terms of increased building costs to meet the needs of the senior classes, the price paid was a heavy one. The assumption of this added financial burden by the parishioners was eventually shown to be justified, even rewarded, when the ceremonial opening of the new St Andrew's Catholic School, paired with the new Houghton Hall, took place on 24 September 1936.

## Noteworthy Teachers

The last head teacher to serve in the old building of 1868 was Frances Ormerod who retired in 1935 after twenty-five years in office. She suffered ill-health during much of her headship but the sound basic teaching she maintained resulted in a succession of senior pupils passing entrance examinations to local grammar and secondary schools. Of the assistant teachers, Eveline Webster's connection with the school was truly remarkable. Entering the school as a pupil in May 1878 at the age of eleven, she subsequently became a monitoress and then a teacher without special training, though as such she was forced to retire from teaching in 1933. She was allowed, nevertheless, to continue instructing children in their religious duties and did so for a further seven years until she collapsed on the school premises and was incapacitated until her death four years later at the age of seventy-seven. In her will she left a substantial sum of money for use by the school, and she is specially commemorated by a plaque erected in the school hall. A colleague of Eveline Webster's for many years was Eleanor Simmons who retired in 1957 after teaching at the school for over forty years. Edward Conybeare, whose close connection with the school is related elsewhere, taught classes during staff shortages and eventually became a school manager. He had a great affection for children and opened up his grounds nearby for their sports and recreation. A strict disciplinarian, he insisted on order and good manners among the children in class and at church, but always delighted in taking pupils for outings and school treats.

## St Andrew's Catholic School

The Official Opening ... children and staff attend Pontifical High Mass High Mass sung by the Rt. Rev. Edward Myers, Bishop of Lamus, with special sermon preached by Archbishop Goodyer on importance of children in Our Lord's Life.

2 p.m. Children, singing 'Faith of Our Fathers', head procession into school while the Bishop of the Diocese blesses exterior of building. Mr Francis Blundell, Chairman of the Catholic Education Council, performs opening ceremony with golden key. Speeches by Bishops of Nottingham and Northampton, Mr Francis Blundell and the Mayor of Cambridge.

Children of Classes II and III sing song of welcome, Class I speaking in unison in explanation (and gratitude) for name of school; and finally sing 'On Wings of Song' (Mendelssohn) (Log Book, 24 September 1936).

Accommodation in the new building (Pl. 29) was provided for 180 junior and senior pupils, the forty infants remaining in their classroom of 1894 which had been considerably enlarged as part of the renovation. As planned and constructed, the new main building consisted of two storeys, the hall and stage occupying the ground floor. The hall itself was 70 feet long by 28 feet wide and 18 feet in height and could be divided by folding partitions to provide classrooms when necessary or space for an assembly area for juniors and seniors. When used for parochial functions the hall, named Houghton Hall like its antecedent, provided seating for 400 people. The upper floor of the building consisted of three classrooms and the head teacher's study, while access to the practical room of 1000 square feet was obtained from a ground floor corridor extending the length of the hall. The modern accommodation even allowed for the provision of school dinners from 1937, cooked on the premises by the caretaker, Mrs Barton, at a weekly cost of one shilling per child, the first time this facility had been offered at any Cambridge school.

The final cost of the refurbishment totalled £14,000, all of which was eventually paid off through parish functions, savings schemes and the generosity of American servicemen based in the region. With the exception of the infants' classroom, the old school buildings then ceased to be used as such and for the next few years provided accommodation for the parish men's club which had lost its premises with the demolition of the old Houghton Hall.

## The Second World War

In spite of its increased capacity, only about 150 children attended the school in 1936 though the number increased to 165 the following year with a staff consisting of the new headmaster, James Bates, and three assistant teachers. By the time the school had really settled down in its new quarters, the shadow of war was again beginning to darken Europe and a conflict was about to erupt which was to affect profoundly all schoolchildren and their parents. During the uncertain years of 1938–9 much attention and practice was given to instructing the children in air raid precautions and the fitting, exercise and storage of respirators.

On the outbreak of war in September 1939, the start of the autumn school term was delayed while the school was used as a dispersal centre for 400 schoolchildren evacuees arriving from the London area for whom temporary homes had to be found in the locality. When St Andrew's eventually reopened on the 18th, the attendance of 200 included 61 children from St Martin-in-the-Fields parochial school who were accommodated in two extra classes in the school hall. With only minor activity of German aircraft over East Anglia in the months immediately following, half the evacuees soon returned to London; a situation reversed by the onset of the Blitz, when a fresh intake of London children arrived:

> Owing to the advent of a large number of London children we have been granted the welcome further assistance of a L.C.C. teacher, Miss Ethel Grady. Mr Bates is now able to organize a full school on really sound lines. (*Cambridge Catholic Magazine*, November 1940).

However, war service was soon to have an impact:

> At the beginning of this term everything was nearly perfect. But then we had the great misfortune of having to let Mr Froud go to the Navy. That had been a great handicap. As master of the senior boys and woodwork teacher he was doing invaluable service. And it is not going to be easy to find a substitute for him ... Meanwhile we wish him luck and Mr Bates and his good staff will bravely do their best to carry on without him (*Cambridge Catholic Magazine*, February 1941).

Staff changes and shortages were not the only factors contributing to the considerable disruption of teaching schedules throughout the war years. Occasional air raids in the area reduced attendances drastically, many parents understandably not wishing their children to be away from home during bombing raids. For instance, only twenty-five pupils attended school on one day in July 1942, though in spite of such difficulties a record number of seven pupils passed an entrance examination for the County School later that month.

Several changes in school times were caused by the total blackout imposed from dusk each day, and the children had necessarily to spend long and short periods in shelters in the rectory garden whenever German aircraft were detected in the vicinity. At the height of the bombing in January 1941, incendiary raids in the area caused chaos when a nearby school suffered much damage. A month later the following was recorded in the school log:

During a heavy raid last night our church was hit and many windows along the north side of the school were shattered as well as doors smashed and cycle shed wrecked. ... Our school now called upon to become a Rest Centre for care of homeless people after Air Raids. Considerable interference due to arrival in school hours of materials and equipment, problems of storage. Head teacher is Superintendent ...

Sometimes, though, light seemed to shine through the trying times:

On the last day of term the entire school sat down to a marvellous Christmas dinner – and perhaps more marvellous still, every child was presented with a slab of chocolate and a bag of boiled sweets, luxuries indeed in these days. ... This exceptionally good Christmas party was made possible by the Catholic Women's League who found the funds and came to help with the work and to clear up afterwards (*Cambridge Catholic Magazine*, February 1942).

By May 1944 Canon Marshall was able to report in his quarterly magazine that there had been a welcome division of the overcrowded infants department into two classes and the appointment of an additional teacher, Miss Joan Gill, to take charge of the extra class. Tragic news soon followed, however:

Since Miss Gill arrived with us she married Flight Sergeant Harrison. Unhappily, he has failed to return from a bombing operation and remains missing. We deeply sympathise with Mrs Harrison and admire the magnificent pluck with which she has carried on without any break at all in her cheery care of her class of babies. She knows how to say her prayers and leave things in God's hands (*Cambridge Catholic Magazine*, August 1944).

Further enemy action soon made an impact when repercussions of the flying bomb offensive against London was felt in Cambridge:

The activities of the Houghton Hall are many and varied. Recently it has been requisitioned again as a rest centre for unfortunate evacuees from the London terror. For several weeks numbers of such sufferers, largely mothers and children, were finding accommodation there until the billeting officers could fix them up somewhere. Mr Bates, in his Civil Defence capacity, had to contend with the running of the centre at the same time that he had his full duties as schoolmaster to cope with (*Cambridge Catholic Magazine*, August 1944).

Mr Bates also served during the war as President of the Cambridge Head Teachers' Association and was awarded the MBE for his services in organizing school savings for the National Savings Movement.

During a 'Wings for Victory' week in May 1943 the children of St Andrew's and their parents contributed no less than £114 to the Movement.

## Post-War Expansion and, eventually, St Alban's

During wartime the number of pupils at the school increased to over 260 with the inclusion of evacuees; even after the latter had returned home the number reduced to only 230 with the inclusion of entries from a long waiting list. Numbers in the school then increased further so that by 1950 overcrowding had again become serious. The problem was contained to some degree by the use of temporary classrooms, one in the rectory garden and others in the assembly hall and the storage area under the hall balcony. Accommodation was thus provided for a total of about 340 children though that number was considerably exceeded during subsequent years. By 1959, when plans for a Catholic secondary school in the city were approved, pupils at St Andrew's totalled almost 400 with a waiting list of about 250 prospective entrants. By then the school staff had increased to a headmaster, ten class teachers and four specialist teachers in Domestic Science, Needlework, Music and Woodwork.

The overcrowding was considerably relieved in 1962 when the senior pupils were transferred to the newly-opened St Bede's School. At that point the status of the school became that of a primary and, for administrative reasons mentioned earlier, its name was changed to St Alban's. With the moving of the senior children, it became possible to double the number of junior classes by admitting an extra 120 children aged between seven and eleven years, making a total in the school of 330 in ten classes. Still further relief from overcrowding came when the new St Laurence's Catholic Primary School opened in Chesterton in 1968.

## A New Broom

James Bates retired in 1968 after thirty-three years as headmaster, by far the longest serving teacher since the school commenced. Without doubt he had done much to improve the overall standard of teaching in the school during difficult times while constant in maintaining its special Catholic character. His successor, Barry Jones, paid immediate tribute to his predecessor 'who during his long service helped to create the wonderful spirit that exists among staff and pupils. I am fortunate to have "inherited" this finest educational aid of all which no amount of money can replace.'

Nevertheless, advances in school building standards in general, witnessed by the facilities offered by St Laurence's and other new schools in the region, contrasted greatly with conditions existing at St Alban's, and the new head at once made a strong case for improvements to be made: 'Due to limited space, amenities and lack of good equipment, the state of the school leaves something to be desired'. By then the hall was being used only infrequently for drama productions and Mr Jones considered it a waste of school space and the basement and upper stage area a fire hazard. The lengthy list of improvements he considered necessary was headed by the outside toilets which were a health hazard and were still open to the elements. In spite of these material deficiencies, he recognized that 'it was a tribute to the spirit, loyalty and hard work of staff that the children of St Alban's received a sound education in a happy atmosphere'. To draw parents closer together in support of the school, he at once launched a parents' association which became an immediate success, year after year running social gatherings and raising much-needed funds for extra equipment and classroom improvements.

In the light of the unsatisfactory state of parts of the school fabric, a considerable body of opinion in the parish questioned whether the school any longer occupied the most suitable site for the Catholic population and whether, therefore, considerable amounts of money should be spent on renovations and improvements. Jones broadly agreed with those sentiments and also pointed out that almost a third of children attending St Alban's were living in villages spread throughout the county with consequent transport problems. A replacement Catholic primary school built near St Bede's School in Cherry Hinton where land was available appeared to many a more logical solution, more especially at a time when a system of comprehensive education was about to be introduced throughout the county.

Yet the position of St Alban's School, close to the parish church and thus complementing the school's special religious ethos, remained the overriding point in a debate which continues to resurface from time to time. However, the lack of modern amenities had to be redressed in some measure and consequently the school was almost continually in the throes of renovations and renewals of one kind or another, the progress of which were often delayed or spasmodic as the general economic situation fluctuated.

When in June 1974 the county council authority took over the local education service from the city council, some restrictions on school budgets were introduced in the form of reduced capitation grants.

Pressure from the managers of St Alban's School for a complete remodelling scheme was resisted by the authorities on the grounds of escalating costs and the current unfavourable economic situation.

Frustrated in his efforts to obtain the improvements he deemed necessary for the school, Barry Jones resigned from St Alban's in 1976 when the opportunity of a headship at a modern city school came his way. His final entry in the school log included a short summary of the state of the school. That year fifty schoolchildren had made their First Confession and there were class and assembly Masses in the school each week. Education attainment was high among all groups, reading throughout the school reached a high standard, and there was a marked improvement in mathematics. Finally, he recorded that he 'was fortunate and happy to have been involved in a very good primary school with the support and kindness of all parties'.

Just a short while into the headship of his successor, Dorothy Head, the much-awaited updated accommodation for infants became a reality. During a night-time gale in January 1978 the temporary Horsa classroom in the rectory garden was demolished beyond repair by a falling tree. With the school lacking adequate accommodation for the infant classes, a speedy solution was sought with plans for a new three-classroom block being drawn up within the space of four weeks. Approval which had been denied for earlier schemes was now given without much delay and work on a new school wing, sited in place of the temporary classroom, commenced the following February, the new block opening in May 1980. With the notorious outside toilets at last replaced by inside facilities as part of the same development and renovation of the cloakrooms completed soon afterwards, the school accommodation was brought up to a reasonably good modern standard, though the school still inevitably lacked suitable space for recreational and sporting activities.

## Long-Serving Teachers

Among a number of teachers who came from local Catholic families, Monica Froud had connections with the school over a period of forty years. She first entered the school as a pupil after the First World War and returned to teach at the school for a brief spell after qualifying in 1933. After subsequent posts elsewhere, she returned to teach at the school from 1938 to 1946, during which period she married another member of the staff, and finally taught infants and juniors at the school from 1959 until 1973 when she retired. In 1980 Eileen O'Connor was awarded the Papal medal *Bene Merente* as a mark of her achievements after teaching at the school for twenty-five years.

# A Proud Record

In 1980 the school managers were re-designated as governors with greatly increased responsibilities including control of capitation grants, involvement with the curriculum, inspection of school fabric and introduction of health and safety exercises. If improvements to accommodation came about only spasmodically or after much delay, the same could not be said of the many changes in teaching methods and the introduction of new subjects which followed each other in rapid succession during the 1970s and afterwards. Advances in science and technology during the post-war years had repercussions down to primary teaching levels, and St Alban's was no exception when in 1986 computers and calculators were first used in the school. The imposition of a National Curriculum was soon to follow, introducing new subjects such as design and technology, health education and basic sex instruction as well as attention to the special needs of disadvantaged children.

But the staff at St Alban's had a long and valued tradition of coping successfully with changes of a varied nature and thus contributing to maintaining a happy atmosphere in which the children were taught. Amid the extra pressures these latest changes brought with them, the school even continued to offer pupils a variety of extra-curricular clubs in guitar, violin, chess, French, football, netball and Irish dancing. Still further improvements to the school accommodation would be needed in the years following to include even an extension to the comparatively new infants' block while the hall stage and basement area would eventually be replaced by a new dining room.

As St Alban's moved towards its 150th anniversary, many would reflect on the wide range of educational opportunities available to present day pupils in stark contrast to the very basic tuition it had been possible to offer the first children of St Andrew's Catholic mission in those humble cottages in Union Road. Nevertheless, during the intervening years the school had remained faithful to its primary commitment to the many generations who had passed through its door, its continued and fundamental aim expressed in a recent school brochure:

> St Alban's exists to provide high quality education within a living Catholic community which values each individual and enables every child to reach its full potential. ... Our life at school has a Catholic ethos which permeates all that we undertake in the education of the children in our care.

# All Clouds have Silver Linings: Reminiscences of 1976–1990

*Stella Fox*

## An Ill Wind?

The great summer drought of 1976 was still having its consequences later that year as tree roots became unstable. At the school, a mature beech tree adjoining the church car park fell in a high wind on Christmas Eve, demolishing a temporary classroom which had housed the top infants' class. Staff had to return hurriedly that day to rescue valuable equipment, and by the start of the next term the top infants were re-housed on a temporary basis, at first in the canteen but later, owing to distracting noise, in very cramped quarters in the staff room. Further trees were to fall during a gale on the night of 12 January 1978, but again the school was empty and no injuries were caused on either occasion. However, disaster turned into good fortune as the opportunity was taken to build the long-hoped-for infants' block on the cleared site between the school and the church car park. All the infants were then housed together in a modern purpose-built block which was light and airy and with sufficient space to allow the children to work on different activities at the same time, thus permitting them a wide curriculum. The playing area, too, was much improved. For the first time the infants were able to play in safer conditions, separately from the juniors, and the grassed area under the shade of the surviving plane tree was put to welcome use on warm summer days for infants' classes and playtimes.

## Falling Rolls

By 1984 a general concern at falling school numbers at all Catholic schools in Cambridge prompted the issue of a publicity brochure entitled *Spectrum – Catholic Education in Cambridge 1984–5*, designed to put this trend into reverse. If there was perceived to be an undercurrent of parental indifference, economic factors played their part as well. There was an increasing reluctance by local authorities to meet the cost of fares for children who, at least in theory, could easily have attended non-denominational schools much closer to their homes. However, such concerns did not signify wholly bad news for St Albans. For the first time in many years class sizes were reduced and the children came to benefit from more individual attention. Those pupils with learning difficulties could be kept in main-stream education and given appropriate attention by the school staff, supported by visiting specialists, part-time teaching staff and classroom assistants.

Under Dorothy Head, the school developed the principle of a caring community while working towards the best education for all. A close working relationship between parents, church and school was seen to offer major benefits for the children. This applied especially in the field of religious education and preparation for the sacraments.

## Fund-raising

Throughout the 1970s and 80s, funding for schools was gradually being curtailed and it became more and more essential to raise funds so that the cutbacks did not impinge on the children's education. Fund-raising events organized at St Alban's proved not only to be very profitable, they served also as ideal occasions for parents to meet socially, particularly valuable for many who lived at long distances from the school. Unlike those at neighbourhood schools, children and their families generally found it more difficult to meet outside school hours owing to St Alban's wide catchment area. Among the events, the summer fairs were always well attended and fun-filled occasions. The dancing displays provided by all the children in the school were a joy for friends and families to watch and enjoy.

## Activities

Outings were always eagerly anticipated by the children. A day out of the classroom visiting exciting places became a valuable part of school life. Visits to museums, wildlife parks, science exhibitions, outdoor activity centres, the seaside, trips on boats, trains and buses, to Ely Cathedral, and frequent outings to the nearby Botanic Garden all enabled the children to enjoy their learning. The top juniors started to benefit from week-long stays at residential centres, an important opportunity to take part in activities that could not be conducted within the school environment.

Sporting activities were never easy as the school lacked its own playing fields and facilities for practice. Even so, the children performed well in football and netball matches in the winter and rounders in the summer. Swimming lessons always proved popular, as did joining with other schools for athletic competitions. The annual sports day, held on Parker's Piece, was an event not to be missed.

Musical and dramatic performances were a highlight of school life. The infants, under the direction of Mrs Angel and accompanied on the piano by Mrs Timbs, provided a deeply religious preparation for Christmas in the Nativity play. Easter gave the juniors the opportunity to present one of many religious musical plays. Two of these proved particularly successful, one about St Alban and the other about St Paul, both specially written by Dorothy Head. Not only were they valuable dramatic productions, they were also an exciting medium for learning about these two important figures and the history of their times. The careful research and preparation of the costumes for these productions were the responsibility of Miss Cracknell.

Throughout this period St Alban's was very fortunate to have a deeply committed and stable staff, enabling the whole school community to be a living Catholic presence in the centre of Cambridge.

# Chapter 32

# St Laurence's School, 1968–1986

*from the reminiscences of Ron Ellison, first headmaster*

## A Second Primary School for Cambridge

St Laurence's School, the second of the Catholic primary schools in Cambridge, owes its existence to the foresight and energy of Fr Patrick Oates, the parish priest of St Laurence's from 1951. Not long after the consecration of his new church in 1958, Fr Oates inaugurated a School Building Fund with the aim of providing a school for the children of his parish. The chosen site, at the northern end of Arbury Road, Cambridge, was at that time far removed from established residential areas, though nowadays the school is surrounded by later housing developments. The project was not included in the Local Education Authority's list of future schools and this meant that instead of receiving an 80% grant towards building costs, the parish had to find virtually the entire cost, about £110,000, when building work started in 1967.

Local authority attitudes towards the project became more favourable as it progressed through the planning stages, though initially the authority was undecided whether the school should become a component in a three-tier system of First School, Middle School and Upper School. This was the plan followed at the outset, sufficient land being purchased to allow for all three schools to be built. The present-day St Laurence's School was to be the First School and that part of the site behind the caretaker's house was to accommodate a Middle School which was never built. For a time St Laurence's was left with unusually large playing fields. Eventually, with a change in policy, the County Council recommended the disposal of the surplus area for housing development. The school governors hastily forestalled this proposal by arranging for another football pitch to be laid out.

Ron Ellison recalls that he was appointed headmaster of the school early in 1967, well over a year before building work was completed, and he started work in September 1967 from an office in Cambridge Guildhall. His first sight of the school was a sea of mud, with planks leading to the footings:

> Later I brought along my wife to see the school. Unfortunately, she slipped off one of the planks and stepped into deep mud, ruining her new suede shoes – she will always remember the first days of St Laurence's School!
>
> Apart from ordering furniture, books and materials, one of my tasks was to visit all the local schools to meet the children who were transferring to St Laurence's School. It was also a good way of introducing myself to the local head teachers. When discussing the children who would be leaving there was usually a pained expression on their faces but occasionally there was a gleam in their eyes and a look of delight – then I knew there was trouble brewing!

The problem of the distance of the new school from most children's homes had to be faced, and it was arranged that the Eastern Counties Bus Company would run a school bus service from Chesterton, along Green End Road, King's Hedges Road and Campkin Road. However, a path across the fields from the school to Northfields Avenue was at first refused, owing, it was said, to lack of council funds.

The school opened after Easter in 1968 with eighty children on the roll that first summer term. There were four classes each of twenty children and with two classrooms spare. A new King's Hedges Junior School was due to open in September 1968 but was running behind schedule. The St Laurence's governors readily agreed to the request from the Local Education Authority (LEA) that the two spare classrooms could be used for the King's Hedges Juniors. 'They say God works in mysterious ways – when the school reopened after the summer holidays, lo and behold, there was a brand new pathway across the fields!' The King's Hedges children stayed for two terms until their own school was ready. The LEA asked that they should have separate playtimes and dinner times to placate parents who were not happy that their children were attending a Catholic school.

An official opening ceremony was performed later by Bishop Charles Grant of Northampton. 'I will never forget that day. It rained so hard there were floods everywhere around the school – even the small car park. The children put on a performance of 'Noah's Ark' which was very apt!'

# Successful Fund-raising

A Parents' Association was soon formed and proved very successful in raising funds for the school through a variety of events. A series of annual garden parties was opened by various popular personalities, among them Miss Rosalyn, the presenter of Anglia TV's 'Romper Room', Percy Edwards, the animal impersonator, and Johnny Ball, the television performer. The funds raised allowed playground equipment to be purchased and the car park to be extended so that parents' cars could enter and leave the school premises safely. Fund-raising for another project, a swimming pool in the school grounds, began with a fashion parade sponsored by Mitcham's, the department store then at Mitcham's Corner in Cambridge. However, the Swimming Pool Fund came to an abrupt end when the City Council announced that they intended to build a pool to serve the local area. They asked the school governors to agree to the pool being built in the school grounds and when this was refused the pool was built just outside the school perimeter fence.

Another extremely successful form of fund-raising was a weekly bingo session held at the school on Sunday evenings for many years. The capacity attendances every Sunday ensured a ready flow of funds which was eventually channelled into the repayment of the school debt, cleared ten years after the school was opened.

Numbers at the school increased rapidly and it was not long before every space, including the library, was used for teaching. One cause for the increased numbers was a request from the army authorities at Waterbeach Barracks to send Catholic children from the base to the school, and up to thirty children travelled from Waterbeach every day in an army bus. The late Vincent Donnelly, a civil engineering contractor and a parishioner, helped ease the pressure on space by donating a Portakabin to the school which was placed in the grounds, wired up by parents and served as a store and for teaching small groups.

# Making its Mark

Before long the school started to make its mark, and to produce satisfying experiences for its pupils. French was a subject on the curriculum at primary schools during the early years, the 'En Avant' course was used for the Junior class and was followed up with a trip to France each year which proved very popular. A visiting violin teacher came for half a day each week, music became a highlight of the school and a school orchestra performed at the school and at outside events. The musicians played regularly at the Children's Mass at St Laurence's and pupils from the Junior classes provided readers and the bidding prayers.

Sport was another area of success, pupils taking part in all the inter-school sports and excelling particularly in football. 'Most of my Saturday mornings', wrote Ron Ellison, 'were spent on a football field somewhere in the City! St Laurence's was probably the most feared team in Cambridge, always at the top of the league table and even representing Cambridge in a national competition, only failing at the semi-finals at Welwyn Garden City.'

St Laurence's School left its mark, too, on Cambridge in a different way during Tree Planting Year in 1973. Scots pines were planted by the top Junior class between the football pitches and other species were planted by the Governors around the car park. Later, each Cambridge primary school was invited to plant a tree alongside the paths on Jesus Green. St Laurence's tree still flourishes there.

## Two Amusing Episodes

'One morning a child turned up with a human skull. I asked him how he came to own it and he said he had swapped his ice-lolly for it. This was reported to the police and that afternoon a man from the Home Office arrived to take it away. It transpired that it had been removed from one of the Colleges.'


'Towards the end of my time a little girl sidled up to me and said "I like your grey suit, sir, it goes with your hair!"'

# Chapter 33

# St Bede's School, Cambridge: A Catholic Secondary School, 1961–1988

*from the memories of George Kent and Colin Ball*

## Plans for Secondary Education

In January 1961, on an open, windswept site off Birdwood Road in the Cherry Hinton district of Cambridge, building work started on what was destined to become St Bede's School, a Catholic Secondary Modern School designed to accommodate the senior pupils from St Andrew's All-Age School in Union Road. The planning for a new school, to relieve the pressure on St Andrew's and to provide secondary education for Catholic pupils on a separate site, had been high on Canon Stoke's list of priorities ever since he had taken over as parish priest in Cambridge in 1946. His vision was that a steep rise in the Catholic population of Cambridge would have to be catered for in educational terms.

According to Colin Ball, an aspiring altar server and schoolboy in 1947 and later to become Deputy Head of St Bede's, Canon Stokes at that time used to speak to him of his hopes for a secondary school for boys in the Cambridge area, to fill a gap which, in the case of the girls, was already occupied by St Mary's School. Fund-raising for such a project was already under way by means of jumble sales, fetes and bingo sessions, and at one point consideration was given to the purchase of Anstey Hall at Trumpington. This was a substantial house with extensive grounds which was being offered for sale by the then Ministry of Agriculture and Fisheries. Unfortunately the grounds were divided by a strip of land in separate ownership which made them unsuitable for school use and the property passed instead into the ownership of the Plant Breeding Institute.

Although other pieces of land in Cambridge were in church owner-ship, all were deemed too small for school building. Hence, in the early 1950s, Canon Stokes obtained outline planning permission for a school to be built on a site between Trumpington Road and the river Cam, but this project was abandoned when the School Commission for Northampton Diocese suggested that the car and bus access to the site was insufficient. The search continued and, in 1957, plans were prepared for a secondary school to be built on a riverside site in Chesterton. The City Council considered the proposals unsuitable owing to lack of playing field space, but at least this led to negotiations with the Council in the course of which they offered to take an exchange of the land in Chesterton for a larger site, in Birdwood Road, Cherry Hinton. It was here that work could start on the planning and construction of St Bede's School.

By this time Colin Ball had entered the teaching profession and in 1960 he moved from his post at Netherhall Secondary School for Boys to become Head of the Upper School at St Andrew's All-Age School, Union Road and, soon afterwards, Deputy Head, under the Headmaster, the late James P. Bates JP, MBE.

Meanwhile, in September 1960, Mr George Kent, a graduate of McGill University, Montreal, was appointed Headmaster of the yet unbuilt school. He moved from a senior teaching post in Corby to occupy an office in Cambridge Guildhall from which he made his plans for the curriculum and staffing of the future St Bede's. Three members of the secondary team at St Andrew's were appointed to the new school: Miss Pauline Baynes (Music and History), Colin Ball (Science), and Tony Froud (Crafts and Technical Drawing).

Colin Ball recalls the building stage:

> Our secondary school was at last under way – in January 1961 access to the site at Birdwood Road, Cherry Hinton, was cleared and building work commenced – visits by the senior boys and myself to look at the holes in the ground were frequent. At last, on a cold wet night in the following July, parishioners and children gathered together on an extremely wet occasion – standing on duckboards with brollies and gas lanterns in the midst of a tangle of iron girders – whilst Bishop Leo Parker of Northampton laid the foundation stone for the newly-named St Bede's (Pl. 30a). Building work continued rapidly and the children moved into the school on 14th May 1962, just sixteen weeks later than scheduled.

# The Best Post-war School in Cambridge

The Cambridge architect David Roberts was chosen for the design of St Bedes. Sir Nikolaus Pevsner, in *Cambridgeshire* (1970), wrote

> This is without any doubt the best post-war school in Cambridge, a model of its kind, inspired perhaps in its effortless C20 classicity by Arne Jacobsen. Red brick, but of pleasant surface, with raked joints, two storeyed with the upper floor all glass and a flat roof, and perfectly symmetrical, from the entrance of the forecourt with the matching brick end walls of the bicycle sheds to the facade and through into the prettily planted inner courtyard, where the hall is placed in the back range.

Equally complimentary are Philip Booth and Nicholas Taylor, in *Cambridge New Architecture* (1970), who make additional points about Roberts's achievement within the stringent cost limits of the then Ministry of Education, and his ability to emphasize the dramatic openness of the site in a theatrical manner with the boiler-house chimney echoing the unpromising form of a distant cement works. It must be said, however, that these very compliments masked some of the difficulties which staff and pupils would have to face when the school was first occupied. Thanks to the 'stringent cost limits', the original school hall had to serve for an inconveniently wide range of uses, from assemblies to gym classes, school Masses to school dinners, to main communication route between the two sides of the school, the inevitably high wear and tear doing nothing to enhance its appearance. As for the newly-sown playing field, the turf would remain thin thanks to the plentiful deposit of dust from the cement works, now no longer operational. The school had cost £122,845 to build.

# The Boys wore Caps, the Girls Brim Hats

The school first opened its doors on Monday 14 May 1962 with 140 pupils, most of whom had transferred directly from the upper forms of St Andrew's School, and a teaching staff of eight. George Kent, the Headmaster, was supported by Sr Margaret, IBVM as Deputy Head, (to be replaced by Colin Ball when she retired in 1970). A pattern of school organization familiar in the early 1960s was adopted, which included navy-blue uniforms with caps for the boys and brim hats for the girls, a three-form entry streamed by ability (Forms Ax, Ay and B in each year) and a house system (Clitherow, Gwyn, Howard and Owen, named after four of the Forty Martyrs) designed to encourage a competitive spirit in both sporting and scholastic fields. A school hymn was composed by Miss Baynes, the first of the annual Sports Days took place on 11 July 1962 and a presentation of the prizes and trophies was combined with the official opening of St Bede's School, which took place on 19 July. George Kent wrote:

> Thursday 19th July was a glorious day full of colour, splendour, pride, hope and ambition. A solemn apostolic blessing for the school was received in the morning by telegram from Pope John XXIII. TV cameras were on hand to film the official opening of the school by Rt Rev. Leo Parker, Bishop of Northampton. The school was packed with parents, pupils and friends. Platform dignitaries, gleaming amongst the floral decorations included: Canons Brewer and Diamond; Chief Education Officers Scarr and Edwards; the Mayor and Mayoress of Cambridge; Architects Roberts and Hall; Catholic Education Council Secretary Cunningham, and Fr Wace.

The school-leaving age in 1962 was fifteen, but to allow the abler pupils to sit O level examinations at the required age of sixteen, children were encouraged to stay on for a voluntary fifth year and O level entries (and successes) started in the summer of 1965. Eventually 60% of children leaving the fifth form went on to further education. Nine years later, in 1971, the school could celebrate ten years of continuous growth, the pupil numbers then being 380, and the teaching staff twenty.

The tenth anniversary of the opening of St Bede's was marked by the inauguration, in October 1972, of substantial extensions to the school which included six new classrooms (Pl. 30b), a biology laboratory, photography room, motor maintenance section, gymnasium and a common room in which older children could meet socially between lessons. These extensions were designed to accommodate another 200 children, partly in response to the raising of the school-leaving age to sixteen, but also in the hope that numbers in the school would increase as a result of an anticipated rising birth rate. The cost of this additional building work was £115,000.

## Too Small A School

By 1972 plans were being made for all Cambridgeshire secondary schools in the council-maintained and voluntary-aided sectors to become comprehensive schools. In a public notice which appeared in the local press in March that year Canon Paul Taylor, chairman of the governors, gave notice of their intention 'to make a significant change in the school by providing for approximately 550 pupils of both sexes and of the full ability range mainly between the ages of 11 and 16. The

School will continue to be conducted as a Voluntary (Aided) School and religious instruction will be given in school hours'.

The transformation of St Bede's from a secondary modern to a comprehensive school proved to be something of a mixed blessing. In spite of all the hopes and intentions for expansion of pupil and staff numbers with consequential opportunities for a wider range of school subjects, for the next seventeen years, despite excellent exam results, the school roll, which was the key to all improvements, never rose to the expected level of 550 pupils. Instead, it remained uncomfortably close to 380, a level which the Local Education Authority regarded as well below the viable limit for a comprehensive school. A small school was deemed to be inflexible because it had fewer teachers than average-sized schools and therefore fewer skills. More than once the school was earmarked for closure or merger. The anticipated rise in the birth rate never took place.

For the Catholic community of Cambridgeshire, however, the closure of St Bede's was unthinkable. This was no school formed merely to serve a given locality but liable to closure or merger if school numbers fell; far too much religious pride, sentiment and devotion had been invested in this school, setting it apart from its neighbours or competitors. By 1974, when the gloomier forebodings first began, the school had already developed its own brand of religious commitment, community responsibility and charitable involvement. Regular school Masses were held in the hall and walking pilgrimages to Walsingham took place each year. Junior St Vincent de Paul and Legion of Mary groups were active in the school and fund-raising events for charitable causes were held from the school's earliest days, including sponsored forty-hour Lenten fasts. Alongside these, more conventional school activities such as Outward Bound scholar-ships, Duke of Edinburgh Awards, school expeditions and camps, a school choir and orchestra, and a full programme of inter-school sports and matches took up much time and energy for pupils and staff alike.

For a Catholic school, special pride will always be reserved for the two boys from St Bede's who found vocations to the priesthood, David Bagstaff (ordained 1976) and Thomas Murray (ordained 1978). Both now serve as priests in the Diocese of East Anglia.

## Good Samaritan Steps Down

Under the headline 'Good Samaritan steps down to save school', the *Cambridge Evening News* reported on 16 September 1983 that George

Kent, the headmaster of St Bede's School, had stepped down to save the school from possible closure:

> Mr Kent resigned his headship after three years of discussions between governors and education officials failed to eradicate the school's 'serious weaknesses'.
>
> The county's senior education officer, Mr David Spreadbury, said the school's 'serious weaknesses' related exactly to its falling rolls.... He said the 380 strong school did not have an adequate educational base and the authority wanted to see the rolls rise to between 500 and 600 pupils.

According to the newspaper, Mr Kent said, referring to his successor, Sr Dolores, 'It was my suggestion that a religious head would bring in the numbers. I feel that the Catholic community will respond to a person who is in a religious order – and that is the experience in the country.'

Four years later, the struggle for survival was continuing:

> St Bede's School in Cambridge is celebrating its silver jubilee today – 18 months after its closure seemed certain. The county council intended to close the Roman Catholic comprehensive school because of falling rolls. But the school just would not give in and after months of campaigning it was given a last minute reprieve. Sister Dolores, who has been head-mistress at St Bede's for almost four years, thinks the school has gained from its struggle to survive.
>
> One of the factors in helping to increase numbers will be plans to turn the school into an inter-denominational centre by 1988 (*Cambridge Evening News*, 14 May 1987).

Eventually, on 4 February 1988, the *Cambridge Evening News* reported:

### New School has backing of Minister

Education Secretary Kenneth Baker has given the go-ahead to turn St Bede's Roman Catholic School into a new inter-church school. It marks the final triumphant move in a turbulent chapter which almost ended with the secondary school being closed down after a drop in the numbers of pupils.

From September it will become an inter-church school, the result of a co-operative venture between the Roman Catholic Church and the Church of England. There are only five other inter-church schools in the country, at Taunton, Oxford, Redhill, Richmond and Torquay.

# Epilogue: an Inter-Church Comprehensive School

On Tuesday 23 May 1989 St Bede's marked its official opening as an Inter-Church Comprehensive School in a ceremony attended by the Rt Revd Alan Clark, Bishop of East Anglia and the Church of England Suffragan Bishop of Huntingdon, Rt Revd Gordon Roe. A little over a year later, in July 1990, Sister Dolores retired as headmistress and was succeeded by Mr Roger Boon from a Church of England school in London. Colin Ball retired at this time, too, from his position as Deputy Head. By 1993 the school was reported to be 'enjoying a popularity boom', with a record 550 pupils at the start of the Autumn term and a waiting list for places.

Inviting prospective families to an Open Evening on 26 January 2000, the School described itself as 'a popular Christian school serving the whole of South Cambridgeshire where the quality of the teaching and relationships was highlighted by OFSTED inspectors in 1999. Priority is given to church attending families and those seeking a Christian education for their children.'

So it is that St Bede's School survives, and with evident success; different in form, yet still owing much to the aims of its original foundation.

## Chapter 34

# Felix Quia Fidelis:
# St Mary's School, Cambridge, 1898–1990

*Christopher Jackson*
*with assistance from Sister M. Gregory Kirkus, IBVM*

### Arrival in Cambridge

Mary Ward (1585–1645), the Yorkshire-born foundress of the Institute
of the Blessed Virgin Mary (IBVM) and a pioneer women's educator,
would have been proud of the five intrepid sisters of her Order,
Mother Stanislaus and Sisters Bernard, Berchmans, Magdalen and
Aloysius, who set out from the Provincial House at Bar Convent, York,
on Tuesday 1 September 1898 with the purpose of setting up a centre
for the accommodation and education of female students and pupils in
Cambridge. Their move was a direct response to the entreaties
received by their Superior from Miss Donelan, a pioneer in the training of Catholic women teachers, who was then active in Cambridge.
Miss Donelan felt it more appropriate that responsibility for the accommodation of Catholic women students in Cambridge should pass from
her to a religious order, leaving her free to move to London to
continue her work there.

If the time seemed right and the place seemed right, this would have
been because Girton College (from 1869) and Newnham College (from
1871) were already admitting female undergraduates to pursue
university studies and Hughes Hall, founded in 1885 by Miss Hughes
as the Cambridge Training College for Women, was offering teacher-
training courses for women. The Catholic student-teachers were
accommodated in a hostel which Miss Donelan had opened in Queen
Anne Terrace, on the south side of Parker's Piece. Moving into
Furness Lodge, on the north side of Parker's Piece, and intending to

continue the work started by Miss Donelan, the newly-arrived sisters from York soon found that there were after all no female Catholic students in need of their accommodation. They had to turn instead to their two alternative objectives, one of which was to help teach the children of Canon Scott's Catholic mission and the other was to establish a girls' boarding school. It seems unduly harsh to suggest that this discovery of actual need, or the lack of it, at local level was a disappointing setback for the sisters. Having arrived on 1 September 1898, they had by 3 October admitted their first pupils (albeit only two, Dorothy and Daisy More of Chesterton), to an embryonic day school and support for their enterprise soon followed when a Miss Corcoran arrived, though with no children for her to teach she turned her educational attentions instead to two later arrivals, Sister Bernard and Sister Joseph. Canon Scott decided to give his Saturday evening lectures at Furness Lodge as the sisters could not be expected to go out in the dark to hear them at his church. Fr Nolan, at that time Master of St Edmund's House and University Chaplain, also called at Furness Lodge to give the nuns lessons in Latin and Scripture. Sister Xavier, a novice, arrived to complete her studies in Cambridge and a young French governess, Mlle Neudin, joined the staff on 14 October. Progress in attracting new pupils was slow during the following spring and summer terms of 1899, but disaster struck at the end of the following year when nine children, virtually the entire enrolment, left the school. Poor teaching may have been a factor, as may have been a suspicion of unhealthy drains at Furness House. Those sisters who were improving their own education by pursuing courses for various subjects in the Cambridge Higher Local Examinations did not fare very well either.

Sr Gregory, IBVM recounts that one of the original sisters at Furness Lodge was Sister Magdalen, a rough diamond from the West Riding of Yorkshire but with a heart of gold. Having arrived in the completely foreign atmosphere of Cambridge in 1898, Sister Magdalen acquired something of a reputation thanks to her service over many years as portress to the community. She had been briefed from the start to expect visits from dons, professors and others from the academic world and opened the door one day to an unknown young man with the greeting 'Are you one of them FELLERS?'.

## Move to Bateman Street

The nuns survived their first few years in Cambridge in conditions of great poverty, even privation, owing to their very limited income from school fees. Eventually the decision was made to move to more promising accommodation, and a fresh start was made when Furness Lodge was sold and the community moved to The Elms, a sizeable family house at the western end of Bateman Street, in March 1904. Bateman Street was to be the location at which all future expansion of St Mary's Convent and its schools in their various forms took place and remains the address of St Mary's School even today.

Conversion work at The Elms and the construction of an additional storey in 1905 allowed the educational work to resume on a better footing and by 1910 the records of the community show that a small but well-established school was operating there for twenty-four boarders with another nineteen day pupils being taught separately at Paston House, a few doors away in Bateman Street, a property which had been acquired in 1909. Mother Salome Oates, a very small and incredibly active figure, almost bird-like in manner, held the positions of Superior of the community and Headmistress of the school at this time. In 1920 she was succeeded by Mother Gertrude as superior of the Convent, by Sister Paul as headmistress of Paston House and by Mother Elizabeth Dunn as headmistress of the Convent School.

## The Era of the Locals

In common with every school offering secondary education in England during the twentieth century, the progress of St Mary's became inevitably linked to the development, in four major phases, of the local examination system. Prior to 1918, local examinations (or 'locals') were offered to secondary schools by four or five of the universities, the lower level after five years of secondary schooling and a 'higher' level after seven. No particular uniformity of standard existed between the examining boards and the results achieved did not necessarily guarantee entrance to universities or professions, nor did they always represent essential entrance qualifications. This relatively casual approach was reflected in the education offered by St Mary's School, and in the expectations of the parents. Most pupils entered the school in their teens and stayed only for two or three years for an education akin to that of a finishing school with a religious dimension, perhaps going beyond what governesses could offer by way of tuition at home. Cambridge Local Examinations did not feature very prominently in the programme. Although life for the nuns remained spartan, a caring and loving approach to the pupils was clearly evident, and care too was taken to give a wider dimension to their education. This was made easier in the Cambridge context by the knowledge and enthusiasm provided by an unfailing supply of kindly academics and other well-wishers who provided talks on general and scientific subjects and acted as guides to local museums and other places of interest. Deserving special mention for their contributions to the school curriculum are Edward Conybeare and Fr Robert Hugh Benson. Conybeare's diaries contain a wealth of detail appertaining to his church and school activities, and during the period 1906–1918 they show him acting as guide to the Convent girls on outings to Ely Cathedral, the Cambridge colleges, museums, the top of the church tower and the May Bumps races, lecturing on subjects as diverse as local archaeological finds, Tennyson, architecture, the microscope and electricity, hosting sketching classes and Morris dancing on his lawn, and frequently a guest at school parties, plays and concerts.

During Fr Benson's time at the Cambridge rectory (1905–8), he too developed a close and cordial relationship with the sisters at St Mary's and their pupils, saying Mass for them at the Convent and frequently visiting the boarders for tea, stories and games. He enjoyed the company of the children immensely and they returned his affection. Their numbers may have been small but even so they succeeded in presenting a series of concerts and plays. They found an ideal collaborator for these performances in Fr Benson, most notably in his production for the School of his specially written *Mystery Play in Honour of the Nativity of Our Lord*, first performed in The Elms in December 1907. For this he painted most of the scenery, designed the costumes, lent some of the 'props', attended the choir practices and ran the rehearsals. This labour of love by a literary figure of Hugh Benson's stature will always be treasured as a unique legacy to St Mary's Cambridge.

> We therefore, too, with good intent,
> The simple story here present
> Here sheep and shepherds you shall see,
> The Holy Child and sweet Mary,
> Great Angels and good Joseph too,
> Merchants and simple folks like you,
> The sturdy landlord of the inn,
> Cold snow without and fire within –
> All shall be shown as best we can,
> In praise of Jesus, God and man.

> Robert Hugh Benson, *A Mystery Play in Honour of the Nativity of Our Lord* (1908).

## A Shelter for Refugees 1914–1918

The space offered by Paston House and its one acre of grounds would one day prove to be an invaluable asset for an expanding school. However, in 1914 the house was far too large for the needs of the twenty day pupils of the school, even allowing for the residential accommodation provided for two or three female students and the occupation of the bedrooms by resident staff and some members of the community. The surplus space was used, whenever the need arose, for meetings, conferences and by various parish organizations, but the situation soon changed after the outbreak of the First World War. Then, a flood of Belgian refugees arrived in Cambridge and two of these refugees, Marguerite and Yvonne de Ley, came for shelter to Paston House. Sadly Yvonne died there in August 1915. Most of the children of the Belgian families billeted in Cambridge came to Paston House for lessons and the concert hall was fitted up as a classroom, with desks lent by the County School. Forty-six children, at first considerably outnumbering the English pupils, were taught there by two French-speaking Ursuline nuns and a Flemish-speaking Belgian. Conybeare records a number of occasions when plays and concerts were staged by the Belgian children at Paston House, mostly in near-faultless English. The Belgians returned home in 1918 and the Belgian Government conferred the Médaille de la Reine Elisabeth on the Superior and the community 'for their services to the Belgian cause'. This medal had been instituted in 1916 for award to women, without regard to rank or class, who distinguished themselves by personal help given to Belgian civilians or soldiers during the First World War.

## School Certificate and Higher School Certificate

The introduction of the School Certificate and Higher School Certificate in 1918 brought officially laid down standards of organization and levels of achievement to the local examination system which before then had been conspicuously absent. From then on, Examination Boards had to receive official recognition, so too did their examination standards. As a result the School Certificate and its 'Higher' cousin became accepted qualifications for school leavers, university and professional entrants, and awards for higher education. Sister Paul's appointment as headmistress of Paston House followed only two years later, in 1920. It fell to her to ensure that the school provided the level of teaching to sixth form level called for by these new educational standards and it is to her credit also that by 1924 the school was recognized as efficient by the Board of Education. Sister Paul encouraged the girls to think of the public examinations as a normal milestone towards higher education, but without losing the caring atmosphere and wider horizons essential in a successful school. The first School Certificate successes date from 1923 and those for the Higher School Certificate from 1928. By the time Sister Paul retired in 1949 after twenty-nine years service as headmistress, St Mary's (by then comprising both St Mary's Convent and Paston House) stood immeasurably higher in reputation and achievements. It is worth noting that until St Mary's Convent and Paston House were combined into a single unit for teaching purposes in the 1930s, the day pupils of Paston House and the boarders at the Convent had been taught separately. Sister Paul was succeeded by Sister Christopher, who had herself been a pupil at the school under Sister Paul from 1920 to 1930.

Numbers at the school had increased out of all recognition since Sister Paul assumed the headship of Paston House in 1920, when there were 100 on the roll. By 1930 there were 200 pupils, rising to 250 by the outbreak of the Second World War in 1939. An influx of evacuees swelled the numbers to more than 300 by 1940 but any hopes that this degree of overcrowding would be eased after the war by a reduction in numbers were not realized.

## The General Certificate of Education

Sister Christopher's appointment as Headmistress preceded by only two years the next major reform in the local examinations system, the introduction of the General Certificate of Education, or GCE, in 1951, with an Ordinary Level to be taken by pupils not before sixteen and an Advanced Level to be taken at the end of a sixth form course. A culture of single subject passes at O level replaced the minimum cluster of subjects required for a School Certificate pass. This may have given encouragement to candidates at the weaker end of the spectrum but also tended to encourage expectations of greater subject opportunities among the more able. Adjustments to syllabuses and staffing were inevitable at St Mary's but at the same time other challenges had to be faced by Sister Christopher. Foremost among these was the severe pressure on space, brought about by an unrelenting demand for places and ever-increasing pressures to improve school facilities. A steady decline in the number of sisters involved in teaching had to be compensated for by engaging increasing numbers of lay teachers, and this diminishing involvement of the IBVM meant that lay support on the governing body became an increasingly important issue. Meanwhile, expansion of the school accommodation under Sister Christopher's headship was addressed by means of a building programme.

## David Roberts, Architect

The physical separation of The Elms and Paston House by the Bateman Street entrance to the University Botanic Garden had long prevented any unified scheme of expansion to solve the pressure on accommodation. At last, in 1952, the University agreed to an exchange of land which allowed these two sites to be merged while the entrance to the Botanic Garden was relocated to its present position further to the east along Bateman Street. This development coincided with a general relaxation of the emergency restrictions on building work which had been in force since 1939 and plans for the much-needed new buildings were put in hand.

The choice of a Cambridge architect, David Roberts (1911–1982), to design the steady succession of additions to the School accommodation between 1955 and 1974 was a fortunate one. The first commission from the School, in 1955, was the largest he had received so far in six years' practice, possibly resulting from his successful completion of a smaller extension for the nearby Perse Girls School. No-one could then have predicted that he would, during his lifetime, acquire a unique reputation for gently understated architecture appropriate both to its purpose and its location. His work for the School over a nineteen-year period stands alongside his many other buildings commissioned by schools, colleges and universities across the country, though it was mostly in the cities of Oxford and Cambridge that his genius seemed to flourish at its best. His work for the School, involving at least nine separate stages, inevitably spread out to match available resources, can be listed as follows:

> **1955** Stage I included a central courtyard (the Cortile), designed to preserve a magnificent magnolia tree and around which were grouped a new assembly hall, dining hall, cycle store and covered way linking existing buildings. These were of economical construction and gave little clue to their existence from the road frontage.
>
> **1959** Stage II – new classrooms, library and art room over the covered way onto Bateman Street and adjoining the existing classroom block (Crush's Building, dating from 1929).
>
> **1962** Stage III – three-storey block adjacent to Stage II in Bateman Street providing classrooms and including alterations to The Elms, completed in 1964.
>
> **1966** Fourth floor added over Stage II Bateman Street building, provid-

ing additional classrooms.

**1967** Fourth floor added over Stage III to provide Study Bedrooms.

**1968** Fourth floor over Stage II building behind Bateman Street to form study bedrooms.

**1969** Fourth floor over existing classroom block (Crush's Building) in Bateman Street.

**1971** Gymnasium and classroom block to east of Crush's Building, completed in 1974.

The buildings comprised in Stages II and III provided a new external appearance to Bateman Street which gave the School its modern image, and David Roberts was commended by Booth and Taylor in *Cambridge New Architecture* for 'a particularly interesting and attractive example of his personal yet functional design with a restrained, precise formality that exactly suits a convent. The planning is excellent and the relationship with the Victorian villas and their neo-Georgian extensions is managed with great delicacy.' The total cost for all this work, spread over the nineteen-year period, was £466,237.

## Transformation from a Convent

From the 1950s onwards St Mary's was to move gradually from being a school existing exclusively under the ownership and control of a religious order to its present day independent status as a girls' school providing a grammar school type of education and accredited to the Girls' Schools Association. In 1951 an instrument of government set up a board of governors, initially with an advisory role only and chaired by successive parish priests, Canon Stokes, Canon Diamond and Canon Taylor. Nomination of members by the Local Education Authority and the University ensured an injection of valuable expertise, but at the same time increasing duties and responsibilities came its way. Local and central government found it convenient to regard it as the body answerable for the performance of the school and for the application of public funding, though in constitutional terms much would need to be done before the IBVM as a religious order could share executive control with the laity. Other factors were at work, however. In the years following the Second Vatican Council it became increasingly apparent that declining religious vocations would lead to an insufficiency of sisters to fill teaching posts and headships in IBVM schools, and lay teachers and lay governing bodies would eventually have to replace them. By 1983 the IBVM was ready for a change of policy and with it a change of status for St Mary's School. After much careful deliberation, a charitable company limited by guarantee was incorporated in 1984 with separate legal and financial status, under the title 'St Mary's School Cambridge'. Three IBVM Sisters were to serve as trustees of the company, together with two Catholic laymen, the first of these being Mr Trevor Gardner and Dr David Blackadder, then respectively Treasurer of the University of Cambridge and Bursar of Downing College. Great care was taken, when framing the School's new constitution, to safeguard its Catholic identity.

## Modern Times, 1972–1990

A final view of the School must be taken, covering the period which saw Sister Christopher's retirement in 1972, to be followed as head by Sister Dominica, succeeded in 1977 by Sister Christina, and then in 1989 by the first lay head, Miss Michele Conway. During this time the building programme was effectively completed, as were the constitutional alterations and the phasing out of the last teaching sisters. Other changes included the removal of the Junior School from Bateman Street, first to Cavendish Avenue from 1968 to 1976, then to 7 and 8 Brookside, where it closed by stages between 1986 and 1989, thus allowing the remaining community of Sisters to move there in 1989, vacating The Elms in the process.

If Sister Dominica saw the expansion of the School to three-stream entry in 1974, Sister Christina was to see it expand yet again to four-stream in 1988, and she gave much attention to the strengthening of the sixth form. This was made necessary to meet serious rivalry from private sector boys' schools where girls were being admitted to sixth forms and from newly established sixth form colleges in the state sector. The success of Sister Christina's efforts can be measured by the standing enjoyed at the end of her headship by a school providing education for 580 girls aged 11–18, fully modernized in all departments, including a well-equipped information technology department and an arts centre, enjoying an enviable record in the all-important public examinations, (GCE O levels having been replaced by GCSEs in 1988) and already planning for further expansion and development towards its centenary in 1998. Describing itself as 'a Catholic foundation which welcomes other denominations', St Mary's School Cambridge remains closely allied by historic links and worship to the church of Our Lady and the English Martyrs, where the staff and pupils attend Mass whenever a feast falls on a school day. Who could wish for a better alternative to a school chapel on such occasions?

# An Epilogue: The Story of St Catherine's School

The prospect of the phased closure of St Mary's Junior School was greeted with dismay by a number of parents, concerned that their daughters would not be old enough to transfer to the Senior School before the closure took place, or that younger daughters would not be able to follow in the footsteps of their older sisters. If an alternative had of necessity to be found for those cases, then why not set up a successor girls' preparatory school catering for the same age group, with the same denominational affiliation, and in close proximity to the Senior School? This at least was the question to which a group of seven parents and others involved in the educational field set out to provide a positive answer. Their advertisement in *The Cambridge Evening News* (13 March 1987) read:

> ST CATHERINE'S PREPARATORY SCHOOL
>
> As a consequence of the announcement in January 1986 of the gradual phasing out of the junior classes of St Mary's School, Cambridge, allowing greater expansion in the senior School, it is intended that a new independent Preparatory School will be established at 1 Brookside, Cambridge, in September 1987.
>
> Applications from 7, 8 and 9 year old girls are invited, as entrance tests will be held before the end of the month.

This announcement, and other arrangements for the formation of the new school which followed, took place with the encouragement of the governing body of St Mary's School. The then headmistress, Sister Christina, interviewed by *The Cambridge Evening News*, spoke for them all when she expressed regret that the junior classes were being discontinued. She said that this step would not have been taken if they had had the room, and they were very pleased that the new school would help to meet the tremendous demand for schooling for children in Cambridge. She hoped that the education would be good so that the children would be able to make a natural progression to the senior School. An endorsement in such terms helped to ensure that when St Catherine's School opened in September 1987, housed in the distinguished Curator's House at 1 Brookside, adjoining the Botanic Gardens, the initial roll comprised fifty girls, a number which has increased over the following years to ninety-four and close to its maximum of 104. The Catholic affiliation ensures that close contacts are maintained with St Mary's School and the local parish, marked, for example, by the formal blessing of the School, on 1 October 1987, by Mgr Anthony Philpot. Little more than a year later, he returned to bless a statue of St Catherine which had been presented by the IBVM sisters for display at the School.

A quotation from a recent scholastic directory perhaps sums up best how the School would wish itself to be seen:

St. Catherine's has a very happy and loving family atmosphere where the girls develop a caring consideration and acceptance of others, combined with the achievement of high academic standards and self-discipline.

# Homily preached by His Eminence the late Basil Hume, Cardinal Archbishop of Westminster, at the Centenary Mass in the Church of Our Lady and the English Martyrs, 12 October 1990

## Opening Remarks by the Parish Priest, Mgr Anthony Philpot

My dear friends, tonight we wish ourselves a happy birthday and we are delighted to welcome His Eminence Cardinal Hume and our own Bishop, who come to celebrate this Mass of Thanksgiving with us; and I would also like to say a great word of welcome to His Worship the Mayor and the Mayoress, to all my friends and collaborators and colleagues from different Christian traditions who have come here, sparing their time so generously, tonight – you are all most welcome; and to all my brother priests of the dioceses of East Anglia and of Northampton, many of whom have worked here over the years; the senior of them, I believe, is Dom Eric Phillips of Downside Abbey who worked here in 1937. They are all most welcome, and it is grand to have this opportunity of together thanking the Lord for all he has done for our parish here in this building.

## The Homily by His Eminence Cardinal Hume

Just two weeks ago I was present at the celebration to mark the centenary of the opening of St James, Spanish Place, opened just two weeks before this church was consecrated and now, today, I am in Cambridge to celebrate your centenary.

1890 was a good year, part of the second spring about which Cardinal Newman had spoken some forty years previously. Newman died, as you know, in 1890, just five or six weeks before this church was opened. There was then new life in the Church; numerically the Catholic community was growing, its influence increasing. Churches were needed and churches were built; priests and laity working hand in hand, and very hard, to provide them. Our laity who had missed so much to keep their faith alive in penal times now provided the new communities with churches in which to celebrate it. Some were rich, like the foundress of this church, but many were poor. But rich and poor shared the same conviction: God must be worshipped in a setting that was both worthy and dignified and His people must find in His house a home where they could be at ease in His presence. So it is right that we should pay tribute to the memory of Mrs Lyne-Stephens, the former Pauline Duvernay, the ballerina. 'If you will allow me, I will build your church', she told Canon Scott and she would provide everything, save for the medieval processional cross, the gift of Baron von Hügel. I think she must have been a very formidable person, but then so was Canon Scott; however, both had vision.

But we must not forget the Canon's predecessor. I find it quite extraordinary that Canon Scott and his predecessor, Canon Thomas Quinlivan, served this parish for a total of seventy-nine years. I don't know whether that is an encouragement or a warning to your present parish priest. But that would be rare today. Canon Scott was to acknowledge at the opening of this church that they must not forget that a great deal of trouble had fallen on his predecessor, Canon Quinlivan, who had many years of anxiety about getting a site. This matter, getting the site, was much helped by the generosity of that remarkable man, Henry, 15th Duke of Norfolk. His intervention was decisive. The site was bought and the church was built. There was no debt and thus the church could be consecrated on completion and that took place on 8 October 1890. *The Cambridge Chronicle* of 10 October described the consecration ceremony in great detail. Would any local paper do that now? All those who write about our affairs these days show the same degree of knowledge of what goes on inside our churches. It was, however, the following week's edition which is of greater interest. It is the account of the opening Pontifical High Mass that took place on the 15th. Many bishops and priests were present, Cardinal Manning was not. He had become ill the day before he was due to preach at the Spanish Place celebrations the previous week. It was a crowded day. Mass at 11 a.m., lunch at 2 p.m. in the Devonshire Assembly Rooms, Green Street, and Vespers at half past six. The presiding celebrant of the Mass was Bishop Riddell, distinguished for opening so many missions in his large Diocese of Northampton. The bishop was a strong, very strong, opponent to Catholics attending the University. That issue divided the hierarchy of the day and the town too. Bishop Riddell, furthermore, was reported to have been quite outraged when it was proposed to open St Edmund's as a house of studies for priests. 'Unthinkable', he said. Canon Scott thought differently. Mr Wilkins, in your admirable commemorative brochure, notes: 'Canon Scott was convinced that when obstacles to University entry were removed the consequent increase in Catholics attending would create the need for a larger church, but other arrangements were made when that permission was forthcoming and the centre of Cambridge Catholic university life was established elsewhere.' It would be improper for me to comment on whether that was good or bad.

The preacher of the Mass was the Benedictine Bishop of Newport, Cuthbert Hedley, in the evening the famous Jesuit, Fr Rickaby. Our newspaper gives a full account of both sermons. The sermons were clearly not short and I would judge, and I trust not rashly, a bit on the heavy side, at least as far as today's tastes are concerned; but it is never prudent for one preacher to comment on another. Bishop Hedley took St Paul's letter to the Romans, chapter 1, verse 5, as his text concerning obedience to the faith. But I was struck by one point he made. If they believed in prayer and the sacraments and their duty to God, the Bishop told his congregation, their belief in those things would become even deeper through the contemplation of the outward manifestations which they would be brought into contact with through the building of the church. There is nothing dated about that! Externals do contribute to the raising of our minds and hearts to God. Beauty is always a word from God to elicit from us a nobler response. And there is nothing dated either in the tribute paid to that great Cambridge figure, John Fisher, by the preacher at Vespers. John Fisher had been beatified just four years previously. It would be wrong for us in Cambridge today were we to fail to recall the memory of that great bishop, a man of great sanctity who would, I think, have been canonized even if he had not been a martyr. Fr Rickaby spoke at length about the Reformation. It was good solid stuff but not notable for delicacy of touch so far as ecumenism is concerned. Far from it. But good relationships with other Christians are required of us by the highest authority in the Catholic Church in our day and the presence of our separated brethren is so important in this celebration this evening. But in our dialoguing with others we must while being respectful in truth always be respectful of persons. 'The harm resulting from the Reformation must be undone', said Fr Rickaby. Indeed, and the need to do so is urgent. Nonetheless, our martyrs who died in defence of the things we hold so dear, for the primacy of the successor of St Peter, for the Mass, for our ancient faith, still speak to us through their witness and their courage. We must have devotion to them while being ecumenical in our dialogue.

I dwelt on the past briefly and perhaps a little bit superficially. Let's look to the future. Our thoughts are centred on this lovely building, God's House. A house of faith, a house of worship, a house of prayer, a house of charity. We must think for a moment about ourselves. 'The Church', in that other sense of the word, the people of God, members of the body of Christ, the dignity which is yours and mine in virtue of our baptism. That was underlined for us just a moment ago by St Peter, 'you are a chosen race, a royal priesthood, a holy nation, God's own people'. We are to hold our heads high and never apologize for what we are. We have a precious gift: our faith and the sacraments to give us the light of Christ, gifts that must be loved and treasured. This great dignity with which we have been endowed in virtue of our baptism is indeed for us to enjoy and rejoice in but it carries with it a duty, and a vital one at that, which is, as St Peter reminded us, to declare the wonderful deeds of Him called out of darkness into his marvellous light. We have a duty to speak of Him and His word. We are to declare the wonderful deeds of God. Eventually that is what will be expected of us in the decade of evangelization which will be announced at Epiphany-time next. No-one may be excused on the grounds of being too small in God's eyes, or even too simple. The Son of Man came to seek and to save the lost – that is us. We heard these words in today's Gospel. Zaccheus was small of stature, and a very imperfect person. But he was bold and enterprising and the Lord was pleased. He climbed the nearest tree to see more clearly and we for our part must in a sense find our sycamore tree and climb as well and look for support and the help that we can get in the Church in order that we should obtain some greater understanding of the things of God and the consequences of our obedience to the faith. That comes from the scriptures, from the sacraments and from prayer.

So, my prayer for you today is that, individually each one of you, and as a parish community, you will prove worthy of your calling as followers of Christ and significantly contribute to the spiritual well-being of this town, as your lovely church contributes so significantly to the beauty of its architecture.

May God then bless you richly and show the strength of His love to each one of you and may you also please remember me in your prayers.

In the name of the Father, the Son and Holy Spirit.

# Appendix 1

# Parochial Organizations

*Margaret Plumb*

## The Guild of the Blessed Sacrament

According to the Parish Magazine of August 1933 the Guild of the Blessed Sacrament was not the longest established of the parochial organizations but it was given pride of place because 'it stands first in dignity. It is an Archconfraternity and it is ordered by Canon Law to be set up in every parish where it is possible to have it.' Its origin is due to St Peter Julian Eymard (1811–1868) who lived, worked and died in the French diocese of Grenoble. He established the Guild of the Blessed Sacrament for laymen. The Guild was established in the English Martyrs parish in 1922, when over twenty men gave in their names in order to elect officers. The Guild actually came into being with forty-six members. They made a corporate Communion once a month, held monthly Guild Services and on days of Exposition watched before the Blessed Sacrament and formed a Guard of Honour in processions. During Quarant' Ore they did the night watchings. The Guild was later established in St. Laurence's parish. It ceased to exist in Cambridge in the 1960s.

## The Children of Mary (COM)

The Children of Mary was founded in 1563 in the Roman College of the Society of Jesus by a Jesuit father, John Leunis and on 5 December 1584 was canonically established by Pope Gregory XIII as a *Prima Primaria* Sodality. At first it was confined to boys in Jesuit colleges but spread rapidly among youths and men, priests and religious through Europe and beyond. The sodality was not extended to women and girls until 1751. It was established in the English Martyrs parish in 1893, three years after the present church was built. According to the *Cambridge Catholic Magazine* of November 1933 Mgr Crook, who was then President of St Edmund's College, Ware, was instrumental in establishing the Sodality in Cambridge. He persuaded Canon Scott that the Children of Mary should have a Cambridge branch and it is said that 'no doubt the priest who had raised this Church to Our Lady's honour did not need much persuading.' Candidates were soon forthcoming. Mgr Crook himself gave a preliminary course of instruction and after three months' probation the first group of Cambridge Children of Mary were consecrated by the rector on Whit Sunday 1893. They were invested with medals attached to white ribbons. The colour was not changed to the regulation blue until 1920. Among the first to be consecrated were Anne Pratt, Elizabeth King, Flora Haslop, Agnes Allen and Eva Webster. Baroness Anatole von Hügel had taken the greatest interest in the foundation and acted as the first president. In honour of the installation she had a party at Croft Cottage. In 1898 the first community of the Institute of the Blessed Virgin Mary arrived at Furness Lodge, Park Terrace. The nuns at once took an interest in the Children of Mary and Sister Mary Hilda acted as President, meetings being held both at the Church and the Convent. The same nuns founded the Girls' Guild, which used to meet in the room in the Rectory. There were close relations between the Sodality and the Guild, and sometimes they would unite to hold a party to which young men were invited. The young men so appreciated the hospitality that they subscribed towards the Children of Mary banner which was carried in procession and has been taken to Lourdes and Walsingham on many occasions. Existing records of the Sodality begin in 1913. In 1915 twenty-four were consecrated Children of Mary. During the war years meetings became intermittent and then dropped, but in 1919 Miss Goss was elected President and in the following year Mother Mary Salome, Reverend Mother of the Convent, became General President of the whole Sodality. Meetings were again held at the convent as well as in the church. Sister Mary Gabriel later became President. It was again slightly moribund until in 1924 it was revived under Canon Marshall, Miss Froude being elected its President. She continued in this Office until 1927 when she was succeeded by Miss Goss. Blue cloaks were worn from the beginning of 1930 and it is said that a small boy once described them as 'the blue ladies who try to be good like Mary'! In 1933, through the kindness of Revd Mother Catherine, association with St Mary's Convent was again established. A monthly meeting was held there in addition to the monthly meeting in church. A corporate Communion was also held at the 8 a.m. Mass on the first

Sunday of the month. Pupils of Paston House were consecrated Children of Mary in the convent chapel and after leaving school some would join the Sodality in the parish. The Junior section was called the Guild of St Agnes; although started, it did not succeed in Cambridge. The Children of Mary ceased to exist in Cambridge in the 1970s.

## The St Vincent de Paul Society (SVP)

The Society was started by Blessed Frédéric Ozanam in Paris in 1833. At the first Conference in May 1833 six young men opened proceedings with a prayer to the Holy Ghost and a reading from the *Imitation of Christ*. They then discussed proposals for working amongst the poor in the spirit of true charity, placing themselves under the protection of St Vincent de Paul, the apostle of the galley-slaves of Paris of 200 years earlier. They chose their officers, made a collection and concluded with the prayer to Our Lady, *Sub tuum præsidium*. This is the procedure now followed weekly by thousands of Conferences all round the world. The first English Conference was established in London in 1844 and that in Cambridge in October 1913 at the instigation of Bishop Keating of Northampton. He turned to Baron Anatole von Hügel and requested him to found a Conference in Cambridge. The brothers were to be recruited from both the University and town. The Baron was made the first President and the other brothers in the Conference were Edward Conybeare, Kenneth Mackenzie, W. O. Aston, Charles Duchemin, Fred Apthorpe, C. E. Lawrence and MacLean Leach. Father Kay was chaplain. It is stated in the *Cambridge Catholic Magazine* of February 1934 that others soon joined. In order that the new brothers might be instructed in the spirit and aims of the Society, Sir John Knill, Bt, came and gave them an address six weeks after the foundation had been made. Sir John Knill, a notable Catholic who had been elected Lord Mayor of London in 1910, was at the time President of the Superior Council of the Society in England. A year later the minutes show a regular weekly attendance of about ten to fifteen members. Meetings were then held fortnightly. On 2 August 1914 the Conference was formally aggregated to the Superior Council and the meetings began to be held weekly according to the rule. Several brothers left for war service but the Conference continued its activities and added to them by taking part in work done for soldiers in camp and hospital; it organized a Soldier's Recreation Room at 30 Regent Street and also assisted the Belgian refugees. In July 1917 the Conference gave a garden party in the rectory garden to wounded soldiers. The Conference was reduced in number by its members going to war and on the suggestion of the President, Baron von Hügel, Belgian brothers among the refugees were invited to join the meetings. They were not expected to take part in the active work of the Conference, but the alliance was valuable for fostering spiritual fraternity. Edward Conybeare succeeded the Baron as President in 1924 and on 16 May 1926 Mr J. H. Britcher became President. To this day the SVP still does valuable work in all the parishes in Cambridge.

## The Third Order of Saint Francis

This Order was founded by Saint Francis of Assisi in the thirteenth century and is unique in sharing its founder with the First and Second Orders. St Francis founded the Order of Friars in 1206 and the Poor Clares, the Second Order, in 1212. Then, in order to assist pious men and women living in the world to advance in the way of holiness he established a Rule of Life for them, which was later formally approved as the Third Order of St Francis by Pope Nicholas IV in 1289. This Order provides the nearest approach to the religious life for secular clergy and people living in the world. It has numbered popes, cardinals, bishops, kings, and queens amongst its members. St Louis IX of France, St Elizabeth, Queen of Hungary, St Elizabeth, Queen of Portugal, St Ferdinand III, King of Castile, St Roch, St Rose of Viterbo, St Margaret of Cortona, many of the Martyrs of Japan and St John Vianney are some of the famous saints of the Third Order. On 1 May 1934 Fr Paul, OSFC, Commissary Provincial of the Third Order in England, formally established a congregation in the English Martyrs parish. He preached morning and evening on Sunday, 29 April, and held a meeting in Houghton Hall. He gave instructions and interviewed callers. Only those who had a serious intention of doing penance and sanctifying their lives were to come forward. Eventually forty-two postulants were invested with the scapular and the cord of St Francis and became novices of the Order. Monthly meetings were held after Benediction on the second Tuesday of each month.

## The Catholic Women's League (CWL)

The League was founded originally in Germany and in 1906 Miss Margaret Fletcher founded the League of England and Wales, modelling it on the German organization. Over a year later it held its first Annual Meeting in the Cathedral Hall at Westminster with the Archbishop in the Chair as its President. Its object was to promote the 'Associated Endeavour' of Catholic women and it adopted as its motto 'Charity, Work, Loyalty'. Branches have been established all over the country. The Union of Mothers, Girl Guides, Welfare Workers, Our Lady's Catechists and numerous other associations of active Catholic women were brought into useful contact by the League organization. In 1920 it was proposed that there should be a Junior League by means of which girls should be brought together to be trained in the spirit of the League so that they might grow up with the desire to work for the Church. This proposal was supported by Miss Froude who established the Junior League in the Parish. The League was founded in the Diocese of Northampton in 1912 when branches were started in Northampton, Norwich and Cambridge. In March 1912 Provost Scott presided over a meeting held at St Mary's Convent which was addressed by Miss Streeter, one of the pioneers who had been associated with Miss Fletcher in founding the League and at that meeting a resolution was made to establish the League in Cambridge. The inaugural meeting was held in April 1912 at St Mary's Convent where meetings continued to be held. Mother Mary Salome was elected its first President and 'for years by her wisdom and guidance was instrumental in inspiring the branch with the right enthusiasm'. The first Executive Committee of the Cambridge Branch of the CWL consisted of the following: President, Revd Mother, St Mary's Convent; Hon. Treasurer, Miss Goss; Hon. Sec., Miss Froude; Council: Mrs Apthorpe Webb, Mrs Henry Arnold, Mrs Baker Smith, Miss Bell, Miss Buckenham, Baroness von Hügel, Mrs Lanham, Mrs McQuaid, Mrs Magoris, Miss Ormrod, Miss Pratt, and Mrs Otto Wehrle. The League linked up all women's activities in the parish and helped to keep them alive, reviving moribund movements and promoting new ones. It was the principal, indeed the only, permanent body for getting work done. During the First World War service was done for men at the front, the wounded in hospital and Belgian refugees. In some of this the CWL co-operated with the SVP and played a leading part in raising money for the School and Hall Building Fund. In 1933 the Cambridge Branch held its twenty-first birthday and to mark the occasion Cambridge was chosen by the Headquarters of the League as the venue for their Annual General Meeting that year. This gathering included the foundress, Miss Margaret Fletcher, Lady Rankeillour, Miss Balfe and other prominent Leaguers. CWL Juniors would organize dances, often fancy dress, in aid of the Shefford Orphanage. The League ceased to exist in Cambridge in the 1980s.

## Work for the Foreign Missions

*1. The Association for the Propagation of the Faith (APF)*

During the 1800s Blessed Pauline Marie Jaricot, a servant girl living in Lyons, led many girls to abandon sinful lives. She then became interested in the work of the foreign missions and became eager to minister to their great needs. She persuaded each of her friends to find ten others who would give a sou a week for the missions. This system spread very quickly, and three years later, in 1822, the Association for the Propagation of the Faith was formally established on Pauline's plan. It is not known when this Association was founded in Cambridge but in the parish library in February 1935 there were copies of the 'Annuals' dating from 1842, the start of the mission in Cambridge, showing that 'the little flock' of the time was already subscribing to the Association. According to the *Cambridge Catholic Magazine* of February 1935 'some tattered copies of the "Annuals" of long ago have been found in the belfry, of all places. On the loose cover of one of them is attached a paper dated August 1876 containing a "list of members" which shows that by then at all events the Association was established here.' Those names were: Canon Quinlivan, Mrs Lespringwill(?), Mrs Colonel Wood (sic), Mrs Mason, Mrs Quilton, Mrs Ventris, Mrs Bossard, Mrs Ryan, Mrs Wehrle, Miss Thurmal, Mr Coe, and Mr Twain. The work of the APF continues in the parishes in Cambridge today and much has been contributed to their funds over the years.

*2. The Catholic Women's Missionary League (CWML)*

The CWML was founded in the Parish in about 1931. Its main work was to send parcels of goods to the missions – vestments and altar furniture, clothes and materials, medicine and soap, toys, trinkets and similar items. In 1935 the Cambridge Branch numbered about forty ladies who made up several parcels a year and sent them to the West coast of Africa.

## The Men's Club

A Catholic Men's Club existed in Cambridge as far back as 1884; its purpose was to encourage social intercourse and to play games. At one time there was a cricket club and classes in gymnastics and shorthand; there was also a small-size billiard table which by 1935 was still being used by the Boys' Club at Paston House. In the early days the members of the club were mainly Irish cattle dealers. It survived until about 1897 but then closed owing to lack of support. In 1907 Fr Kay came to Cambridge and soon afterwards efforts were made to revive the club. The billiard table, still preserved in the school, was cleaned and repaired and taken to the guild room (later the parish library) in the rectory, where a few men would meet on one evening a week. The club started to flourish and a full-sized billiard table was purchased for £45 from the Mitre Hotel in Bridge Street. In order to afford larger premises the club ran entertainments in the school which proved so successful that a platform was purchased which eventually formed the stage in Houghton Hall. Some of the members turned to bell-ringing and with assistance from Mr Taylor, the senior ringer at Great St Mary's, and some of his friends, they were able to peal the church bells. Baron von Hügel became the first President and was generous both in money and goods, giving them a piano and £50 towards a building fund, shortly followed by another £50. He also had plans prepared for a fine hall and club rooms. During the Great War the club was used by Belgian refugees and soldiers. After the war an approach was made, with the permission of the rector, to a contact at the Eastern General Hospital, and through him a prefabricated building was purchased for £250. It was reassembled by parishioners in the back garden of the rectory, given the name Houghton Hall, and part of it was allocated to the club. (The contact, later ordained as Fr Moir, became a curate in the Cambridge parish.)

A supper was held in Houghton Hall on 8 October 1936 to mark the club's move to Union Road. The President at this time was Canon Marshall, Vice-Presidents were Fathers T. K. Phillips, J. H. Mullett, E. H. Watkis and A. N. Gilbey and Messrs. Fred. Apthorpe, Henry Arnold, H. Fleming Stewart and A. G. Swannell. Mr. Hugh Venables was the Chairman and the Committee consisted of Messrs. Ron Markham, H. Wilkins, L. Daisley, Eustace Ward, Alfred Bull and W. Thompson. The club had a very successful billiard team which competed in the Murratic Cup. After a thirteen-year stay in Union Road, premises were purchased in Cambridge Place and on 17 May 1949 a dinner was held there to mark the opening of the new club. The President was Canon Stokes, Vice-Presidents were Fathers Alfred Bull and Gerard Hulme and the Chairman was Harold Runham. The club ceased to exist in the 1980s.

## The Archconfraternity of St Stephen

In his preface to the manual of the Archconfraternity of St Stephen, Cardinal Bourne wrote: 'No ministry, except that of those who by ordination are set apart for the service of the altar, deserves greater thought and consideration than the duty of those laymen and boys who have the office of assisting the Priests of God in the discharge of their sacred functions.' This Archconfraternity was formed in 1906 by Fr Hamilton Macdonald, son of General Macdonald CB, of the Bombay Staff Corps. He became a Catholic after some years in the Anglican ministry. After studying at the Beda College in Rome he was ordained priest by Cardinal Vaughan in 1901. The Cardinal made him his secretary and appointed him chaplain to the Sacred Heart Convent at Hammersmith and it was during this time that Fr Macdonald conceived the idea of the Archconfraternity. Having had opportunities for many years, and in many countries, of observing the rites of the Church, he took a great interest in the ceremonies of the sanctuary and in those who, as servers, assist the priest. He organized classes to train boys to serve. The Cardinal took an interest in the servers, encouraged them and desired to see the Guild extended, so in January 1905 at Archbishop's House, Westminster a committee was formed. Among those who took an interest in the Guild were the Duke of Norfolk and the Marquess of Ripon and through their generosity it was possible to print and publish the Manual. (Today, *The St Stephen's Handbook for Altar Servers*, the essential guide, is published by Gracewing.) In May 1906 St Pius X gave his approbation to the canonical erection in Westminster Cathedral of the Guild of St Stephen for Altar Servers and in December of that year the Sacred Congregation of Rites made the Guild an Archconfraternity *Prima Primaria*, with power to affiliate to itself confraternities established elsewhere. It was also enriched with grants of indulgences. The Guild flourished but like other organizations it suffered during the Great War. However, after the War it was revived to such an extent that there were branches not only in the Archdiocese of Westminster and the provinces, but also in Africa and India. Until February 1934 the Papal Rescripts applied only to the Province of Westminster but on 19 February 1934 the privileges and indulgences were extended to the whole British Empire. Sanctioned by Cardinal Bourne, the Guild of St. Stephen was formed in Cambridge on 15 September 1932 when Canon Marshall gave an address to fifteen boys. He pointed out the privilege and the dignity of the altar server and explained to them the objects of the Guild. The general Communion of the Guild, preceded by a short instruction, took place on the third Sunday of each month at the 8.30 a.m. Mass. Its first Secretary was 'Master Maurice Wilkins'. This Guild still flourishes in the present three parishes in Cambridge. Girls are now also admitted to membership.

# Knights of St Columba (KSC)

The Knights of St Columba were formed in Glasgow in 1919 in the aftermath of the First World War. The founding fathers took as a model the Knights of Columbus, a thriving American Catholic society. The new society was to be one with its membership confined to Catholics and practising the fundamental virtues of charity, unity and fraternity. It would be neither a confraternity nor purely religious but it would be benevolent, social, educational and composed of men who would be a credit both to their faith and to their country. Catholic clergy would be welcomed and their spiritual guidance appreciated.

In the *Cambridge Catholic Magazine* of August 1934, Canon Marshall wrote:

> I recently called a meeting of men of the parish to consider some sort of organisation for Catholic action such as is being called for by the Pope and Hierarchy. The meeting was not well attended. We have in the parish the Blessed Sacrament Guild, a Conference of S.V.P. and a Circle of Catenians. These are all admirable bodies adequately performing the work that belongs to them. But none of them provide the link with public affairs nor the stimulus to be and up doing that the C.W.L. does for the women. I would like the men to read the article on the C.W.L. in this magazine. The Archbishop of Birmingham once said 'I wish we had a Catholic Men's League'. It seems to me that perhaps the Knights of Saint Columba meet the need that I feel. Some Knights came to address the meeting, and it may be that a Cambridge council will be formed.

The Cambridge Council was inaugurated in the original Houghton Hall in 1935 and held its meetings there, but now meets at St Laurence's.

A junior section, the Squires of St Columba, was started in Forest Gate in 1926 and flourished for some years, including a branch in Cambridge. The Second World War took many senior members away. Membership declined for various reasons after the war and the movement was closed down in 1968; the Cambridge branch had ceased to exist in the early 1950s.

# The Catenian Association

The Catenian Association was founded as 'The Chums Benevolent Association' in Manchester in 1908, but changed its name to 'The Catenian Association' in 1910. Its purpose, then as now, was to provide society and support to Catholic business and professional men, prompted by the less than welcoming attitudes to such individuals among the non-Catholics of those days. Mr C. T. Wilkins was already a member of the Association when he moved to Cambridge and was instrumental in the foundation of a branch, or Circle, in Cambridge, inaugurated on 11 November 1920. Virtually all the foundation members of the Cambridge Circle were also members of the Cambridge parish. This situation continued for the next thirty years or more, giving the Circle the appearance of a parish-based organization during that time, especially on account of its willingness to support parish activities and needs. Less than a year after their inauguration, brothers of the Cambridge Circle earned a commendation from Cardinal Bourne for their part in the organization of the Catholic Bible Congress in July 1921 and they provided a rota of Sunday morning lifts for Cambridge curates to the Mass Centre at Papworth for a number of years from 1929. The twenty-fifth anniversary of the Circle in November 1945 was greeted with warmth and affection by Canon Marshall in the *Cambridge Catholic Magazine*. As a result of the creation of daughter parishes at Chesterton and Sawston, and due also to increased mobility during the 1960s and 70s, the membership of the Cambridge Circle became more widely based, with brothers resident in at least eight other parishes and only a minority still resident in Cambridge. The Circle makes a point of offering hospitality to Cambridge clergy but can strictly speaking no longer claim the character of a parish organization.

## The Catholic Scout Troop and Boy's Club

The foundation of the Boy Scouts by General Sir Robert Baden Powell, the hero of Mafeking, in 1908, had led to a rapid spread of the movement across the country. By 1910 a Catholic Scout Troop, the 14th Cambridge, had been formed with enthusiastic support from such leading figures in the Catholic community as Canon Scott, Mgr Barnes and Baron von Hügel. Inevitably, a church-linked troop required a Catholic scoutmaster and when the first scoutmaster, G. Roe, left Cambridge in 1911, not long after the participation of the troop in that year's Scout Rally, it proved impossible to find a successor and the troop was disbanded.

A new troop, the 17th Cambridge, was formed in 1913 at the initiative of two Catholic scoutmasters, Cutting, a townsman, and Duchemin, an undergraduate. A promising fresh start was made with a church parade on the feast of the Dedication of the Church in October 1913, followed by an inspection and blessing of the troop by the Bishop of Northampton. In July 1914 the scouts provided a guard of honour for the reception of the Princes of Uganda at the Church during their official visit to Cambridge (Pl. 6a). Although overshadowed by the outbreak of the First World War and the enlistment of two patrol leaders and two of the scoutmasters, the troop flourished for a time, increasing in numbers from twelve to twenty-four that year, adding a Wolf Cub pack and acquiring new headquarters at 6 Parkside with club facilities for the scouts and other boys of the parish. A trek cart provided by the Catholic Women's League proved invaluable to the troop in the collection of gifts for the Belgian war refugees arriving in Cambridge. As the war progressed, numbers slowly declined as senior members of the troop joined the forces, a total of ten seeing active service of whom three lost their lives. By early 1915, Scoutmaster Duchemin had left for Rome to study for the priesthood and Scoutmaster Cutting had enlisted. Assistant scoutmasters were by then virtually unobtainable and the troop had to function under the leadership of its chaplain, Fr Kay. Numbers and attendances at parades grew ever fewer, and by September 1916 the decision was taken to disband the troop, at least for the duration of the war. The boys' club continued, though with some difficulty.

The arrival of Fr Charles Davidson in the parish in 1919 marked a change in the fortunes of the Scout Troop. Under his keen guidance as their new chaplain the troop quickly re-formed and by 1922 enjoyed a particularly successful summer camp at Sheringham and took part in the Prince of Wales Rally at Alexandra Park that autumn. Part of the newly-erected Houghton Hall was at this time allocated to a junior club for 14–18 year olds, offering a library, a debating society and a variety of indoor games, and a cricket club had encouraging results.

By 1924 the scoutmaster and the chaplain had both left the area and the troop was run on an interim basis by Canon Marshall and a five-man committee until the arrival of a new curate, Fr George Webb, in 1925. Fr Webb appeared well-suited to take over the position of scoutmaster, and in August that year he led a party of nine scouts from the 17th Cambridge Troop on what would prove to be the proudest episode in its history – participation in the International Holy Year Scout Pilgrimage to Rome (Pl. 32a). The 750-strong British contingent of Catholic Scouts was received in London by Cardinal Bourne and the Chief Scout who sent them on their way with strong words of encouragement. The pilgrimage reached its climax in Rome with Mass in St Peter's, an address from the Pope who received a salute of banners, and an audience with the Holy Father for the scoutmaster and the Cambridge contingent. A welcome from their families in the rectory awaited the scouts on their return to Cambridge, and the flag which had accompanied them to Rome was paraded up the nave of a crowded church for evening Benediction.

The troop flourished under Fr Webb's leadership, reaching a membership of forty, including a re-formed Wolf Cub pack, and moved to newly refurbished headquarters at Paston House, lent to them by St Mary's Convent. Fr Webb's departure in 1928 was only one contributory factor in the eventual decline of the troop. Canon Marshall made every effort to strengthen its fortunes, seeing it as the only organization available for Catholic youths in the district, especially those attending non-Catholic schools. Eventually the falling numbers as senior members left were unmatched by new recruits from the younger boys, and a widespread shortage of scoutmasters led to the final suspension of the troop in 1930. Canon Marshall could at least be consoled by the reinstatement of the junior club for youths in the 14–18 age group which took over the former scout premises at Paston House. At first this came under the supervision of the SVP Conference, but later under the care of a new curate, Fr James Mullett, who also organized successful summer camps for boys from the parish during the years 1934–6.

## The 16th Cambridge Girl Guide Company

In 1921 a Catholic Girl Guide company was formed at the Catholic Church, under the captaincy of Miss Goss, with Miss Watts as Assistant Guider (Pl. 32b). In the 1920s the Girl Guide Association in Cambridge did not allow 'closed' units (i.e. units based on a church and restricted to one faith), but as the Catholic Guides had connections to the Catholic Women's League they were probably sponsored by them. Funds for the thirteen-strong unit were donated from the 1921 Christmas Fair. In 1922 a Junior Catholic Women's League based on the Guides was started (and maybe contributed to the Guides' eventual collapse).

The most important event in 1922 was the participation of the now seventeen-strong 16th Cambridge with other local companies in the International Girl Guide Conference. This camp, held in Cambridge, was linked to the inauguration of Foxlease, the Guide Association International Training House. International delegates spent the first part of their trip to England in Cambridge where Cambridge Guides including the 16th provided hospitality by inviting them into their homes and acting as runners and message-takers at the campsite. The delegates then left Cambridge to attend the opening of Foxlease.

The usual guide activities were enthusiastically undertaken by the Catholic Guides (according to the late Doris Kriesi (née Flaxman). Of especial note was a summer camp at Leiston in Suffolk. They entered keenly into learning outdoor skills: knots, open-fire cooking and square lashing, as well as housekeeping achievements (cooking, sewing and hostessing). Singing around the camp fire was a highlight. The Guides demonstrated their folk dancing ability at the parish fête in 1924, earning their Entertainers' Badge, and in 1925 worked towards their Hostess Badge by waitressing at the fête assisted by the Junior Catholic Women's League.

It was with sadness and regret that Miss Goss closed the 16th Cambridge Girl Guide Company in 1926 due to lack of numbers. One cannot help wondering if the small parish of that time could not sustain two groups for young girls. The funds left from the 16th Cambridge were handed over to the Catholic Women's League for safekeeping.

## The Walsingham Association

Originally known as the 'Guild of Our Ladye of Walsingham' the Association was founded in 1933 and has branches throughout the country. The Association exists primarily to spread devotion to Our Lady of Walsingham and encourage pilgrimage to her Shrine. Like the CWL, KSC and COM the Association is not parish-based but covers a large area. A branch was started in Cambridge in 1989 and meets once a month at St Laurence's church, while others also meet at the English Martyrs church to say the Association prayers.

## St Laurence's Ladies' Guild

This Guild was formed in 1978 for ladies who did not wish to attend meetings of the Catholic Women's League. Membership is open to all ladies of the parish and their friends, Catholic or non-Catholic. The purpose is to encourage friendship and the sharing of information among its members. Meetings are held in the parish room on the first Thursday of each month when there is a speaker or an outing. Money collected at the meetings goes towards expenses for speakers and the annual charities to which the Guild chooses to contribute at its Annual General Meeting held in September. A Mass for all the ladies of the parish is held each September.

# Appendix 2

# The Catholic Clergy of Cambridge from 1841

## St Andrew's, Union Road/ Our Lady & The English Martyrs

| | |
|---|---|
| Bernard Shanley | 1841–2 |
| H. Norbert Woolfrey | 1842–3 |
| Canon Thomas Quinlivan, Mission Rector | 1843–83 |
| Robert Pate | 1883 |
| Henry F. C. Logan | 1877–84 |
| Canon Christopher Scott, Mission Rector | 1883–1922 |
| George Page | 1883–99 |
| William H. Reade | 1899–1905 |
| R. Hugh Benson | 1905–08 |
| Alfred Wilson | 1907–08 |
| Andrew J. Kay | 1909–18 |
| Charles Davidson | 1919–21 |
| John W. Cosser | 1922 |
| Canon J. Bernard Marshall, Mission Rector | 1922–46 |
| R. Pilkington | 1923–4 |
| George W. H.Webb | 1925–8 |
| R. Moir | 1925–30 |
| John Ketterer | 1929–30 |
| Christopher G. McGregor | 1931–6 |
| James H. Mullett | 1932–7 |
| Thomas K. Phillips | 1934–8 |
| Edward H. Watkis | 1936–41 |
| Eric Phillips | 1937–46 |

| | |
|---|---|
| Charles Grant | 1939–43 |
| Maurice Ryan | 1941–5 |
| Patrick Oates | 1943–4 |
| R. Fawsitt | 1944–7 |
| Gerard Langley | 1945–7 |
| Revd Guy Pritchard, Parish Priest | 1946–7 |
| A. Throckmorton | 1946–8 |
| Canon Edmund H. Stokes, Parish Priest | 1948–61 |
| J. Devaney | 1947–50 |
| Christopher Roberts | 1947–58 |
| A. Bull | 1949 |
| L. F. Howlin | 1954–7 |
| P. Nightingale | 1955–61 |
| J. Parr | 1957–62 |
| J. Wallace | 1957–59 |
| Henry M. A. Wace | 1959–66 (Priest in charge 1961) |
| Canon Frank Diamond, Parish Priest | 1961–8 |
| B. Nightingale | 1964–9 |
| A. Berrell | 1962 |
| Raymond Kerby | 1962–4 |
| G. Moorcroft | 1964–7 |
| Anthony Foreman | 1965–75 |
| Paul Hypher | 1967–70 |
| Canon Paul Taylor, Parish Priest | 1968–80 |
| T. Feighan | 1970–1 |
| J. Koenig | 1971–3 |
| G. Thornton | 1973–5 |
| Francis Selman | 1975–7 |
| Anthony Rogers | 1977–9 |
| J. McNally | 1977–9 |
| M. Finch | 1977–80 |
| Patrick Cleary | 1978–82 |
| Mgr Anthony Philpot, Parish Priest | 1980–94 |
| Gerard Quigley | 1981–3 |
| Gary Dowsey | 1980–3 |
| Peter Leeming | 1983–6 |
| Brendan Moffatt | 1984–7 |
| Michael Vulliamy | 1982–5 |
| Rafael Esteban | 1986–present |

| | |
|---|---|
| David Finegan | 1986–9 |
| Gary Cawthorne | 1987–90 |
| C. Cook | 1989–92 |
| James Caulfield | 1990–3 |
| Russell Frost | 1991–5 |
| Adrian Gates | 1990–3 |
| David Jennings | 1993–8 |
| Mgr Anthony Rogers, Parish Priest | 1994–present |
| Robert Penhallurick | 1996–9 |
| David Ward | 1998–2000 |
| John Minh | |
| (Nguyen Minh Hoan) | 1999–present |

## St Laurence, Cambridge

*Parish Priests*

| | |
|---|---|
| Gerard Hulme | 1947–51 |
| Patrick Oates | 1951–68 |

*Curates*

| | |
|---|---|
| Peter Stoyle | 1963–4 |
| Paul Hypher | 1964–7 |
| Norman Smith | 1968–9 |
| Derrick Morgan | 1967–70 |
| Liam Brady | 1969–72 |
| John Drury | 1970–2 |
| John Drury (Parish Priest) | 1972–7 |
| Timothy Russ | 1972–6 |
| Richard Wilson | 1977–82 |
| Francis Selman | 1976–9 |
| Peter Wynekus | 1982–8 |
| Michael Vulliamy | 1980–2 |
| Michael Griffin | 1988–96 |
| Michael Ryan | 1981–3 |
| Joseph Farrell | 1983–6 |
| David Paul | 1997–present |

# Our Lady of Lourdes, Sawston

*Parish Priests*

| | |
|---|---|
| Christopher Roberts | 1958–69 |
| Laurence O'Toole | 1969–2000 |
| David Hennessey | 2000–present |

# St Philip Howard, Cambridge

*Parish Priests*

| | |
|---|---|
| Anthony Rogers | 1978–84 |
| Michael Edwards | 1984–5 |
| Michael Vulliamy | 1985–92 |
| Neil Crayden | 1990–3 |
| Henry McCarthy | 1992–4 |
| Richard White | 1994–6 |
| Mgr Eugene Harkness | 1996–present |

*Curate*

| | |
|---|---|
| Peter Edwards | 1997–present |

# Appendix 3

# Religious Orders in Cambridge in the Nineteenth and Twentieth Centuries

*Enikö Regös*

These lists have been compiled from the *Catholic Directory*, and from the archives of the Bar Convent, York, and various convents in Cambridge. Until 1976 Cambridge belonged to the Diocese of Northampton; since then it has been part of the Diocese of East Anglia.

## MEN

### Benedictines (English Congregation) (OSB)

House 1896, Chapel 1938, St Benet's House, 32 Hobson Street, House of Studies for Benedictines.
1898: Edward Cuthbert Butler, Arthur Benedict Kuypers
1900: Richard Hugh Connolly (in 1900, and 1905–16)
1917–1918: closed during the war
1920: Downside House of Studies, 13 Park Terrace
1920: Reginald Bede Camm MA, FSA, Charles Mervyn Pontifex
1928: moved to Brooklands Avenue
1939: Nicholas Wilfrid Passmore MA (Superior)
1940: Roy Mark Pontifex MA (Superior)
1939: moved to Benet House, Mt Pleasant
1946–1950: closed temporarily
1970: Richard Adrian Morey Litt.D., Ph.D., MA, F.R.Hist.S. (Superior)

1991: David Nicholas White
Closed in 1996.


## Dominicans (OP)

First founded 1238, destroyed 1538, restored 1938 as Priory of St Michael, Buckingham Road.
Vicars, 1938–69; Priors from 1969:
1938: Adrian English STL, B.Sc.
1938–45: John-Baptist Reeves BA
1945–6: Bernard Delany, B Litt
1946–8: Ambrose Farrell, STL, JCD
1948–52: Cuthbert Bretherton
1952–3: Fabian Dix PG, BA
1953–8: Kenneth Wykeham-George STL, JCL, B Litt
1958–64: Very Rev. Thomas Gilby STL, Ph.D.
1964–9: Kenelm Foster STL, MA, Ph.D.
1969–72: Gerard Meath MA
1972–5: Thomas Gilby STL, Ph.D.
1975–80: Cyril Hodsoll
1980–4: Robert Pollock MA
1984–90: Robert Ombres STL, LLB, LLM
1990–2: Richard Conrad, MA, Ph.D. (Cantab), MA (Oxon)
1992–8: David Sanders, BA, Dip.Theol, S.T. Lic., MH
1998–: Aidan Nichols STL, MA, Ph.D., Dip.Theol.


## Franciscans (Friars Minor, OFM)

Founded *c.* 1225, restored 1938.
1939: Dominic Devas (Superior)
1940: St Bonaventure's, 17 Trumpington Street, Franciscan House of Studies
1940: Alphonsus Bonnar DD, STL, M.Sc. (Guardian)
1949: Anthony Rickards (Guardian)
1955: Ethelbert Cardiff MC (Superior)
1957: Gilbert Sisam (Superior)
1962: John Berchmans Dockery MA, F.R.Hist.S. (Superior)
1967: Alan Keenan MA (Guardian)
House was closed in 1970.

## Christian Brothers of Ireland

1952: Edmund Rice House of Studies, 8 Brookside
1956: moved to 221 Hills Road
Closed in 1968.

## Institute of Charity (IC)

1951: Rosmini House, 6 Grange Road, House of Studies.
1951: Gilbert Sisam (Superior)
1952: William D. Murray MA (Rector)
Closed in 1968.

## Brothers of the Christian Schools (DLS, De la Salle)

1943: La Salle House of Studies, 7 Brookside. [FSC.].
1943: Bro. Baptist BA (Director)
1949: Bro. Anthony (Director)
Closed in 1976.

## Jesuits (SJ)

1994: 26 Kinghome Close.
1995: Christopher Moss, Stephen Buckland, Daniel Sweeney
1997: listed under St Laurence's, Arrupe House, 116 Milton Road,
      Louis Caruana, Gangolf Schussler
1999: Michael Barnes, John Montag

## WOMEN

## Institute of the Blessed Virgin Mary (IBVM)

1898: St Mary's Convent, The Elms, Bateman Street, Grammar and
      Preparatory School for Girls, also for the Local Examinations at
      the University of Cambridge, the Royal College of Music, and
      the South Kensington Examinations.
1988: moved to 8 Brookside.
1898–1901: M. Stanislaus Dagnall (Superior)

1901: no record, possibly M. Josepha Noble
1904–06: M. Stanislaus Dagnall
1906: M. Salome Oates
1920: M. Gertrude Murphy
1932: no record
1934: M. Paul Murphy
1940: M. Elizabeth Dunn
1946: M. Paul Murphy
1952: M. Elizabeth Dunn
1955: M. Campion Davenport
1961: M. Ancilla Barton
1964: M. Gregory Kirkus
1970: M. Clare Goodman
1976: M. Bridget Geoffrey-Smith
1982: M. Thomas Williams
1985: M. Clare Goodman
1991: M. Francis North
1997: M. Armine Radley
Catholic House of Residence, Paston House, Bateman Street (day students of the course at the Cambridge Training College for Women).

## Canonesses Regular of St Augustine (Augustinians of the Assumption)

1938: **Congregation of Our Lady** (Roman Union)
Lady Margaret House, 12 Grange Road, Oratory for Women Students at University and House of Studies for Girls, from age 17.
Hostel of Residence for Women Students, 10 Grange Road.
The community is of the Couvent des Oiseaux of Paris.
1937: M. Mary Joseph Walters (Superior), M. Thomas More Grimes, M. St Anselm Roberts, M. Mary Rosario de Fischer, M. Emmanuel Athill, M. St Paul Evans, Sr Françoise Georgeault
1973: Sr Marie-Claire Sellen (Sister in Charge)
1973: Sr Patricia White
1978: Sr Philippa Wright
1990: Sr Emma Athill
1992: Sr Philippa Wright
1944: Chaplain: Humphrey Johnson MA; later: Chaplain from St Edmund's House.

## Convent of Sisters of Hope of the Holy Family of Bordeaux

1947: listed also as **Sisters of the Immaculate Conception**
Hope House Nursing Home, Brooklands Avenue.
Trained nurses, looking after a limited number of lady patients, irrespective of creed.
1940: M. Wenceslas Butler
1948: M. Michael Reynolds
1951: M. Frances Phelan
1957: M. Matilde Harney
1963: M. Michael Reynolds
1969: M. Agnes Scully
1976: M. Francis Phelan
1982: M. Michael Reynolds
1988: M. Cecilia McKay
1995: M. Clare Marie O'Connell

## Convent of the Sisters of Our Lady (Mülhausen)

1947: St Edmund's House
1980: moved to 9 Rotherwick Way
Closed in 1988.

## Carmelite Convent, discalced (OCarm)

1923: 104–106 Chesterton Road.
Moved to Waterbeach in 1937.

## Sisters of Adoration Reparatrice

1983: 94 Norwich Street
1986: moved to 17 Glisson Road.
Founded in Paris in 1848. Mother General Sr Marie Dolores (Paris) sent Sisters to Cambridge in November 1982 to begin Exposition of the Blessed Sacrament at Our Lady and the English Martyrs.
Sister in Charge: Sr Christina Mary
M General 1984: Sr Thérèse Emmanuel
            1996: Sr Cecilia

# Religious of Jesus and Mary

From 1984, in 1984, Sisters of Jesus and Mary, c/o the Convent, Bateman Street,
1985: 41 Mill End Road, Cherry Hinton.
Closed in 1998.

# Appendix 4

# List of Heads of Schools, St Edmund's College and the University Chaplaincy

## Union Road /St Andrew's/St Alban's School Heads

| | |
|---|---|
| James O'Brian | 1847–9 |
| Hugh McCormack | 1849–50 |
| Sisters of the Order of the Infant Jesus | 1850–52 |
| Patrick Smith | 1853 |
| Genevieve Hexley | 1855–8 |
| Mary Jane Hexley | 1858–63 |
| Mary Maloney | 1863–8 |
| Mary Trehearne | 1868–92 |
| Hannah McHale | 1892–4 |
| Janet Hill | 1894–6 |
| Margaret Ellis | 1896–1902 |
| Nellie O'Connell | 1902-03 |
| Helen Jennings | 1903-08 |
| Frances Ormerod | 1908–35 |
| James Bates | 1935–68 |
| Barry Jones | 1968–76 |
| Dorothy Head | 1976–91 |
| Anne Hargreaves | 1991–2000 |
| Valerie Pye | 2000– |

## St Bede's School Heads

| | |
|---|---|
| George Kent | 1962–83 |
| Sister Dolores | 1983–90* |
| *inter-church from 1988 | |
| Roger Boon (inter-church) | 1990–2001 |

# St Laurence's School Heads

| | |
|---|---|
| Ron Ellison | 1968–86 |
| Patricia Flett | 1986–93 |
| Brigida Martino | 1993–2001 |
| Anne Rutherford | 2001– |

# Paston House/St Mary's School – Headmistresses

| | |
|---|---|
| Sr M Paul, IBVM | 1917–49 |
| Sr M Christopher, IBVM | 1949–72 |
| Sr M Dominica, IBVM | 1972–7 |
| Sr M Christina, IBVM | 1977–89 |
| Miss Michele Conway | 1989–97 |
| Mrs Morag Chapman (Acting Head) | 1997–8 |
| Mrs Gina Protrowska | 1998–2000 |
| Dr Alf. Jackson (Acting Head) | 2000–2001 |
| Mrs Jayne Triffitt | 2001– |

# St Catherine's School Heads

| | |
|---|---|
| Mr Salt | 1987–8 |
| Mrs Sheila Salt | 1988–97 |
| Mrs Deirdre O'Sullivan | 1997– |

# Fisher House Chaplains

| | |
|---|---|
| Edmund Nolan | 1896–1902 |
| Arthur Barnes | 1902–16 |
| J.Byrne O'Connell (acting) | 1917 |
| J.Blundell (acting) | 1918 |
| J.Bernard Marshall | 1918–22 |
| John Lopes | 1922–8 |
| George McGillivray | 1928–32 |
| Alfred Gilbey | 1932–65 |
| Richard Incledon | 1966–77 |
| Maurice Couve de Murville | 1977–82 |
| Christopher Jenkins, OSB | 1982–8 |
| John Osman | 1988–94 |

Allan White, OP                          1994–2000
Alban McCoy, OFM Conv.                   2000–

## St Edmund's College Masters

Revd William O. Sutcliffe          1897–1904
Mgr Edmund Nolan                   1904–09
Revd Thomas L.Williams             1909–18
Revd Joseph L. Whitfield           1918–21
Revd John F. McNulty               1921–9
Revd Cuthbert L. Waring            1929–34
Revd John E. Petit                 1934–46
Revd Raymund Corboy                1946–64
Revd Garrett D. Sweeney            1964–76
Revd John Coventry SJ              1976–85
Dr Richard M. Laws                 1985–96
Prof. Robert Brian Heap            1996–

# Bibliography

**General**

Atkinson, Thomas Dinham, and Clark, John Willis, *Cambridge Described and Illustrated* (London, Macmillan, 1897).

*Cambridge Catholic Magazine*, 1931–54, 1959–61.

*Cambridge Parish Diary and Blotter*, 1923–31.

Conybeare, Edward, *Highways and Byways in Cambridge and Ely* (London, Macmillan, 1910).

Cooper, Charles Henry, *Annals of Cambridge*, 5 vols (Cambridge, various publishers, 1842–1908).

Couve de Murville, Maurice N. L., and Jenkins, Philip, *Catholic Cambridge* (London, Catholic Truth Society, 1983).

Hicks, Carola (ed.), *Cambridgeshire Churches* (Stamford, Paul Watkins, 1997).

Lack, William, Stuchfield, H. Martin, and Whittemore, Philip, *The Monumental Brasses of Cambridgeshire* (London, Monumental Brass Society, 1995).

Pevsner, Nikolaus, *Cambridgeshire*, 2nd edn (Harmondsworth, Penguin, 1970).

Royal Commission on Historical Monuments (England), *An Inventory of the Historical Monuments in the City of Cambridge*, 2 vols (London, HMSO, 1959).

Saint Francis' Diocesan Magazine, 1926–33.

Taylor, Alison, *Cambridge: A Hidden History* (Stroud, Tempus, 1999).

Taylor, Nicholas, and Booth, Philip, *Cambridge New Architecture*, 3rd edn (London, Leonard Hill, 1970).

*The Victoria History of the County of Cambridgeshire and the Isle of Ely*, 10 vols (London, University of London Institute of Historical Research, 1938–2002).

## Roman Britain

Clarke, L.C.G., 'Roman Pewter Bowl from the Isle of Ely', *Proceedings of the Cambridge Antiquarian Society*, 31 (1931), pp. 66–75.

Thomas, Charles, *Christianity in Roman Britain to AD 500* (London, Batsford, 1981).

Painter, K. S., *The Water Newton Early Christian Silver* (London, British Museum Publications, 1977).

Watts, Dorothy, *Christians and Pagans in Roman Britain* (London, Routledge, 1991).

## Medieval Cambridge

Bateson, Mary (ed.), *Cambridge Gild Records* (Cambridge, Cambridge Antiquarian Society, 1903).

Binns, John, and Meadows, Peter (eds), *Great St Mary's: Cambridge's University Church* (Cambridge, Great St Mary's, 2000).

Brooke, C. N. L. 'The churches of medieval Cambridge', in Derek Beales and Geoffrey Best (eds), *History, Society and the Churches: Essays in honour of Owen Chadwick* (Cambridge, Cambridge University Press, 1985), pp. 49–76.

Foster, J. E. (ed.), *Churchwardens' Accounts of St Mary the Great, Cambridge, from 1504 to 1635* (Cambridge, Cambridge Antiquarian Society, 1905).

Gray, J. Milner, *Biographical Notes on the Mayors of Cambridge* (Cambridge, the author, [1922]).

Haslam, Jeremy, 'The Development and Topography of Saxon Cambridge', *Proceedings of the Cambridge Archaeological Society*, 72 (1982–3), pp. 13–29.

Lobel, M. D., *Cambridge* (London, Scolar Press, 1974).

## The University and Colleges

Attwater, Aubrey, *Pembroke College, Cambridge: A Short History*, ed. S. C. Roberts (Cambridge, Cambridge University Press, 1936).

Baker, Thomas, *History of the College of St. John the Evangelist, Cambridge*, ed. John E. B. Mayor, 2 vols (Cambridge, Cambridge University Press, 1869).

Brooke, Christopher, *A History of Gonville and Caius College* (Woodbridge, Boydell Press, 1985).

Brooke, Christopher N. L., 'The Dedications of Cambridge Colleges and their Chapels', in Patrick Zutshi (ed.), *Medieval Cambridge: Essays on the Pre-Reformation University* (Woodbridge, Boydell Press, 1993), pp. 7–20.

Cobban, A. B., *The King's Hall within the University of Cambridge in the Later Middle Ages* (Cambridge, Cambridge University Press, 1969).

Crawley, Charles, *Trinity Hall: The History of a Cambridge College, 1350–1975* (Cambridge, Trinity Hall, 1976).

Cunich, Peter, Hoyle, David, Duffy, Eamon, and Hyam, Ronald, A *History of Magdalene College Cambridge, 1428–1988* (Cambridge, Magdalene College Publications, 1994).

Emden, A. B., *A Biographical Register of the University of Cambridge to 1500* (Cambridge, Cambridge University Press, 1963).

Hackett, Michael, *The Original Statutes of Cambridge University* (Cambridge, Cambridge University Press, 1970).

Hall, Catherine P., 'The Gild of Corpus Christi and the Foundation of Corpus Christi College: An Investigation of the Documents', in Patrick Zutshi (ed.), *Medieval Cambridge: Essays on the Pre-Reformation University* (Woodbridge, Boydell Press, 1993), pp. 65–91.

Leader, Damian Riehl, *A History of the University of Cambridge, I, The University to 1546* (Cambridge, Cambridge University Press).

Mayor, J. E. B., (ed.), *Early Statutes of the College of St. John the Evangelist in the University of Cambridge* (Cambridge, Macmillan, 1859).

Miller, Edward, *Portrait of a College: A History of the College of Saint John the Evangelist, Cambridge* (Cambridge, Cambridge University Press, 1961).

Stokes, H. P., *The Chaplains and the Chapel of the University of Cambridge* (Cambridge, Cambridge Antiquarian Society, 1906).

Twigg, John, *The University of Cambridge and the English Revolution, 1625–1688* (Woodbridge, Boydell Press, 1990).

Venn, J., and Venn, J. A., *Alumni Cantabrigienses: A Biographical List of All Known Students, Graduates and Holders of Office at the University of Cambridge, from the Earliest Times to 1900* (Cambridge, Cambridge University Press, 1922–54).

Willis, Robert, and Clark, John Willis, *The Architectural History of the University of Cambridge*, 4 vols (Cambridge, Cambridge University Press, 1886).

**Religious Houses**

Brooke, Rosalind B., *The Coming of the Friars* (London, Allen and Unwin, 1975).

Clark, John Willis (ed.), *The Observances in Use at the Augustinian Priory of S. Giles and S. Andrew at Barnwell, Cambridgeshire* (Cambridge, Macmillan and Bowes, 1897.

Gray, Arthur, *The Priory of Saint Radegund, Cambridge* (Cambridge, Cambridge Antiquarian Society, 1898).

Gumbley, Walter, OP, *The Cambridge Dominicans* (Oxford, Blackfriars, 1938).

Haigh, David, *The Religious Houses of Cambridgeshire* (Cambridge, Cambridgeshire County Council, 1988).

Moorman, John R. H., *The Grey Friars in Cambridge, 1225–1538* (Cambridge, Cambridge University Press, 1952).

Ombres, Robert, OP, *The Dominicans in Cambridge 1238–1538*, exhibition catalogue (Cambridge, University Library, 1988).

Salway, Peter, 'Sidney before the College', in D.E. D. Beales and H. B. Nisbet (eds), *Sidney Sussex College, Cambridge: Historical Essays in Commemoration of the Quatercentenary* (Woodbridge, Boydell Press, 1996), pp. 3–34.

Wayment, Hilary, 'Ten Carmelite Roundels at Queens' College Cambridge', *Proceedings of the Cambridge Antiquarian Society*, 82 (1993), pp. 139–56.

Zutshi, Patrick and Ombres, Robert, OP, 'The Dominicans in Cambridge 1238–1538', *Archivum Fratrum Praedicatorum*, LX (1990), pp. 313–73.

### St Simon Stock and the Scapular Vision

Breeze, M. S. Gabrielle, *Our Lady of Cambridgeshire* (Cambridge, W. Heffer & Sons Ltd, 1933).

Xiberta, Bartholomaeus F. M., *De visione Sancti Simonis Stock* (Romae, apud Curiam Generalitiam, 1950).

### Lady Margaret Beaufort

Cooper, Charles Henry, *Memoir of Margaret, Countess of Richmond and Derby* (Cambridge, Deighton Bell, 1874).

Jones, Michael K., and Underwood, Malcolm G., *The King's Mother: Lady Margaret Beaufort, Countess of Richmond and Derby* (Cambridge, Cambridge University Press, 1992).

### St John Fisher

Bradshaw, Brendan, and Duffy, Eamon (eds), *Humanism, Reform and the Reformation: The Career of Bishop John Fisher* (Cambridge, Cambridge University Press, 1989).

Hatt, Cecilia A. (ed.), *English Works of John Fisher, Bishop of Rochester (1469–1535): Sermons and other Writings, 1520–1535* (Oxford, Oxford University Press, 2002).

Rex, Richard, *The Theology of John Fisher* (Cambridge, Cambridge University Press, 1991).

Reynolds, E. E., *Saint John Fisher* (London, Burns & Oates, 1955).

### Cambridge Martyrs

Burton, E. H., and Pollen, J. H. (eds), *Lives of the English Martyrs, Second Series* (London, Longmans & Co., 1914).

Camm, Bede (ed.), *Lives of the English Martyrs declared Blessed by Pope Leo XIII in 1886 and 1895*, 2 vols (London, Burns and Oates Ltd., 1904–05).

Camm, Bede (ed.), *The English Martyrs: Papers from the Summer School of Catholic Studies, held at Cambridge, July 28–Aug. 6, 1928* (Cambridge, W. Heffer & Sons, 1929).

Camm, Dom Bede, *Nine Martyr Monks* (London, Burns Oates & Washbourne, 1931).

Caraman, Philip, *Henry Morse: Priest of the Plague* (London, Longmans, Green and Co., 1957).

Challoner, Richard, *Memoirs of Missionary Priests*, ed. John Hungerford Pollen (London, Burns, Oates & Co., 1924; repr. Farnborough, Gregg, 1969).

Thomas, D. Aneurin (ed.), *The Welsh Elizabethan Catholic Martyrs: The Trial Documents of Saint Richard Gwyn and of the Venerable William Davies* (Cardiff, University of Wales Press, 1971).

Whatmore, L. E., *The Carthusians under King Henry the Eighth*, Analecta Cartusiana, 109 (Salzburg, Institut für Anglistik und Amerikanistik, 1983).

### Catholics, 1559–1829

Husenbeth, F. C. (attrib.), 'Notes on the Early Missions in the Diocese of Northampton', (manuscript, *c.* 1850, Northampton Diocesan Archives).

Anstruther, Godfrey, *The Seminary Priests: A Dictionary of the Secular Clergy of England and Wales, 1558–1850*, 4 vols (Ware, St Edmund's College; Ushaw, Ushaw College (vols 2–4 Great Wakering, Mayhew-McCrimmon), [1968]–1977).

Bellenger, Dominic Aidan, *The French Exiled Clergy in the British Isles after 1789* (Stratton on the Fosse, Bath, Downside Abbey, 1986).

Bossy, John, *The English Catholic Community, 1570–1850* (London, Darton, Longman & Todd, 1975).

Brady, William Maziere, *Annals of the Catholic Hierarchy in England and Scotland A.D. 1585–1876* (Rome, Tipographia della Pace, & London, Thomas Baker, 1877).

Foley, Henry, SJ, *Records of the English Province of the Society of Jesus*, 7 vols in 8 (London, Burns and Oates, 1875–83).

Foster, Michael, 'Walter Montague, Courtier, Diplomat and Abbot, 1603–77', *Downside Review*, 96 (1978), pp. 85–102, 208–25.

O'Leary, J. G., 'Recusants among our Neighbours: Cambridge and Ely', *Essex Recusant*, 9 (1967), pp. 66–71.

Rowlands, Marie B. (ed.), *English Catholics of Parish and Town, 1558–1778* (London, Catholic Record Society, 1999).

Ward, Bernard, *The Eve of Catholic Emancipation 1803–1829*, 3 vols (London, Longman & Co., 1911).

**Joshua Basset**

Goldie, Mark, 'Joshua Basset, Popery and Revolution', in D. E. D. Beales and H. B. Nisbet (eds), *Sidney Sussex College, Cambridge: Historical Essays in Commemoration of the Quatercentenary* (Woodbridge, Boydell Press, 1996), pp. 111–30.

Rogers, Nicholas, 'Basset, Joshua', in *New Dictionary of National Biography* (Oxford, Oxford University Press, forthcoming), s.v.

**Sawston Hall and the Huddlestons**

Huddleston Papers (Cambridgeshire County Record Office, Ref 488/C1/EH 61–73).

Bircham, Ronald, *Introduction to the History of the Church of Saint Mary the Virgin, Sawston, Cambridgeshire, Part One, 970–1800* (Stapleford, [the author], 1981).

'History from Sawston', *Cambridge Catholic Magazine*, 11 (1941), pp. 56–7.

Hodgetts, Michael, 'A House with Three Priest-Holes,' *Country Life*, 22 March 1962, pp. 662–3.

Holt, T. G., SJ, 'An Eighteenth Century Chaplain: John Champion at Sawston Hall,' *Recusant History*, 17 (1984) pp. 181–7.

Teversham, T. F., *A History of the Village of Sawston*, 2 vols (Sawston, Crampton and Sons, Ltd, 1942–7).

**Seventeenth- and Eighteenth-Century Cambridge**

Cambridgeshire Quarter Session Records, 1778–1848 (Cambridgeshire County Record Office).

Cambridge Town Sessions Records, 1770–1847 (Cambridgeshire County Record Office).

Cooper, Trevor (ed.), *The Journal of William Dowsing: Iconoclasm in East Anglia during the English Civil War* (Woodbridge, The Ecclesiological Society, 2001).

Palmer, W. M., *William Cole of Milton* (Cambridge, Galloway & Porter, Ltd., 1935).

**Nineteenth-Century Catholicism**

Beard, Madeleine, *Faith and Fortune* (Leominster, Gracewing, 1997).

'The Beginnings of the Cambridge Parish', *Cambridge Catholic Magazine*, 3 (1933), pp. 43–5.

Fitzgerald-Lombard, Charles, *English and Welsh Priests 1801–1914: A Working List* (Stratton on the Fosse, Bath, Downside Abbey, 1993).

Gorman, W. Gordon, *Converts to Rome: A Biographical List of the More* ·

*Notable Converts to the Catholic Church in the United Kingdom during the Last Sixty Years*, new edn (London, Sands, 1910).

Lance, Derek, *The Returning Tide (1850–2000): A History of the Northampton Diocese over the last 150 years* (Northampton, Diocese of Northampton, 2000).

Marshall, J. B., 'The First Post-Reformation Mass in Cambridge', *Cambridge Catholic Magazine*, 4 (1934), pp. 15–17.

Ryder, Cyril, *Life of Thomas Edward Bridgett* (London, Burns and Oates, 1906).

Trappes-Lomax, T. B., *The Diocese of Northampton Centenary Souvenir 1850–1950* (London, Hoxton & Walsh, [1950]).

Ward, Bernard, *The Sequel to Catholic Emancipation 1830–1850*, 2 vols (London, Longman & Co., 1915).

Young, Urban, *Life of Father Ignatius Spencer C.P.* (London, Burns, Oates & Co., 1933).

## Canon Quinlivan

Philip S. Wilkins, 'Glimpses of Canon Thomas Quinlivan' (a paper presented to the Quinlivan Research Association, February 1999).

## Nineteenth-Century Cambridge

Murphy, Michael J., *Cambridge Newspapers and Opinion 1780–1850* (Cambridge, Oleander Press, 1977).

Bury, M. E., and Pickles, J. D. (eds), *Romilly's Cambridge Diary, 1842–1847* (Cambridge, Cambridgeshire Records Society, 1994).

## Pugin and St Andrew's church, Union Road

'Parish Return of 1858 to Bishop Amherst' (OLEM Parish Archives HA1/22)

'Ecclesiastical Census, 30 March 1851' (PRO/HO/129/188)

Belcher, Margaret, *A. W. N. Pugin: An Annotated Critical Bibliography* (London, Mansell, 1987).

'Consecration of the Old Church of St. Andrew', *Cambridge Catholic Magazine*, 3 (1933), pp. 55–7.

O'Donnell, Roderick, '"Blink by [him] in silence"? The Cambridge Camden Society and A. W. N. Pugin', in Christopher Webster and John Elliott (eds), *'A Church As It Should Be': The Cambridge Camden Society and Its Influence*, (Stamford, Shaun Tyas, 2000), pp. 98–120.

Pevsner, Nikolaus, *Bedfordshire and the County of Huntingdon and Peterborough* (Harmondsworth, Penguin Books, 1968), p. 336.

Pugin, A. Welby, *The Present State of Ecclesiastical Architecture in England* (London, Charles Dolman, 1843; repr. Oxford, St. Barnabas Press, 1969).

Stanton, Phoebe, *Pugin* (London, Thames and Hudson, 1971).

Wedgwood, Alexandra, *A. W. N. Pugin and the Pugin Family* (London, Victoria and Albert Museum, 1985).

## Our Lady and the English Martyrs

*The Catholic Church in Cambridge. A Guide to the Present, with Notes on the Past* ([Cambridge, The Rectory], n.d. [1920s]).

Croucher, Maurice, 'The Opening of the New Catholic Church in Cambridge', *Cambridge Catholic Magazine*, 3 (1933), pp. 57–61.

Devas, Raymund, OP, 'Pre-Reformation Dominican Statue of Our Lady of Grace', *Hawkesyard Review*, N. S., 4 (1912), pp. 94–6.

M[acgregor], C. G., *The Church of Our Lady and the English Martyrs, Cambridge* (Gloucester, British Publishing Company, [1936]).

[Sayle, C. E., and Scott, C.], *The Church of Our Lady & the English Martyrs*, Cambridge ([Cambridge, The Rectory, 1890]).

Marshall, J. B., 'The Ancient Statue of Our Lady in the Church', *Cambridge Catholic Magazine*, 2 (1932), pp. 41–3.

Wilkins, P. S., *The Church of Our Lady and the English Martyrs, Cambridge* (Cambridge, The Rectory, 1955; 2nd edn, 1965; 3rd edn, 1985; 4th edn, 1995).

Wilkins, Philip S., *The Church of Our Lady and the English Martyrs, Cambridge, 1890–1990: A Centenary Commemoration* ([Cambridge, The Rectory, 1990]).

## Canon Christopher Scott

'Mgr. Provost Scott, D.D.,V.G.', obituary, *The Tablet*, 25 February 1922, pp. 265–6.

## Mrs Lyne-Stephens

Beaumont, Cyril W., *Three French Dancers of the 19th Century: Duvernay, Livry, Beaugrand* (London, C.W. Beaumont, 1935).

*Enciclopedia dello Spettacolo*, IV (Roma, Casa Editrice Le Maschere, 1957), cols 1219–20.

Guest, Ivor, *The Romantic Ballet in England: Its development, fulfilment and decline*, 2nd edn (London, Pitman, 1972), pp. 70–5.

[Scott, Christopher], *In Memoriam. A Sermon preached in the Church of Our Lady and the English Martyrs, Cambridge, at the Pontifical Requiem for the Repose of the Soul of Yolande Marie Louise Lyne-Stephens, the Church's Foundress* (Cambridge, [Canon Scott], 1894).

Wilson, G. B. L., *A Dictionary of Ballet*, 3rd edn (London, Adam & Charles Black, 1974), pp. 173–4.

**Baron von Hügel**

Froude, Mary C., 'The History of the Chapel at Croft Cottage', *Cambridge Catholic Magazine*, 2 (1932), pp. 17–23.

Haddon, A. C., 'Baron Anatole von Hügel, M.A., Sc.D., K.C.S.G.', *The Cambridge Review*, 12 October 1928, p. 7.

Hügel, Anatole von, *Charles von Hügel, April 25, 1795–June 2, 1870* (Cambridge, privately printed, 1903 (2nd issue, 1905)).

**Edward Conybeare**

The Diaries of J. W. E. Conybeare (Cambridgeshire County Record Office, R84/75).

'The Death of Mr. Conybeare', *Cambridge Catholic Magazine*, 1 (1931), pp. 15–16.

Obituary, *The Cambridge Chronicle*, 18 February 1931.

Colombs, Brenda: *Victorian Country Parsons* (London, Constable, 1977), pp. 249–65.

Emery, Jane, *Rose Macaulay: A Writer's Life* (London, John Murray, 1991).

**Robert Hugh Benson**

Cornish, Blanche Warre, Leslie, Shane, et al., *Memorials of Robert Hugh Benson* (London, Burns & Oates, 1915).

Grayson, Janet, *Robert Hugh Benson: Life and Works* (Lanham, Md, University Press of America, 1998).

Marshall, George, 'Two Autobiographical Narratives of Conversion: Robert Hugh Benson and Ronald Knox', *Recusant History*, 24 (1998), pp. 237–53.

Martindale, C. C., SJ, *The Life of Monsignor Robert Hugh Benson*, 2 vols. (London, Longmans, Green and Co., 1916).

Monaghan, M. St Rita, *Monsignor Robert Hugh Benson: his apostolate and its message for our time* (Brisbane, Boolarong Pub., 1985).

Symons, A. J. A., *The Quest for Corvo* (London, Cassell & Co., 1934), pp. 189–204.

**Edward Bullough**

Stopp, Elisabeth, 'Remembering Edward Bullough, 28.3.1880 – 17.9.1934', typescript (Blackfriars, Cambridge).

**First World War**

*Hügel Homes for Belgian Refugees, Cambridge, 1914–1919* (Cambridge, Committee of the Hügel Homes, 1920).

**Catholic Bible Congress**
Westall, L. M. A., and Wilkins, Charles T. (eds), *Handbook for the Bible Congress Commemorating the XVth Centenary of Saint Jerome. Cambridge, July 1921* (Cambridge, Cambridge Chronicle for the Congress Committee, 1921).

**Second World War**
Bowyer, Michael J. F., *Air Raid!: The enemy air offensive against East Anglia 1939–45* (Wellingborough, Patrick Stephens,1986).
Marshall, J. B., 'The Parish in War Time', *Cambridge Catholic Magazine,* 15 (1945), pp. 39–44.

**Canon Diamond**
Obituary, *Northampton Diocesan Directory,* 1993.

**Parish Organizations**
'The Cambridge Sodality of the Children of Mary', *Cambridge Catholic Magazine,* 16 (1946), pp. 45–6.
'Parochial Organizations', *Cambridge Catholic Magazine,* 3 (1933), pp. 69–72, 83–7; 4 (1934), pp. 17–21, 43–5, 65–9; 5 (1935), pp. 17–19, 35–41, 65–70.

**St Laurence's, Chesterton**
'Saint Laurence's, Chesterton', *Cambridge Catholic Magazine, 9* (1939), pp. 79–81.

**Blackfriars**
Letter from Fr Delany to Mrs Bullough, 20 September 1937 (English Dominican Archives, 25 George Square, Edinburgh).
Gaine, Simon Francis, OP, *Obituary Notices of the English Dominicans from 1952 to 1996* (Oxford, Blackfriars Publications, 2000).
Nichols, Aidan, OP, *Dominican Gallery: Portrait of a Culture* (Leominster, Gracewing, 1997).

**Carmelites**
'The Carmelites at Waterbeach', *Cambridge Catholic Magazine,* 7 (1937), pp. 83–7.
'The Departure of the Carmelites', *Cambridge Catholic Magazine,* 7 (1937), pp. 55–7.

**University Chaplaincy**
Evennett, Outram, 'The Cambridge Prelude to 1895: The Story of the Removal of the Ban on the Universities told from the Cambridge

Angle', *The Dublin Review*, 218 (1946), pp. 107–26.

E[vennett], H. O., '29 Years in Cambridge', *Cambridge Catholic Magazine*, 17 (1947), pp. 9–12.

E[vennett], H. O., *Fisher House, Cambridge* (Cambridge, Fisher House, 1958).

Gregory-Jones, Peter, *A History of the Cambridge Catholic Chaplaincy 1895–1965* (Cagliari, the author,1986).

Reeves, Norman C., and others, *John Ludlow Lopes M.A., D.D., 1882–1961* (n.p., n.d. [1980s]).

Watkin, David (ed.), *Alfred Gilbey: A Memoir by Some Friends* (Wilby, Michael Russell, 2001).

### St Edmund's College

McClelland, V. Alan, 'St. Edmund's College, Ware and St. Edmund's College, Cambridge: Historical Connections and Early Tribulations', *Recusant History*, 23 (1997), pp. 470–82.

'The Relic of the True Cross at Cambridge', *Cambridge Catholic Magazine*, 3 (1933), pp. 35–7.

Sweeney, Garrett, St Edmund's House, Cambridge, The First Eighty Years: A History (Cambridge, St Edmund's House, 1980).

Walsh, Michael, *St Edmund's College, Cambridge, 1896–1996* (Cambridge, St Edmund's College, 1996).

### Polish Community

*Polska Wspólnota Katolicka w Cambridge: Kronika Jubileuszowa 1948–1974* (Cambridge, Polska Wspólnota Katolicka, 1974).

*Polska Wspólnota Katolicka w Cambridge: Kronika Jubileuszowa* (Cambridge, Polska Wspólnota Katolicka, 1998).

Suchcitz, Andrzej, *Poland's Contribution to the Allied Victory in the Second World War* (London, Polish Ex-Combatants Association in Great Britain, 1995).

### The Organ

Hale, Paul, unpublished report on the Organ, May 1999, rev. March 2000.

Sayer, Michael, 'Abbott & Smith', in *The New Grove Dictionary of Musical Instruments*, ed. Stanley Sadie, 3 vols (London, Macmillan, 1984), I, p. 2.

Scott, Christopher, 'The Roman Catholic Revival at Cambridge' (OLEM Archives HA1/12).

Thistlethwaite, Nicholas, *The Organs of Cambridge: An Illustrated Guide to the Organs of the University and the City of Cambridge* (Oxford, Positif Press, 1983), pp. 14, 56.

**Union Road School**

School Log Books, 1887–1986 (Cambridgeshire County Record Office).

'Eva Webster', *Cambridge Catholic Magazine*, 14 (1944), pp. 43–5.

*Opening and Blessing of the New Building of Saint Andrew's Catholic School, Cambridge, September 24th, 1936. Commemorative Programme* (Cambridge, St Andrew's School, 1936).


**St Mary's Convent and School**

Kirkus, Sr Gregory, IBVM, *An I.B.V.M. Biographical Dictionary of the English Members and Major Benefactors (1667–2000)* (London, Catholic Record Society, 2001).

McElroy, Vernon, Hall, Peter, and Thurlow, David (eds), *David Roberts, Architect: A Commemoration* (Orwell, Foxhollow Press, 1984).

[Oates], Mother Mary Salome, 'The Coming of the Nuns: The Founding of St. Mary's Convent, Cambridge', *Cambridge Catholic Magazine*, 1 (1931), pp. 45–8.

*A Will to do Well: A History of St Mary's School, Cambridge* (Cambridge, St Mary's School, 1999).

# Index